SCRIPTS AND LITERACY

NEUROPSYCHOLOGY AND COGNITION

VOLUME 7

The purpose of the Neuropsychology and Cognition series is to bring out volumes that promote understanding in topics relating brain and behavior. It is intended for use by both clinicians and research scientists in the fields of neuropsychology, cognitive psychology, psycholinguistics, speech and hearing, as well as education. Examples of topics to be covered in the series would relate to memory, language acquisition and breakdown, reading, attention, developing and aging brain. By addressing the theoretical, empirical, and applied aspects of brain-behavior relationships, this series will try to present the information in the fields of neuropsychology and cognition in a coherent manner.

The titles published in this series are listed at the end of this volume.

SCRIPTS AND LITERACY

Reading and Learning to Read Alphabets, Syllabaries and Characters

Edited by

INSUP TAYLOR

The McLuhan Program in Culture and Technology, University of Toronto

and

DAVID R. OLSON

The Ontario Institute for Studies in Education

KLUWER ACADEMIC PUBLISHERS

DORDRECHT / BOSTON / LONDON

Library of Congress Cataloging-in-Publication Data

Scripts and literacy : reading and learning to read alphabets, syllabaries, and characters / edited by Insup Taylor and David R. Olson.
p. cm. -- (Neuropsychology and cognition ; v.7)
Papers presented at a conference held June 1-4, 1988, Toronto, Canada.
Includes bibliographical references and index.
ISBN 0-7923-2912-0
1. Writing. 2. Literacy. 3. Graphemics. 4. Reading (Early childhood) 5. Reading, Psychology of. I. Taylor, Insup. II. Olson, David R., 1935- . III. Series: Neuropsychology and cognition ; 7.
P211.S42 1994
302.2'244--dc20 94-20325

ISBN 0-7923-2912-0

Published by Kluwer Academic Publishers,
P.O. Box 17, 3300 AA Dordrecht, The Netherlands.

Kluwer Academic Publishers incorporates
the publishing programmes of
D. Reidel, Martinus Nijhoff, Dr W. Junk and MTP Press.

Sold and distributed in the U.S.A. and Canada
by Kluwer Academic Publishers,
101 Philip Drive, Norwell, MA 02061, U.S.A.

In all other countries, sold and distributed
by Kluwer Academic Publishers Group,
P.O. Box 322, 3300 AH Dordrecht, The Netherlands.

Printed on acid-free paper

Printed in the Netherlands

TABLE OF CONTENTS

PART III: EARLY STAGE OF LEARNING TO READ

PART IV: COGNITIVE AND METALINGUISTIC IMPLICATIONS OF LEARNING TO READ

PREFACE

Literacy is of concern to all nations, developed or under-developed, of the world. In recognition of this fact, the year 1990 was designated by the United Nations as the International Year of Literacy. A literate person is one who is able to read and write so as to function adequately in society. And reading and writing is done in a particular writing system or script. What kind of scripts are used in the world today and how do they influence the acquisition, use, and spread of literacy?

To address this important and timely question, a group of international scholars were invited to participate in the conference, 'Scripts and Literacy: East and West' in Toronto on June 1–4, 1988. This volume is an outgrowth of that conference.

Altogether 32 speakers presented 26 papers, of which 20 have been selected as chapters for this volume. Three additional papers were solicited to round out the content of the volume.

The 23 chapters discuss learning and processing of a wide variety of scripts, some familiar and some unfamiliar, such as Chinese, Japanese, Korean, Arabic, Hebrew, Devanagari, and Cree. The chapters are organized in four major sections: 'I. Optional and Optimal Scripts,' 'II. Reading Processes for Different Scripts,' 'III. Early Stages of Learning to Read Eastern and Western Scripts,' and 'IV. Cognitive and Metalinguistic Implications of Learning to Read Various Scripts and Script Types.'

We thank the following organizations for funding the conference: the Social Sciences and Humanities Research Council of Canada, the Connaught Foundation, the Japan Foundation, and the Joint Council of the University of Toronto/Ontario Institute for Studies in Education. We also thank Sylvia Wookey and Marie McMullin for looking after the many and varied needs of the participants at the conference, Denese Coulbeck and J. Wibier for their assistance in the preparation of this volume.

Toronto, Canada I. T. and D. R. O.

INSUP TAYLOR AND DAVID R. OLSON

1. AN INTRODUCTION TO READING THE WORLD'S SCRIPTS

A script or writing system represents spoken language in visible form. Scripts are diverse in their origin and history, in the linguistic units they code or represent, in the shape and number of signs they use, and in the rules relating signs to their spoken forms. They are conventionally classified into two main types, logographic and phonetic, on the basis of the ways they represent language. A logograph (logo = word; graph = written sign) represents primarily the meaning of a word or morpheme and secondarily its sound. A sign of a phonetic script represents primarily a sound unit, either a syllable or phoneme, and through a sequence of sounds and signs, the meaning of a word or morpheme. Not all scholars agree on this classification, as can be seen in this volume.

This volume examines many questions about the relations between scripts and literacy, such as their effects on learning to read, on word recognition, literacy levels, and the cognitive processes. In particular it examines on the differences and similarities between logographic and phonetic scripts. In this introduction, we concentrate on describing various scripts, leaving the reading processes for the contributors to discuss.

SCRIPTS: OVERVIEW

Writing systems appeared in Egypt and Mesopotamia around 3500 BC, in the Indus River valley around 2800 BC, in China around 2000 BC, and a millennium later in Mesoamerica. These ancient scripts used pictographs, word signs, syllable signs, determinative, as well as combinations of two or more of these diverse signs (e.g., Coulmas, 1989; Gaur, in this volume and 1984; Gelb, 1952; Jensen, 1970; Sampson, 1985).

Of these ancient scripts, only the Chinese script is still used, if with some modification. Furthermore, Chinese characters still remain basically logographic. Most, though not all, of other scripts examined in this volume evolved from the Phoenician script (16th Century BC) and are primarily sound-based.

The diverse scripts discussed in this volume by different contributors are listed in Table 1.

Scripts are written in various directions. In East Asia, Chinese characters, Japanese Kana, and Korean Han'gŭl were traditionally written vertically, but in modern times, have come to be written either vertically or horizontally. Alphabets are all written horizontally, most from left to right, but Hebrew, Arabic, and Urdu are written right to left (Vaid in this volume).

I. Taylor and D.R. Olson (eds.), Scripts and Literacy, 1–15.

The scripts listed in Table 1 are briefly described below.

TABLE 1
The scripts discussed in the volume

Script type	Script	Region of use
MEANING BASED		
Logography	Chinese characters	China, Taiwan (Korea, Japan)
SOUND BASED		
Syllabary	Kana	Japan
	Cree, Ojibwe	Canada
Syllabo-alphabet	Devanagari, Kharosthi	India
Alphabetic syllabary	Han'gŭl	Korea
Consonantal alphabet	Arabic, Urdu	Middle East, Pakistan
	Hebrew	Israel
Latin/Roman alphabet	English, Spanish, Athapaskan	UK, U.S.A., Spain, Canada
OTHER	Braille	

LOGOGRAPHIC CHINESE CHARACTERS

Logographic Chinese characters are used in China (the People's Republic of China) and Taiwan (the Republic of China), as well as by overseas Chinese in different parts of the world. They are used also in Japan and South Korea, where they are supplemented by phonetic scripts (Taylor and Park, in this volume).

A logograph represents primarily the meaning of a morpheme and secondarily its sound. There is nothing in a simple character that codes the sounds of a morpheme. (A compound character is described later.) Thus the same logograph may be given different sounds in different dialects, languages, and times, while maintaining more or less the same meaning. Consider the character 十 that represents the morpheme 'ten'. Its sound is *shi* in Mandarin; *sap* in Cantonese; *sip* in Korean, and *tō* in Japanese. (An overbar represents a lengthened vowel in Japanese.) The syllable in Mandarin and Cantonese has a tone, not necessarily the same tone, but not in Korean or Japanese. A character can also have multiple sounds: the character for 'ten' has the sounds of *to-, tō, jū, jitt-, jutt* in Japanese. The case is analogous to the Arabic numeral 10 being read *ten* in English, *dix* in French, and *Zhen* in German. Note that *ten*, a word in a phonetic script, cannot be read arbitrarily as *tom* or *net*.

Since each logograph represents a morpheme, there have to be as many logographs as there are morphemes in a language. A large dictionary may contain as many as 50,000 characters, though a literate Chinese may use only about 3,500 characters. The number of characters is not only large but also unspecifiable. Numerous characters have to be complex in shape to be discriminated from each other.

While the majority of characters are semantic-phonetic compounds that contain phonetic components, the phonetic is no longer a reliable guide to the tone syllable of a character after an extensive sound change over hundreds of years (Leong in this volume). For example, 江 ('river') contains the phonetic *gong* (level tone; right component) but has the sound *jiang* (level tone). (The left, semantic component represents 'water'.) To ease the learning of the sounds of characters, auxiliary phonetic scripts are used in China and Taiwan (see Lee, Uttal, & Chen, in this volume).

In spite of the disadvantages of logographic characters described above, characters have been used continuously for thousands of years by a huge number of people, because they have some important advantages. The Chinese language, which uses about 400 syllables or 1,300 tone syllables, and whose morphemes are monosyllabic, is full of homophones. The Chinese dictionary *Cihai* (1979), which contains 14,872 characters, lists no fewer than 150 morphemes with the same sound *yi* (falling tone). Each of these numerous morphemes has its own distinct character. Thus characters are useful in differentiating abundant homophones of the Chinese language. (To minimize ambiguity, this morpheme tends to be combined with another morpheme to form a compound word). Logographic characters are also useful in unifying the vast land of China populated by people speaking mutually unintelligible dialects, because a Chinese character, though pronounced differently in different dialects, maintains more or less the same shape and meaning.

PHONETIC SCRIPTS

In a phonetic script one graph represents a unit of sound, either syllable or phoneme, of a language. The meaning of a word or morpheme is then obtained in a sequence of sounds and signs, as *t, e, n,* in that sequence expresses one meaning and in the reverse sequence *n, e, t* expresses another meaning. There are basically two types of phonetic scripts: in a syllabary one sign represents one syllable, and in an alphabet one letter represents one phoneme. Some scripts can be described as alphabets with syllabic features.

Syllabary: Japanese Kana

In the Japanese Kana, one sign represents one syllable, and this sign cannot be analyzed into the consonant and vowel parts. For example, the three Kana signs かけた (*ka ke ta*) the first and the second signs code the same consonant *k*, while the first and the third signs code the same vowel *a*, but one would not know such a relation from their shapes.

There are a little over 100 Kana signs (46 basic, 25 secondary, and 35 compound) to represent that many syllables of the Japanese language.

(Strictly speaking, a Kana sign represents a "mora", a time to pronounce a short syllable, which may not contain a vowel.) Kana comes in two forms: cursive Hiragana tend to be used to write grammatical morphemes, while squarish Katakana tend to be used to write European loan words and onomatopoea.

Syllabary: Cree and Ojibwe

In the Cree syllabary used in northern Canada, the syllables *ka, ke, ki, ko* are represented by the signs *b, q, p, d,* respectively, while the syllables *na, ne, ni, no* are represented by the same signs written sideways. In other words, the shapes of the signs represent consonants, while the orientations of the signs represent vowels. There are a few auxiliary signs for final consonants: mat = L′. The Ojibwe syllabary is modelled on the Cree syllabary (see McCarthy, in this volume).

Alphabet or Syllabary: Devanagari and Kharosthi

The Devanagari and Kharosthi scripts used in East India have been described as types of alphabets (Gelb, 1952). Because some alphabetic letters are clustered into blocks, the scripts may also be described as syllabaries (Patel, in this volume; Prakash and Joshi, in this volume). Each consonant (C) letter actually represents "C + vowel *a*"; if a vowel other than *a* is required, some mark can be put on or under each consonant. For example, Devanagari syllable sign क represents *ka*. But to represent the syllables *ke, ku,* and so on, the sign for *ka* is now taken as a consonant sign so that *ku* is कु and *ke* is के . And two consonants without vowels form a ligature. The same principle applies to Kharosthi.

Alphabetic Syllabary: Han'gŭl

Han'gŭl is the sole script in North Korea and the major script in South Korea, which uses also some Chinese characters for some content words (Taylor and Park, in this volume). Han'gŭl is an alphabet, in that its letters represent phonemes. Unlike other alphabets used in the world that can be traced, directly or indirectly, to the Phoenician script, Han'gŭl was created in Korea in the mid-15th century and has some unique features. "Complex" sounds have complex shapes. For example, the basic letter ㄱ represents *k* or *g*; this letter with a stroke inside ㅋ represents *k′* (*k* aspirated); the letter repeated ㄲ represents the tense consonant *kk*. Han'gŭl is used like a syllable in writing and reading: two or more consonant and vowel letters are packaged into a syllable block, as in *k* + *a* + *k* = *kak* 각, in which the final consonant, -C, is put under CV. By packaging the 24 letters of the alphabet in a systematic way, over 12,700 CV, CVC, and CVCC syllable blocks can be generated, out of which about 2,000 are used in the language.

Consonantal Alphabet: Hebrew, Arabic, and Urdu

Consonantal alphabets, all deriving from the Phoenician script, have a distinctive letter for a consonant but not for a vowel. In Semitic and Hamitic languages that use such alphabets, consonants express the root of a word, while vowels express grammatical variations of the word. Modern consonantal alphabets have a small set of diacritics that can indicate vowels.

Alphabet: Greek, English, Spanish

The Greek alphabet, which was derived from the Phoenician script, is the first alphabet that contained letters for both consonants and vowels. It is the ancestor of the Latin alphabet, which in turn is the ancestor of most contemporary alphabets used in Europe, including English and Spanish. Because of sound changes over time, letter-sound correspondence is not always maintained. In English, for example, the letter *a* has several different sounds, as in *father, ant, cake*, and *all*. Yet there is some regularity in this complex sound-letter relation (Venezky in this volume). In other alphabets letter-sound relation tends to be simple and regular: Spanish (Koda in this volume) and Greek (Chitiri's paper presented but not included in the volume).

PURPOSE OF THE VOLUME

To reiterate the purpose of this volume, the contributors examine how scriptal differences affect such important issues as learning to read, reading achievement, word recognition, sentence and text comprehension, phonological recoding in reading, brain mechanisms, the role of metalinguistic knowledge, transfer of reading skills to other domains of activity, and levels of literacy in a culture.

As editors we tried to include many diverse scripts and views on reading these scripts. Not surprisingly, the contributors do not always agree with each other, thus making the debate lively and interesting. Later we will close this "Introduction" by drawing some conclusions from the diverse views.

We now introduce these contributions organized in four parts: optional and optimal scripts; reading processes for different scripts; early stages of learning to read; and cognitive and metalinguistic implications of learning to read.

Part I: Optional and Optimal Scripts

Chapter 2. Scripts and Writing Systems: A Historical Perspective

Albertine Gaur (British Library) challenges both of the assumptions underlying the conventional theory of the history of scripts, namely, that scripts are the attempt to represent the sounds of a language and that the differences among scripts are to be explained on evolutionary or progressive theories. Rather, she argues that scripts evolve for the preservation and communication of information – this applies equally to scripts and to modern communication technology – and that scripts take the form they do for a variety of reasons including the form of the language, the cultures they reflect, and the functions they serve. She examines the history of the major world scripts, pointing out how they came to take the forms that they did – Chinese serving to unite a variety of dialectical groups, for example, and alphabets evolving in the attempt to make a script devised for one language and culture serve the needs of a quite different language and culture.

Chapter 3. Optimal Orthographies

Henry Rogers (University of Toronto) addresses the issue of optimal orthography, i.e., the possibility that some types of writing systems are more suited than others to represent one language or group of languages. An optimal orthography should not only be efficient for an experienced reader and writer but also easily acquired by a beginning reader and writer. Rogers considers the linguists' notion that an underlying representation is the best level for an orthography: a morpheme should have a single representation, and different morphemes should be written differently. Syllabic orthographies would be appropriate for language with certain specific phonotactic configurations, while a phonemic orthography is preferable for a language with a high degree of fusion. A language with a high degree of homophony would be best written with a logographic system. For most areas of the world, an alphabetic system is the only new one that could be introduced, although a syllabic system would be acceptable in certain cultural situations.

Chapter 4. Logographic and Semasiographic Writing Systems: A Critique of Sampson's Classification

J. Marshall Unger (University of Maryland) and John DeFrancis (University of Hawaii) question the classification of writing systems into logographic and phonographic categories. They argue that no ordinary writing systems ever depend exclusively on morphological aspects of language. Rather, any practical system must convey a certain minimum amount of phonetic information, if it is to represent everything that could be said. They argue strongly that, on the broad theoretical spectrum from purely phonographic to purely logographic systems, all ordinary writing systems are clustered within a relatively small range. Although Chinese writing may be near the logographic extreme of this range, there are non ordinary writing systems, such as military codes, that are far better examples of true logography. (Likewise, they might have added, Finnish orthography is said to be a prime example of phonography, but is under-specified compared with some of the unwieldy but precise notational systems used by phoneticians.) The often striking differences among scripts is thus more apparent than real and mask an essential unity that embraces all writing systems.

Chapter 5. The Cree Syllabary and the Writing System Riddle: A Paradigm in Crisis

Suzanne McCarthy (Ontario Institute for Studies in Education) also challenges the classification of writing systems into phonographic and logographic systems, since this does nothing to illuminate the distinctions between alphabets and syllabaries. Although the Cree syllabary appears to outsiders to have analytic aspects to it, she argues that the Cree themselves have used it primarily as a "pure" syllabic system. She suggests that it is the unique characteristics of a syllabary which cause the Cree to so closely identify syllabics with their language and culture. She proposes a paradigm for writing systems in which the primary division is between syllabic (wholistic) systems and alphabetic (analytic) systems. Within each category a continuum exists, the first, ranging from "pure" syllabic, i.e. Cree, to morphosyllabic, i.e. Chinese; and the second, from relatively phonemic, i.e. Finnish, so morphophonemic, i.e. English. Within this paradigm all full writing systems have a phonographic base: none are purely morphemic.

Chapter 6. Developing Orthographies: The Athapaskan Languages of the Northwest Territories, Canada

Keren Rice (University of Toronto) discusses the range of cultural and political factors involved in the development of orthographic conventions for one of the languages of the Athapaskan family in the Northwest Territories of Canada, the Dene. Decisions regarding the development of the orthography involved a series of compromises between such factors as accuracy of representing a particular dialect against applying the orthography to a larger community, and precision in representing speech units against the ease of visual recognition of morphemic constituents. In the choice of a writing system, linguistic and social factors sometimes outweighed the factors of ease of reading and writing and the resulting script, although basically alphabetic, employs some syllabic and logographic signs.

Chapter 7. Orthography and Reading in Kannada – A Dravidian Language

P. Prakash (University of Mysore, India) and R. Malatesha Joshi (Oklahoma University) provide an enlightening account of the history of the two Indian scripts, Kharosthi, written from right to left, and Brahmi, written from left to right. One Brahmi script is used to represent Kannada, a major south Indian language belonging to the Dravidian language family. This writing system is a mixture of syllabic and alphabetic principles with a grapho-phonological mapping of sign to syllable, and each syllable, in turn, being analyzable into consonant and vowel sounds. But as Kannada is a poly-syllabic agglutinate language with numerous inflections, written words can be long and have complex internal structures. (Faced with a similar problem, Rice in this volume reports that the Athapaskan script inserted word spaces between inflectional morphemes.) Although the Brahmic script is readily learned, traditional pedagogic methods often allow children to confuse reading with memorization. Reform in instructional method is required.

Part II: Reading Processes for Different Scripts

Chapter 8. How English is Read: Grapheme-Phoneme Regularity and Orthographic Structure in Word Recognition

Richard Venezky (University of Delaware) has examined the complex and devious ways that English spelling relates to punctuation. A series of studies attempted to determine which of these relations are exploited in word recognition, especially if word recognition relies on phoneme recognition. He concludes that the regularity of the relations between sound and letter has no effect on word recognition: readers do not recognize words by generating their phonological form on the basic of their spelling. Phonological recycling occurs when the form has to be held in memory while other aspects of processing occur. This view is similar to that reported by Leong for Chinese (this volume).

Chapter 9. Getting at the Sound and Meaning of Logographic and Alphabetic Scripts

Rumjahn Hoosain (University of Hong Kong) provides an extensive summary of his own and others' research on word recognition in logographic and alphabetic scripts. By comparing the reading of Chinese with the reading of English, he finds that meaning extraction is faster with single logographic characters than with single alphabetic words, whereas pronunciation is faster with alphabetic words than with logographs. But he points out that fast meaning extraction of Chinese characters does not translate into faster reading of Chinese text because of other factors, such as those sequential factors responsible for the comprehension of propositions and texts. A similar conclusion is formulated in neuro-linguistic terms. Whereas earlier studies had indicated that logographs are processed by the right and alphabets by the left hemisphere of the brain, Hoosain provides more recent data suggesting that both are processed in the left, though possibly in different areas of the left.

Chapter 10. Script Factors that Affect Literacy: Alphabetic vs Logographic Languages

In-Mao Liu (National Chung-Cheng University, Taiwan) reports on eight studies conducted to examine a series of hypotheses about how alphabetic words and logographs are processed. Like Hoosain he concluded that, counter to the conventional belief that Chinese characters map directly into meaning while alphabetic characters map to sound, both scripts involve word or morpheme recognition rather than meaning recognition and in that sense provide indirect routes to meaning. Some differences do appear. Logographs provide graphic visual clues, in addition to word retrieval, thus facilitating memory. Also the minimal representation of sound by Chinese characters results in it taking longer to voice low-frequency logographs than low-frequency English words. Finally, for Chinese, unlike for English, context does not aid the rapid pronunciation of characters. These conclusions provide detailed information on how similarly or differently Chinese characters and alphabets are pronounced.

Chapter 11. Orthographic and Psycholinguistic Considerations in Developing Literacy in Chinese

Che Kan Leong (University of Saskatchewan, Canada) extends the preceding arguments of Hoosain and Liu. First he explains Chinese phonology and how Chinese characters represent sounds and how characters represent the morphemes of the language. He goes on to present research evidence that access to the Chinese lexicon in the form of a mental dictionary is most efficient via a visual or orthographic route but that phonetic recoding is also needed at times, particularly for storing items in working memory during comprehension of a text.

Chapter 12. Differential Processing of Content Words and Function Words: Chinese Characters vs Phonetic Scripts

Insup Taylor (University of Toronto) and Kwonsaeng Park (Keimyung University, Korea) carried out five experiments to see how script manipulations (e.g., Hancha-Han'gŭl mix, Han'gŭl only) influence reading Korean and also English texts. In a Korean text, important content words (CWs = nouns, verbs, adjectives, and some adverbs) can be written in visually complex logographs, i.e. Hancha, while unimportant grammatical morphemes (GMs = postpositions, verb or adjective endings) are written in visually simpler phonetic scripts, i.e., Han'gŭl. In English, a passage with CWs in boldface and function words (e.g., *in, the, of*) in plain font was read faster than a passage with all words in plain font. In Korean, however, a passage with CWs in Hancha and GMs in Han'gŭl was read slower than a passage with all words in Han'gŭl. In a Japanese study, a Kanji-Hiragana mixed text was read much faster than an all-Hiragana text. Why do the results differ between Japanese and Korean? The learning and use of Kanji are extensive in Japan, whereas they are limited in South Korea. Enhancing visual distinction between CWs and FWs/GMs can speed reading, but only when readers are equally familiar with the fonts, script, and orthographies in which the two different types of words are printed.

Part III. Early Stages of Learning to Read

Chapter 13. Teaching Japanese Toddlers to Read Kanji and Kana

The Japanese script is a mixed system that is composed of Kanji, borrowed Chinese characters, and two forms of Kana that represent syllables. In six years of primary school, Japanese children learn about 1,000 of the 2,000 official Kanji. In view of the commonly held assumption that Kanji (unlike the syllabic Kana) are difficult to learn it is interesting to read the report of Miho Steinberg (Nagoya Gakuin University, Japan) which shows that a few hundred Kanji and Kana can easily be taught to toddlers in some 15 minutes per day using a whole word, then a phrase, then a sentence method.

Chapter 14. Asymmetries Between Reading and Writing for Japanese Children

Jun Yamada (Hiroshima University) examined the errors school children (in grades four, five and six) make in learning to read and write Kanji. He found important asymmetries between reading and spelling. But whereas for the reading of English these asymmetries can be explained by suggesting that beginners use a visual strategy for reading but a phonological strategy for spelling (Bryant and Goswami, 1990), Yamada attributes the asymmetries for Kanji to such factors as homophony, homography, graphic complexity and the transparency of a script. In contrast to the relative ease with which preschoolers learn a few hundred Kanji (Steinberg, this volume), Yamada found that school children's mastery of Kanji both in writing and reading was poor (perhaps due to multiple readings associated with each Kanji).

Chapter 15. Reading Disabilities in Japan: Implications from the Study of Hemispheric Functioning

Takeshi Hatta and Takehito Hirose (Osaka University of Education) report a series of experiments on the reading abilities of Japanese school children. They find that 11% of fifth grade children are two or more grade levels behind in reading scores, thus dispensing with the common view that reading disability does not occur with logographic scripts and that Japanese children have no reading disabilities. Rather than claiming that logographs are processed by the right hemisphere of the brain, a view criticized in Chapters 5, 6, and 7, they suggest that both left and right hemispheres of the brain are involved in high verbal ability. The possibility remains that the relatively poor reading of Japanese children is identical in form to the poor reading of alphabet-using children. This possibility is examined more closely in the following chapter.

Chapter 16. Writing Systems and Acquisition of Reading in American, Chinese, and Japanese First-Graders

Shin-Ying Lee, David Uttal, and Chuansheng Chen (University of Michigan) compared the initial acquisition of literacy among children learning to read Chinese, Japanese, and English. Their study is exemplary in the care given to selecting comparable populations of subjects, in equating educational experiences, and in designing comparable measures of learning. Earlier studies by their group, led by Harold Stevenson, had shown that the percentage of children falling behind by two or more years was similar for the three countries. In the present study, American children, compared to Chinese or Japanese children, did worse in reading words at the end of the first grade, but did better in reading words that had not yet been taught and in answering comprehension questions beyond their grade level. Furthermore, the variability or spread in scores among American children was larger than that among Chinese children. They conclude that reading success and failure cannot be simply attributed to the orthographic differences; each system has easy and difficult features.

Chapter 17. Brahmi Scripts, Orthographic Units and Reading Acquisition

P. G. Patel (University of Ottawa) examines the linguistic organization underlying the writing system known as Brahmi. The ancient Hindu scholars designed Brahmi to represent syllabo-alphabetic units, which can be interpreted in terms of the current phonological terms "mora" (short, one-beat syllable) and "extra-metrical element". In the different Indian scripts, which are based on Brahmi, moras and extra-metrical elements function as orthographic units that provide intraword segmentation. Patel discusses the relevance of the syllabo-alphabetic writing system to reading acquisition and presents some data on Gujurati-speaking children from Baroda, India.

Chapter 18. Orthographic and Cognitive Processing in Learning to Read English and Hebrew

Esther Geva (Ontario Institute for Studies in Education) studies children who are learning to read in two scripts, English and Hebrew. Both are alphabets, but English is a Roman alphabet that is read from left to right, whereas Hebrew is a Semitic alphabet that is read in the reverse direction (like Arabic and Urdu). Despite the differences in the shapes of letters and reading direction, children who were good readers in one language-script tended to be also good readers in another language-script. The finding suggests that language and cognitive abilities more general than those specifically involved in decoding a specific orthography are central to reading.

Part IV: Cognitive and Metalinguistic Implications of Learning to Read

Chapter 19. Script Directionality Affects Nonlinguistic Performance: Evidence from Hindi and Urdu

Jyotsna Vaid (Texas A & M University) examines the effect of reading directionality, left to right versus right to left, by comparing the reading of Hindi and Urdu words and sentences. Hindi uses the Devanagari script derived from Sanskrit, while Urdu is a form of Nasta'liq, an Arabic script. Yet Hindi and Urdu have the same dialectical base, essentially the same grammar and a common core lexicon. Thus, one language is written in two different scripts. (This event may be contrasted to China, where several different dialects share a common written form). Hindi and Urdu permit one to examine the effects of directionality of script on the more general cognitive and representational processes. In a drawing task, Hindi subjects begin at the top left of the page, while Urdu subjects begin at the top right, just as they do in writing. Further, Hindi subjects tend to draw objects facing leftward, a tendency previously attributed to lateralization of hand and brain. Most interestingly, Hindi subjects also tended to scan pictures from left to right, a tendency also previously attributed to cerebral dominance. So, reading habits do influence perceptual and cognitive activities.

A propos to this study, and anecdote illustrates the effect of reading directionality. Proctor and Gamble have a well-known advertisement for laundry detergent, which shows a pile of dirty clothes on the left, a box of Tide in the middle, and clean folded clothes on the right. The ad worked very well in North America and Europe. But in Arabia, sales of P & G products dropped. Why? Arabic readers viewed the ad from right to left, associating Tide not with the clean folded clothes but with the dirty ones on the left!

Chapter 20. Cognitive Consequences of L1 and L2 Orthographies

Keiko Koda (Ohio University) examined the possibility that the effects of learning to read a first language (L1) in one orthographic system influences learning to read a second language (L2) involving a different orthographic system. Readers of alphabetic scripts for L1 were disrupted by the presence of unpronounceable words in L2 much more seriously than were readers of morphological scripts in L1. Reading strategies for L1 therefore transferred to the reading of a new script.

Chapter 21. Lexical Representation of Script Variation: Evidence form Korean Biscriptals

Kwonsaeng Park (Keimyung University, South Korea) and Jyotsna Vaid (Texas A & M University) explored incidental memory for the script in which words were presented. Subjects were more likely to recall the script in which a word was written when it was in Hancha than when it was in Han'gŭl. Similarly, memory for Hancha words was enhanced when the words were copied. Even when Hancha words were read aloud (auditory processing) subjects were more likely to remember the script type when it was Hancha than when it was Han'gŭl. On the other hand Han'gŭl words, being in phonetic scripts, were named faster than Hancha words. The authors acknowledge that some of their results may have been affected by subjects' greater familiarity with Han'gŭl. The effects of familiarity also affected the findings of Taylor and Park (this volume).

Chapter 22. Syllabic Literacy and Cognitive Performance Among the Cree and Ojibwe People of Northern Canada

John Berry and Jo Anne Bennett (Queen's University) report on the acquisition and use of a syllabic writing system among the Ojibwe people of Northern Canada. Knowledge of the Cree syllabary is widespread, serving a variety of local and interpersonal purposes. The Cree syllabary is easily learned and is becoming increasingly important in fostering native identity. This form of literacy, unlike systematic schooling, however, bears little relation to other cognitive skills including the high levels of spatial ability usually reported among Arctic hunter-gatherers.

Chapter 23. Orthography, Vision, and Phonemic Awareness

Robert Scholes (University of Florida) presents an ingenious method of examining the relation between a script and linguistic awareness. Capitalizing on the fact that braille represents words in three different ways, namely, logographically or syllabically or alphabetically, he examined the possibility that phoneme deletion would be easy for words represented alphabetically but not for words represented logographically. In fact, orthographic form was found to have no effect on task performance. This work is compared to results of studies of phoneme deletion in sighted readers of English who show a reliance on spelling in such tasks. Based on this and others' work, the author suggests that the acquisition and use of literacy in any type of orthography – so long as the orthography represents the morphology of the language – can lead to an awareness of purely abstract linguistic constructs, i.e., to constructs (here termed "intensional") whose reference is internal to the grammar itself (as opposed to reference to elements of the extra-linguistic universe).

CONCLUSIONS

The 23 chapters of this volume reported on reading and literacy in more than a dozen different writing systems, with particular attention to two major types, logographic and phonetic scripts. The logographs examined were the Chinese characters used by Chinese, Japanese, and South Koreans. The phonetic scripts examined were the variety of alphabets (English, Spanish, Hebrew, Arabic, Urdu, and Athapaskan), syllabaries (Japanese Kana and Cree), and alphabets with syllabary features (Korean Han'gŭl, East Indian Brahmi, Kharosthi, Devanagari). One chapter deals with Braille, a script for the blind.

Some of the chapters point out similarities among different scripts and reading processes, while others point out differences. Differences are found most often in word recognition. Readers extract meaning faster from logographs than from words in a phonetic script, whereas they pronounce words in a phonetic script faster than from logographs. Visual memory for logographs is better than for words in a phonetic script.

In reading text, however, scriptal differences tend to disappear. Readers, in whatever script, may resort to phonetic coding to store linguistic items in working memory during comprehension. They also may use the strategy of processing important information more deeply than unimportant information. Good readers in one language-script tend to be good readers also in another language-script.

Both logographs and phonetic signs appear to be processed in the left hemisphere of the brain. After all, when individual graphs – be they Chinese characters, syllable signs, or alphabetic letters – form a word, sentence, and text, they have to be processed sequentially, and at certain stages phonetically. A sequential-phonetic processing is the province of the left hemisphere. But within the left hemisphere, logographs and phonetic signs may be somewhat differently represented.

Both logographs and words in a phonetic script can be learned by a whole word/logograph method, even by toddlers. But at some stage of learning, a phonics method (letter-to-sound translation) can be used with phonetic scripts but not with logographs. Taught by the phonics method, children can sound out even new words not yet taught.

In learning to read and write at school, children will always differ in their performance, but kinds and sources of difficulties differ for different scripts. For example, irregular spelling and pronunciation present difficulties for English-speaking children; multiple readings for one Kanji present problems for Japanese readers; the complexity of shapes and a large number of Chinese characters present problems for their users.

So, logographs and phonetic scripts are different or similar, depending on which aspects are examined. The differences tend to be found in word recognition, whereas the similarities tend to be found in text reading.

BIBLIOGRAPHY

Cihai ('A grand dictionary of Chinese words'). 1979, Shanghai Dictionary Press, Shanghai.
Coulmas, F.: 1989, *The writing systems of the world*, Basil Blackwell, Oxford.
Gaur, A.: 1984, *A history of writing*, British Library, London.
Jensen, H.: 1970, *Sign, symbol and script: An account of man's effort to write*, George Allen & Unwin, London.
Maddieson, I.: 1984, *Patterns of sounds*, Cambridge University Press, New York.
Sampson, G.: 1985, *Writing systems*, Stanford University Press, Stanford, CA.
All the chapters of this volume.

PART I

OPTIONAL AND OPTIMAL SCRIPTS

2. SCRIPTS AND WRITING SYSTEMS: A HISTORICAL PERSPECTIVE

Evaluations of writing systems, or a particular script, are all too often based on the twin assumption that it is the purpose of writing to make language visible; and that the alphabet is best suited to achieve this. Such a Euro-centric approach ignores both history and facts.

It is difficult to see how the alphabet can be the best and most unambiguous medium to make, for example, the English language visible. One has only to remember that there are at least five different ways of pronouncing the vowel sign *a*, or look at words like: 'drought', 'love', 'shut', 'belief', 'receive', 'reed', 'read', 'bread', 'food', 'nude' etc. Contrast this with words written in one of the syllabic Indian scripts, namely Malayalam:

Kēraḷapāṇinīyam

Garuḍasendēśām

Malayavilāsam

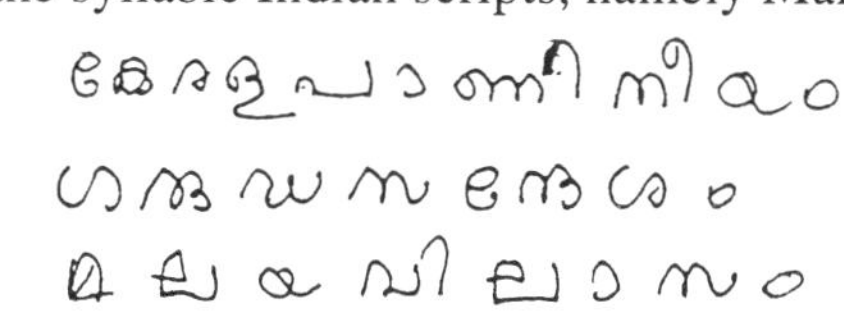

In the case of the latter the phonetic elements (phonemes) are represented in a consistent and unambiguous fashion by one character only. Having been taught the Malayalam script it would indeed be possible to transcribe those words into the alphabet and back again into Malayalam characters without knowing their meaning. The reason is simple: Indian (Brahmi derived) scripts are especially designed to fit the peculiarities of Indian languages, the same can not be said of modern European languages and the alphabet.

Is the visible representation of language really the primary and (as some would have it) only purpose of writing? Has this been the motivation behind the development and the continuation of the various writing systems? What are the systems which have come into existence over the last six millennia and how are they read and used?

It is generally accepted that systematic writing, using codified graphic symbols, came into existence in Egypt and Mesopotamia sometimes between 4000–3000 BC, probably around 2800 BC in the valley of the River Indus, c. 2000 BC in China and perhaps over a millennium later in Central America. The common factor which necessitated such developments has often been pointed out: a move from various levels of subsistence farming to communal labour which allowed for the production of surplus, the consequent creation of large settlements (cities), an organised exchange of property (trade), and a need for agencies to safeguard the new prosperity (centralized organisation and states).

The scripts used by those communities were highly sophisticated, and,

I. Taylor and D.R. Olson (eds.), Scripts and Literacy, 19–30.

though vastly different in appearance, they have certain elements in common. They all make use of pictorial representations (humans, animals, plants, objects, actions) which are often borrowed from earlier property marks (Mesopotamia), heraldic symbols, name and/or office identifications (Indus Valley, China), iconographic elements (Central America) and cult symbols (Egypt). Together with an effective representation of sound elements, Rebus (transfer), and the use of determinatives to clarify ambiguities, they are far from primitive. They were also highly effective forms of writing. The Egyptian system of writing could for example express gender, numbers, cases and prepositions. The Aztek script had similar flexibility. Two days after Cortez landed in Vera Cruz, Moctecuma received a written account of the Spaniards' arrival, describing their ships, their horses (unknown in Mexico), and their weapons. The Aztec empire perished not because it lacked effective means of communication and information storage but because its political leaders failed to act upon the information received.

How did those systems function and what was their exact relationship to language and speech?

The Egyptian script which developed around 3100 BC (and remained basically unchanged for nearly three and a half thousand years) structures itself around a number of basic components:

(1) Logograms, represented by drawings depicting objects or actions (i.e. the drawing of a leg means 'leg', the drawing of two legs can mean 'to go' and so on).

(2) The concept of Rebus (transfer); i.e. logograms are additionally used to write words, or parts of words, to which they bear no relation but which share the same consonants. This allowed for a high degree of flexibility; if, for example, we transfer this idea to English, the drawing of a sun disc meaning 'sun' and containing the consonants s-n could be used for writing 'sun', 'Sun-day', 'sun-ny', 'sin-ging', 'son-g', 'son' etc. In theory an Egyptian scribe could write a word consisting of more than one consonant in a number of different ways.

'Pyramid', for example, could be written:

1. By simply using the logogram

2. 'Linguistically'; by using the double consonant sign which stood for the phonetic representation of the word

 = m – r

3. By using the double consonant sign and the two single consonant signs, adding the determinative (which in this case is the logogram for 'pyramid')

 = m; = r:  = m – r (pyramid)

This seems to indicate great complexity but in reality the full range of possibilities was rarely used and the spelling was sufficiently standardized to make the words easily recognizable.

In addition to the (less than hundred) biconsonatal, and the (40–50) triconsonatal signs, there were also some 24 single consonant signs which could adequately have been used for the writing of the Egyptian language (a branch of the Hamito-Semitic family where the structure of the word depends on the consonants).

(3) To eliminate any remaining ambiguities the Egyptians employed determinatives, 'sense-signs' (other logograms) which, added to a particular word, indicated the sphere to which this word belonged. To return to English: the sign of a man added to the sign of a sun disc could only mean 'son'.

Why then did the Egyptians 'fail' to take the 'obvious step' and develop a full consonantal system? Those convinced of the inherent superiority of alphabetic scripts see in it proof for a general lack of abilities. But the answer may not be so simply. Despite the 'disadvantage' of a large number of signs (c. 700 were probably in regular use though the total number of known hieroglyphs is about 6,000) the mixed orthography of the Egyptian writing system creates visually distinctive word patterns which in fact greatly enhance legibility. Greek influenced experiments in the Late Period to write texts in an unbroken line, with a succession of consonants, were difficult to read and short lived. In addition, because of their relation to religious art, Egyptian hieroglyphs were capable of conveying additional (extra-linguistic) information, they could be cryptographic manipulated to increase the potentialities of the texts (similar to the way Hebrew letters are used to express cabbalistic thoughts).

Another important factor was the role played by scribes in Egyptian society. Scribes were members of a powerful and influential cross section, dominating both secular and religious administration. Moreover, the well-being of Egyptian society, its prosperity and security over several millennia was rooted in the consistency of its institutions and the hegemony of the realm. The brittle utilitarianism of the trading empires along the western seashore of the Mediterranean which eventually moved towards 'simpler' scripts did not yet recommend itself as progress.

A good example of the way in which a linguistically unsuitable system can provide a serviceable infrastructure is the cuneiform script of Mesopotamia. The earliest tablets (late 4th millennium) from what is now Syria, Iraq and Iran are inscribed with numbers, pictures and seals impressions, and related to business activities. ("Writing" as Walker puts it "was invented to record business activities in the Near East"; 1989: p. 7). The change from pointed to blunt-edged reed stylus (writing materials and writing implements have always played an important part in the developments of scripts) changed the appearance of the individual characters from thinly drawn picture to wedge-shaped cuneiform (Lat. *cuneus* – wedge).

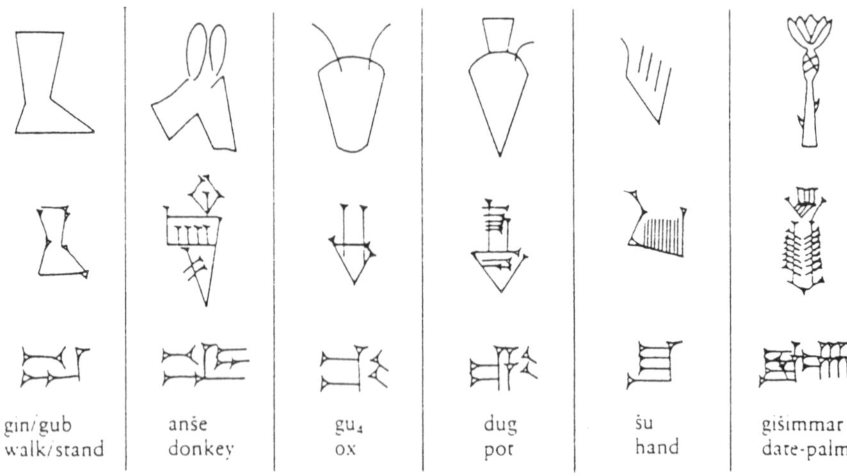

Fig. 1. From Walker, C.B.F.: *Reading the past: cuneiform* (1989), p. 10.

Originally logographic, the script acquired phonetic elements (and determinatives) similar to the Egyptian manner. But there are differences. The Sumerian language is agglutinative and rich in monosyllabic (verbal root) words, but, unlike Egyptian, vowels are important. Phonograms stood for syllables which could either be used directly or like a rebus. This was still relatively simple; problems arose when after 2800 BC the Semitic Akkadians (Babylonian/Assyrians) began to establish their dominance in Mesopotamia. Culturally less advanced, they took over certain vital features of Sumerian life; among them script and language (though the latter receded into a position similar to that of Latin in medieval Europe). Since the cuneiform script is ill-suited to accommodate the structure of a Semitic language, a number of compromises became necessary. Thus the Akkadians continued to use the Sumerian logograms but substituted the Semitic equivalent for the Sumerian word (if we transfer this situation to English and German, the drawing of a sleep could now be read as 'Schaf'); in addition they also made use of the original (Sumerian) phonetic value of the (written) syllables. The total number of distinct cuneiform signs was by then about 600, but the number of possible values and variations was of course much higher. Nevertheless, during the 2nd millennium BC Babylonian-Assyrian written in cuneiform script became the language of international diplomacy and was used as such from Persia to Anatolia, from the Caspian Sea to the Nile. The cuneiform script was also transmitted to various foreign peoples such as the Elamites, Hittites, Chaldean and Hurians, and the technique, thought not the system, formed the basis of Old Persian and Ugaritic (which used the cuneiform signs in a consonantal manner).

A similar situation can be observed in relation to the Chinese script which during the 4,000 years of its estimated history has undergone only comparatively minor changes. It is still basically a word, or better, a concept script with all the disadvantages and advantages such a system entails. The disadvantages are the large number of signs necessary – 50,000 altogether, though for everyday use 2,000 to 4,000 may suffice. The advantages are that as a concept script Chinese does not depend on the spoken word; it can be read without regard to, or even knowledge of, the spoken language. This made it, throughout Chinese history, an ideal means of communication in an empire whose people spoke a large number of different dialects, yet were all ruled from the same centre. For administrators and scholars alike, the Chinese script was the least ambiguous (and therefore simplest) form of communication.

It was also unnecessary for the written language to follow the development of the spoken language; indeed, modern Chinese do not need to know the ancient pronunciation of the words to read the classical texts. On the other hand the many homonymous (monosyllabic) words of the Chinese language make it sometimes necessary to refer to a written character for clarification. For example the word *fu* can mean: to return, to send, kingdom, father, woman, skin – but a separate character is used for each meaning. This is very different from the Mesopotamian usage where a single cuneiform character can be used to form the syllabic components of a number of different words. Another unique feature of the Chinese script is the emphasis it places on appearance. The formation of the characters must not only be correct, it must also be aesthetically pleasing; calligraphy, closely connected with painting, is (at least) as important as 'orthography'.

According to archaeological evidence Japan first came into contact with the much more advanced Chinese civilization during the Han dynasty (206 BC–220 AD). From the beginning of the Christian era the Chinese script was known in Japan through contacts with Korea, though only to a very small circle of people. In the 6th century Buddhism became the official state religion of Japan, with the result that a much larger section of society was now 'Chinese-educated'. From then on Japanese scholars went regularly to China for further studies, and in 645 AD a centralized administration, based largely on Confucian ideas, was installed which lasted until the end of the Heian period (12th century). Chinese writing techniques too were adopted: the brush, the ink, the ink-stone and, after 600 AD, the manufacture of paper.

How then was the Chinese script (designed for a largely monosyllabic language with hardly any grammar) adapted to the polysyllabic, agglutinative Japanese language full of formal words? Basically by the addition of simplified Chinese characters used in a syllabic manner. It is true that as a concept script the Chinese characters could simply have been read in Japanese. But the Japanese syntax is vastly different from Chinese, an additional difficulty which had to be overcome by adding special notations to indicate the order in which the (Chinese) characters should now to be read. The next step was the modification and simplification of some phonetic (Chinese) characters to form a systematic syllabary (*kana*) with fixed phonetic values. Between the 8th and the 10th century two such syllabaries evolved. Theoretically, Japanese could now have been written entirely in *kana* syllables and much poetry and prose literature of the Heian period (794–1192 Ad) was indeed composed in this way – but mainly by women authors. Chinese was too deeply entrenched as a prestigious form of writing to make its abolition feasible. After the end of the Second World War a mission consisting of twenty-seven American educationists recommended to General MacArthur a drastic overhauling of the Japanese education system. They called especially for the abolition of the "Chinese-derived ideograms", since otherwise Japan could never hope to achieve technological parity with the West!

It seems that between 1800–1300 BC sporadic attempts were made among Semitic people living on the eastern shore of the Mediterranean to arrive at a purely phonetic form of writing. The eastern shore of the Mediterranean was a highly cosmopolitan area, a meeting-place between Egypt, Babylon, the Agean and the rest of western Asia. The international character of the coastal towns required a knowledge of several languages and made much demand on the scribes who had to be conversant with different systems of writing. This was especially true for scribes in the employment of traders – for traders want to be understood, unlike politically dominant priests and administrators who can put the onus for understanding on others.

The question of the origin of the Semitic script is one of the most debated subjects in the history of writing and has occupied scholars from antiquity to the present day. Was it can independent unique invention (unlikely), a development on the basis of existing forms (probable), or an adapted borrowing from one of the existing forms of writing – Egyptian (still a strong favourite with many scholars), cuneiform, Cretan, Hittite or Cypriote? Whatever the exact origin of the Semitic script, there can be no doubt that it became one of the most powerful instruments for the dissemination of knowledge, stimulating the development and growth of new and highly efficient forms of writing in Europe and Asia, and becoming the vehicle for the spread of three major religious cultures: Christianity, Hinduism/Buddhism and Islam, while at the same time safeguarding, if not spreading Judaism – which after the rise of Christianity had turned into a non-proselyting religion.

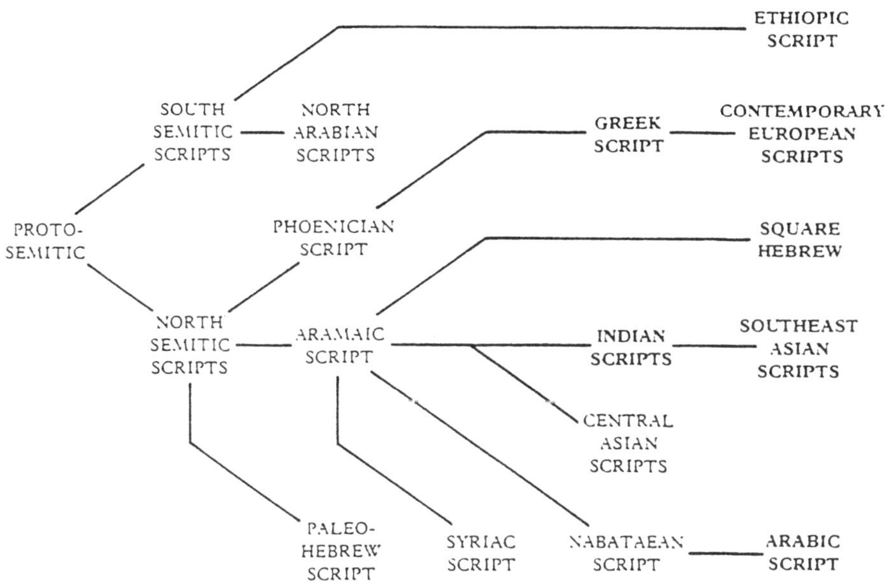

The chart shows the development of modern scripts (given in bold) from Semitic sources. From Gaur, A.: *A history of writing* (1987), p. 105.

There exist altogether three distinctly different though equally effective forms of purely phonetic writing which relate mainly to the way sounds are broken down into their most basic units: syllabic scripts, consonantal scripts and alphabetic scripts.

In the case of a syllabic script the basic sound unit represented by a graphic symbol is the syllable. Such a syllable can consist of: consonant plus vowel; vowel plus consonant; consonant plus vowel plus consonant; or a vowel on its own. Graphically a syllable can be represented by one individual sign, or by a combination of consonant signs plus an (abbreviated) vowel sign. In the case of a consonantal system words are represented by their consonants which carry the meaning, vowels serve mainly to fashion grammatical forms (k t b can thus stand for all words associated with writing depending on the interpolated vowels). Vowel indicators may and do develop but their use is nearly always auxiliary and optional. The exact opposite is true in the case of an alphabetic script. Here vowels and consonants are of equal value, and, at least in theory, each phoneme is represented by a single sign.

Greek tradition and modern scholarship alike consider the Greek alphabet a successful mutation of the Phoenician consonant script. When exactly this transfer took placed remains speculative, the earliest inscriptions so far discovered date from the 8th century BC. By then the Greeks had twice tried to borrow a script for the use of their language: the syllabic Cypriote script and Cretan Linear B, both highly unsuitable and short lived. In their original form the 22 Phoenician (consonant) signs were even less suited; Greek is an Indo-European language and vowels are important. But this time the Greeks went beyond mere borrowing and established a convention by which Phoenician consonant signs, for which the Greek language had no corresponding sounds, were used to represent vowels (a, e, i, o). In the course of time further modifications were made but none was quite as important and far reaching as the stabilization of vowel representations and their continuous use. At first a number of local variations of the alphabet arose to fit the various dialects but around 403 BC the Athenians passed a law which made the use of the Ionian alphabet compulsory in official documents. Eventually the Ionian alphabet superseded all other forms, and from then on the Greek alphabet underwent no further radical changes.

Diringer has called the alphabet a 'democratic' script (1953: 214), as opposed to the scripts of Egypt, Mesopotamia and China, since it was accessible to a wider section of society and dispensed with the necessity for an expensively trained elite; and Greek society had indeed reached a stage where it was in need of such a means of information control. Under Athenian democracy all (free male) citizens were actively involved in the affairs of state. The machinery of government depended not on scribal coordinators but on the contribution of its citizens who performed duties which would today be undertaken by permanent civil servants, and in previous societies by professional scribes. The spread of democracy relied on the spread of literacy.

It seems that during the 8th century BC Greek settlers brought the alphabet to Italy where it was adopted (subject to some alteration and still written in the old Semitic right-to-left direction) by the Etruscans. Out of the various Etruscan alphabets the Roman (or Latin) alphabet, documented from the 7th/6th century BC onwards, evolved, and became in due course the script of the western half of the Roman empire. It was a highly successful and timely arrangement. In fact the level of literacy which prevailed in Rome during the 1st century AD was never again reached in western Europe until the 19th century (Michelle Brown, lecture, 1990).

In 311 AD Christianity became the official religion. A century later Rome was sacked by the Goths and the organized way of life which had marked the empire came to an end; and with it the need for common literacy decreased. Without the Christian church, which inherited the mantle of Rome, it may well have vanished. But as a proselyting religion Christianity depended on written texts and during the 7th/8th century the new faith spread along the old (Roman) lines of communication taking the Bible, the vellum codex and the quilt pen to the new centres of (Christian) learning and (Christian) control. By the late medieval ages the alphabet had travelled a long way and became the vehicle for a good many languages other than (and not always directly related to) Greek and Latin.

Writing systems are not only enabling agents, they also set norms. Once committed to writing the written language does not easily follow changes in the spoken language. In the 15th century an event took place which increased this distance even further, namely printing. As a commercial enterprise printing aimed at mass production; to be widely understood (and bought), standards had to be set (sometimes artificially) as far as the texts, their interpretation and the spelling of words was concerned. Printing also shifted the basic of support from patronage to capital, unlike the monks who worked in the monastic *scriptoria* the printer could no longer rely on a ready made clientele of *cognoscenti*, who had similar tastes and a similar level of education – he had to attract a largely anonymous general public. Language and text, and the spelling of words, had to become sufficiently uniform to be understood in different parts of the country (countries), by different classes of people. Orthography gained in importance. Now a highly (over?) priced criterion by which the level of education is all too often assessed, it is good to remember that it was originally just a practical, if not purely commercial, tool.

As far as Indian scripts are concerned (our second example at the beginning of this text), the situation was vastly different.

It is generally assumed that a knowledge of writing was brought to India by (Semitic) traders, not later than the 7th or 6th century BC. But orthodox Hindu society, which assigns special privileges and special duties to each caste, was not instantly receptive. The memorizing and the recitation of the sacred Vedic hymns, which ensured the well-being of the community and the continuation of the universe, was the carefully guarded property of certain Brahminical sub-castes whose position at the apex of the hierarchy depended on the retention of this monopoly. Manu and other Brahmanical law givers (500 BC–500 AD) degreed that a Shudra who accidentally heard the recitation of the hymns should have his ear filled with molten lead and his tongue torn from the mouth to prevent him repeating what he had heard (Kane, 1968: 306–349). Buddhism disrupted the established order by propagating a heterodox movement which rejected caste, ritual and occupational exclusiveness, and the first literary evidence indicating a more widespread use of writing (other than for purely commercial purposes) comes indeed from Buddhist sources of the 5th century BC. The earliest epigraphic records of a decidedly Indian form of writing are the edicts of the emperor Ashoka (272–231 BC) written in Kharoshthi (a geographically limited, short lived and mainly clerical script) and Brahmi (the basis of all Indian and most Southeast Asian scripts).

One of the difficulties when assessing origin and early development of scripts lies in the fact that we usually come across them, already fully developed, in the form of inscriptions. Much that must have been recorded before on perishable material (bark, leaves etc.), which would allow us a clearer understanding, is no longer available and we have to rely, to a large extent, on speculation. The Brahmi script of the 3rd century BC was already a most rational and scientific script, and one which provided Indian languages with an exact reflection of their pronunciation. (More so than the alphabet it 'made language visible'.) Since the correct pronunciation of the Vedic hymns had always been an essential part of the ceremonial aspect of Hinduism, an exact, orally transmitted knowledge of phonetics existed long before the Sanskrit grammarians codified the language in the 5th century BC, and long before it was committed to writing. This was an uniquely Indian situation which does however demonstrates that evolution need not necessarily take the same linear course in different civilisations.

Indian scripts are syllabic and consist (with the exception of Tamil) of about 48–54 basic signs which allow for a sophisticated level of manipulation. (1) All consonants are perceived syllabic, containing a short *a*, a vowel which occurs most frequently in Indian languages. (2) Vowel signs are written in their full form only if they are on their own or in an initial position; in conjunction with a consonant they are abbreviated to auxiliary signs before, after, below, or above the consonant. (3) Consonants without a vowel are if possible amalgamated, usually by writing one above the other, forming ligatures, or having a special sign added to them. (4) Arrangements of letters are strictly phonetic: vowel signs follow diphthongs (as understood in India), and the consonants are then arranged in seven groups indicative of the way in which they are pronounced. (5) The direction of writing is left-to-right, though early Brahmi (and Kharoshthi) were written right-to-left, indicative of the Semitic connection.

What then is the primary purpose of writing? From the above it appears that suitability to express language can easily be compromised when the script comes to serve political (China) needs, or when questions of prestige (Japan) are concerned. A well developed writing system, once firmly established, can have great staying power (cuneiform); compromise rather than total revision are often chosen to cope with linguistic (or other) changes (alphabet). Only the Indian syllabic script, designed on the basis of strong oral traditions of handling language and pronunciation outstayed the course. But this too only as long as it restricted itself to Indian languages. In the first Christian millennium a great cultural expansion into Southeast Asia took place which brought Buddhism, Buddhist manuscripts and Indian scripts to ethic groups which had no writing systems of their own. The languages spoken in those areas did not always fit easily into the Indian system, yet the scripts which consequently developed are still in use. Just as the development of early writing systems was mostly based on commercial and political needs (religion being in most cases only the continuation of politics by other means), those same needs have usually a say in their retention.

What then of the future? Throughout most of the 19th, and at least the first half of the 20th century, universal literacy and the alphabet were seen as the panacea for all social, economic and (in countries under colonial rule) political ills. As late as 1972 Gustav Barthel wrote in his study of the history of writing "im einundzwanzigsten Jahrhundert wird es auf Erden kaum noch Analphabeten geben" (p. 455), thus confidently confirming not only the arrival of universal literacy but associating it, exclusively, with the use of the alphabet. Only twenty years later the prophecy seems, to say the least, ill founded. What happened?

It is here perhaps time to ask ourselves two questions: what exactly is writing, and who needs it? Looking at the way scripts developed it is perhaps right to say that writing is basically an attempt to store information. What kind of information? To begin with, mostly information related to trade, administration and politics; in other words, information essential to the survival of a particular group. Religion and literature, 'texts', have for long been able to manage perfectly well within the framework of oral traditions. Only as a result of certain historical events such as the high death rate after 633 AD among the *Huffaz* who traditionally memorized and recited the Koran, or a situation where the endless number of commentaries and sub-commentaries began to outstrip human memories (India), or where critical interpretation became important, did it become necessary to store 'texts' in written form. Greek democracy, and in more recent times industrialization and colonial expansion demanded a wider spread of literacy. Now that we have firmly passed into the post-industrial period much has changed. The growing sophistication of electronic information storage is beginning to rival, and indeed often outstrip, writing. To function in this new world children have not only to be taught how to read and write, they must also be 'computer-literate'. It seems that information is again stored in memory (the electronic memory of the computer) the way it was once stored in human memory and unlike the way it is stored in books. There are indeed strange ritualistic elements in the logistics of computer usage: the need for a password to enter a particular system (to prove ones belonging to the circle of initiates), the formality of address and answer, the limitation of the subject that can be discussed. Any dialogue with a computer is based on computer rules, or rather on rules programmed into the computer by somebody else. The result is increased efficiency but also a loss of originality and independence. The risk is that of a divided society, divided not only into the 'information poor' and the 'information rich' (with the latter mainly to be found among technologically affluent nations) but also the creation of a new class system among the 'information rich': those who know how to handle, manipulate, select and create information, and those who passively accept information. The progressive decline in literacy and the ability to read and write among school children may in fact simply be a sign that out society no longer needs writing, and written information storage, in quite the same way. (There is also the sudden outburst of pictorial signs to aid us at every step of everyday life.) If this is the case, questions about the quality of teaching and the ideological defensibility of a particular teaching method alone will not solve the problem. We will have to ask ourselves in addition: what exactly is the society in which we are living, where will it lead us, and how can we best learn to cope with it?

REFERENCES

Barthel, G.: 1972, *Konnte Adam schreiben: Weltgeschichte der Schrift*, Koln.

Brown, M.: 1990, *A guide to western historical scripts from antiquity to 1600*, London.

Davis, W.V.: 1990, *Egyptian hieroglyphs*, London.

Diringer, D.: 1953, *The alphabet: a key to the history of mankind*, London.

Gaur, A.: 1987, *A history of writing*, London.

Gelb, I.J.: 1963, *A study of writing, the foundations of grammatology*, Chicago.

Harris, R.: 1986, *The origin of writing*, London.

Healy, J.F.: 1990, *The early alphabet*, London.

Jensen, H.: 1970, *Signs, symbols and script: an account of man's effort to write*, London.

Kane, P.V.: 1968, *History of the Dharmasastra: ancient and medieval religious and civil law in India*, Vol. i., Poona.

Laver, M.: 1980, *Computer and social change*, New York.

McArthur, T.: 1986, *Worlds of reference: lexicography, learning and language from the clay tablets to the computer*, Cambridge.

Sampson, G.: 1985, *Writing systems*, London.

Schmitt, A.: 1980, *Entstehung und Entwicklung der Schriften*, Köln.

Walker, C.B.F.: 1987, *Reading the past: cuneiform*, London.

Wellisch, H.H.: 1978, *The conversion of scripts: its nature, history and utilization*, Maryland.

HENRY ROGERS

3. OPTIMAL ORTHOGRAPHIES

INTRODUCTION

This paper examines the question of what constitutes a good writing system. I have taken it as given that some writing systems are better than others. This question could certainly be debated. The opposite position would be that all writing systems are equally good for all languages, that it simply makes no difference which writing system is used. As far as I know, very few people have held this position, either academics or lay people. Consider the presence of proposed spelling reforms for English, the recent character simplifications of China, and the considerable thought that is often given to establishing an orthography for a previously unwritten language. All these are clear testimony to the fact that people generally feel that some writing systems are better than others. (Berry, 1977; Justeson, 1988; Sampson, 1985; Winter, 1983)

An optimal writing system should have the following characteristics: it should be efficient for the experienced reader and writer, and it should be efficient for the person learning to read and write. Note that efficient is not the same as simple. Efficiency can be measured in terms of the time required and the number of mistakes made. It is difficult to determine the criteria for measuring simplicity. Who would claim that dividing nouns into classes like gender is simple; yet gender is a common linguistic phenomenon, with no obvious disadvantage to those languages having it. There is no obvious correlation between what seems simple to intellectual study and what seems simple to human psychological processes.

Despite any assumption that a particular writing system may be better or worse for a particular language, it should be pointed out that probably any writing system could be made to work for any language. Speaking only of alphabets, Pike (1947) says, "People can be taught to read any alphabet provided ample time is given and provided they desire to read strongly enough." An interesting example comparing alphabetic and non-alphabetic reading is the success that Rozin, Poritsky, and Sotsky (1973) had in teaching reading by means of Chinese characters to English-speaking children with reading problems. DeFrancis (1984) has a very amusing tongue-in-cheek discussion of various ways of writing English using Chinese characters.

This paper does not go into the very interesting question of the optimal shape of symbols (Spencer, 1959). I have mentioned at the end, however, that recent changes in technology have made innovation in symbol shape,

I. Taylor and D.R. Olson (eds.), Scripts and Literacy, 31–43.

as well as the use of less popular writing systems, more economically possible than in the past.

The study of writing systems is as subject to ethnocentric bias as most work in cultural areas. Titles like *Our Glorious Alphabet* are somewhat extreme, but at a more subtle level, there is no lack of articles extolling the virtues of a particular writing system, articles which happen to be written by speakers of that language. Obviously such work must not be arbitrarily discounted, but it must be used with care.

A second problem is that a large proportion of the research that has been done on reading has been done on European languages and on Japanese (Paradis, Hagiwara, and Hildebrandt, 1985). Undoubtedly, this non-random selection of languages has not given us a true picture of reading.

A further problem in research on reading is much more difficult to deal with. Reading is a skill taking years to develop fully. It is difficult to develop an experiment which matches the experienced reader's expertise in one writing system with a similar level of expertise reading the same language in a different writing system. If we want, for example, to compare reading in English using traditional orthography with reading in English using a different system, we generally do very limited studies. Work like that mentioned above by Rozin, Poritsky, and Sotsky (1973) compares traditional orthography with Chinese characters for reading English. Such a study tests the effect of the novel system for a short period of time, say a few weeks or months, and then generalises from the results of people who have read less text than what would constitute a typical novel. Proficiency in reading, however, requires thousands and thousands of hours of practice. It would be very difficult, however, to mount an experiment which compares experienced readers' ability to read English in traditional orthography with their ability to read English in Chinese characters. The cost and effort of producing such materials would be prohibitive, and it would probably be considered immoral to have children devote that much of their youth to an end with little direct and lasting advantage to them.

One possible area where comparative work can fruitfully done is in those situations where the same language is written with two different writing systems. Serbo-Croatian uses a roman and a cyrillic alphabet. Hindi-Urdu is written with the devanagari and Arabic alphabets.

In this paper I enclose phonemic transcriptions in solidi /x/, phonetic transcriptions in square brackets [x], morphemic transcriptions in curly brackets {x} and orthographic transcriptions in angle brackets ⟨x⟩.

GENERAL CHARACTERISTICS

This section examines what linguists and psychologists have considered a good writing system. In certain respects their views have been fairly compatible and have moved from an older to a newer view along the same lines (Venetzky, 1977).

Linguistic

The older view is typical of most western linguistics in the first half of this century. Linguists in this period were concerned with speech and not writing. This lack of interest was partially a reaction to an older view that writing was 'good' and speech was 'fallen'. Modern linguists of the twentieth century were eager to examine language as it actually existed, i.e., was naturally spoken, rather than as a record of carefully, edited 'good' usage (Sampson, 1955). The upshot of this view was that, with some exceptions (e.g. Chao, 1968; Trager, 1972), linguists viewed writing with a little disdain. To the degree that writing was considered at all, a good writing system was one that mirrored the phonological system of the language. The essential principle was that each phoneme should have one and only one written symbol. The best writing system for a language was essentially a phonemic transcription. Such a position rejected homographic English spellings such as ⟨blue, blew⟩ and tolerated spelling allomorphs differently as would be the case if *south* and *southern* were spelled phonemically, i.e., /ˈsawθ – ˈsʌðəɹn/.

Obviously with this frame of mind, logographic and syllabic systems were sadly deficient. Only alphabets had any claim to adequacy. Orthographic systems like those of Spanish or Finnish, which mirror the phonological system fairly closely, were held up as ideals. English orthography was an embarrassment. Hockett's (1958) view was that, when first introduced, a writing system was fairly good. Over time, however, the writing system failed to keep up with changes in the language and became an increasingly archaic anomaly.

Since the 1960's, adopting the views of the generative phonologists, linguists have generally altered their view of the phonology. This view takes the position that an abstract level of representation known as the underlying level has a significant importance in the structure of a language. This underlying level removes all predictable aspects of phonology. Having done this for English, Chomsky (1970) saw that the resulting underlying representation had much in common with the traditional English orthography. To illustrate this, the words *sane – sanity* are shown in Table 1.

TABLE 1
Representation

Surface	Underlying	Orthographic
[sejn]	/sān/	⟨sane⟩
[sæn–ɪti]	/sān–ɪti/	⟨sanity⟩

At the surface level, the two allomorphs are written differently in [sejn – sæn]. In the underlying representations for both forms, the root morpheme is identical – /sān/. The traditional orthography writes this the same as well – ⟨san⟩. Chomsky's claim that traditional English orthography is almost perfectly suited as a writing system for English is perhaps overstated, but is has been quite therapeutic in countering the view that English spelling is an unmitigated disaster.

There are a number of places where an underlying representation is obviously different from the spelling. There is, for example, no need whatsoever to posit an underlying /k/ in *knee*, /b/ in *debt*, or the first /l/ in *colonel*. See Sampson (1985) and Francis (1970) for other criticism. Sampson describes Chomsky's view as "extravagant and unsupported". Note very carefully that Sampson does not argue against an underlying representation as a good orthography, but against the extreme claim that English orthography is near-perfect. Sampson agrees with Albrow's (1972) more restrained version that English spelling shows fairly regular phoneme/grapheme correspondences. Justeson's (1988) review of Sampson leaves a false impression.

Authors sometimes use representations like /bɔj–pl/ for the sake of clarity in their presentation of the moment. Such a representation is mixed: phonological for /bɔj/, and morphological for /pl/. Occasionally, people have seen such representations and concluded that there is some sort of major difference in the representation at the underlying level between lexical morphemes like /bɔj/ and inflexional morphemes such as the plural morpheme. There is, in fact, no reason not to represent the form above as /bɔj-s/, which would be a more consistent representation at the underlying level.

From the changes in phonological theory, linguistics adopted a new view of what constitutes a good writing system. The principles that emerge are:

1. The underlying level is the best level for an orthographic representation.
2. Each morpheme should have one and only one representation without showing allomorphic variation.
3. Different morphemes should be represented differently.

Principle 1 supports representations like ⟨sane, sanity⟩, but not ⟨knee, debt⟩. Principle 2 follows from principle 1, and supports representations like ⟨south, southern⟩, but not ⟨duke, duchess⟩. Principle 3 supports representations like ⟨blue, blew⟩, but not ⟨well, well, well⟩ for the words meaning respectively 'healthy', 'in a good fashion', 'water hole'. Where principles 1 and 3 come into conflict, it is expected that 3 would generally override 1. Thus, ⟨blue, blew⟩ as dictated by principle 3 is preferred to writing them both with the same underlying form.

Chomsky (1970; see also Klima, 1972) points out that underlying representations are useful in that they preserve the semantic similarity of related words, they undergo change more slowly than do the surface forms, and they tend to be the same for various dialects.

Psychological

Psychology, in investigating writing, and particularly reading, has held views fairly similar to those of linguistics. The earlier view was that writing was a manifestation of the sound system of a language. Psychologically, writing was related to language via phonology.

The view generally held today is that writing is related to language as a whole; it is a system for making language, not just speech, visible. This means that writing may have connections to the morphology, syntax, lexicon, or semantics of a language which totally bypass the phonological system. The so-called *pictographic, ideographic*, and *compound ideographic* characters of Chinese (Chao, 1968) represent morphological or lexical units in Chinese and have no particular connection to the phonology.

These views are closely tied to notions of how we read. Readers have two different ways of reading at their disposal (Ellis, 1984). They may read by ear (Kavanagh and Mattingly, 1972). For this purpose a transcription which permits letter-to-sound conversion is most useful. This is particularly true in sounding out an unknown word (Goswami and Bryant, 1990; Goswami, 1992). Most English speakers have probably never heard the word *xylophilous* 'growing in wood' actually pronounced; certainly I never have. A familiarity with the standard letter-to-sound conversion rules is very likely to allow a guess which coincides with the dictionary's pronunciation of /ˌzajˈlɑfɪləs/. We might even be able to guess that British speakers would have /ˌzajˈlɒfɪləs/. This type of approach is typical of learners; they 'sound out' a new word. Experienced readers use this technique for new or unfamiliar words.

Readers also read by eye (Kavanagh and Mattingly, 1972). They recognise the entire word as a single lexical unit. For this type of reading, it is most helpful to have a transcription which writes homophonous words differently. Thus, the English spellings ⟨blue⟩ and ⟨blew⟩ help English readers grasp the meaning more quickly with less chance of error than if they saw an undifferentiated /blu/. This type of reading is characteristic of experienced readers. These people read most efficiently if the writing system is closely linked to the morphology: namely, with the same morpheme always written the same way and different morphemes written differently.

An ideal system would allow experienced readers to read morphemically, the most efficient way for them; yet, it would allow them to sound out unfamiliar words, as well as helping learners acquire reading and writing skills efficiently. Unfortunately, these goals are at odds with each other. In many cases, pursuit of one goal hinders achieving success in the other. With this in mind an optimal writing system is one which balances these conflicting ideals as well as possible. At the moment, we do not have an algorithm for achieving this balance.

One view is that writing systems tend to optimise themselves in time. This is a kind of Darwinian theory of natural selection. Writing systems will change in time so as to be optimally suited to their language. Olson (1988) in his article for the *Encyclopædia Britannica*, sets out the position that all writing systems represent relatively optimal solutions to a large and unique set of constraints, including: a. the structure of the language represented, b. the functions that the system serves, and c. the balance of advantages to the reader as opposed to the writer.

This view obviously supports Chomsky's view of English orthography and is completely at odds with Hockett's view (1958). On the other hand, it is hard to know whether a specific changes such as the recent character reforms in China (DeFrancis, 1977) are unnecessary or are a part of Olson's process.

Even if Olson's view is correct, linguists and psychologists continue to ponder the problem of what constitutes an optimal system. Partly from a curiosity as to how people read and write and partly from practical needs. There is an unwillingness to wait until a particular language has developed its optimal writing system, and there is a need to create new systems for previously unwritten languages and a desire to revise old ones as quickly as possible. Scholars working in education need to be able to advise on the best way for children to learn to read and write.

SPECIFIC CHARACTERISTICS

The following discussion attempts to see what characteristics would make a particular language more or less suitable for a particular writing system. Logographic and alphabetic systems are considered first. Because of their peculiar status, syllabaries are considered separately later.

I will use the terms *logographic, syllabic*, and *alphabetic* in their usual sense that a symbol represents a morpheme, a syllable, or a phonological segment, respectively (Sampson, 1985; Taylor, 1980). If we view these terms as theoretical ideals, we can fairly confidently say that no writing system is pure and fits any category absolutely. It is, however, convenient to use them as describing the overall tendencies of a writing system. Undoubtedly, most established writing systems are mixed. Chinese writing is fairly logographic although there is a phonetic component is most characters (DeFrancis, 1984). English is primarily alphabetic although spelling differences such as ⟨blue blew⟩ are logographic in nature.

Linguists have traditionally classified languages typologically using concepts such as synthesis and fusion. Comrie (1981a) suggests establishing a continuum for each of these notions and indexing languages along each continuum. The further notions of variation and homonomy are also considered.

Synthesis

Synthesis is the number of morphemes per word. It can be seen as a continuum. Languages with few morphemes per word are called isolating; languages characterised by polymorphemic words are called synthetic. Thus, English *boy* has only one morpheme and is at one end of the scale. By way of contrast, Svan is a Caucasian language, a group known for its high degree of synthesis. The Svan word /jə-q'ɑ-l-c'ɑ-k°ón/ 'she used to do it several times' (Comrie, 1981b) has six morphemes divided here by /–/.

isolating ⟵⟶ synthetic

Probably no language is completely isolating in that it has only one morpheme per word, although Chinese and Vietnamese seem to be situated towards the isolating end of the continuum. Inuit, Aztec, and the Caucasian languages all allow a fairly large number of morphemes in a single word. English is probably slightly on the isolating side. Language like Turkish with large sequences of affixes fall somewhere in the middle of the synthetic side.

It is often said that isolating languages are naturally better-suited for logographic systems. I find this notion hard to understand. Two principles follow from such a notion; for it to be true, at least one of them should be true.

a. An isolating language is ill-suited for a phonographic system.
b. A synthetic languages is ill-suited for a logographic system.

Vietnamese, a fairly isolating language, is written with an alphabet, phonographic even to the point of indicating tone. Also, with experience, Chinese speakers can read romanised Chinese. These two examples contradict point a.

In examining the second point, I have tried to see how difficult it would be to write Turkish, a fairly synthetic language with a logographic system. The simple word *evlerimizde* is shown below divided into its constituent morphemes. I have transcribed each morpheme with a logogram. The logograms are simply symbols which are available on my computer easily and which have some mnemonic value.

ev –	ler –	im –	iz –	de	'in our houses'
house	pl	1st	pl	in	
∩	. . .	♥	≈	⊕	

Obviously, producing logograms for the entire lexicon would be a considerable task, but no more so than starting over for Chinese. This observation contradicts point b above. In summary, I can find no merit in the notion that there is some natural connection between logographic systems and isolating languages.

Fusion

non-fusing ⟵——⟶ fusing

The second typological parameter to consider is fusion, the degree to which morpheme divisions are transparent. The English word *roasted*, for example, is transparently divisible into the two morphemes {roast} and {ed}. On the other hand, the word *went* is completely opaque in this respect. We require specific lexical knowledge to divide *went* as {go} and {ed}. We can speak of the morphemes in *went* as fused, as opposed to those of *roasted* which are not fused. Languages can be characterised according to the degree of fusion they exhibit.

An alphabetic writing system can represent both fused and non-fused forms equally well. A logographic system has more difficulty with fused forms. Assuming that such a system would represent *roasted* as a sequence of two symbols, there are two ways it could handle *went*. On the one hand, it could create a special symbol for *went*, different from the normal symbols for *go* or for *past*; or it could represent *went* as a sequence of ⟨go – ed⟩. In the latter case the reader is required to interpret the sequence ⟨go – ed⟩ as an unpredictable phonological sequence /wɛnt/. Either way is somewhat more complex than the representation for *roasted*; either an extra symbol is required or an extra burden is placed on the reader.

Variation

The third aspect of language to be considered is variation. To show this, I will consider three examples of variation in English:

leaf	[lif]	leav-es	[liv – z]
sane	[sejn]	san-ity	[ˈsæn – ɪti]
south	[sawθ]	southern	[ˈsʌð – əɹn]

All three of these examples show allomorphic alternation. In the first, the alternation is overtly marked with an orthographic alternation ⟨f – v⟩; in the second, the alternation is less obviously marked, but consistent with the ordinary spelling conventions of English. The third is unmarked. (Note the variation in the pronunciation in the name of the news service *Southam* [ˈsawðəm – ˈsʌðəm]; presumably, the spelling conventions of English do not give readers any sure direction here.) The alphabetic system used in English allows orthographic representations of allomorphic variation along a continuum, ranging from fully marked to completely unmarked.

A logographic system operates most comfortably at a more abstract level. It is likely to leave such allomorphic alternations unmarked. By using separate symbols for each of the allomorphs, this variation could be marked. In a strictly logographic system, however, no information as to the phonological nature of the alternation would be given.

Homonomy

A fourth consideration is the degree of homophony present in a language. How many separate lexical units sound alike? Chao (1968) says that in Chinese the syllable /xi/ has 116 characters in one dictionary. This figure is undoubtedly high on two accounts: first, it merges the tonally distinct syllables /xī xí xǐ xì/, and second, it includes some very rare items. Nevertheless, it is obvious that Chinese still has a very high degree of homophony.

Homophony is simply not a problem for a logographic writing system. As many symbols can be created for morphemes as may be required; their sound is irrelevant. Sampson (1985) cites a poem made entirely of the syllables /ī í ǐ ì/, and Chao (1968) gives one entirely with /xī xí xǐ xì/. Chinese readers can read the text when written in characters but have great difficulty in reading the same text written in romanisation, no matter how familiar they may be with the romanisation. The diversity of characters supplies the information as to which homophonous morpheme is intended.

An alphabet can deal with a limited amount of homophony. English, for example, has quite a number of homophones, although rarely more than two or three for any particular syllable shape: *to, too two; meat, meet; so, sow, sew; you, ewe, U, yew*. Taking the syllable /tu/ as an example, English orthographic conventions could possibly be stretched to provide distinct spellings for some 10–15 homophonous lexical items: ⟨to too two tu tuw tuu tuuw twu twuu twuh tuh tuuh⟩.

If a language has a large amount of homophony, a logographic system clearly is advantageous in this respect. It must be remembered, however, that there is some trade off here between reading and writing. Different orthographic representations (heterographs) are beneficial to the reader, but they require the writer to be careful in choosing the correct one. Conversely, undifferentiated orthographic representations (homographs) are easier to write, but harder to read by requiring the reader to figure out which one is intended. Furthermore, homography is usually not so great an impediment to reading as might be first thought. If the words written the same occur in different structures in the language, it is likely that the appropriate reading is the one the will occur most readily to the reader. In English, for example, the three lexical items all written ⟨well⟩ meaning 'water hole', 'healthy', or 'in a good fashion' are respectively noun, adjective,and adverb. The structure of sentence usually makes the choice quite easy with little ambiguity or confusion.

To summarise the discussion so far, whether a language is synthetic or isolating is irrelevant to choice of writing system. Fusion and variation in a language are more easily dealt with an alphabet. Homophony is more easily handled by a logographic system. Obviously, the amount of fusion, variation, and homophony must be taken into account.

SYLLABARY

The advantages of a syllabic writing system are two-fold. It has flexibility and capacity for innovation like an alphabet. Second, the same amount of text requires less writing and fewer individual symbol identifications in reading than does an alphabet. It has been argued as well that the syllable is a more salient psychological unit than the single segment (Ladefoged, 1982).

Syllabic writing systems seem appropriate for languages with certain specific features. A language is best suited for a syllabary if it has a fairly small number of possible syllable shapes. Japanese has primarily syllables with a consonant-vowel shape; syllable-final consonants and consonant clusters are severely limited. A Japanese syllabary has some 75 symbols which is quite a manageable number.

English has a much larger number of possible syllable shapes, certainly in the thousands (Read, 1983). Undoubtedly it is possible to have a syllabary with such a large number of symbols, but it seems of questionable utility to have one symbol for *sick*, a different symbol for *six*, a third, completely different symbol for *sixth*, and yet a fourth symbol for *sixths*. A very large syllabary would in fact function as a logographic system in many instances.

A syllabic system also functions best if the morpheme boundaries coincide with syllable boundaries. Consider two possible cases. In the first, there are two lexical morphemes /ka/ and /di/, and there are two inflexional morphemes /po/ and /gu/ which are suffixed to both of the lexical morphemes. In the column showing the morphemic representation, the /+/ indicates a morpheme boundary. The phonological representation is next with /–/ indicating a syllable boundary. The third representation is orthographic with the syllable shapes arbitrarily represented by the numerals 1–4. A syllabary can represent this sort of situation quite well because the syllable boundaries coincide with the morpheme boundaries.

Morphemic			Phonological		Orthographic	
{ka}	{ka + po}	{ka + gu}	/ka – po/	/ka – gu/	1–3	1–4
{di}	{di + po}	{di + gu}	/di – po/	/di – gu/	2–3	2–4

Consider now a slightly different situation. The lexical morphemes are /kap/ and /dig/; the inflexional morphemes are /o/ and /u/. Here the orthographic representation requires six syllabic shapes because the morphological and phonological boundaries do not coincide.

Morphemic			Phonological		Orthographic	
{kap}	{kap + o}	{kap + u}	/ka – po/	/ka – pu/	1–3	1–5
{dig}	{dig + o}	{dig + u}	/di – go/	/di – gu/	2–6	2–4
{kat}	{kat + o}	{kat + u}	/ka – to/	/ka – tu/	1–7	1–8

In the second situation, the visual unity of the morphemes has been lost. Note the forms for an additional morpheme {kat}. The forms /kapo/ ⟨1–3⟩ and /kapu/ ⟨1–5⟩ are no more related than are /kapo/ ⟨1–3⟩ and /kato/ ⟨1–7⟩, even though the former have the same roots and the latter have different roots.

CULTURAL

Arguments about writing often touch sensitive cultural concerns. Geerts, van den Broeck and Verdoodt (1977) outline the tension of spelling reform in Dutch. Norway now has two official dialects of Norwegian, each with its own orthography; school boards choose by local option. The Otomí Indians of South America rejected an orthography for themselves which contained such bizarre elements as a c-cedilla and certain accents, items unfamiliar to them from their acquaintance with Spanish (Grimes and Gordon, 1980). The simplification of Chinese characters has left a situation where their use or non-use may brand a writer with strong political overtones. In this volume, Rice (1994) states the cultural problems for setting out a common orthography for the various Slave groups.

Speakers may like the idea that language is written, but have little intention of doing much reading. In my own work, I have found Scottish Gaelic speakers, particularly in Protestant areas, who are resistant to the idea of anything but the Bible being printed in Gaelic. Presumably books in English have less resistance, or are considered beyond the pale. Rice (1994) reports that the Slavey people use writing not for creative activities but only for reciting known cultural material.

We often hear that the effort needed to learn characters is responsible for the low literacy rate in China. Given that Japan has a negligible illiteracy rate, and a more complicated writing system than Chinese, this position seems untenable (Martin, 1972). Literacy is primarily determined by a society's priorities and the amount of time the society is will to place on teaching reading and writing.

TECHNOLOGY

In the nineteenth century, typefounding and typesetting were fairly inexpensive; the result was that a good deal of diversity was possible in printed materials. In this century, circumstances have changed this. First, typefounding and typesetting became much more expensive, encouraging the use of what was already available, rather than innovation. Second, the introduction of typesetting machines limited the ease of typographical variation. The typesetting industry became geared to alphabetic writing systems, with a bias towards the roman alphabet. Third, the easy availability of typewriters meant that writers were essentially limited to the number of symbols printable on a standard keyboard. All of these influences acted together to discourage symbol innovation and the use of uncommon scripts.

The availability of micro-computers in this decade has reversed this trend. For computers, symbols are simply instructions on how to draw a figure. They easily handle a much larger number of symbols than does a typewriter. The author essentially acts as the typesetter. The result has been an enormous increase in the flexibility of printed output using all sorts of orthographies. There are hundreds of roman fonts available for computers. In the United States, two companies have managed to establish themselves offering dozens of non-roman fonts for the Apple Macintosh alone. There are now systems for Chinese, Japanese, and Korean. The micro-computer has taken away any serious need for undesired transliteration or romanisation.

CONCLUSION

There is probably no situation where a new writing system could be introduced uninfluenced by cultural considerations and determined only by linguistic and psychological considerations. For most areas of the world, an alphabetic system it the only new one which could be introduced, although a syllabic system would be acceptable in certain cultural situations.

The linguistic and psychological considerations argue that an underlying representation is the best level for an orthography. The principles set out above are that a morpheme should have a single representation and that different morphemes should be written differently. The result would be a mixed system, basically phonographic with a logographic element in that different morphemes would have different representations. Syllabic writing systems would be appropriate for language with certain specific phonotactic configurations. The balance between these two elements must be found by experience. Over time, the system should tend to improve.

BIBLIOGRAPHY

Albrow, K.H.: 1972, *The English Writing System: Notes towards a Description*, Longman, London.

Berry, Jack: 1977, '"The making of alphabets" revisited', in Fishman, 3–16.

Chao, Yuen Ren: 1968, *Language and Symbolic Systems*, Cambridge University Press, Cambridge.

Chomsky, Noam: 1970, 'Phonology and Reading', in Levin and Williams, 3–18.

Comrie, Bernard: 1981a, *Language Universals and Linguistic Typology*, Basil Blackwell, Oxford.

Comrie, Bernard: 1981b, *The Language of the Soviet Union*, Cambridge University Press.

Coulmas, Florian and Ehlich, Konrad (eds.): 1983, *Writing in Focus*, Mouton, Berlin.

DeFrancis, John: 1977, 'Language and Script Reform in China', in Fishman, 121–148.

DeFrancis, John: 1984, *The Chinese Language: Fact and Fantasy*, University of Hawaii Press, Honolulu.

Ellis, Andrew W.: 1984, *Reading, Writing and Dyslexia: A Cognitive Analysis*, Lawrence Erlbaum, London.

Fishman, Joshua A. (ed.): 1977, *Advances in the Creation and Revision of Writing Systems*, Mouton, The Hague.
Francis, W. Nelson: 1970, 'Linguistics and Reading: A Commentary on Chapters 1 to 3', in Levin and Williams, 43–56.
Geerts, G., van den Broeck, J., and Verdoodt, A.: 1977, 'Successes and Failures in the Creation and Revisions of Writing Systems', in Fishman, 179–246.
Goswami, Usha: 1992, *Analogical Reasoning in Children*, Lawrence Erlbaum, Hove.
Goswami, Usha and Bryant, Peter: 1990, *Phonological Skills and Learning to Read*, Lawrence Erlbaum, Hove.
Grimes, Joseph E. and Gordon Jr., Raymond G.: 1980, 'Design of New Orthographies', in Kavanagh and Venezky, 93–103.
Hockett, Charles F.: 1958, *A Course in Modern Linguistics*, Macmillan, New York.
Justeson, John: 1988, Review of Sampson, 1985. Lg., **64**: 421–425.
Kavanagh, James F. and Mattingly, Ignatius G. (eds.): 1972, *Language by Ear and by Eye: The Relationships between Speech and Reading*, MIT, Cambridge, Mass.
Kavanagh, James F. and Venezky, Richard L.: 1980, *Orthography, Reading, and Dyslexia*, University Park Press, Baltimore.
Klima, Edward S.: 1972, 'How Alphabets Might Reflect Language', in Kavanagh and Mattingly, 57–80.
Kolers, Paul A., Wrolstad, Merald E., and Bouma, Herman (eds.): 1980, *Procession of Visible Language*, 2, Plenum, New York.
Ladefoged, Peter: 1982, *A Course in Phonetics*, Harcourt, Brace, Jovanovich, New York.
Levin, Harry and Williams, Joanna P. (eds.): 1970, *Basic Studies on Reading*, Basic Books, New York.
Martin, Samuel E.: 1972, 'Nonalphabetic Writing Systems: Some Observations', in Kavanagh and Mattingly, 81–102.
Martlew, Margaret (ed.): 1983, *The Psychology of Written Language: Developmental and Education Perspectives*, John Wiley, Chichester.
Olson, David R.: 1988, *Encyclopedia Britannica* 'Writing', 982–1033.
Paradis, Michel, Hagiwara, Hiroko, and Hildebrandt, Nancy: 1985, *Neurolinguistic Aspects of the Japanese Writing System*, Academic Press, Orlando.
Pike, Kenneth L.: 1947, *Phonemics: A Technique for Reducing Language to Writing*, University of Michigan Press, Ann Arbor.
Read, Charles: 1983, 'Orthography', in Martlew, 143–162.
Rice, Keren: 1994, 'Developing Orthographies: The Athapaskan Languages of the Northwest Territories, Canada', in Taylor and Olson, 77–94.
Rozin, Paul, Poritsky, Susan, and Sotsky, Raina: 1973, 'American Children with Reading Problems can Easily Learn to Read English Represented by Chinese Characters', in Smith, 105–115.
Sampson, Geoffrey: 1985, *Writing Systems: A Linguistic Introduction*, Stanford University Press.
Spencer, Herbert: 1959, *The Visible Word*, Lund Humphries, London.
Taylor, Insup: 1980, 'The Korean Writing System', in Kolers, Wrolstad, and Bouma, 57–82.
Taylor, Insup and Olson, David R. (eds.): 1994, *Scripts and Literacy*, Kluwer, Dordrecht.
Trager, George L.: 1972, *Language and Languages*, Chandler, San Francisco.
Venetzky, Richard L.: 1977, 'Principles for the design for practical writing systems', in Fishman, 37–54.
Winter, Werner: 1983, 'Tradition and innovation in alphabet making', in Coulmas and Ehlich, 227–238.

J. MARSHALL UNGER AND JOHN DeFRANCIS

4. LOGOGRAPHIC AND SEMASIOGRAPHIC WRITING SYSTEMS: A CRITIQUE OF SAMPSON'S CLASSIFICATION

INTRODUCTION

The composer John Cage once remarked that silence is the sound the environment makes. Though Cage showed insight by noting that we rarely if ever experience a total lack of sound, one could hardly imagine a worse definition of the word "silence". Cage's observation is an oxymoron: its truth derives from the rhetorical force of a contradiction, which in turn depends on the fact the word "silence" denotes the absence of sound, not its presence. Anyone who thought Cage had actually improved on the definition of silence would simply be missing the point.

It seems to us that many scholars misunderstand the plain meaning of the words "writing" and "system" in exactly this way. From them, virtually any collection of permanent symbols, manipulated under any set of rules, qualifies as a writing system. The recent work of British linguist Geoffrey Sampson is a case in point.[1] Sampson rejects the usual definition of writing – "a system for representing utterances of spoken language by means of permanent, visible marks" – preferring to say that to write is "to communicate relatively specific ideas by means of permanent, visible marks" (Sampson, 1986: 26). In this paper, we shall argue not only that this broader definition is incorrect, but that the traditional definition can be sharpened considerably. Specifically, we claim that there is a limit on the number of logograms that any practically learnable system of writing can contain. (By logograms, we mean units of writing that do not provide a visual clue to the pronunciation of the speech strings they represent.) We will discuss this claim in regard to Chinese and Japanese writing, but shall also deal with the so-called picture writing of the Yukaghir in the course of developing our thesis.

1. SEMASIOGRAPHIC VERSUS GLOTTOGRAPHIC WRITING

Following Haas (1976), Sampson divides all writing into semasiographic and glottographic systems. The main reason for changing the definition of writing from "representing utterances of spoken language" to "communicat[ing] relatively specific ideas" is that Sampson believes "[t]here are forms of communication which one might want to describe as 'writing' but which are not in any sense dependent on spoken language" (1985: 28).[2] As examples of semasiographic writing systems, Sampson cites,

I. Taylor and D.R. Olson (eds.), Scripts and Literacy, 45–58.

besides the Yukaghir pictures, mathematical notation and international road signs. Because these systems are, to use Sampson's words, "not in any sense dependent on spoken language," the meaning of "writing" has to be stretched to accommodate them. In our view, this procrustean stretching must be rejected for two reasons.

First, it distorts reality. Any physical act or thing whatsoever can serve as a signal provided its users make suitable prearrangements. Because such prearrangements ultimately depend on speech for their very existence, it is at best an exaggeration to claim that there are forms of writing that do not depend on speech "in any sense." The magnitude of Sampson's exaggeration is most clearly seen in his hypothetical example of a tribe that "expanded a semasiographic system, by adding further graphic conventions, until it was fully as complex and rich in expressive potential as their spoken language" (Sampson, 1985: 30). Sampson is correct when he says that the tribe would then ". . . possess two fully-fledged 'languages' having no relationship with one another", but errs crucially when he adds that "there would appear in principle to be no reason why" such a thing could not happen. His argument is circular: a semasiographic system that had the full "expressive potential" or communicative power of a natural language could not be constructed by people who did not share a spoken language in the first place.[3]

Second, Sampson's expanded definition of "writing" makes it so vague as to be useless as a technical term. Not all gesture is dance; not all landscapes are maps; not all human noises are music. Why must all intentional visible marks be writing? As Sampson himself notes (1985: 26), communicative acts such as sign language and painting can be excluded from writing, as he defines it, only arbitrarily, on the grounds that the visible markings are not permanent or that the ideas communicated are insufficiently explicit. He is thus in the same position as someone, to use our opening analogy, who insists that silence is the sound the environment makes and then hastens to add that certain manmade noises don't count. Furthermore, as Sampson tacitly acknowledges in invoking his hypothetical tribe, we have no choice but to use language as the standard by which to judge the systematic power of all other modes of communication-call it "expressive potential," as does Sampson, generative capacity, comprehensiveness, closure, completeness, or what you will. Glottographic writing systems (i.e. *all* writing systems under the traditional definition) are necessarily complete in this sense, since they are coextensive with language itself; mathematical notation, international road sings, and similar collections of symbols obviously are not.[4] Calling them systems of writing is like saying that chess is a language. Saussure made use of this metaphor to explain the difference between diachronic and synchronic descriptions, and it underlies the often heard claim that good chess-playing computer programs somehow prove the feasibility of artificial intelligence. But chess is in fact not a language, and chess-like models of language are seriously misleading (Lakoff, 1987). Likewise, specialized signs and notations lack the essential completeness characteristic of all true writing systems.

2. YUKAGHIR PICTURE WRITING

In light of these twin problems with Sampson's redefinition of writing, one cannot help asking whether there are, in fact, any forms of communication worthy of the name writing system that do not depend on language "in any sense." Let us examine Sampson's prime example of a semasiographic writing system to see if it qualifies.

Figure 1 shows what Sampson calls "a copy of a letter sent by a girl of the Yukaghir tribe of northeastern Siberia to a young man" (Sampson, 1985: 28–29). He describes it thus:

> The conifer-shaped objects . . . are people. The second from the right is the writer (the row of dots represents plaited hair and thus shows that she is a woman); the next one leftwards, the recipient of the letter, was previously her lover, but has now gone off to live with a Russian woman (plaited hair, together with a skirt with panniers distinguishing Russian from Yukaghir costume). The Russian woman, naturally, has broken up the relationship between writer and addressee (line from head of the Russian woman cutting through the lines joining the two Yukaghir); nevertheless, the new *ménage* is stormy (criss-cross lines linking the two). The writer is unhappy (crossed lines) alone in her house (the rectangular enclosing structure), and she is still thinking of the addressee (curly tendril reaching toward him). On the other hand the addressee should bear in mind that there is another young man at home (far right) sending a tendril toward her. If the addressee wants to act on the message, he had better hurry before his new household has children (two small conifers on the left). (Sampson, 1985: 28–29)

Although Sampson does not provide so much as a footnote explaining how he came upon this interpretation, he obviously did not arrive at it on his own. (If he had, how would he know he were right?) He must have copied both Figure 1 and its interpretation from an earlier source. This deduction does not by itself prove that Figure 1 did not, at some time or in some place, convey specific ideas directly rather than by reference to language; it does, however, raise the question of whether or not it is really a form of communication or part of a system, as Sampson assumes. Only by going back to the original source can we answer this crucial question.

With no help from Sampson, DeFrancis (1989: 24–35) has reconstructed the lineage of this Yukaghir "love letter," tracing it back to an original sketch by a Russian named Shargorodskii (1895). The discrepancy between original (Figure 2) and Sampson's reproduction is striking, and in itself casts grave suspicion on the claim that the "letter is capable of communicating its meaning independently of speech. But even more important, the picture in question turns out to be the remnant of a Yukaghir party game, akin to charades, in which girls carved pictures on birchbark about their love lives, challenging onlookers to guess their riddle-like meanings. The picture is not

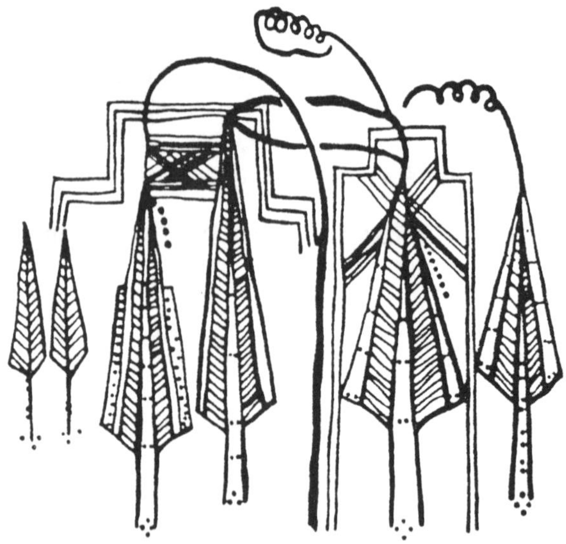

Fig. 1. Illustration in Sampson, 1985.

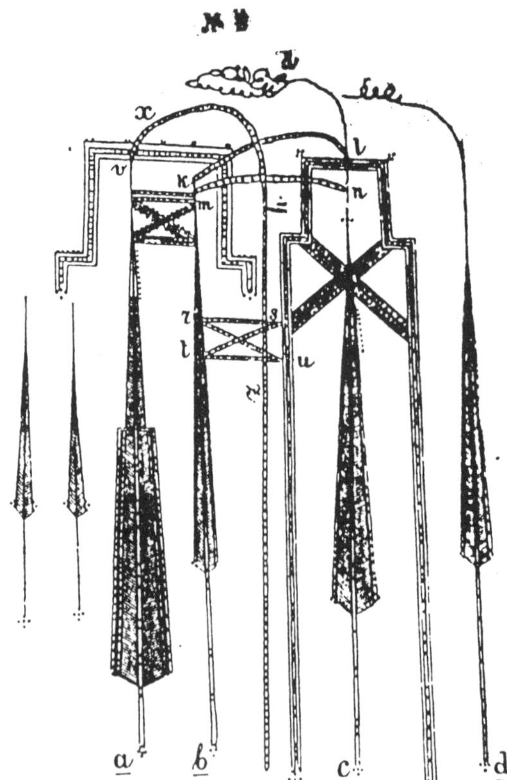

Fig. 2. Illustration 3 in Shargorodskii, 1895.

a letter at all. It may look like writing, and its visible structure may not have anything to do with language, but it is merely the token of semiritualized play. It was never intended as a form of communication in the sense obviously meant by Sampson, and therefore cannot be an example of semasiography. Indeed, were it not for the fact that there is an unbroken line of language-mediated communication leading step by step from the carver through Shargorodskii to the generations of writers who have cited this so-called letter, its message would be lost forever.

3. LOGOGRAPHIC VERSUS PHONOGRAPHIC WRITING

The lesson of this non-example of semasiographic writing is easily summarized: a collection of symbols cannot be both totally independent of language and also a genuine system of visible communication. The usual definition of writing, which restricts the field to what Sampson calls glottographic systems, is therefore the broadest that can be justified. Let us next consider Sampson's two divisions of this category, logographic and phonographic systems, turning our attention from Siberia southward to China and Japan.

Chinese characters are frequently called ideograms; Sampson chooses to use the term semasiographic rather than ideographic only because the latter is sometimes applied to Chinese and other scripts that he considers logographic (Sampson, 1985: 34, 149).[5] We of course agree that Chinese characters are not ideograms, in either Chinese or Japanese writing (DeFrancis, 1984; Unger, 1987), but not for the reasons Sampson gives. In our view, one cannot legitimately apply the label "logogram" to all Chinese characters under all circumstances; moreover, even if we were to grant that logographic units play a relatively greater role in Chinese or Japanese orthography than in, say, that of English, we find no basis for separating those systems that do and do not make use of Chinese characters into distinct types.

According to Sampson, the logogram/phonogram distinction is justified by Martinet's well-known observation that language is "doubly articulated": logograms are based on units of meaning (i.e. morphemes); phonograms are based on units of phonological structure (i.e. syllables, phonemes, or subphonemic features) (Sampson, 1985: 32–33). This dichotomy fails to take the essential role of context into account, however. In both Chinese and Japanese, it is easy to find cases in which characters are used merely for their phonetic values, to represent a syllable or part of a syllable, without regard to the conventional "meaning" associated with them. For example, the common noun *dōngxi* 'thing', written 東西, which must be logographically interpreted as 'east-west', is obviously not a compound of morphemes meaning 'east' and 'west'. It is simply an unanalyzable dissyllabic noun for the transcription of which the characters 東 and 西 have been pressed into service willy-nilly.[6] Evidently a character may be highly motivated or iconic in one functional context but highly arbitrary in another; hence, it makes little sense to insist that it is a logogram or a phonogram once and for all.

Furthermore, there is no guarantee that the smallest graphic units of a writing system are necessarily its basic functional units as well. Experienced readers of English, for example, perceive syllable- or word-length chunks; they do not "sound out" pronunciations letter by letter – in fact, in many cases, they couldn't if they tried. To say that the letters of the alphabet are phonograms is thus at best a half-truth. The orthographic word, flanked by spaces or punctuation marks, is the basic functional unit of written English; if Chinese characters have an analog in English, it is the word, not the letter.

In recognition of these two weaknesses in Sampson's definitions of logogram and phonogram, we propose the following replacements:

A *logogram* is a unit of writing that stands for a morphophonemically definable string (its reading) that cannot be inferred by inspection; e.g., the symbol ⟨&⟩ used in an English text for the word *and*. Note that the reading of a logogram may but need not be the realization of a morpheme.

A unit of writing that does provide a phonetic clue, no matter how crude, to its reading is a *phonogram*; e.g., the letter combinations ⟨write⟩ and ⟨right⟩, each of which stands for a word pronounced /rayt/ in English.

Notice that these definitions do not refer to "smallest units" or require that a logogram or phonogram always represent a specific kind of linguistic structure. The only material question is whether a discernible functional unit of writing (an English orthographic word, a Chinese character) does or does not provide a clue to its reading. What makes a functional unit a logogram is its opacity with respect too the linguistic form for which it stands in a particular context; on the other hand, a symbol is a phonogram by virtue of the reader's knowledge of its systematic relationship with other phonograms in terms of the phonological structure of the language being written. The mere fact that we can count and compare individual characters does not mean that each has only one function in a writing system or that they necessarily form the units of that system.

If distinguishing individual logograms and phonograms is problematic, so much the more so is the classification of entire systems of writing into logographic or phonographic varieties. Many scholars have cited Chinese an Japanese script as classic instances of logographic writing systems, but there are other systems that in fact are far better examples. These are the codes used by commercial, military, and espionage organizations. Most linguists who talk about logograms (with the notable exception of Barber [1974]) have conveniently overlooked them.

A code (as opposed to a cipher) involves the arbitrary substitution of words, e.g. *eggplant* for *President*. The distribution of the codeword *eggplant* in an encoded message might provide a clue to its plaintext equivalent, but its form cannot. This is an important advantage of encoded over enciphered messages, the overt form of which can be analyzed for clues to the rules of encipherment and their inverses. Indeed, were it not for the fact that large codes require the use of codebooks, the distribution of which compromises security, there would be little need to use cipher systems, which give prying cryptanalysts more to work with. To put it historically, there has always been a strong incentive for users of large codes to devise ways to make them easy to learn and easy to recall with a high degree of accuracy.

That no one has ever succeeded in doing so is therefore a highly significant fact, for what is true of codes must also be true of all so-called logographic writing systems, such as the Chinese. In a memorable review of Morris Halle, Wang (1980: 200) put his finger on exactly this point. According to Halle (1969: 18), learning Chinese characters is like remembering so many arbitrary telephone numbers. Wang observed that this "is to compliment the Chinese for memory feats of which few mortals are capable." Just so: Halle should have said that learning *a truly logographic* writing system would be like memorizing thousands of phone numbers; therefore, Chinese script can *not* be a logographic system.[7]

The fact of the matter is that the Chinese writing system is far from being truly logographic. The statistically typical Chinese character contains a graphic component that gives some indication of the pronunciation of the syllable the character stands for. In the parlance of sinology, these components are called *phonetics*, *phonetic elements*, or *phonetic indicators*.

Linguists and sinologists have been slow to grasp the importance of these phonetic indicators though their presence in the overwhelming majority of Chinese characters was established long ago (Boodberg, 1937; 1940; 1957). Indeed, Boodberg goes so far as to claim (1937: 345–347) that, apart from "a few exceptional cases", there is simple no such thing as a class of characters constructed on semantic principles. The "exceptional cases" comprise chiefly those (no more than about one percent of all Chinese characters) of direct pictographic origin, such as 馬, 羊, and 女, which stand for modern Mandarin *mǎ* 'horse', *yáng* 'sheep', and *nyǔ* 'female', respectively. Although semantic indicators (*radicals*, *keys*, or *significs*) are also present in characters with syllabic/phonetic components, "[c]haracters were not invented by just putting together two or more elements based on their semantic values alone" (Boltz, 1986: 428), even in the early stages of the script. "At least one of the components must have had a phonetic function" (ibid.), and, for the most part, that component was the core of the character, the so-called radical being a mere embellishment of secondary status (Barnard, 1978).[8] Even if the preponderance of historical evidence suggested the opposite, it would not make any difference synchronically:

if Chinese characters really gave as little information about the phonetic structure of the syllables they represent as telephone numbers provide about their owners' names, no one could learn the system.

The traditional characters used to write Mandarin, for example, can be divided into unitary (unanalyzable) forms, of largely pictographic origin, and compound forms, which are traditionally analyzed as consisting of a phonetic indicator and a radical; the letter conveys at best very general information of the thesaurus type (e.g. 'vegetation', 'mineral', etc.) as against the specific information of the phonetic indicators. These comprise a sort of capricious syllabary according to which various scholars have attempted to classify Chinese characters in general.[9]

The complex forms can be separated into four types depending on the amount of information about the syllable represented by the phonetic indicator, if present: (1) all the phonemes, including tone; (2) all the segmental phonemes; (3) most of the segmental phonemes; and (4) few if any phonemes.[10] The ratios of these categories are shown in Table 1. In 42 percent of all characters, the phonetic indicator provides so much accurate information about the structure of the syllable represented that omitting the radical would not result in any confusion in most contexts.[11] In another 24 percent, the radical does serve a useful function (it makes up for he lack of complete phonemic information) but the phonetic indicator is still reliable enough to allow for a good guess at the syllable in context. Thus, 66 percent of all the traditional characters used for Mandarin are functionally syllabograms.[12]

TABLE 1
Types of traditional characters for Mandarin

Kind of Character	Example		Ratio
Unitary:	馬 mǎ 'horse'		1%
Complex:			99%
Phonetic indicator specifies			
all phonemes	蝗 huáng "locust"	25%	
all segmental phonemes	媽 mā "mother"	17%	
majority of segmentals	澆 jiāo "sprinkle"	24%	
few or no phonemes	下 xià "down"	33%	

Source: DeFrancis, 1989: 113.

Furthermore, although a majority of Chinese morphemes are monosyllabic, the majority of Chinese words are not, and a significant number cannot be analyzed into monosyllabic morphemes. The fact that they must be written syllable by syllable in the traditional orthography is misleading (recall the foregoing example of *dōngxi*). Thus, the apparent lack of a visually distinct phonetic indicator is no guarantee that a character cannot function as a syllabogram. As already remarked, a character can legitimately be described as a logogram only when it stands for a word or morpheme of which it gives no syllabic or phonemic clue.

This is equally true in the case of Japanese writing, which some might argue provides an even better example of logographic writing than Chinese. In Japanese, some Chinese characters, or *kanji*, can stand for native (i.e. non-Chinese) words or morphemes; in such cases, phonetic indicators embedded in the graphic structure of the *kanji* should not matter. In fact, however, the strings for which *kanji* stand in the Japanese writing system can be longer or shorter than actual morphemes. Furthermore, even when the reading of a *kanji* happens to coincide with an actual allomorph, it may not correspond to a productive morpheme of the modern language because of semantic changes that have occurred over the centuries. In some cases, called *ateji*, the lack of a grapheme/morpheme correspondence was consciously introduced into the orthography, just as in the example of Chinese *dōngxi* already mentioned; i.e., *ateji* exploit rebus-like combinations of *kanji* that bear no relationship to the etymology of the word being written. There are even instances (called *jukujikun*) in which a distinct reading for each of two or more *kanji* cannot identified because the *kanji* string stands for only a single, unanalyzable morpheme. Thus, the *kanji* component of the Japanese writing system can legitimately be called logographic only under the fallacious assumption that every *kanji* reading is ipso facto a morpheme. A more accurate description of *kanji* usage is to say simply that *kanji* are conventional abbreviations for certain strings of moras in certain words.

4. CONCLUSION

A code can *either* be learnable *or* comprehensive but it cannot be both. For that reason alone, any writing system people actually use must incorporate a certain amount of "cipher", i.e. include a minimum core of elements that can be analyzed or assembled by rule in terms of the forms of a particular language. Thus, while individual logographic symbols exist in many, perhaps all writing systems, no entire system (except a genuine code) can be called logographic. In the same way, an ideographic or semasiographic writing system is a contradiction in terms.[13] Therefore, a typology of writing systems such as the one illustrated in Figure 4, which gives due recognition to the difference in learnability and practicality of ordinary and special-purpose writing systems, is superior to the typology shown in Figure 3, which ignores the existence of extreme cases and therefore exaggerates the differences among ordinary writing systems.

It might be objected that writing systems should nevertheless be classified into predominantly logographic and predominantly phonographic types, according to the proportion of logograms to phonograms they employ,

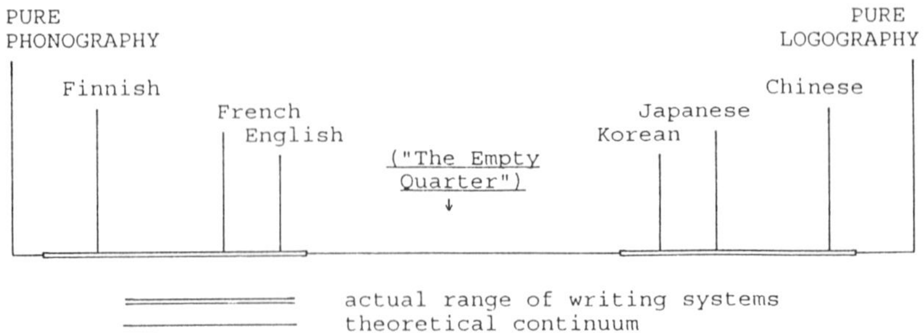

Fig. 3. Naïve (Bimodal) view of writing system typology.

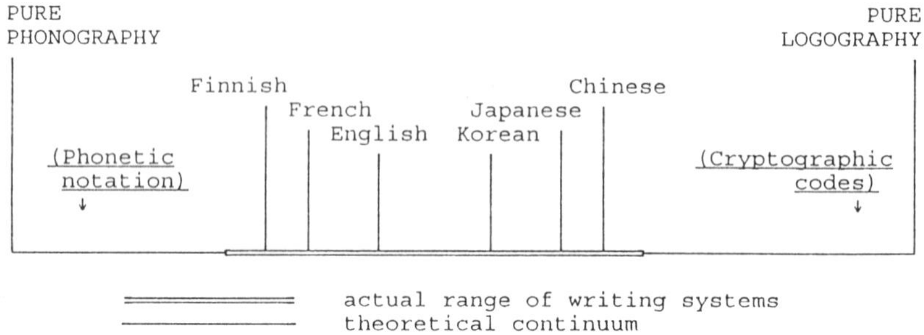

Fig. 4. Realistic (Unitary) view of writing system typology.

even though the difference between these types pales into insignificance when either is compared with a true code.[14] The question, however, is not whether such a typology is possible but whether it is useful. Are there real-world correlates of this distinction between "largely logographic" and "largely phonographic" writing systems, or is drawing such a distinction simply a facile, dead-end exercise of no consequence? Let us look at relevant empirical research:

An exhaustive survey of experimental results in psycholinguistics and the allied medical literature going back to 1901 has turned up no solid evidence for hemispheric lateralization effects attributable to the difference between *kanji* and *kana* in Japanese script (Paradis *et al.*, 1985).

A careful analysis of errors in the writing and reading of Chinese characters made by educated by Japanese has yielded impressive statistical evidence that *kanji* are primarily associated with phonological strings and only secondarily with categories of shape or "meaning" (Horodeck, 1987).

A thorough comparative study of reading among Japanese and American elementary school students shows that the use of *kanji* confers no special benefits on the Japanese learners and, in fact, makes progress for them more difficult over the long run (Stevenson *et al.*, 1986).

Experiments with very young children suggest that reading acquisition is facilitated when graphic units corresponding to whole words are taught first rather than the smallest units of the writing system, which usually do not correspond to linguistically meaningful units (Steinberg & Yamada, 1979). The overt visual form of the whole-word graphic units is immaterial.

An examination of the history of Japanese literacy makes it clear that cultural factors other than the writing system itself have been primarily responsible for setting the direction of development (Unger 1987: 83–98, 104–108).

As far as we can see, there are no real-world facts to be found that justify a naive typology of writing systems into "largely logographic" and "largely phonographic" types. The gross visual differences between alphabetic scripts and those that incorporate Chinese characters, though obvious, are ultimately trivial. They do not reveal a fundamental dichotomy but rather mask an essential unity that embraces all writing systems.

NOTES

[1] See also Vachek, 1973 and Haas, 1970.

[2] Sampson does say "that written language is not a straight-forward transcription of spoken language" (1985: 26), but concludes that the various under- and overspecificities of writing vis-à-vis speech do not require a change in the usual definition of writing; we agree, and so will not bother with this point further.

[3] Some might argue that the existence of sign languages refutes this charge of circularity, though Sampson himself takes the position that signing does not qualify as a form writing. Haas, for example, disputes the claim that writing is dependent on speech by saying, "We might as well argue that deaf-and-dumb language can convey no meaning to those who are deaf and dumb" (Haas, 1970: 12). All sign languages of which we are aware, however, include a significant amount of finger spelling, reflect various distinctive structural features of the surrounding spoken language, and were originated primarily by hearing individuals. Likewise, we are not persuaded by the claim that "[t]he biological and historical precedence of speech is no *logical* priority" (ibid.). Since the priority of speech over wiring is recapitulated in the life of each individual speaker, it has just as much synchronic reality as diachronic.

[4] Part of the problem here is that Sampson (1985: 34–37) uses "completeness" in a different sense. For him, writing systems are more or less complete to the extent they reflect the detail of whatever level of linguistic structure they are supposed to represent; thus, virtually all writing systems turn out to be incomplete to some degree. Our point is precisely that such incompleteness, being universal (and almost impossible to quantify), is trivial; on the other hand, the obvious limitations of international road signs or mathematical notation with respect to the whole realm of thought expressible through ordinary language make them hard to compare in any meaningful way with genuine writing systems, like those of English and Chinese.

[5] For Sampson, "logographic systems based on units longer than single morphemes" are "a hypothetical rather than an actual possibility" (1985: 39); thus, when he cites Chinese writing as an example of a logographic system, he means that it is morphemic. This is a weaker claim than that of Saussure (1959: 25–26), Giedon (1966: 90), and others who think that Chinese characters represent ideas rather than speech; for them, Chinese writing is truly

ideographic, i.e. semasiographic. Kolers (1969: 353) seems to agree with Sampson, but for many scholars, such as Geoghegan et al. (1979: 131), the terms "logographic" and "ideographic" are virtually interchangeable.

[6] The dissyllabic word *shānhù* 'coral' provides a somewhat more subtle example. The two characters used to write it (珊瑚) occur in no other combination; although both contain the so-called 'jade' radical, *shānhù* is not a compound. Moreover, although the phonetic indicator of the first character is read *cè*, which has no synchronic phonemic similarity with *shān*, the second has a fully useful indicator read *hù*.

[7] A parallel argument about allegedly pure phonographic writing systems can be made. Finnish orthography, for example, though recognized as highly regular, is a far cry from the narrow phonetic transcriptions used by phoneticians. Like all practical writing systems, it leaves out a great deal of phonetic information that the reader (because he or she knows the language) can fill in with virtually no conscious effort. And beyond phonetic notation, there is still the possibility of analog or digital representations of speech in two visual dimensions (e.g. spectrograms, computer-readable arrays of bits) that are totally unusable for ordinary purposes of communication by people but meet all the requirements of a writing system (e.g. they can be transmitted and played back with the proper equipment).

[8] Gelb (1963: 104) gets this backwards: the semantic indicators, or radicals, were not the principal characters; they were added (often in graphically reduced forms) to the so-called phonetic indicators, not the other way around.

[9] E.g. Karlgren (1940), on the basis of historical phonology, and Soothill (1942), on a pedagogical basis more in keeping with the way ordinary readers see characters. Our analysis is based on the "Soothill Syllabary" of 895 phonetic indicators. Lest this figure seem unacceptably large for a syllabary, it should be noted that a syllabary of 819 unrelated signs was standardized for the Yi languages spoken in Southwest China in 1975 and has been used since then in education, publication, and other areas (DeFrancis, 1989: 144–149).

[10] Specialists in Chinese historical phonology might be able to detect some phonemic clues lurking in the structure of some of the characters in class (4), but for ordinary readers, they are entirely opaque, especially since the analysis of characters into semantic and phonetic elements is often done quite mechanically by simply subtracting the key or radical and calling what remains the phonetic. This approach ignores the exceedingly complex problem of the changes the distortions many individual characters have undergone in their long and checkered histories.

[11] Lest it be thought that a lack of tonal indicators creates intolerable ambiguities, it should be noted that, since the early 1950s, a Cyrillic orthography that does not indicate tones has been used in newspapers and other publications in the Dungan dialect of Chinese spoken by some 36,000 people in Soviet Asia (Comrie, 1981: 273–274, 280; Rimsky-Korsakoff, 1967; Rimsky-Korsakoff Dyer, 1987).

[12] Recent script simplifications have only increased the number.

[13] Although individual ideograms or semasiograms, like individual logograms, may exist, it is doubtful, despite the example of mathematical notation, whether there are many that transcend the boundaries of a single cultural community. For "experience does not *determine* conceptual systems, but only *motivates* them," as Lakoff notes.

[T]he same experiences may provide equally good motivation for two somewhat different conceptual systems. For example, the concept *front* has its basic characterization in the body and then is extended metaphorically to other objects. In English, it is extended to objects like bushes as follows: If you are looking at a bush, the "front" of the bush is the side facing you. In Hausa, the reverse is true: the "front" of the bush would be the side facing *away* from you, that is, in the same direction in which you are facing. (Lakoff, 1987: 310)

[14] Or a highly detailed phonetic transcription (see note 7). In this paper, we have highlighted the fact that codes are true examples of purely logographic writing because we are

concerned primarily with the false belief that Chinese characters are always and entirely logograms. We have not highlighted the fact that narrow phonetic transcription systems are examples of nearly pure phonographic writing because most people seem to understand without difficulty that the letters of the alphabet are not always and entirely phonograms. Of course, both facts are equally important.

REFERENCES

Barber, E.J.W.: 1974, *Archaeological Decipherment: A Handbook*, Princeton University Press, Princeton.

Barnard, Noel: 1978, 'The Nature of the Ch'in "Reform of the Script" as Reflected in Archaeological Documents Excavated under Conditions of Control', in David T. Roy and Tsuen-hsuin Tsien (eds.) *Ancient China: Studies in Early Civilization*, Chinese University Press, Hong Kong.

Boltz, William G.: 1986, 'Early Chinese Writing,' *World Archaeology* **17.3**: 420–436.

Boodberg, Peter A.: 1937, 'Some Proleptical Remarks on the Evolution of Archaic Chinese', *Harvard Journal of Asiatic Studies* **2**: 329–372.

———. 1940, '"Ideography" or Iconolatry?' *T'oung Pao* **35**: 266–288.

———. 1957, 'The Chinese Script: An Essay on Nomenclature (the First Hecaton)', *Bulletin of the Institute of History and Philology, Academia Sinica* **39**: 113–120.

Comrie, Bernard.: 1981, *The Languages of the Soviet Union*, Cambridge University Press, Cambridge.

DeFrancis, John: 1984, *The Chinese Language: Fact and Fantasy*, University of Hawaii Press, Honolulu.

———. 1989, *Visible Speech: The Diverse Oneness of Writing Systems*, University of Hawaii Press, Honolulu.

Gelb, I.J.: 1963, *A Study of Writing*, Second edition, University of Chicago Press, Chicago.

Geogheghan, Sheila *et al.*: 1979, *Languages Files*, Advocate Publishing Group, Reynoldsburg, OH.

Giedon, S.: 1966, 'Symbolic Expression in Prehistory and in the First High Civilizations', in György Kepes (ed.) *Sign, Image, Symbol*, George Braziller, New York.

Haas, William: 1970, *Phono-Graphic Translation*, Manchester university Press, Manchester.

———, 1976, 'Writing: The Basic Options', in William Haas (ed.) *Writing without Letters*, Manchester University Press, Manchester.

Halle, Morris: 1969, 'Some Thoughts on Spelling', in Kenneth S. Goodman and J.T. Fleming (eds.) *Psycholinguistics and the Teaching of Reading*, International Reading Association, Newark, Del.

Horodeck, Richard Alan: 1987, 'The Role of Sound in Reading and Writing Kanji', Ph.D. dissertation, Cornell University.

Karlgren, Bernhard: 1940, *Grammata Serica: Script and Phonetics in Chinese and Sino-Japanese*, Reprinted from the Bulletin of the Museum of Far Eastern Antiquites 12. MFEA, Stockholm.

Kolers, Paul A.: 1969, 'Some formal characteristics of pictograms', *American Scientist* **57**: 345–363.

Lakoff, George: 1987, *Women, Fire, and Dangerous Things: What Categories Reveal about the Mind*, University of Chicago Press, Chicago.

Paradis, Michel, Hagiwara, Hiroko, and Hildebrandt, Nancy: 1985, *Neurolinguistic Aspects of the Japanese Writing System*, Academic Press.

Rimsky-Korsakoff, Svetlana: 1967, 'Soviet Dungan: The Chinese Langauge of Central Asia', *Monumenta Serica* **26**: 352–421.

Rimsky-Korsakoff Dyer, Svetlana: 1987, 'Sulian Dungan minzu yuyan, xianzhuang, ji qi shi'er yue ge [The Language, Current Condition, and Twelve-Month Poems of the Soviet Dungan

Nationality]', in *Wang Li xiansheng, jinian lunwen*, Zhongguo yuwen xuehu, Hong Kong, pp. 233–280.

Sampson, Geoffrey: 1985, *Writing Systems: A Linguistic Introduction*, Hutchinson, London.

Saussure, Ferdinand de: 1959, *Course in General Linguistics*, Translated by Wade Baskin. Philosophical Society, New York.

Shargorodskii, S.: 1895, 'Ob Yukagirskikh pis'menakh', *Zemlevedeniye* **2/3**: 135–148.

Soothill, W.E.: 1942, *The Student's Four Thousand Character and General Pocket Dictionary*, 16th ed., Kegan Paul, London.

Steinberg, Danny D. and Yamada, Jun: 1979, 'Are Whole Word Kanji Easier to Learn Than Syllabic Kana?' *Reading Research Quarterly* **14.1**: 88–99.

Stevenson, Harold W., Lee, Shin-ying, and Stigler, James in collaboration with Kitamura, Seiro, Kimura Susumu and Kato Tadahisa: 1986. 'Learning to Read Japanese', in H. Stevenson, H. Azuma, and K. Hakuta (eds.) *Child Development and Education in Japan*, Freeman, New York, pp. 217–235.

Unger, J. Marshall: 1987, *The Fifth Generation Fallacy: Why Japan Is Betting Its Future on artificial Intelligence*, Oxford University Press, New York.

Vachek, Josef: 1973, *Written Language: General Problems and Problems of English*, Mouton, The Hague.

Wang, William S-Y.: 1980, Review of Winfred P. Lehman (ed.): Language and Linguistics in the People's Republic of China. *Language* **56.1**: 197–202.

SUZANNE McCARTHY

5. THE CREE SYLLABARY AND THE WRITING SYSTEM RIDDLE: A PARADIGM IN CRISIS

In October of 1840, in Norway House on the northern tip of Lake Winnipeg, the Wesleyan Methodist minister, James Evans, printed the first copy of the Cree Syllabary. The syllabary was a highly structured chart which displayed consonant values down the left-hand side and vowel qualities across the top. Each symbol occurred twice, the second time in a broken form to indicate an added feature of vowel length. In less than a year two more symbols were added to represent /w/ and /h/. Thus all the refinements necessary to represent a "mature spelling style" (Nichols, 1984) were completed.

Since the symbols may be analysed for consonant value by shape and vowel quality by orientation, it can be interpreted as behaving like an alphabet. In addition, the symbols for final consonants and the diacritics for long vowels, /w/ and /h/, appear to be alphabetic in nature. Therefore the Cree Syllabary is regarded as a mixed syllabic and alphabetic system (Nichols, 1984; Ellis, 1983).

A syllabic writing system is classified as a variation of phonographic writing, in which symbols represent sound. The main entry in this category is, of course, the alphabet. The only other category of writing system is logographic, in which symbols represent meaning, e.g. Chinese (Rogers, this volume; Scribner and Cole, 1981: 32). Therefore, a syllabary is considered to have similar characteristics to an alphabet and to function in a similar way. A syllabic writing system, however, is generally used only for languages which have a certain type of sound structure. Otherwise, linguists sum up a consideration of writing system types by saying "Whatever is true of alphabets is also true for syllabaries" (Rogers, this volume).

But the Cree nation became fully literate in the syllabic writing system in a brief ten years, from 1841 to 1851. In fact, there was a higher incidence of literacy among the Cree than among the English and French communities in Canada at that time (Murdoch, 1981; Berry and Bennett, 1989). Monolingual men, women and children were able to become literate in their own language without formal education. The puzzle is how a predominantly oral culture could become a culture of mass literacy in less than one generation. I suggest that the Cree nation adopted the symbols of what appeared to be an analytic syllabarium and adapted then to a non-analytic form of writing which would function within their culture. The ensuing syllabic literacy, then, would bear no more resemblance to alphabetic literacy than it would to literacy in Chinese, possibly less.

I. Taylor and D.R. Olson (eds.), Scripts and Literacy, 59–75.

(Nichols, 1984)

Vowel only	ē ᐁ	i ᐃ	o ᐅ	a ᐊ	Finals: Moose	Finals: Western
p	ᐯ	ᐱ	ᐳ	ᐸ	ᑉ	ᑊ
t	ᑌ	ᑎ	ᑐ	ᑕ	ᑦ	ᐟ
c	ᒉ	ᒋ	ᒍ	ᒐ	ᒡ	-
k	ᑫ	ᑭ	ᑯ	ᑲ	ᒃ	ᐠ
m	ᒣ	ᒥ	ᒧ	ᒪ	ᒻ	c
n	ᓀ	ᓂ	ᓄ	ᓇ	ᓐ	)
l	ᓓ	ᓕ	ᓗ	ᓚ	ᓪ	{, ᐪ
r	ᕃ	ᕆ	ᕈ	ᕋ	ᕐ	}
s	ᓭ	ᓯ	ᓱ	ᓴ	ᔅ, ᔥ -sk	ᐢ
š	ᔐ	ᔑ	ᔓ	ᔕ	ᔥ	
w	·ᐁ	·ᐃ	·ᐅ	·ᐊ	o	o
y	ᔦ	ᔨ	ᔪ	ᔭ	•, ᔾ	•
h					■	■, × -hk

(Ellis, 1983)

The Syllabary is a so-called "mixed system", partially syllabic, partially alphabetic.

Fig. 1. Syllabic chart from 1841 hymnal (retouched).

In short, I am convinced that the native way of writing syllabics, developed in the last century and existing to this day, can have no more in common with the western way of writing in an alphabet than traditional Cree society has in common with Euro-Canadian society. How do the qualities of the syllabic script contribute to this distinctive form of literacy which has such an integral function in native Cree society?

CURRENT DISCUSSION OF SYLLABIC LITERACY

Most current studies on script choice focus on the following variables. The first would normally be the relationship between the sound structure of the language and the symbols. A syllabic system best suits a language with a fairly simple syllable structure and few consonant clusters. Cree fits this pattern. If, in fact, the Cree adopted syllabics simply because of this structural suitability, the question remains, why did not other language groups as readily adopt an alphabet, which would be suited to the sound structure of their languages?[1]

Another variable commonly considered is that of efficiency or economy. A syllabic character represents a complete syllable so language can be written with fewer characters, which saves both time and materials, a significant consideration in a hunter-gatherer community (Murdoch, 1981). This may be a contributing factor but again seems insufficient to explain how the concept of literacy was so easily attained and transmitted throughout the Cree nation within a decade.

However, it is also widely recognized that the initial learning process is much easier with syllabic writing than with an alphabet (Gelb, 1952; Gibson and Levin, 1975). So after experiencing little success with an alphabet in Ojibway, Evans influenced by his knowledge of Oriental languages and shorthand to seek another solution (Murdoch, 1981).

THEORETICAL APPROACH

For an outsider of Cree society to understand exactly how the Cree both learn and continue to read syllabics throughout their life, it is not enough to simply lean the Cree language and memorize the syllabic chart. While most Cree read aloud, first interpreting symbol into sound and then from sound into meaning (Burnaby and McKenzie, 1985), some English literates who become fluent in Cree naturally develop a style of silent reading that corresponds to English literacy. Therefore, the conclusions of Basso and Anderson (1977) that "knowledge necessary to become literate" is the key to obtaining an insider's view of a writing system, is not sufficient. This does not, however, negate their basic premise that unless one establishes "concepts . . . considered meaningful by the users of the system, the resulting description is almost certain to suffer from bias and distortion" (p. 79).

In this paper I wish to present a variety of syllabic spelling styles and how they reflect language structure. Then, I will discuss the physical activity of learning to read and write syllabics. Literacy depends on perceiving an association between symbols and language. The characteristics of a particular writing system enable beginning readers to learn certain types of associations more easily than others and the manner in which one learns establishes these notions more firmly. I hope to describe how these notions fit into the culturally preferred mode of expression among the Cree. Finally, I suggest that instead of undermining Cree social structure, as one might expect a foreign technology to do, syllabic literacy supports it.

THE EVOLUTIONARY WRITING SYSTEM PARADIGM

It is a basic tenet of social anthropology that symbolic systems reflect and reinforce the organization of society (Keesing, 1981). This school of thought became prominent in the 1950's when Radcliffe-Brown (1953) used Durkheim's social theory to describe the functional unity of a social system. That this principle must also apply to writing systems was recognized by Sjoberg, who stated that "relationships between writing and speech vary significantly with the nature of the socio-cultural order" (1966: 260). Unfortunately this led to many false conclusions at the time, since the characteristics of a writing system were usually organized according to a paradigm which has now been rejected. This evolutionary model of writing systems indicated a progression from logographic to syllabic systems, culminating in the alphabet (Diringer, 1948; Gelb, 1952). It was assumed that the alphabet as the highest and most modern type of writing must be most suited to mass literacy and modernization, the goals of a democratic society (Sjoberg, 1966: 265).

The most obvious argument against this interpretation is the example of Japan, where a mixed syllabic-logographic writing system does not prevent Japan from having one of the highest literacy rates in the world (Gibson and Levin, 1975). Another protest comes from a scholar of cuneiform, a type of syllabic writing, who comments,

> the inescapable conclusion is that the introduction of the alphabet, by itself, has had little effect upon the reduction of functional illiteracy, and thus, its importance in the history of human development has been overestimated, whereas that of cuneiform has probably been underestimated (Powell, 1981).

CURRENT PARADIGM FOR WRITING SYSTEMS

The current paradigm for writing systems which offers only two major classifications, phonographic, writing units of sound; and logographic, writing units of meaning (Sampson, 1985; Rogers, this volume), is a direct consequence of these arguments. Therefore, a syllabic system must be classified along with an alphabet as a phonographic system. Makita and Sakamoto (cited in Burnaby and Anthony, 1985: 113) also accept this basic classification. There is no longer vocabulary or a theoretical framework available for discussing a qualitative difference between an alphabet and a syllabary. The bias against such an interpretation is so strong that Scribner and Cole (1981) do not consider the fact that the Vai script was a syllabary as a variable for many aspects of their landmark study on the psychology of literacy. They simply classify it as a sound-based script, similar to an alphabet (p. 32) and add that they "certainly do not want to ascribe the principal restrictions on Vai literacy to the fact that the script is a syllabary" (p. 240). However, they also manage to put an evolutionary bias on this two-category paradigm, claiming "sound-based scripts are considered the most advanced" (p. 32).

Now a new approach to the Chinese writing system has challenged the logographic-phonographic dichotomy. With more awareness that each Chinese character not only represents a morpheme but also a syllable, it can be more correctly termed a morphosyllabic system (DeFrancis, 1989). This establishes the phonographic principle for Chinese and leads Unger and DeFrancis to argue "for an essential unity that embraces all writing systems" (this volume).

Emphasizing the similarities between the English, morphophonemic system and the Chinese, morphosyllabic system, has potential usefulness and may be long overdue. However, the question remains, why continue to lump syllabic and alphabetic systems together as phonographic and not consider the implications of classifying systems by their level of representation, i.e. phonemic or syllabic.[2]

A paradigm for writing systems that has been collapsed from three categories to two, and now possibly to one, may have considerable usefulness in understanding the universal aspects of literacy but does little to illuminate the culturally diverse characteristics which remain. Recognition of a qualitative difference between Cree society and Euro-Canadian society remains. The Cree themselves would be the first to confirm this. They claim that the syllabic writing system functions in their society in a way that the alphabet cannot.

THE BASIC CREE WRITING STYLE

In order to understand the essential difference between a syllabic system and an alphabetic system, one must first look at some of the different styles of writing syllabics which have developed apart from the influence of missionaries. The style which could be considered the most basic, or most informal way of writing Cree syllabics is qualitatively different from the form of writing found in the prayer books, hymnals and catechisms and is used for writing letters and record-keeping.

In this most informal style of writing syllabics only symbols which represent a full syllable of speech are employed. All full syllabic characters are included along with the row designating vowels only, since a vowel by itself is a syllable. The symbols for final consonants are usually not used although a tick or other mark may be inserted to indicate that a final consonant is there in speech. Anecdotal evidence suggests that those syllable final consonants which are continuants, that is have the capacity to be produced as a syllable, i.e. /m/ and /n/ and /s/ would be represented by the final consonant symbol or a full syllabic character while final consonants which are stops such as /p/, /t/, and /k/ would be omitted. There is wide regional and dialectal variation here.

The only diacritic to be employed is the dot which occurs at midline preceding (or following) a full syllabic character and represents the sound /w/. This sound is derived from the vowel /o/ and can be pronounced as a syllable without distorting the language structure.[3] The symbol for /h/ and the superscript dot to indicate vowel length are usually omitted.

Therefore, while a mix of symbols from the syllabic chart may be found even in this informal or basic way of writing, all these symbols represent full syllables which may be pronounced and perceived audibly in isolation. There may not even be breaks to mark word boundaries so a continuous stream of characters would be written to be pronounced in isolation from each other (Murdoch, 1981). This style of writing is similar to that found among the Liberian Vai (Scribner and Cole, 1981).

While the physical appearance of the Cree symbols would suggest that a mix of syllabic and alphabetic symbols are being used, that is not, in fact, the case. Therefore, the usual textbook designation of the Cree writing system as mixed syllabic and alphabetic does not apply to the basic syllabic literacy which was adopted by the Cree in the 1840's and spread without the direct teaching of Euro-Canadians. This style of writing seems to be a direct consequence of the native style of learning to read and could be fairly accurately labelled "pure" syllabics.

LEARNING TO READ SYLLABICS OUTSIDE OF SCHOOL

Learning to read syllabics started with memorizing the 48 symbols of the syllabary chart. This was usually done by reciting row after row of symbols from left to right and top to bottom. There was typically no attempt to analyse each character for symbol shape and orientation. While this pattern is evident, the effect of the rotation of the symbol is usually one of confusing rather than assisting the reading process.[4] Although the syllabary looks analytic, readers learn each symbol as a unique unit, as is the case in the Japanese and Vai syllabary. One could therefore suggest that most Cree did not traditionally either perceive or employ the analytic features of the syllabary which were provided by James Evans.

Syllabic learners then read out loud from a text. First, they read each symbol in succession without grouping the syllables into words. The next step involved rereading the text this time as a meaningful utterance. Writers would say a sentence slowly syllable by syllable out loud and write the symbol for each spoken syllable. The writing closely reflects dialect patterns and individual differences. In brochures printed recently, the spelling of some words varied according to author, although it is also possible to find writers who, themselves, vary the spelling of certain words within a single text.

The relationship between speech and writing then is between the smallest, audible unit of speech which can be pronounced in isolation and the symbol which stands for it. At least this is how a Euro-Canadian would express it. However, the native Cree speaker would correct you and rephrase it. The symbol does not "stand for" the sound, it "is" the sound. The quality of the association between symbol and sound is one of metaphor not analogy. There is identity of sound and symbol rather than comparison. This relationship also exists between the spoken language as a whole and the written language as a whole. Therefore, Bennett and Berry (1987) found it impossible to discuss the syllabic script with native speakers without discussing the language itself. They state,

> The confusion goes deeper, however, than a semantic identity between language and script. Despite our persistent efforts to disentangle the two strands of script and speech, people would still "forget", and tell us that it was important to learn to read the syllabic script "because it's the language for the Indian people, the same as whites have to learn their language" (p. 246).

It is essential to realize that it is the syllabic script itself which makes possible a metaphorical association between audible sound and visible symbol. There is no need for the rule-governed logic and prerequisite ability to separate or abstract smaller segments of sound from a spoken unit or syllable, required by a alphabetic literacy. Rather than representing atomistic fragments of speech a syllabic system deals with whole, concrete units of sound. For this reason, I refer to the Cree way of writing as wholistic in this paper.

SYLLABICS AND CULTURE

The Cree were able to adapt the James Evans syllabary, by excluding the analytic elements, to a wholistic mode of writing which would function within their existing conceptual framework. Barnett's theory of cultural change holds that an element in a new configuration must be identified with an element in a familiar configuration before it can be accepted by a society (1952: 188). The innovator must be within the culture in order to perceive that the innovation is an extension of a cultural pattern which already exists. It seems that the syllabic script was accepted, then, because it made possible a mode of writing in which the relationship between speech and symbol reflected the preference for metaphorical expression found in a wholistic society, not simply because they were easier to learn or more economic to write.

SYLLABICS AND THE SOCIAL ORDER

Not only might syllabics reflect Cree culture, they also appear to reinforce the social order of a traditional Cree community. Cree social structure is horizontal, where "political leadership tends to be . . . carried out by egalitarian decision-making or consensual support" (Keesing, 1981: 129). Traditionally everyone had to learn the basic skills to survive equally well since people moved around in small family groups (Murdoch, 1981: 168). Parents passed these skills on to their children and education was obtained within the family group. Syllabic literacy could also be passed on this way. Birchbark and charcoal or animal blood provided the first materials for writing. Since syllabic skill was learned from parents as were other skills no generation gap was created by this new literacy. There was no valid or invalid way of writing since everyone wrote as they spoke: there were simply dialect or family differences even within one community. Syllabic literacy did not require that schooling be introduced into the nomadic lifestyle of the Cree. Therefore this new mode of communication reinforced existing social relationships as outlined in Bennett and Berry (1987) who state,

> In general the Cree have a distaste for giving/receiving orders, for making commands or demands on others – in short, a distaste for anything which looks like an exercise of power by one person over another. For most purposes the Cree have no "proper" or "best" method of proceeding. If they have a preference at all, it is a preference for avoiding rule-bound situations and rule-making people, a preference for flexibility and economy . . . (p. 245).

Syllabic literacy is also close to the oral tradition of Cree society. The fact that the script is usually read aloud corresponds well to the communal lifestyle. It would only seem natural to read aloud for the benefit of whoever else would be present and discuss the information within the group. Knowledge would not be seen as belonging to the individual nor would anyone want to study new information silently. An English style of literacy would not be appropriate in the traditional Cree society although it has been adopted recently along with corresponding changes in lifestyle. Since in every way syllabic literacy seems to authenticate Cree society, it is hardly surprising that there has been strong resistance to its replacement by a Roman orthography.

Scollon and Scollon (1981) came to the same conclusion comparing syllabic literacy with English essayist style literacy. "Learning literacy in these patterns does not threaten to produce changes in ethnic identity the way essayist literacy does" (p. 55). They also consider the role that script characteristics may have played in the development of syllabic literacy, challenging the fact that "Goody (1968; 1977) more recently has played down the importance of the actual script" and affirming that "It seems important to keep the arena open for investigation because some cases of native American literacy have involved non-alphabetic scripts" (p. 46).

In summary, Cree syllabic literacy is equally accessible to each individual in Cree society and serves to support the strong oral tradition already present. It has not traditionally been used by the Cree either to build a literature of indigenous knowledge, – most syllabic texts are translations from English, although some journals and diaries have been written, – or to establish a hierarchy within society based on education and leadership.

This type of system supports the horizontal social organization of Cree society and reinforces respect for diversity and the autonomy of the individual. It might also function as an auxiliary system in a more hierarchical society.[5] The main characteristics of a syllabic script are that it can be learned outside of formal schooling and that it is read initially for sound and secondly for meaning.

VARIATIONS ON NATIVE CREE SYLLABICS

The Cree do use the alphabetic symbols when writing in a more formal or careful style. However, this is not characteristically on the "alphabetic" principle,[6] to create a phonemically consistent spelling, or a one-to-one correspondence between each segment of sound and symbol.

First, the symbols for final consonants would be used where final consonants occur. However, most non-continuant final consonants occur in word final position and represent grammatical morphemes, so they are relatively available to perception. Therefore, syllabic writers who use final symbols for these consonants may have learned the spelling word by word, or for each grammatical ending, rather than through developing an analytic approach to representing speech sounds. Further research would be helpful here.

Next, the diacritic symbol for aspiration is used to mark a difference in meaning between two words which differ only in the presence or absence of this feature. This symbol may appear within the word, in a position which corresponds to where it occurs in speech or it may simply be written at the beginning of the word to indicate that the reader must understand the meaning to be the one other than that indicated by the syllabic characters alone.

In fact, some writers use a diacritic or alphabetic symbol which has no sound relationship to the additional feature which must be read. In this case the alphabetic symbol appears to act as a determiner to establish that the reader must be aware that the word intended differs in some way from the syllabic spelling.

I believe that these patterns of symbolization should be recognized as following a morphemic principle of writing, creating distinct forms for distinct meanings. This is summarized in Rogers (this volume) simply as "Different morphemes should be represented differently". Since there is no rule to symbolize these sounds each time they occur, the phonemic principle is not involved.

Finally, in some cases these alphabetic symbols and diacritics can be used to enhance a text, without having any phonographic significance whatsoever. They either make the text appear more sophisticated or they may identify the writer with a particular religious tradition or community. I would conclude that the more formal Cree writing is basically syllabic with some morphemic patterns of symbolization, combined with an aesthetic approach to symbol use.

So far, however, only one aspect of morphemic representation in writing has been considered. Another aspect of morphemic representation is that "each morpheme should have one and only one representation" (Rogers, this volume). This would occur as the result of standardization, created either by the publication of a lexicon prescribing spelling rules, or by the establishment of some text or body of textual material which would be considered authoritative. For most of the syllabic tradition religious texts have functioned as standards to which the Cree ascribe in varying degrees.

One might expect that a consequence of morphemic standardization would be morphemic literacy, a sight-word reading strategy in which the reader silently perceives the meaning of a word from the pattern which the letters in the word create. Nevertheless, those who read Cree as their first language of literacy rarely develop this style of reading.[7] The same effect is manifested among Vai literates (Scribner and Cole, 1981). The Cree community read church texts in the typical syllabic style and accept it as a distinct dialect of Cree.

However, morphemic literacy, or sight-word approach to reading has been initiated by non-native instructors in different school systems (John Nichols, Arlene Stairs, pers. communication). The young people are now beginning to develop morphemic literacy and reading for meaning. Morphemic literacy, then does not appear to occur outside of formal education, but within a school system standardized syllabics can be read by a morphemic literacy style as easily as any other script.

Standard morphemic representation also enables a common text to be used throughout many dialect areas and provides a basis for unity among different groups. This has happened through religious texts in one dialect being used throughout several dialect areas. The question is how much this more unified and hierarchic use of texts represents Cree culture and society and how much it represents the structure of the church which introduced the texts. There seem to be two distinct traditional uses of syllabics, one informal and "pure" syllabic use, and the other that of liturgical texts and more formal writing. The first is "pure" syllabic literacy and the second, syllabic influenced by morphemic principles. In any case the church and its texts and literacy have become an integrated with Cree society to a large extent.

Therefore, although the Cree have an inventory of both syllabic and alphabetic symbols, I would conclude that Cree writing is basically syllabic with an auxiliary morphemic component. However, it functions in Cree society as a syllabic system which reflects the Cree tendency not to standardize their language and create a right and wrong way of doing things.

SCHOOL BOARD REFORMS

In an attempt to make Cree syllabics meet the needs of education and modernization, a syllabary reform has been undertaken by some school boards and other institutions. These reforms include both reducing ambiguities in syllabic spelling by using diacritics on a consistent "scientific" basis, and publishing a dictionary which provides a standard spelling for each word according to territory.

Although it may be premature to draw conclusions, in one particular instance, two interesting patterns have emerged. First, the dictionary can only be used by a trained "elite"; and second, the diacritic for aspiration is now most commonly used where it is non-phonemic but easily perceptible, and ignored where it is phonemic. The use of the distinctive symbol for aspiration could be interpreted as providing group identity, distinct from other Cree communities and symbolizing participation in the modernization process. However, it does not seem to indicate a more analytic approach to symbolizing their language for most members of the group.

So the two processes, moving in the direction of phonemic representation, and standardizing morphemic representation, have not yet been readily assimilated by the Cree. The theory was that these processes had taken place in Inuktitut, also written in syllabics, so they should have been possible to duplicate.

In fact, Inuktitut for a variety of reasons developed a slightly different function before the writing system reform evolved. In *Language Planning and Social Change* (1989) R. Cooper argues that standardization reflects an existing standard rather that creating one, i.e. normalization precedes codification. "Corpus planning prior to changes in the function for which the language is used is likely to be ineffective" (p. 171). However, can scripts characteristics be related to the function for which they are used?

ALPHABETS AND MORPHEMIC WRITING SYSTEMS

In order to better understand the role of a syllabic writing system, it is essential to compare it with the two other basic types of systems, an alphabet and morphemic systems. The letters of the alphabet represent abstract segments of sound which may be described as atomistic or fragmented. These sounds can be arrived at by analysing words to derive smaller discrete units of sound which cannot be pronounced in isolation. This is part of the general language awareness children develop through experimenting with words which begin with the same sound and words which rhyme, i.e. Helen begins with "H" and John rhymes with leprechaun. Letters of the alphabet "stand for" these sounds but are not identical with them. Regardless of the teaching approach in school, the home and peer environment, and Sesame Street promote this awareness.

However, readers also learn morphemic literacy or sight-word literacy by becoming familiar with the form of each frequently occurring word in any text they are likely to read. This kind of reading is done by pattern recognition and may not, in fact, require the same analytic skills involved in decoding an alphabetic script. In alphabetic literacy, then, the reader may use either or both analytic decoding and pattern recognition.

The type of writing system which is read on a purely morphemic basis with no reference to the sound structure of the language also exists in the context of native literacy. The still partially extant ideographs of many native nations of North America are also described as wholistic by Battiste (1985). These largely pictographic texts were read directly for meaning but did not have the capacity to represent speech sounds and so did not become a complete writing system able to record speech. They "supplemented the oral traditions with ideological catalogues" (Battiste, 1985: 9). So the purely morphemic symbols were an auxiliary mode of communication in an oral society and did not become a full writing system. They can be used as a mnemonic for religious services but, unlike the syllabic Cree literature where all religious material exists as translations from other languages, an ideographic system may be used to develop a "native theory of knowledge, predicated on the existence of spirits, power or medicine" (Battiste, 1985: 10).

The Chinese writing system is the most morphemic of all full writing systems and is classified as a morphosyllabic system (DeFrancis, 1989). Each character represents a distinct morpheme and each morpheme is a single syllable. Auxiliary phonetic systems, either syllabic or alphabetic, have long been used to provide the pronunciation of a new word. However, in reading the Chinese script itself, no abstract analysis of segments of sound is required. This kind of morphosyllabic writing has also been called wholistic (Wang, 1981: 232). In this type of writing system morphemic literacy is learned immediately.

NEW PARADIGM FOR WRITING SYSTEM CLASSIFICATION

I maintain that there are indeed two distinct types of scripts. However, these are not phonographic and logographic, but rather alphabetic, i.e. analytic; and syllabic, i.e. wholistic. The syllabic systems have been identified as wholistic by native speakers. This might imply a combination of factors. First, symbols represent segments of speech which are concrete and easily available to awareness. There is also a relationship of identification rather than representation between symbol and sound or possibly, symbol and meaning. Finally, the aesthetic or sentimental function of the script is not separated from the instrumental function. All of these factors combine to form a close relationship between the writing system and the language and culture of a people.

The alphabet is an analytic system, providing a more remote representation and a more flexible relationship between sound and symbol. It is readily adaptable to other languages and the form of the symbols themselves are not always elaborated to create unique appearances for each language and culture they represent. In actual fact, it seems that many writing systems combine features of both wholistic and analytic systems. The Japanese syllabary has some analytic features and eastern alphabets are often grouped in syllables and develop an artistic form which expresses group identity.

Within these two basic categories of wholistic and analytic systems all full writing systems represent speech on the phonographic principle but vary to the extent that they also represent the morphology of the language. However, all writing systems can also be read directly for meaning, so in that sense literacy may be understood as universal. Although I would propose that there is a significant correlation between both the type of script, including the way the script is perceived; and the socio-cultural order, that does not have to imply corresponding psychological differences in literacy activity.

TABLE 1

	phonographic	logographic
wholistic	syllabic	morphosyllabic
analytic (alphabetic)	phonemic	morphophonemic

However, there do seem to be three different manifestations of literacy which can occur in any culture. These were outlined by Tolstoy (1967),

> One pupil has a good memory, and it is easier for him to memorize the syllables themselves than to comprehend the vowellessness of the consonants; another reflects calmly and will comprehend a most rational sound method; another has a fine instinct and grasps the law of word combinations by reading whole words at a time.

Syllabic literacy is sufficiently different from alphabetic literacy to warrant a classification of its own. While morphemic literacy might be encouraged by a morphophonemic or morphosyllabic system, it seems that any written language can be read for meaning. Pictographic or "pure" morphemic representation apart from phonographic representation seems to function only as a system of communication which complements an oral tradition or another phonographic writing system. It is sometimes called visual literacy and exists in most societies but seems remote from representing language and verbal thought (Unger and DeFrancis, this volume). However, it deserves attention as part of the constellation of communication systems interacting on both local and global levels.

The "phonographic"/"logographic" spectrum is still important. A truly phonographic system, such as a "pure" syllabic system, reflects the speech of the individual or the community and reinforces respect for diversity, non-interference and autonomy. The predominant social functions for syllabic literacy are correspondence, newsletters, records, journals and oral reading in church rather than transmitting indigenous knowledge. This both reflects and supports a horizontal social order.

A more logographic system, and this includes all written languages standardized by either dictionaries or a body of literature, reflect a societal norm and have to be learned as part of a prescriptive process even if that means referring the corrective task to a "spell-checker". However, morphological representation unites speakers of various dialects across a wider territory and promotes a more unified or hierarchical social organization.

The ideal is perceived in our society as an appropriate combination of the two extremes with channels for accommodating diversity within a single state. Other modes of communication, such as television and radio on the one hand, and oral submissions and call lines to government on the other, increasingly complement English language literacy to maintain social cohesion and serve the goal of respecting autonomy. While a language with a large literature and a function in government is complemented by the electronic media, the Cree syllabary is in the process of being replaced by telecommunications systems on the one hand and English literacy on the other (Bennett and Berry, 1987).

Since it is necessary to consider all modes of communication which function in a society, one cannot correlate the nature of the socio-cultural order with script type quite as easily as Sjoberg suggested. However, some historic patterns of association may still be evident and we can certainly try to learn from them.

If, in fact, there is any correlation between script type and cultural and social factors, then non-native linguists who are involved in creating and revising writing systems need to take this into consideration. Even though many historic systems are a mixture of wholistic and analytic, as well as phonographic and logographic, this is no justification for altering a script by changing its characteristics unless there is a specific preceding change in the socio-cultural order or the function of the script. Any reform will have an effect which will ripple through the system and repercussions will occur.

However, if the function of literacy does not expand, full standardization may never occur and the vernacular might not be used across the school curriculum. This would not prevent the written language from continuing to play a vital role in native society. In fact, a literacy that is not acquired through formal education might be better suited for use in the home, community or church. It would then be up to these institutions to see that native literacy was maintained.

The lack of an adequate classification for writing systems has also compounded the problem. There has been a long-standing custom in this century, carried out by many institutions and governments around the world, of bestowing an alphabet on "pre-literate" peoples, and tidying up awkward systems of "primitive" groups so they work a little more like an alphabet. Maybe it is time to stand back and allow writing system development to evolve by adoption and consensus from within the group – as, in fact, some are beginning to do.

It is interesting to read that the Wesleyan James Evans returned to England and died shortly after his work on the syllabary. Neither he nor the Wesleyan church were in any position to impose syllabics on the Cree. By the time the Anglican and Catholic churches continued the work left off by Evans, they found that the syllabary was already used widely among Cree communities beyond missionary influence. Their decision to accept syllabics went against their usual practice of transcribing native languages in an alphabet. According to this interpretation syllabics came to be used for religious texts because the Cree themselves had already claimed it as their own script.

ACKNOWLEDGEMENTS

I would like to acknowledge the financial support of the Council of Native Ministries of the Anglican Church of Canada and the sponsorship of the Diocese of Moosonee, in particular Rev. J. Collins.

Thanks to Annie Loon, Bertha Metat, Evelyn Martin and the Ojibway and Cree Cultural Centre in Timmins for Cree lessons and literacy training. Arlene Stairs, Faculty of Education, Queens University, and Marguerite McKenzie, Memorial University, provided further information and encouragement.

Finally, I am indebted to Henry Gleason in general linguistics, Marvin Mayers in anthropology and Carol Eastman in language planning for their class lectures.

NOTES

[1] R. Cooper expresses the same sentiment with reference to the Vai syllabary (1989: 131). "Vai is a language with a predominantly consonant-vowel structure, for which a syllabary is well-suited. But it is unlikely that such technical considerations were responsible for the script's acceptance. In fact the syllabary is relatively inflexible (Kotei, 1972). Rather, a unique script was consistent with the African tradition of using indigenous symbols for magical purposes, a use which was surrounded by a 'high degree of mystery and secrecy' (Dalby, 1968)."

[2] DeFrancis does, in fact, use this typology to organize the chapters of Visible Speech (1989), but doesn't develop the idea.

[3] Syllabic writers do not seem to transfer this derivation of /w/ over to English. Thus an attempt by a well-educated biliterate Cree woman to write the name "Wilbert" in syllabics was abandoned as too difficult.

[4] In the school system a current teaching method encourages the teachers to present symbols with dissimilar shapes together and separate those symbols with a similar shape.

[5] "Pure" syllabic scripts have been used for centuries by women in Japan and China.

[6] Writing on the alphabetic principle uses a symbol for every segment of sound which can vary the meaning of a word in a particular language on a consistent basis.

[7] Native priests have possibly developed a morphemic literacy also through continuing use of text. According to Walker (1969) there are two different categories of readers of the Cherokee syllabary, those who read aloud in church and those who read silently in private to study indigenous "Indian doctor" knowledge. While the morphemic literacy of the Cherokee does not take place within the context of western schooling it is still only acquired by those adults who dedicate themselves to the study of indigenous knowledge (Walker, 1969).

BIBLIOGRAPHY

Barnett, H.G.: 1953, *Innovation: The basis of cultural change*, McGraw Hill Book Company, New York.

Basso, Keith H. and Anderson, Ned: 1977, 'A Western Apache writing system: The symbols of Silas John', in Joshua Fishman (ed.) *Advances in the Creation and Revision of Writing Systems*, Mouton, The Hague, pp. 77–104.

Battiste, Marie: 1985, 'An Historical Investigation of the Social and Cultural Consequences of Micmac Literacy', in B. Burnaby (ed.) *Promoting Native Writing Systems*, OISE Press, Toronto.

Bennett, J.A.H. and Berry, J.W.: 1987, 'The Future of Cree Syllabic Literacy in Northern Canada', in D.A. Wagner (ed.) *The future of literacy in a changing world*, Pergamon Press, Oxford.

Berry, J.W. and Bennett, J.A.: 1989, Syllabic literacy and cognitive performance among the Cree, *International Journal of Psychology* **24**: 429–450.

Burnaby, Barbara (ed.): 1985, *Promoting Native Writing Systems*, OISE Press, Toronto.

Burnaby, B. and Anthony, R.J.: 1985, 'Orthography Choice for Cree Langauge in Education', in B. Burnaby (ed.) *Promoting Native Writing Systems*, OISE Press, Toronto.

Burnaby, B. and McKenzie, M.: 1985, 'Reading and Writing in Rupert House', in B. Burnaby (ed.) *Promoting Native Writing Systems*, OISE Press, Toronto.

Cooper, Robert: 1988, *Language Planning and Social Change*, Cambridge University Press, Cambridge.

DeFrancis, John: 1989, *Visible Speech: The Diverse Oneness of Writing Systems*, University of Hawaii Press, Honolulu.

Diringer, David: 1948, *The Alphabet, A key to the history of Mankind*, Philosophical Library, New York.

Ellis, C.D.: 1983, *Spoken Cree* (Revised ed.), Pica Pica Press, Edmonton.

Fishman, Joshua, A.: 1969, *Language and Nationalism: Two Integrative Essays*, Newbury House, Rowley, Mass.

Fishman, Joshua (ed.): 1977, *Advances in the Creation and Revision of Writing Systems*, Mouton, The Hague.

Gelb, I.J.: 1952, *A Study in Writing*, University of Chicago Press, Chicago.

Gibson, E. and Levin, H.: 1975, *The Psychology of Reading*, MIT, Cambridge, Mass.

Keesing, Roger, M.: 1981, *Cultural Anthropology: A contemporary perspective* (second ed.), Holt Rinehart and Winston, New York.

Ladefoged, Peter: 1975, *A Course in Phonetics*, Harcourt Brace Jovanovich, Inc.

Murdoch, J.S.: 1981, 'Syllabics: A Successful Educational Innovation', Master's thesis, University of Manitoba, Winnipeg.

Nichols, J.D.: 1984, 'The composition sequence of the first Cree hymnal', in H.C. Wolfart (ed.) *Essays in Algonquian Bibliography, Algonquian and Iroquoian Linguistics*, pp. 1–21.

Powell, M.A.: 1981, 'Three problems in the history of cuneiform writing: origins, direction of script, literacy', *Visible Language* **15**: 419–440.

Radcliffe-Brown, A.R.: 1953, 'On the Concept of Function in Social Science', *American Anthropologist*. Vol. 37, pp. 394–402, July–Sept.

Rogers, Henry: *Optimal Orthographies* (this volume).

Sampson, Geoffrey: 1985, 'Writing Systems. A Linguistic Approach, Hutchison, London.

Scollon, Ron, and Suzanne: 1981, *Narrative, Literacy and Face in Interethnic Communication*. Ablex Publishing Corporation, Norwood, New Jersey.

Scribner, Sylvia and Cole, Michael: 1981, *The Psychology of Literacy*, Harvard University Press, Cambridge, Mass.

Sjoberg, Andree: 1964, 'Writing, speech and society: some changing interrelationships', in H. Hunt (ed.) *Proceedings of the ninth international congress of linguists*, Mouton, The Hague.

Sjoberg, Andree: 1966, 'Socio-cultural and linguistic factors in the development of writing systems for pre-literate peoples', in W. Bright (ed.) *Sociolinguistics* (Januarum Linguarum XX), pp. 260–273.

Tolstoy, Leo: 1967, 'On Teaching the Rudiments', in Leo Wiener (ed.) *Tolstoy on Education*, University of Chicago Press, Chicago.

Unger, J.M. and DeFrancis, J.: Logographic and Semasiographic Writing Systems: A Critique of Sampson's Classification (this volume).

Wagner, Daniel (ed.): 1987, *The Future of Literacy in a Changing World*, Pergamon Press, Oxford.

Walker, Willard: 1969, 'Notes on native writing systems and the design of native literacy programs', *Anthropological Linguistics* **11:5**: 148–166.

Wang, W.S.Y.: 1981, 'Language structure and optimal orthography', in O.J.L. Tseng and H. Singer (eds.) *Perception of Print: Reading research in experimental psychology*. Hillsdale, New Jersey, pp. 223–236.

KEREN D. RICE

6. DEVELOPING ORTHOGRAPHIES: THE ATHAPASKAN LANGUAGES OF THE NORTHWEST TERRITORIES, CANADA

Over the past several years, there has been a focus on literacy in the native American languages of the Northwest Territories, Canada. I have been involved in a committee that is concerned with the development of orthographic conventions for one of the languages of the Athapaskan family in the Northwest Territories. This language, defined largely on geographical and political grounds rather than on linguistic grounds, is usually called North Slavey or Dene.[1] In this paper, I discuss a process that is part of the development of literacy for North Slavey, a process that is designed to lead to orthography standardization.

The paper is organized as follows. Section 1 is a description of the Athapaskan languages and of dialect variation in North Slavey. Section 2 is a brief history of literacy in North Slavey. Section 3 presents the terms of reference given to the orthography committees. Section 4 deals with background issues and with the actual decisions that have been made.

1. THE DENE LANGUAGES

North Slavey is a language complex consisting of three major dialects that are usually called Hare (spoken in Fort Good Hope and Colville Lake), Bearlake (Fort Franklin), and Mountain (Fort Norman). These dialects differ in several ways, largely phonological and lexical. In this section, several linguistic characteristics, both shared and varying, of the language are examined. The variation is important since it is the differences between dialects that were problematic in establishing a standardized orthography.

1.1. *Shared Characteristics*

The Dene languages show many shared characteristics that do not enter into decisions about orthographic standardization. A major area of importance in looking at standardization is the sound system. The Dene languages have large sound systems, with a typical inventory including thirty-five consonants and six vowels, with vowels occurring with or without tone and nasalized or non-nasalized. A typical consonant inventory, this one for Bearlake, is shown in (1). The inventory is given in phonetic symbols, with orthographic symbols in parentheses where they differ from phonetic symbols.

I. Taylor and D.R. Olson (eds.), Scripts and Literacy, 77–94.

(1)	labial	dental	alveolar	lateral	alveopalatal	velar	labiovelar	glottal
stops and affricates								
aspirated		t	ts	tł	č (ch)	k	kw	
plain	b	d	dz	dl	ǰ (j)	g	gw	
ejective		t′	ts′	tł′	č′ (ch’)	k′	kw′	ʔ
continuants								
voiceless			s	ł	š (sh)	x	w̥ (wh)	h
voiced			z	l	ž (zh)	γ (gh)	w	
sonorants								
nasals	m	n						
other		r			y			

The sound differences between Bearlake and the other dialects, Hare and Mountain, will become clear in later sections.

There are six distinctive vowels in Slavey, /i/, /e/ (orthographic ⟨ə⟩), /ɛ/ (orthographic ⟨e⟩), /a/, /o/, and /u/. Each vowel can bear high tone, marked with an acute accent ´ in the orthography, or low tone, unmarked in the orthography. In addition, all vowels but /e/ can be nasalized, marked by a hook under the vowel, ˛, in the orthography.

In addition to complex sound systems, Athapaskan languages exhibit complex morphophonemics, or alternations of sounds in phonologically predictable environments. Thus a single morpheme can be pronounced in a variety of ways. I will give a few examples in order to help make sense of some of the problems faced in standardizing the orthography.

In Bearlake and Mountain, many d-initial prefixes show [d] phonetically word-initially and [r] phonetically after a vowel. Examples are given in (2), where the underlined segment is the same morpheme.

(2) a. <u>d</u>éhtła ‘s/he started out on land’
na<u>r</u>éhtła ‘s/he started back on land’

b. <u>d</u>ék′ǫ ‘it burns’
ʔek′a<u>r</u>ék′ǫ ‘candle (fat burns)’

In Hare, a prefix begins with [n] if the following vowel is nasalized and with [r] if the following vowel is oral. (3) illustrates this. The underlined segment is the initial consonant of the same morpheme.

(3) k′ína<u>n</u>į́yo ‘you sg. drive around’
k′ína<u>r</u>eyo ‘s/he drives around’

The actual phonetic pronunciation of an Athapaskan word can thus be quite different from its underlying representation.

1.2. *Variation*

Within North Slavey, there is variation found in all dialects and there is variation between dialects.

1.2.1. *Variation Throughout the Language*

In all North Slavey dialects, variation between [zh] and [y] is found. All /zh/'s can be pronounced as [y]. The factors that control this variation are uncertain; they seem to include a combination of discourse and dialect factors. Examples of alterative pronunciations are given in (4).

(4)	zh-y variation		
	z̲h̲a	y̱a	'snow'
	nágoz̲h̲ə	nágoy̱ə	's/he plays'

Underlying /y/'s do not vary with [zh], as shown in the words in (5), in which only [y] occurs.

(5)	y only	
	ˀeghálay̱ehda	'I work'
	y̱iˀá	'I ate'

This is just one example of a widespread phenomenon in North Slavey. There are many other similar variations in pronunciation. For stance /gh/ may be pronounced [w], but /w/ cannot be pronounced [gh].

1.2.2. *Between-dialect Variation*

There is a second kind of variation within North Slavey. The three dialect differ in several ways, largely phonological and lexical. Some of the major phonological correspondences found between dialects are discussed in section 1.2.2.1. Section 1.2.2.2 is a brief description of lexical variation.

1.2.2.1. *Sound Correspondences.* There are regular correspondences between consonants in the North Slavey dialects. For example, whenever [kw] is found in Bearlake, [f] occurs in Hare and [p] in Mountain. Likewise, where [kw′] is found in Bearlake, [w′] occurs in Hare, and [p′] in Mountain. There are also regular correspondences between Bearlake [gw], Hare [gw] or [b], and Mountain [b], between Bearlake [wh], Hare [w], and Mountain [f], and between Bearlake [w], Hare [w], and Mountain [v]. These correspondences are shown in (6).

(6)	Bearlake	Mountain	Hare	
a.	kw: sekwí	p: ṡepí	f: sefí	'my head'
b.	kw′: kw′á	p′: p′á	w′: w′á	'dish, plate'
c.	gw: nágwe	b: nábe	b/gw: rábe/rágwe	'she, he stays'
d.	wh: wheda	f: feda	w: weda	'she, he sits'
e.	w: ˀewé	v: ˀevé	w: ˀewé	'skin, hide'

In Hare, the affricates /ts/, /tł/, and /ch/ have been largely lost phonetically, with the fricatives [s], [ł], and [sh] occurring instead. This deaffrication process is illustrated in (7).

(7)	Bearlake	Mountain	Hare	
a.	ts: tsá	ts: tsá	s: sá	'beaver'
b.	ch: choh	ch: choh	sh: shoh	'feather'
c.	tł: tłe	tł: tłe	ł: łe	'lard, oil'

1.2.2.2. *Lexical Variation.* There is a second major type of variation, lexical variation between dialects. Examples are given in (8).

(8)	Bearlake	Mountain	Hare	
	tehmį́	tehmį́	ˀǫ́hshú	'pack'
	nazha	nazha	lalén	'wool'
	bé	ˀį́yę	ˀį́yę	'meat'

1.2.3. *Sources of Variation*

The types of variation identified so far are phonologically (e.g. [d]-[r] alterations) or geographically determined (e.g. sound correspondences between dialects). There are additional factors that control variation in North Slavey. As well as between-community geographical variation, there is within-community variation. This variation is determined by a variety of factors. First, each community was settled by groups of people who came from different places, and the various origins are reflected in the speech of people within the community today. Second, there is variation which is determined by age, or more exactly by conservatism of the speaker, variation which is determined by sex, variation due to speech style, variation due to the degree of assimilation, and other sources. The committee established to propose a standardized orthography attempted to deal with geographical variation, both within and between community, and with differences between conservative and innovative speech, and it is how these areas were dealt with that I will concentrate on.

2. HISTORY OF WRITING

Before turning to recent work in the development of orthographic conventions, it is useful to review the history of writing of these languages.

North Slavey was first written in a systematic way by Oblate priests, beginning in the latter part of the nineteenth century. The Oblates did extensive language work, writing dictionaries and grammars, translating hymns and prayers, and preparing hymnals and prayer books in the native languages. They introduced two writing systems, a phonetically-based alphabetic system taking French as its basis and a syllabic system. Both systems are problematic in some ways.

The French-based Alphabetic System

The alphabetic system is phonetically based, with each symbol designed to represent a single sound. While the principle on which this orthographic system is based is still in use, the implementation of the French system is problematic in that it does not give an accurate representation of the range of sounds in the languages. In particular, it sometimes underdifferentiates the consonants and sometimes uses more than one symbol for a particular sound. Some examples from Petitot (1876) are shown in (9).

(9)	French orthography		current orthography	correspondence French-current
a.	tl'in̨	'dog'	tłį	tl'-tł
	'kla, tla	'bottom'	tł'á	'kl-tł', tl-tł'
	klô	'grass'	tł'o	kl-tł'
	glure, klu	'mouse'	dlǫ	gl-dl, kl-dl
	'klié	'squirrel'	dliye	'kl-dl
b.	tchô, χô	'big'	cho	

Two problems with the French orthography can be seen in (9). First, a single symbol may represent more than one sound. This is evident in (9a), the lateral affricates, where the symbol ⟨'kl⟩ represents [tł'] or [dl]. Second, a single sound may be represented by more than one symbol, as in (9a) and (9b). In (9a), [tł'] is written in three different ways, ⟨'kl⟩, ⟨tl⟩, and ⟨kl⟩. [dl] is also written in three different ways, ⟨'kl⟩, ⟨gl⟩, and ⟨kl⟩. In (9b), the sound [ch], usually written ⟨tch⟩ by Petitot, has a variant spelling ⟨χ⟩.[2]

The French writing system, while designed to be a phonetically-based orthography, did not meet that goal and is thus to some extent an unsuccessful system. The fact that the second language of the Dene is English rather than French also contributes to the unpopularity of the French-based orthography. It is important to keep in mind, however, that the problems with the French system are in implementation rather than concept: current orthographies rely on the same basic principle of sound-symbol correspondence.

2.2. *The Syllabic System*

The syllabic system is based on the syllabary developed by Reverend James Evans for Cree and widely used for Algonquian languages and Inuktitut. The syllabic system is phonetically based, with each symbol representing a single syllable. Examples of symbols used in this system are given in (10).

(10)	te	ᑌ	ti	ᑎ	to	ᑐ	ta	ᑕ
	se	ᓭ	si	ᓯ	so	ᓱ	sa	ᓴ
	she	ᔐ	shi	ᔑ	sho	ᔓ	sha	ᔕ

The shape of the symbol indicates the consonant and the direction the vowel quality. Some North Slavey words written in this system are shown in (11).

(11)	orthography	syllabics	
	shá	ᔕ	'knot'
	sa	ᓴ	'sun'

This writing system is hampered for Athapaskan languages. A major problem arises from the fact that North Slavey has six distinctive vowels, with vowels having nasalized and oral counterparts and high and low tone counterparts. The syllabic system used for North Slavey relies on directionality, and there are only four distinctive directions, as in (10). It therefore cannot capture a six vowel distinction and is thus inadequate to handle the range of vowels. While it theoretically could use diacritics for tone and nasalization, this was not done. In addition, the consonant inventory of North Slavey is larger than that of Cree, the langauge for which the syllabary was developed. Additional symbols which are interpretable directionally and diacritics would have to be introduced to capture the range of consonantal sounds as well.

2.3. *Use of the French-based Orthography and Syllabics*

How did the French-based and syllabic writing systems fare with respect to literacy? This is perhaps not a fair question since it is unclear that literacy was perceived to be an important goal when these systems were introduced. As noted earlier, hymnals and prayer books were written in these orthographies. These are ritual materials, not meant to be read in a creative sense of reading. It appears that while there are some readers of syllabics and the French-based orthography, at least some of the people who read syllabics and the French-based orthography do not so much interpret new material as recite known material.[3]

2.4. *Recent Orthographies and the Push for Standardization*

The next major step in the development of literacy was the introduction of a phonemic writing system by missionaries in the 1950's. This writing system was based on an interpretation of a principle current in linguistics, "one sound, one symbol; one symbol, one sound." Behind this orthography was a different goal than that of the Oblates. The missionaries aimed at literacy, with their personal goal being Bible translation. They felt the need to create literacy materials in the native languages so that people could be taught to read, and eventually be able to read the Bible. The missionary movement began the current phase of literacy work.

Until the mid 1970's, major literacy work was carried out by missionaries, with some materials, largely prepared by missionaries, published by the government of the Northwest Territories. In the mid 1970's, a major effort was made by the government to introduce the teaching of native languages in the schools, to develop curriculum materials in the native languages, and to introduce literacy in the native languages. At this time, native people, missionaries, and linguists interested in the native languages formed a group under the name of Athapaskan Languages Steering Committee which was directed to introduce a standardized orthography. The committee interpreted 'orthography' in a narrow sense, and concentrated on developing a single set of symbols for use in all of the Athapaskan languages in the Northwest Territories. The committee made some progress in this; however, even in choice and use of symbols it left question unanswered.

2.5. *Why Standardization?*

In 1985, the government of the Northwest Territories established a Task Force on Aboriginal Languages. A recommendation of the Task Force was that committees be established for each of the Dene languages to make recommendations about orthography standardization. The reasons for suggesting standardization were many. The most salient reason given in the report concerns official language status. I quote from the report:

> Developing a standardized Dene writing system would strengthen the Dene languages as a whole, and would overcome some of the barriers to official status. However, it would not be an easy task. It would have to be done by the speakers of the languages, and would particularly involve elders. Once achieved, a widespread public education campaign would be necessary to familiarize all Dene with the new system. (p. 20)

It was pointed out in the Task Force report that standardizing writing does not imply standardizing speech:

> Standardizing the writing system for the Dene languages may mean that all speakers of the Dene languages would write and read the same symbols. Some speakers suggest that over a long period of time, the various Dene languages will become more understandable to each

other. Standardizing the writing system does not, however, mean standardizing the spoken languages. (p. 19)

The Task Force recommended that efforts to standardize the writing systems of the Dene languages be made a high priority and that funds be made available for this work under the direction of the Ministry of Aboriginal Languages and Cultures.

In other discussion of the need for standardization, the issue of official language status also arose as a primary motivation for standardization. Chambers (1986), for instance, discusses the position of the Dene Nation, the political organization representing all descendants of the Dene tribes in the Northwest Territories, with respect to the need for the protection of aboriginal rights, including that of language. Chambers remarks that the enshrinement of the Dene languages as official languages is considered to be an aboriginal right, a right that must be protected by legislation. In order to use the Dene languages in Denendeh, the Dene name for the Dene territory in the Northwest Territories, Chambers suggests that a campaign of literacy is required. With a standardized writing system, all written government communication (legislation, documents, advertisements, etc.) could be produced in one rather than numerous writing systems, making the notion of official language status a feasible one. While much work has been done on standardization, the issue of official language status remains an important one, and one of growing political importance as of the late 1980's.

Another reason for standardization has been cited. There has been a push to teach the Dene languages in the schools as both first and second languages. In the first language schools, early schooling is done in the native language, with reading taught in the native language. A prerequisite to the development of reading skills is that words and grammatical conventions be the same across speakers. In the type of system in use, each reader is taught the letters of the alphabet. Because the alphabet is largely phonemic, it is considered that once the sound associated with each symbol is known, a person can read and write. The result is that even for an individual, a word is not always written in the same way. This is shown in (12).

(12) a. ya, zha 'snow'
b. weda, wada 's/he sits' (Hare dialect)

A given speaker might pronounce the word in (12a) sometimes with [y] and sometimes with [zh]. This person would write the word in two different ways. The word in (12b) is sometimes pronounced with [ɛ] and sometimes with [a] as the first vowel. Again, a single speaker can use both pronunciations and therefore would have alternative spellings for the same word.

When writing across individuals within a dialect and between dialects is examined, there is a great variety in how words are spelled. When words are not always written in the same way, a reader cannot easily develop strategies for productive reading.

Finally, finances are an oft-cited reason for developing a standardized writing system. More writing systems means more money for production of materials, and, given a fixed budget, means fewer overall materials.

Thus, in the fall of 1987, committees were established for each of the Dene languages in the Northwest Territories. Each committee consisted of a number of native people including native language teachers, teachers who are natives, native language curriculum developers, interpreters, and a linguist as a resource person. It is basically the deliberations of the North Slavey committee that I will discuss in the remainder of this paper.

3. TERMS OF REFERENCE

The orthography standardization committees were given guidelines by a planning committee consisting largely of people working in the areas of language education and interpreting in the Northwest Territories. The goal of the committees as laid out by the planning committee in April 1987 was to devise a set of writing conventions for the language. These conventions were to include decisions about (i) choice of orthographic symbols, (ii) use of orthographic symbols, (iii) guidelines on dealing with within- and between-dialect variation, (iv) word divisions, and (v) punctuation.

All committees were required to use an alphabetic system similar to the one in current use. There was to be no returning to the syllabic writing system. It might be noted that throughout the meetings several people suggested using syllabics despite the problems with it. The syllabic system is in many ways viewed as a true writing system for native languages, while the Roman alphabet system is viewed as a writing system imposed by whites.

The committees were instructed to develop a consistent system of symbols to be used for writing the languages so that all of them would use a particular symbol for a common sound. (This became a point of controversy.) They were instructed to inquire how far towards uniformity of spelling it is possible to go between significantly different dialects of a major grouping. The committees were also directed to develop guidelines on dividing words, to develop guidelines for writing conservative vs. innovative and formal vs. informal forms, and to consider intonational tones. The committees were also instructed that in general more conservative forms of speech should be represented in the writing system. Several specific orthography questions were also identified.

It should be noted that the guidelines did not always give clear guidance. In particular, there was a conflict between two goals. The goal of maintaining a one sound-one symbol correspondence and that of developing uniformity of spelling between different dialects is a particularly thorny one, and one that occupied much of our time.

4. BACKGROUND ISSUES

Before turning to a discussion of orthographic decisions, it is useful to outline some of the major background considerations that were important in making decisions on the orthography questions.

4.1. *Types of Standardization*

There was major discussion within the North Slavey committee as to just what standardization means. The committee recognized three possible levels of standardization: individual standardization, community-based standardization, and regionally-based standardization.

4.1.1. *Individual Standardization*

By individual standardization, we meant that each person would be consistent in his or her own writing, but need not strive to make his or her writing consistent with that of others. Some advantages were recognized to this system. Prime among these were that little training is required and that different dialects, both within a community and between communities, are preserved. However, there are drawbacks to such a system. Most important of these is that there is no single established writing system. As noted above, a major argument for standardization is that a fluent reader reads many words as chunks rather than sound by sound; the more possible ways of writing a particular word that exist, the less likely it is that a learner will become a fluent reader. In addition, it was recognized that there would be considerable problems in producing teaching materials since the teacher might write in a different way than that used in the teaching materials.

4.1.2. *Community Standardization*

Standardization at the community level was a second possibility. By this we meant that one orthographic system would be chosen for each community despite differences in pronunciation within that community. For instance, some Hare speakers use [gw] while others use [b] (see (6)). In the orthography system in use for Hare, a community-based decision was made and all speakers write ⟨gw⟩ even if they use [b] when they speak. There would then be essentially three orthographies in North Slavey, one for Hare, a second for Bearlake, and a third for Mountain. While these orthographies would be similar, there would be differences between them.

Many advantages to this system were apparent. Because all speakers within a community would use the same orthography, the problems for the reader noted with an individual orthography would be largely overcome. However, the system does allow the community of origin of the reading material to be readily identified.

Another advantage noted for this system in comparison to a regional system (section 4.1.3) is that because the sound-symbol correspondences in the Dene language are similar to those in English, transference of reading skills between languages would be enhanced. In the regionally-based system, transference could be impeded, depending on choice of symbols.

There were a number of negative points recognized with a community-based orthography. First, if a teacher or child moved from one community to another, as often happens, she or he would have to learn to write in the system of the local dialect. Second, while some of the problems of use of materials noted under an individual standardization approach would disappear, the cost of materials under this system would still be high since materials would have to be printed for each of the three dialects. Third, with basically as many writing systems as there are communities, there are problems with the recognition of the native languages as official languages since the cost of preparing materials in numerous dialects makes it less feasible for native languages to be regarded as official languages.

4.1.3. *Regional Standardization*

The third possibility for standardization offered was what we termed regional standardization. By this, we meant that one orthographic system would be chosen for all dialects within the language, despite differences between the dialects. Each reader would read this writing system as she or he spoke. For instance, for a word like 'rock' which is pronounced [kwə], [fə], and [pə] depending on dialect, we might chose to use a slash (/) to represent this sound and write the word as ⟨/ə⟩. Speakers would each bring their own pronunciation to this word.

Several advantages were recognized. First, costs are kept down. The need for preparing materials for each community is lessened, allowing for the production of more materials. It also makes it more feasible to consider official language status. Problems of movement between communities are lessened when the communities use the same writing system.

Some negatives were recognized. Primary among these is that major changes in current practices become necessary. People who now read and write would require retraining. In addition, teacher training would require rethinking since the system generally used for teaching reading and writing would cease to be adequate. The need for resource materials such as dictionaries becomes even stronger. Finally, it was felt strongly that there is a danger that individual-community dialects and within-community dialects could be lost since they are not directly expressed in the writing system.

As a whole, the committee felt that regional standardization should be aimed for. As we shall see, social reasons prevented this from being adopted in full blown form.

4.2. *Other Considerations*

As a committee, we took a variety of other factors into account in coming to decisions about orthography standardization, including literacy (reading), social, political, and linguistic considerations.

4.2.1. *Reading Considerations*

Several issues concerning reading were considered to be important to decisions about a standardized orthography. One concerned the type of orthography to be used, a phonemically-based orthography, as is currently used, or a more abstract morphophonemic orthography. (We did not seriously entertain returning to a syllabic system.) A writing system must allow an adult to read rapidly and effectively and must also provide cognitive clarity in learning to read. As discussed in Burnaby & Anthony 1986 and other sources, a phonetic system is easier for a learner. However, there is some indication that the early advantages to a phonetic writing system are lost in the intermediate grades, and that a morphophonemic system, which gives some clues about the structure of the language, is easier for readers at an intermediate level. For mature readers, Burnaby & Anthony state that it does not matter whether a phonetic or morphophonemic system is used. Burnaby & Anthony also point out that transference of reading skills between languages is facilitated when both languages have the same type of writing system. The transference problem suggests that a morphophonemic writing system might be more suitable for North Slavey. While we considered such issues, they were not very important in actual decision making. Moving to a morphophonemic writing system was with few exceptions thought to be too great a shift from the current orthography for the people that now know how to read and write.

A reading consideration that was felt to be quite important in our decisions concerned word recognizability. Given the complex nature of the Athapaskan word, we agreed that a reader needed certain guidelines in reading to recognize words. Many of our decisions about whether sequences should be written as one or two words were based on this criterion.

4.2.2. *Social and Political Considerations*

A second area of concern in making decisions was social and political considerations. While it was recognized that regional standardization need not create a levelling of dialect differences, there was considerable discussion about how people would respond to regional standardization. Fear was expressed that standardization at a regional level would make all dialects the same. In addition, in two of the North Slavey communities the language is a second language for most speakers. Many people felt that while regional standardization has advantages, given the actual language environment a regionally standardized system in a community where most people read English would probably create a situation where people from different dialects pronounce the words the same way. The need to retain dialect differences in the spoken language was an overriding consideration, often overshadowing other reasons for adopting regional standardization.

Linguistic considerations separate from reading considerations played a role in decision making as well. The clearest area in which this can be seen was in choice of symbols. I will return to this below.

5. THE ACTUAL DECISIONS

I now turn to some of the decisions made by the North Slavey committee. I look at the different areas in which we were required to make decision and discuss some of the criteria used in coming to decisions.

5.1. *Regular Correspondences Across Dialects*

One of the harder areas to deal with was dialect variation. As discussed above, there is considerable predictable variation between dialects. Because the differences are predictable (e.g. whenever one says [kwə], the second says [fə], and the third [pə] 'rock', etc.), it should theoretically be possible to develop one symbol to represent the sounds /kw/, /f/ and /p/, with the speaker learning which way to pronounce it in his or her own dialect. Because of a variety of problems including transference from English, I suggested that nonalphabetic symbols found on a typewriter keyboard be used, symbols like >, /, etc. Examples of possible choices are shown in (13).

(13)

orthography	pronunciation			
	Bearlake	Mountain	Hare	
>ə	kwə	pə	fə	"rock"
>'ih	kw'ih	p'ih	w'ih	"mosquito"
ná/e	nágwe	nábe	rágwe, rábe	"s/he stays"

There was considerable understanding in the committee about why such a system would be good – it would facilitate exchange of materials between dialects, it would allow more materials to be produced, it would foster the goal of the aboriginal languages being recognized as official languages. Despite this, social reasons prevailed, with people feeling that this sound difference was important in dialect identity and it would represent too much of a loss to the individual dialects if a standardized system were use.

Another predictable differences between dialects can be seen in the affricates. As discussed in section 1.2.2.1, there is a correspondence between aspirated affricates in Bearlake and Mountain and voiceless fricatives in Hare. With respect to this issue we faced a two-fold problem. We first dealt with the affricates [ts] and [tɬ] and the corresponding Hare forms [s] and [ɬ]. The question that arose was whether we should use [ts] and [tɬ] in all dialects, including Hare, compromising the principle of one symbol-one sound, but creating more standardized material. Several linguistic considerations guided us. While Bearlake and Mountain [ts] is [s] in Hare, there is a difference in patterning between the [s]'s in Hare that come from [ts] and the [s]'s that correspond to [s]'s in the other dialects. An example is given in (14).

(14)

Bearlake	Hare	
s-s correspondence		
sa	sa	'month'
bezá	bezá	'his, her months'
ts-s correspondence		
tsá	sá	'beaver'
betsá	besá	'his, her beaver'

While Hare [s] corresponding to Bearlake [s] voices when a prefix is added, Hare [s] corresponding to Bearlake [ts] fails to voice in the same environment. Thus, the two [s]'s in Hare pattern differently. Based on evidence such as this, the committee at first agreed that a Hare speaker would benefit by using ⟨ts⟩ and ⟨tɬ⟩ in writing despite the fact that she or he did not use these sounds. It was thus primarily linguistic evidence that led to this decision. However, reconsideration took us back to the 'one sound-one symbol' principle, and the final decision was to maintain the writing system as is, with ⟨s⟩ representing two different patterns in Hare. The alveopalatal affricate caused additional difficulties. In the established writing system, this sound was written ⟨ch⟩. We noted that if we adopted the proposed revision for ⟨ts⟩ and ⟨tɬ⟩ (which was later rejected), a simple rule of thumb could be given to Hare readers – do not pronounce the initial ⟨t⟩. This did not hold true for the alveopalatal affricate. In order to maintain this rule, we suggested that the alveopalatal affricate be written ⟨tsh⟩ rather than ⟨ch⟩. This proposal was based on linguistic and reading factors, and such a decision leads to the goal of facilitating exchange between dialects. This decision was not well-received by the other standardization committees. They did not require such a change in orthography, and in order to keep the orthography as close as possible to the current system were not keen to change. Based on their input, the North Slavey committee reconsidered its decision, and decided to maintain the status quo.

We see then that while the need for facilitating exchange between dialects is important, this was not the only factor involved in coming to decisions. Social and political reasons sometimes led to avoiding a standardized system, while linguistic and reading reasons led to a standardized system. However, social and political reasons sometimes created standardization while reading reasons led to the avoidance of standardization. I will not look at the other areas of between-dialect variation since the types of criteria used in making the decisions are similar to those outlined for the two examples given above.

5.2. *Variation Within All Dialects*

As discussed in section 1.2.1, in addition to between-dialect variation, there is variation found within all of the North Slavey dialects. Some of this variation appears to be free, others is controlled by linguistic factors. In recognizing the need to have a single way of writing a particular lexical item, we came to a general principle to deal with such variations. If a particular morpheme could be pronounced with only one of the two sounds, it is to be written with the symbol for that sound. For instance, the word ⟨ˀeghálayehda⟩ "I work" can be pronounced only with a [y], and is thus to be written with a ⟨y⟩. If the morpheme can be pronounced with either of the two sounds, it is to be written with the varying one. For example, the word 'snow' is pronounced [zha] or [ya]. It is to be written with ⟨zh⟩ since ⟨y⟩ is reserved for the nonvarying sound. There is a linguistic basis for this decision, with a general principle required in order to facilitating readability.

5.3. *Morphophonemic Alternations*

In all dialects, there are predictable morphophonemic alternations, as discussed in section 1.1. In dealing with these variations, it was decided that the words should be written the way they are pronounced. This is illustrated for the d-r alternation in (15).

(15)	orthography	pronunciation	
	déhtła	déhtła	's/he started out'
	naréhtła	naréhtła	's/he started back'

Thus in dealing with dialect variation and morphophonemic alternations, many factors, including literacy, social, and linguistic considerations, contributed to the choices made. We arrived at a symbol system that is a hybrid between community-based and regional standardization. Perhaps over time we will move towards regional standardization; perhaps we will develop a system of materials exchange and people will find themselves able to read the different dialects. This remains to be seen.

5.4. *Word Divisions*

The area in which linguistic and readability considerations were of greatest importance is that of where to divide between words. As pointed out earlier, all major category lexical items (noun, verb, postposition) have a stem, the final element of the word. However, stems can be followed by clitics that indicate tense, mode, and aspect. These clitics are phonologically bound to the noun or verb. Some examples are given in (16).

(16)	shénetį	'you sg. eat'
	shénetį íle, shénetį́ le	'don't you sg. eatl'
	shéwohtį wolé	'I am going to eat'

Because the clitics are phonologically part of the stem, it was suggested that they be written as part of the same word. However, based on facilitating word recognizability, the committee decided against this position, and decided that clitics are to be written as separate words. This allows a reader to recognize the final syllable as the stem, the part of the word that carries the main lexical (as opposed to grammatical) meaning. Similarly, because the subject immediately precedes the stem in verbs, it also allows a ready strategy for identifying the subject of the verb.

A similar rationale was used for deciding how to write compounds and deverbal (or desentential) nouns. Compounding is highly productive in Slavey. Compounds in Slavey often have meanings that cannot be easily derived from the meaning of the pieces of the word. (17) is an example.

(17)	góhsimį́lé	'rainbow'
	góhsi 'spider' + mį́lé	'net (possessed form)'

Because compounds function as a single lexical item rather than as two lexical items, it was agreed to write them as a single word.

Nominalizations provided a somewhat greater problem. Nouns can be derived from a single verb, from a phrase, and from an entire sentence. Some examples are given in (18).

(18)	nádu	'snake, s/he crawls around'
	satsóné helu	'siren, metal rings'
	zhú behé k′enáˀenetsi	'washing machine, clothes are washed with it'

In general, it was decided that phrasal compounds should be written as separate words since this would enhance ease of readability. If they were written as a single word, the word could be long, and thus difficult to decipher. However, in a few cases, it was decided that phrasal nominalizations had to be written as a single word because the phonology so strongly suggested this. An example is given in (19).

(19)	ˀek′a dék′ǫ	[ˀek′a dék′ǫ]	'fat burns'
	ˀek′a 'fat' + dék′ǫ 'it burns'		
	ˀek′arék′ǫ	[ˀek′arék′ǫ]	'candle'

In the noun, it is impossible to separate the two pieces and within-word phonology, with /d/ becoming [r], is found. In the sentence, it is possible to put other items (e.g. adverbs) between the noun and the verb and the /d/ is always pronounced [d]. In cases like this then, it was felt that it was important to write the noun as a single word. It might be noted that all such cases that we could think of involved relatively short items, as in (19).

6. CONCLUSION

In developing conventions for writing, we began with an alphabetic system, and with the basic principle one symbol-one sound. In making decisions about choice and use of symbols, language variation, allomorphy, and word divisions, various considerations were taken into account, including reading, linguistic, social and political factors. We aimed for standardization among three dialects that differ in some significant ways in their sound systems. This goal was not reached, and the reasons for not reaching it have largely to do with the strongly felt need to have dialect identity reflected in the writing system. The work of the committee is ongoing, and perhaps we will later find other criteria to bring to decision making and set other goals that might differently affect decision making.

NOTES

1 The word "dene", pronounced [dɛnɛ], means "person, man" in the native languages. This word is used both for the particular language and for the all the Athapaskan languages of the Northwest Territories. The word "Slavey" is pronounced [slevi]. I use angled brackets ⟨ ⟩ to enclose orthographic forms, where necessary. Slashes / / are used to represent underlying representations and square brackets [ ] to represent actual pronunciations. In general, orthographic symbols are used throughout the paper unless otherwise noted.

2 Petitot (1876) notes that ⟨χ⟩ is an abbreviation for ⟨tch⟩.

3 I should note that this has not been tested beyond mere observation. Several of the elders who were taught syllabics can read and write, and will send notes to each other in syllabics.

REFERENCES

Burnaby, B. and Anthony, R.: 1985, 'Orthographic choice for Cree language in education', in B. Burnaby (ed.) *Promoting Native Writing Systems in Canada*, OISE Press, Ontario Institute for Studies in Education, pp. 105–126.

Chambers, C.: 1985, 'Practical suggestions for making Dene literacy function', in B. Burnaby (ed.) *Promoting Native Writing Systems in Canada*, OISE Press, Ontario Institute for Studies in Education, pp. 159–174.

Petitot, E.: 1876, *Dictionnaire de la langue Déné-dindjíe*, Ernst Laroux, Paris. *The Report of the Task Force on Aboriginal Languages*, 1986.

P. PRAKASH AND R. MALATESHA JOSHI

7. ORTHOGRAPHY AND READING IN KANNADA: A DRAVIDIAN LANGUAGE

The objectives of this chapter are:

1. to present a brief sketch of the origin of Indian scripts and the general features of the scripts;
2. to illustrate the specific features of Kannada orthography and how they represent the language; and
3. to discuss briefly reading, writing and teaching of Kannada and to list some research implications.

ORIGIN OF INDIAN SCRIPTS[1]

Paleographers have recognized two main writing system in India – Brāhmī (derived from *Brahma* meaning God of creation; origin) and Karosthī (possibly derived from Armaic word *harūttā*, meaning writing/engraving, or persian word *Khār-ustar*, meaning ass-camel, implying a caravan of merchants). Of these, Karosthī was in use mainly in North-West regions of India between 300 BC and 400 AD. As this script was written from right to left, the origin of Karosthī is unequivocally connected with the semitic group. Brāhmī – the basis of all modern Indian languages except the Arabic, a late-comer – was written from left to right, hence the controversy over its origin. Buhler (1892) was of the opinion that even Brāhmī was originally written from right to left and therefore argued in favor of semitic origin of Brāhmī. The other approach often employed is to derive the script from somc pictographic writing of the Indus valley. The earliest recorded Brāhmī is from the inscriptions of Ashoka (272–231 BC).

Indian Writing System

The precedence of grammar over the script is the hallmark of Indian writing system. Long before there was any script, they had developed the concept of letters (akšara), consonants (vyanjana) and vowels (svara). Phonetic analysis of 'mantras' and its recitation from generation to generation was transferred orally in the absence of any writing system. Therefore, we see a systematic arrangement of letters in the script. The whole set of basic letters are arranged in a phonetic order. Vowels come first in the arrangement (akšaramala, the string of letters) followed by the consonants grouped together on the basis of their articulation (velars, pre-palatals, retroflexes, dentals and labials, in that order). All the consonant letters have an inherent vowel 'a' with them (unless or otherwise specified by other explicit vowel signs attached).

I. Taylor and D.R. Olson (eds.), Scripts and Literacy, 95–108.

The vowels are in the order of short (hrisva), long (dīrgha), medial (guna) and dipthongs (vriddhi):

Short	*Long*	*Medial*	*Dipthong*
a	ā	e	ai
i	ī	o	au
u	ū		
r	r̄		

Of the consonants, 25 have been grouped into five classes, four semi-vowels, three sibilants, one aspiration, one pure nasal and three voiceless spirants. Each class of consonants consists of hard and soft consonants, their aspirators and a corresponding nasal:

Hard	*Aspirate*	*Soft*	*Aspirate*	*Nasal*
ka	kha	ga	gha	ṅa
ča	čha	ja	jha	ña
ṭa	ṭha	ḍa	ḍha	ṇa
ta	tha	da	dha	na
pa	pha	ba	bha	ma

Four semi-vowels:	ya, ra, la and va
Three sibilants:	s̄a, ṣa, and sa
Aspirate:	ha
Pure nasal:	ṁ (anusvara)
Three voiceless spirants:	ḥ (visarga)
	ḥ̤ (jihvāmūtīya) and
	ḥ̤ (upadhmānīya)

The basic structure of all the Indian scripts is the same until the present day, though anusvara and visarga are placed now along with vowels. There are also a few additions/omissions of graphemes in different languages, particularly South Indian languages. For instance, in Kannada there are graphemes for long medial vowels and an additional lateral ḷa. In Tamil, a single grapheme is used to represent both hard and soft consonants of each consonant class.

ON DRAVIDIAN LANGUAGES

Indo-Dravidian (or Dravidian) languages constitute one of the major language families existing in India (the other three being Indo-Aryan, Sino-Tibetian and Austro-Asiatic). This family of language is supposedly the fifth or sixth largest language family of the world. However, the exact number of languages (and dialects) which can be grouped under the Dravidian family is debatable. Whatever may be the differences of opinions among the linguists regarding the number of languages to be included in the Dravidian group, of all the Dravidian languages only Tamil, Telugu,

Kannada and Malayalam have their own writing systems. Some of the other Dravidian languages employ one of the four Dravidian scripts (in South India) or a neighboring script (in other parts of the country) for their writing. Some of the characteristics that distinguish the Dravidian languages from Indo-European are that in Dravidian languages:

a. all nouns denoting inanimate objects are of the neuter gender;

b. there is no passive voice;

c. nouns are inflected not by means of case terminations but by suffixed postpositions;

d. there is no nominative case; and

e. there are no copulative verbs.

KANNADA ORTHOGRAPHY

Kannada is one of the major Dravidian languages of South India. It is the state language of Karnataka, and is spoken by about 20 million people. It has a long history of about 1,500 years. The earliest documented inscription is from Halmidi inscription dated 450 AD and has a literary tradition of about 1,200 years (Kavirājamārga of the ninth century, is the first literary work available). The language naturally has undergone a number of changes in phonology and morphology throughout its history (Rajapurohit, 1982). Though several geographical and political factors have resulted in at least seven clearly identifiable dialects, there is always a notion of 'standard Kannada' which is followed in writing.

Kannada Alphabet (Akšara)

Modern Kannada has 50 basic letter symbols which are arranged in the same general Indian script order described earlier. Schematically it can be presented as follows:

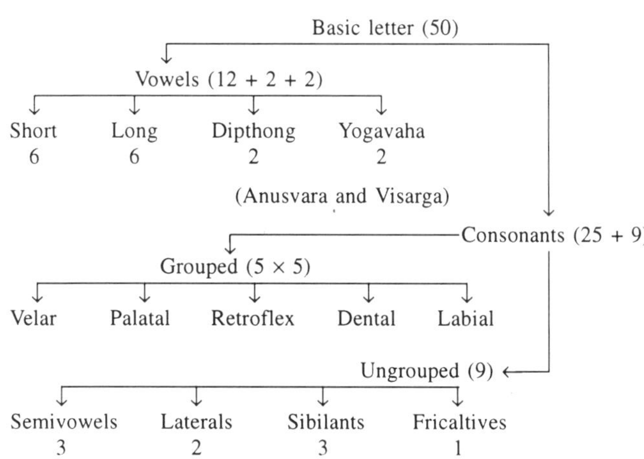

Figure 1 shows the alphabet in the way it occurs. Kannada has six short vowels, six long vowels (including ṛ and ṝ, which are rarely used in some Sanskrit loan words) and two dipthongs (ai and au). After these, there are two features called anusvara (0 – a pure nasal sound) and a visarga (: – a fricative). Visarga is a very rarely used sign in actual writing. Anusvara and Visarga are also referred to as *yogavaha*, meaning the articulation of these signs depends on the phonemic context they occur. This is followed by consonant classes – velar, palatal, retroflex, dental, and bilabial – each having corresponding hard/soft, aspirated/non-aspirated consonants and a nasal. At the end there are nine unclassified letters. Three of them (ya, ra, va) are semivowels, three are sibilants (śa, ṣa and sa), two are laterals (ḷa and la) and one is a glottal fricative (ha).

The following contrast features to English can be noted:

a. phonetic arrangement of the script
b. inherent 'a' in consonants
c. short and long vowel differentiation
d. existence of retroflex consonants
e. aspiration/non-aspiration differentiation

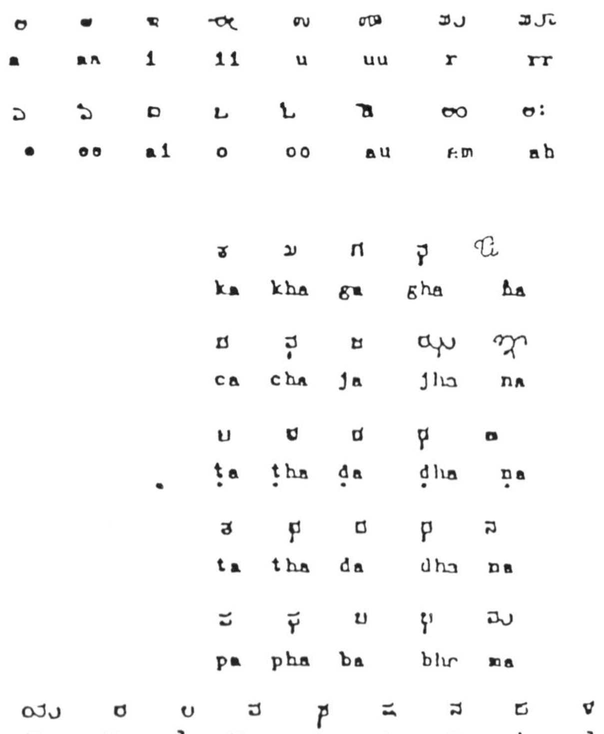

Fig. 1. Kannada alphabet

f. differentiation between ḷa and la; ṇa and na

g. ṛ and ṝ among the vowels. These differentiate the representations like Pṛthvi, Tṛpti from Prathvi and Trapti

h. Many of the nasals are hardly used; all aspirated forms are used only in Sanskrit words. Thus, the script follows some ideal format presumably developed for Sanskrit in earlier days.

Kannada script presents a mixture of syllabic and alphabetic principles (like Korean Hangul). There is almost one to one graphophonological equivalents expressed in syllable structure, regular signs of vowels being attached to the basic consonant forms. Ideally, each syllable form can be analyzed into its consonant and vowel components. And also a consonant can combine with any of the sixteen vowels to form a corresponding syllable. This form is illustrated by the syllable matrix (Figure 2). Each of the thirty-four consonants results in sixteen syllable forms when combined with the same number of vowels (including anusvara and visarga).

Figure 2 also illustrates that each of the vowels, in addition to its syllabic (primary) form, has an intrasyllable (secondary) form which is used in writing a cv syllable. These intrasyllabic forms are attached to the consonants in a regular fashion – the right, above and/or below of the consonant. The intrasyllabic forms of vowels are illustrated with an imaginary consonant form X in Figure 3.

Conjunct Consonants

In order to maintain the syllabic representation in conjuncts, all consonants have a conjunct form (used while in position C_2 or C_3 in a consonant cluster) in addition to their primary forms. The conjunct forms are mostly truncated forms of their primary forms – this is apparent in some of the forms and inherent in others. The general rule of writing a conjunct is shown in Figure 4. Conjuncts involving initial /r/ are written, however, with a special independent sign 'arka' and they are exceptions to the above rule. The consonant cluster in Kannada script does not exceed C C C V complexity.

Kannada is a polysyllabic agglutinative language with numerous inflections. There are six cases (*vibhakti*) to denote the relationship of nouns and pronouns with others in a sentence context (Eight *vibhakti* cases are found in all Indian language grammar books, though no language perhaps uses all the eight cases). The language is so highly inflected that it is often very difficult to get into the root of a word. These characteristics have resulted in some properties that are in contrast to English.

Because of the cases and other inflections, word order is not particularly affected by the sentence types. For instance, both active and passive forms can follow the same order S-O-V (which is the general form of sentences in Kannada) by attaching appropriate cases in each of the categories.

ವ್ಯಗಳು ಸ್ವರಗಳು ಹಾಗೂ ಅವುಗಳ ಗುರುತುಗಳು

ಅ	ಆ	ಇ	ಈ	ಉ	ಊ	ಋ	ೠ	ಎ	ಏ	ಐ	ಒ	ಓ	ಔ	ಅಂ	ಅಃ
-	ಾ	ಿ	ೀ	ು	ೂ	ೃ	ೄ	ೆ	ೇ	ೈ	ೊ	ೋ	ೌ	ಂ	ಃ
ಕ	ಕಾ	ಕಿ	ಕೀ	ಕು	ಕೂ	ಕೃ	ಕೄ	ಕೆ	ಕೇ	ಕೈ	ಕೊ	ಕೋ	ಕೌ	ಕಂ	ಕಃ
ಖ	ಖಾ	ಖಿ	ಖೀ	ಖು	ಖೂ	ಖೃ	ಖೄ	ಖೆ	ಖೇ	ಖೈ	ಖೊ	ಖೋ	ಖೌ	ಖಂ	ಖಃ
ಗ	ಗಾ	ಗಿ	ಗೀ	ಗು	ಗೂ	ಗೃ	ಗೄ	ಗೆ	ಗೇ	ಗೈ	ಗೊ	ಗೋ	ಗೌ	ಗಂ	ಗಃ
ಘ	ಘಾ	ಘಿ	ಘೀ	ಘು	ಘೂ	ಘೃ	ಘೄ	ಘೆ	ಘೇ	ಘೈ	ಘೊ	ಘೋ	ಘೌ	ಘಂ	ಘಃ
ಙ	ಙಾ	ಙಿ	ಙೀ	ಙು	ಙೂ	ಙೃ	ಙೄ	ಙೆ	ಙೇ	ಙೈ	ಙೊ	ಙೋ	ಙೌ	ಙಂ	ಙಃ
ಚ	ಚಾ	ಚಿ	ಚೀ	ಚು	ಚೂ	ಚೃ	ಚೄ	ಚೆ	ಚೇ	ಚೈ	ಚೊ	ಚೋ	ಚೌ	ಚಂ	ಚಃ
ಛ	ಛಾ	ಛಿ	ಛೀ	ಛು	ಛೂ	ಛೃ	ಛೄ	ಛೆ	ಛೇ	ಛೈ	ಛೊ	ಛೋ	ಛೌ	ಛಂ	ಛಃ
ಜ	ಜಾ	ಜಿ	ಜೀ	ಜು	ಜೂ	ಜೃ	ಜೄ	ಜೆ	ಜೇ	ಜೈ	ಜೊ	ಜೋ	ಜೌ	ಜಂ	ಜಃ
ಝ	ಝಾ	ಝಿ	ಝೀ	ಝು	ಝೂ	ಝೃ	ಝೄ	ಝೆ	ಝೇ	ಝೈ	ಝೊ	ಝೋ	ಝೌ	ಝಂ	ಝಃ
ಞ	ಞಾ	ಞಿ	ಞೀ	ಞು	ಞೂ	ಞೃ	ಞೄ	ಞೆ	ಞೇ	ಞೈ	ಞೊ	ಞೋ	ಞೌ	ಞಂ	ಞಃ
ಟ	ಟಾ	ಟಿ	ಟೀ	ಟು	ಟೂ	ಟೃ	ಟೄ	ಟೆ	ಟೇ	ಟೈ	ಟೊ	ಟೋ	ಟೌ	ಟಂ	ಟಃ
ಠ	ಠಾ	ಠಿ	ಠೀ	ಠು	ಠೂ	ಠೃ	ಠೄ	ಠೆ	ಠೇ	ಠೈ	ಠೊ	ಠೋ	ಠೌ	ಠಂ	ಠಃ
ಡ	ಡಾ	ಡಿ	ಡೀ	ಡು	ಡೂ	ಡೃ	ಡೄ	ಡೆ	ಡೇ	ಡೈ	ಡೊ	ಡೋ	ಡೌ	ಡಂ	ಡಃ
ಢ	ಢಾ	ಢಿ	ಢೀ	ಢು	ಢೂ	ಢೃ	ಢೄ	ಢೆ	ಢೇ	ಢೈ	ಢೊ	ಢೋ	ಢೌ	ಢಂ	ಢಃ
ಣ	ಣಾ	ಣಿ	ಣೀ	ಣು	ಣೂ	ಣೃ	ಣೄ	ಣೆ	ಣೇ	ಣೈ	ಣೊ	ಣೋ	ಣೌ	ಣಂ	ಣಃ
ತ	ತಾ	ತಿ	ತೀ	ತು	ತೂ	ತೃ	ತೄ	ತೆ	ತೇ	ತೈ	ತೊ	ತೋ	ತೌ	ತಂ	ತಃ
ಥ	ಥಾ	ಥಿ	ಥೀ	ಥು	ಥೂ	ಥೃ	ಥೄ	ಥೆ	ಥೇ	ಥೈ	ಥೊ	ಥೋ	ಥೌ	ಥಂ	ಥಃ
ದ	ದಾ	ದಿ	ದೀ	ದು	ದೂ	ದೃ	ದೄ	ದೆ	ದೇ	ದೈ	ದೊ	ದೋ	ದೌ	ದಂ	ದಃ
ಧ	ಧಾ	ಧಿ	ಧೀ	ಧು	ಧೂ	ಧೃ	ಧೄ	ಧೆ	ಧೇ	ಧೈ	ಧೊ	ಧೋ	ಧೌ	ಧಂ	ಧಃ
ನ	ನಾ	ನಿ	ನೀ	ನು	ನೂ	ನೃ	ನೄ	ನೆ	ನೇ	ನೈ	ನೊ	ನೋ	ನೌ	ನಂ	ನಃ
ಪ	ಪಾ	ಪಿ	ಪೀ	ಪು	ಪೂ	ಪೃ	ಪೄ	ಪೆ	ಪೇ	ಪೈ	ಪೊ	ಪೋ	ಪೌ	ಪಂ	ಪಃ
ಫ	ಫಾ	ಫಿ	ಫೀ	ಫು	ಫೂ	ಫೃ	ಫೄ	ಫೆ	ಫೇ	ಫೈ	ಫೊ	ಫೋ	ಫೌ	ಫಂ	ಫಃ
ಬ	ಬಾ	ಬಿ	ಬೀ	ಬು	ಬೂ	ಬೃ	ಬೄ	ಬೆ	ಬೇ	ಬೈ	ಬೊ	ಬೋ	ಬೌ	ಬಂ	ಬಃ
ಭ	ಭಾ	ಭಿ	ಭೀ	ಭು	ಭೂ	ಭೃ	ಭೄ	ಭೆ	ಭೇ	ಭೈ	ಭೊ	ಭೋ	ಭೌ	ಭಂ	ಭಃ
ಮ	ಮಾ	ಮಿ	ಮೀ	ಮು	ಮೂ	ಮೃ	ಮೄ	ಮೆ	ಮೇ	ಮೈ	ಮೊ	ಮೋ	ಮೌ	ಮಂ	ಮಃ
ಯ	ಯಾ	ಯಿ	ಯೀ	ಯು	ಯೂ	ಯೃ	ಯೄ	ಯೆ	ಯೇ	ಯೈ	ಯೊ	ಯೋ	ಯೌ	ಯಂ	ಯಃ
ರ	ರಾ	ರಿ	ರೀ	ರು	ರೂ	ರೃ	ರೄ	ರೆ	ರೇ	ರೈ	ರೊ	ರೋ	ರೌ	ರಂ	ರಃ
ಲ	ಲಾ	ಲಿ	ಲೀ	ಲು	ಲೂ	ಲೃ	ಲೄ	ಲೆ	ಲೇ	ಲೈ	ಲೊ	ಲೋ	ಲೌ	ಲಂ	ಲಃ
ವ	ವಾ	ವಿ	ವೀ	ವು	ವೂ	ವೃ	ವೄ	ವೆ	ವೇ	ವೈ	ವೊ	ವೋ	ವೌ	ವಂ	ವಃ
ಶ	ಶಾ	ಶಿ	ಶೀ	ಶು	ಶೂ	ಶೃ	ಶೄ	ಶೆ	ಶೇ	ಶೈ	ಶೊ	ಶೋ	ಶೌ	ಶಂ	ಶಃ
ಷ	ಷಾ	ಷಿ	ಷೀ	ಷು	ಷೂ	ಷೃ	ಷೄ	ಷೆ	ಷೇ	ಷೈ	ಷೊ	ಷೋ	ಷೌ	ಷಂ	ಷಃ
ಸ	ಸಾ	ಸಿ	ಸೀ	ಸು	ಸೂ	ಸೃ	ಸೄ	ಸೆ	ಸೇ	ಸೈ	ಸೊ	ಸೋ	ಸೌ	ಸಂ	ಸಃ
ಹ	ಹಾ	ಹಿ	ಹೀ	ಹು	ಹೂ	ಹೃ	ಹೄ	ಹೆ	ಹೇ	ಹೈ	ಹೊ	ಹೋ	ಹೌ	ಹಂ	ಹಃ
ಳ	ಳಾ	ಳಿ	ಳೀ	ಳು	ಳೂ	ಳೃ	ಳೄ	ಳೆ	ಳೇ	ಳೈ	ಳೊ	ಳೋ	ಳೌ	ಳಂ	ಳಃ

ಕ್ಷ ಕ್ಷಾ ಕ್ಷಿ ಕ್ಷೀ ಕ್ಷು ಕ್ಷೂ ಕ್ಷೆ ಕ್ಷೇ ಕ್ಷೈ ಕ್ಷೊ ಕ್ಷೋ ಕ್ಷೌ ಕ್ಷಂ ಕ್ಷಃ
ಜ್ಞ ಜ್ಞಾ ಜ್ಞಿ ಜ್ಞೀ ಜ್ಞು ಜ್ಞೂ ಜ್ಞೆ ಜ್ಞೇ ಜ್ಞೈ ಜ್ಞೊ ಜ್ಞೋ ಜ್ಞೌ ಜ್ಞಂ ಜ್ಞಃ

Fig. 2. Syllable matrix

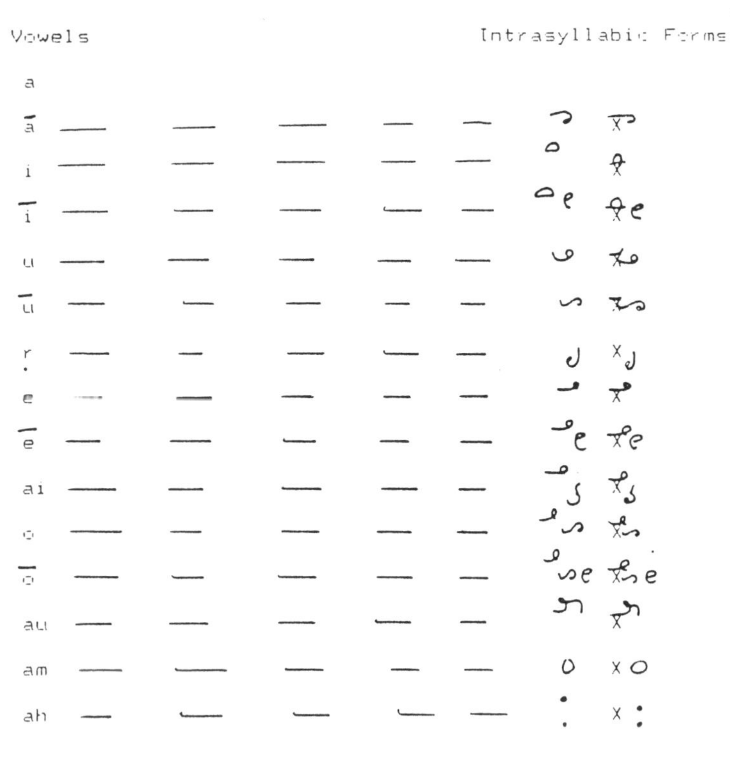

* ṝ is never used.

Fig. 3. The intrasyllabic forms of vowels with an imaginary consonant

A particular word order selected often depends on general usage and some times intentional emphasis on a specific point.

E.g.,

Avanu mavinahannannu tindanu (He mango ate)	– Active (S-O-V)
Avaninda mavinahannu tinnalpattitu (Him by mango eaten)	– Passive (S-O-V)
Mavinahannu avaninda tinnalpattitu (Mango him by eaten)	– Passive (O-S-V)

A very high grapheme-phoneme correspondence has resulted in the absence of irregular spellings and homonyms (thereby presumably reducing related reading problems). In Kannada, all homophones are homographs (except a few discussed in the paper). However, the absence of these useful/popular tools in reading research need not, perhaps, imply the absence

The general rule of writing a conjunct can be represented as follows:

C_1C_2V $\quad\quad$ $C^1{}_{C'_2}V$

or

$C_1C_2C_3V$ $\quad\quad$ $C^1{}_{C'_2}{}_{C'_3}V$

where,	C_1	primary form
	C'_2 & C'_3	conjunct forms
	V	intrasyllabic form

E.g.,

tna	t_na	(ತ್ನ)
trya	$t_{ry}a$	(ತ್ರ್ಯ)
gni	g_ni	(ಗ್ನಿ)

The initial consonant is written with the vowel in its intrasyllabic form attached on to its primary form, following consonants are represented below the initial consonant in their conjunct forms.

Fig. 4.

of corresponding processing difficulties in Kannada. Features like anusvara, arka could provide some alternatives to study the issue.

Sandhi

The agglutinative character of Kannada has resulted in a grammatical rule called 'Sandhi' (meaning 'union' or 'joining'). In Sandhi, two or more words/morphemes fuse together, resulting in a single 'compound' word. The morphophonemic changes occurring at junctural points, i.e. the ways in which vowels and consonants combine or get modified in the formation of new compound words, are explained by 'Sandhi rules'. There is also another related grammatical function called 'Samasa' – which explains the semantic relation of agglutives to their component words. For instance:

Arasana + mane = Aramane	Tampada + gali = Tangali
(king's + residence) = (palace)	(cold + wind = cold wind)

Tense Markers

There are three main tense markers:

utta	–	in present tense
da	–	in past tense
va	–	in future tense

These markers come in between verb (root form) and its inflexions. For instance, with avanu (he), hogu (go) takes the following forms:

hogu + utta + ane	hoguttane	(present)
hogu + da + anu	hodanu	(past)
hogu + va + anu	hoguvanu	(future)

Because of the complexities involved with inflexions and sometimes mysterious verb forms, a grammatical expertise is required to analyse any sentence at that level. However, the tense classes are not sub-divided and all English tense classes cannot be represented satisfactorily in Kannada. And also in speech, present tense forms are generally used in place of future tense.

Writing – 'Letter Types'

The script is written from left to right. The curved, round shape of the letters are believed to be a consequence of early practice of writing on palm leaves with stylus.

The punctuation marks are exactly the same as in English, but there are no letter types (Italics, Upper case of Lower case). The emphasis in writing is often conveyed by thick prints, larger prints and/or underlines. The loan words (from other languages, mainly English) which are already common in Kannada, are written in transliterated way of their Kannadized forms (e.g., bus/bussu). The sounds which do not have graphemic representations in Kannada are represented with their nearest phoneme symbols existing in the language with a diacritical mark below them.

E.g.,	pha	for	/f/	
	ja	for	/z/,	etc.

Typewriters have been introduced in recent years, but the existing types do not exactly represent the fused form of syllables.

KANNADA TEACHING

Kannada in primary schools is taught syllabically. Elaborate phonetic arrangement of the script, the articulation principle, linguistic characteristics of vowels and consonants, consonant classification, phonemic-graphemic fit are hardly made explicit in teaching. Instead, it is mechanically taught from one end of the script to the other. Interestingly, reading and writing are taught simultaneously in the earlier grades. A child begins to trace vowel forms, consonants and simultaneously learning to identify the syllables and indulging in a kind of logographic reading. Gradually, the child starts reading words with picture (given in the text), and quickly moves on to short phrases and simple sentences. However, all the while syllabic strategy is emphasized. For illustration, a typical lesson in the middle of Grade I text book may read like this:

Basava get up	Kamala get up
it is seven o'clock	it is time to go to school
Basava got up	Kamala got up
washed their faces	ate their breakfast
got ready to go to school	

GET UP SCHOOL FACE BREAKFAST

Pattanayak (1981) documents that children in a tribal school failed even to differentiate reading from memorization. They 'read' with the books closed. However, generally the child is expected to learn all the basic syllabary forms and some other syllables by the end of first year of schooling. By the second year, they are expected to decode all syllables, even though they may fail to decode some of the conjunct words. Grammar as a part of the curriculum starts in the third grade. In fifth grade, explicit teaching of morphophonemics starts with the introduction of Sandhis. English is introduced in the fifth grade where Kannada is the medium of instruction.

Of interest is the new method of teaching by some practitioners in Mysore (P. Karanth, personal communication). The method is phonemic, teaching syllables in alphabetic principle. This method could well be the acknowledgement of alphabetic features of the script. It may be worthwhile to note that in Korea, Hangul, a semi-syllabic script, was at one time taught as an alphabet and later on was taught as a syllabary. The syllabary method was found to be more successful and is still practised (Taylor and Taylor, 1983).

READING AND READING RESEARCH IN KANNADA

It seems perfectly logical to think that, all other things being equal, the type of orthography a person is exposed to should have some role to play in literacy acquisition and reading failures. English orthography is a morphophonological transcription which represents a word as a systematic sequence of phonemes, while at the same time capturing its constituent morphemes and underlying phonology. Phoneme awareness is found to be very closely linked with English and other alphabetic scripts. But it could be a different story in scripts like Kannada. Generally all the previous comparative studies have been conducted in pure logographic or pure syllabic scripts. The semi-syllabic scripts like Kannada provide yet another dimension for comparison.

Some varieties of reading problems are linked to the type of scripts. For instance, it is reported that about 10% of the first graders in France have difficulty in learning French (Ruthman, 1973), while about 5% of German speaking children have difficulty in acquiring reading skills (Klassen, 1972). The highest percentage reported is for English speaking countries (Critchley, 1970), while the lowest reported is in a survey by Makita (1968) for Japanese children which was less than 1% of the population and further dyslexia is considered a rare phenomenon in Japan. However, the incidence of reading problems reported for Japanese and other languages with close correspondence between sound and symbol may be much higher than it was reported earlier (see Stevenson, Stigler, Lucker, Lee, Hsu, and Kitamura, 1982).

There is not much work done regarding the nature and incidence of reading problems in Kannada. One study by Rama, Miles, and Lalithamma (1993) showed that there were 14 children who were classified as dyslexics out of a total of 246 third and fourth grade children. The following criteria were used to identify dyslexia:

a. 8 years of age or higher
b. normal auditory and visual functioning
c. normal intelligence as measured by Raven's Progressive Matrices.

Additionally, 43 children in the same population were classified as non-dyslexic poor readers. Thus, it appears that reading problems can occur in a langauge like Kannada, which has an almost perfect sound-symbol relationship. As Hatta reported in this conference, nearly 11% of the Japanese 11 year-old children were reading at least two grade levels below their expected grade level. Further, he attributes cognition to be a determining factor in reading disabilities than perception (see also Hirose and Hatta, 1988). Thus, the low incidence of reading problems reported in some languages may be an artifact of measurements and techniques used. In Prakash's (1987) study, children could decode in Oriya, another Indian language with almost perfect sound-symbol relationship but could not comprehend what was read.

An interesting observation has been made by Karanth (1992) about a multilingual dyslexic subject. The subject A.K. was 9 years old and had a full scale IQ of 112. He was exposed to reading and writing in three languages but his writing errors in English and Hindi were of phonetic nautre while errors in Kannada were substitutions of visually similar symbols. Similar observation has also been made in a 56 year old Kannada-English bilingual alexic, N.R. (Karanth, 1981; 1985). Although N.R.'s recognition of orally spelled words was good both in Kannada and English, he read Kannada with more difficulty than English, and furthermore, N.R. took more time to read Kannada than English. Due to the orthographic nature of Kannada, one would expect Kannada to be easier to read than English. According to Karanth (1985), however, ". . . the greater difficulty that N.R. faces in a syllabic orthography like Kannada can only be explained in terms of the greater number of graphemes and their relative complexity, which call for finer discrimination" (p. 258).

Thus, there is a need to clarify the different types of reading disorders before examining the relationship between scripts and literacy. Frith's (1985) model on literacy acquisition presents a promising framework to study the reading acquisition and developmental dyslexia across the scripts. It hopes to capture the underlying universal process unfolding in a script specific situation along with the interacting variable of specific teaching method. In the Appendix some of the orthographic features that could be helpful in testing the model in Kannada are listed.

ACKNOWLEDGEMENTS

We are indebted to Drs. John Morton and Uta Frith for stimulating and helpful discussions during the first author's stay at MRC Cognitive Development Unit, London. Grateful appreciation is expressed to Dr. Prathibha Karanth of All India Institute of Speech and Hearing, Mysore, India, for her comments and encouragement.

APPENDIX: ORTHOGRAPHIC FEATURES THAT ARE HELPFUL IN TESTING THE MODEL IN KANNADA.

a. *Anusvara*: Is a nasal grapheme (represented by 'o') which represents more than one phonemic value. It represents /m/, /n/, /ṇ/, /ṅ/ and /ñ/. Its phonetic value is context dependent but rule governed. It is given a nasal sound of the consonant class to which the anusvara following consonant belongs. Otherwise, i.e., when followed by unclassified consonants or in word last position, it is always actualized as /m/. E.g.:

manga	vanga	/ṅ/
mancha	lancha	/ñ/
ganḍa	banḍi	/ṇ/
tanda	bindu	/n/
tumba	amba	/m/

It is the only such grapheme represented by an independent characteristic 'O' in Kannada. It has been noticed that poor readers have difficulty in realizing its phonemic value while reading. Though words having anusvara follow a definite rule, they could serve as a good candidate to study logographic representation of the feature. In later stages, overreliance on syllabic strategy may result in reading this erroneously and with self-corrections.

b. *Arka*: Is another characteristic sign 'ϛ' which stands for secondary form of /ra/. It is an extra sign which behaves like any other secondary form. It does not follow the general pattern of conjunct representation described earlier.

C_1C_2V $\quad C_{1_{C_2'}}V$ $\quad$ general rule

with Arka,

C_1C_2V $\quad C_2V\,C_1$ $\quad C_1$ – arka

$C_KV_AC_MV_AC_1$ $\quad C_R$ – arka i.e., when regular /r/ secondary form is used (which follows the general rule).

$C_KV_AC_{R_{C_M}}V_A$

Thus, it is an exceptional secondary feature. With its characteristic shape and independent occurrence at nonconventional position may well be a feature that marks the whole range of development from stage one of the model to stage three through stage two. Intuitively, it is a very appropriate candidate for logographic representation and if it is so, a child should read a word with arka (even if other letters are changed) sign in it, and should fail to read the same word using regular secondary form of /ra/ (which follows the general rule of conjunct representation and equally (?) acceptable). In the second stage, the same child should find it hard to read and write arka words than when the same words are written in non-arka fashion – if they adhere to the sequential syllabic strategy. But this difficulty should cease to occur once he reaches the orthographic stage (say, there should not be any difference in time taken to process arka words and their non-arka counterparts).

c. *Unmarked aspiration and homophonic effect of sibilants in speech*: These are two more seemingly powerful features which could be very suitable to test stage 2 level acquisition. In ordinary speech, both aspirated and unaspirated consonants are spoken unaspiratedly. There is also not any fine difference in pronouncing s and ş sibilant words. Therefore, children adopting an alphabetic strategy are prone to commit errors in writing the words contaning aspirated consonants and these two sibilants. Differentiating between these features calls for orthographic representation of these (aspirated/sibilant) words.

d. *Conjuncts*: It is interesting because of the secondary forms coming below the primary forms of C (initial consonant). A child employing syllabic strategy is prone to read, for example, Ishwara (written as Isha̭ra) as Ishawara. Children do find it difficult to read/write conjunct words (observation).

e. *Alternate homophonic unacceptable spellings of words*: E.g.,

Unacceptable (nonsense) homophones	Acceptable
vuguru	uguru
vūru	ūru
yili	ili
yīga	īga
wondu	ondu
hau	havu
bai	bayi

May be these features can be used in lexical decision tasks where the words are exposed for a brief time. The children employing the pre-lexical grapheme-phoneme strategy might perform poorly with nonsense homophones.

f. *Phonologically guided spelling resulting in erroneous syllable form*: The feature referred to is /aī/, a long dipthong which does not exist in the language but employed while writing. Thailand ($Th\bar{a}_{ai}land$), Tenginakai ($Tenginak\bar{a}_{ai}$ – coconut), Rama naik (Rama $N\bar{a}_{ai}ka$ – to differentiate from another community spelt as as Nayaka) are some of the examples where 'ai' intrasyllabic sign is often attached to 'ā' intrasyllabic form, resulting in a new syllable.

NOTE

[1] Dani (1963) is the main source for what follows in this section.

REFERENCES

Buhler, J.G.: 1892, *On the origin of the Indian Brahmi alphabet*, Trubner, Strassburg.

Caldwell, R.: 1974, *The comparative grammar of the Dravidian or South-Indian family of languages*, (3rd Ed.), Oriental Books Reprint Corporation, New Delhi.

Critchley, M.: 1970, *The dyslexic child*, Heinemann, London.

Dani, A.H.: 1963, *Indian paleography*, Clarendon Press, Oxford.

Frith, U.: 1985, 'Beyond the surface of developmental dyslexia', in K.E. Patterson, J.C. Marshall, and M. Coltheart (eds.) *Surface dyslexia: Neuropsychological and cognitive studies in phonological reading*, Erlbaum, London, pp. 301–310.

Hirose, T. and Hatta, T.: 1988, 'Reading disabilities in modern Japanese children', *Journal of Research in Reading* **11**: 152–160.

Karanth, P.: 1981, 'Pure alexia in a Kannada-English bilingual', *Cortex* **17**: 187–198.

Karanth, P.: 1985, 'Dyslexia in a Dravidian language', in K.E. Patterson, J.C. Marshall and M. Coltheart (eds.), *Surface dyslexia: Neuropsychological and cognitive studies in phonological reading*, Erlbaum, London.

Karanth, P.: 1992, 'Developmental dyslexia in bilingual-biliterates', *Reading and Writing* **4**: 297–306.

Klassen, E.: 1972, *The syndrome of specific dyslexia*, University Park Press, Baltimore.

Makita, K.: 1968, 'The rarity of reading disability in Japanese children', *American Journal of Orthopsychiatry* **38**: 599–614.

Pattanayak, D.P.: 1981, *Multilingualism and mother-tongue education*, Oxford University Press, Delhi.

Prakash, P.: 1987, 'Development of reading proficiency: Relationship with metalinguistic awareness and cognitive processing skills', Unpublished Ph.D. thesis, Utkal University, India.

Rajapurohit, B.B.: 1982, *Acoustic characteristics of Kannada*, Central Institute for Indian Languages, Mysore.

Rama, S., Miles, T.R., and Lalithamma, M.S.: 1993, 'Processing difficulty in the Kannada language', *Reading and Writing* **5**: 29–41.

Ruthman, P.: 1973, 'Reading in France', in J. Downing (ed.) *Reading: Cross national studies of behavior and processes in reading and writing*, McMillan, New York.

Stevenson, H., Stigler, J., Lucker, G., Lee, S., Hsu, C., and Kitamura, S.: 1982, 'Reading disabilities: The case of Chinese, Japanese and English', *Child Development* **53**: 1164–1181.

Taylor, I. & Taylor, M.: 1983, *The psychology of reading*, Academic Press, New York.

PART II

READING PROCESSES FOR DIFFERENT SCRIPTS

RICHARD L. VENEZKY

8. HOW ENGLISH IS READ: GRAPHEME-PHONEME REGULARITY AND ORTHOGRAPHIC STRUCTURE IN WORD RECOGNITION

Almost all of the methods for introducing reading instruction in the U.S.A. attend, sooner or later, to the complexities of translating from spelling to sound. Although reading programs differ in the number of grapheme-phoneme patterns they introduce and in the manner in which letter sounds are identified, they nevertheless use similar methods for generating sound from spelling. Concepts about the relationships of spelling to sound and about the role which grapheme-phoneme correspondences play in learning to read, although seldom clearly stated, can nevertheless be inferred from the activities and rhetoric of these reading programs.

Psychologists, on the other hand, have been somewhat more forthcoming about their notions on orthography in reading and, in particular, in the recognition of printed words. From Cattell's studies on reading in the 1880s until the middle 1950s, orthography was never mentioned as a potential factor in word recognition. Shannon's work in the late 1940s on redundancy in information transmission led in the early 1950s to empirical investigations of the statistical properties of English orthography and their influence on recognition and recall of letter strings (Miller, Bruner, and Postman, 1954).

The first speculations on the role of grapheme-phoneme correspondences in word recognition came in the work of Gibson, Pick, Osser, and Hammond (1962) who found that letters of pronounceable pseudowords were more easily recalled in a full report paradigm than were letters of unpronounceable pseudowords (e.g., *dink* vs. *nkid*). The authors hypothesized that the operative unit in word perception was not the letter (or whole word), but a sequence of letters which had an invariant letter-sound relationship. However, Gibson, Shurcliff, and Yonas (1970) obtained the same results with congenitally deaf subjects, thereby demonstrating that orthographic structure alone could account for the response differences.

Two influential studies on word recognition in the early 1970s, Rubenstein, Lewis, and Rubenstein (1971) and Smith and Spoehr (1974), defined the debate over grapheme-phoneme correspondences for the next decade. Both Rubenstein *et al.* (1971) and Smith and Spoehr (1974) assumed that lexical access was made on the basis of a phonological code. However, Rubenstein *et al.* (1971) assumed that grapheme-phoneme codes were used to generate a phonological representation while Smith and Spoehr (1974) assumed that the grapheme string was first parsed (or "unitized") into syllabic units (vocalic center groups) and then phonological codes assigned

I. Taylor and D.R. Olson (eds.), Scripts and Literacy, 111–129.

to these units. In contrast, Gibson *et al.* (1962) assumed that word recognition occurred on the basis of higher-order visual units which the reader formed through experience with grapheme-phoneme translation.

The potential role of grapheme-phoneme correspondences in pre-lexical access became a subject of considerable debate in the 1970s and continued to be in the 1980s (e.g., Meyer, Schwaneveldt, and Ruddy, 1974; Baron and Strawson, 1976; Coltheart, 1978; Bauer and Stanovich, 1980; Humphreys and Evett, 1985). Although alternative models for generating phonology from graphemic input were proposed (e.g., Glushko, 1979; Henderson, 1984), most phonological access models persisted in postulated one form or another of grapheme-phoneme translation (see Henderson, 1984, for a review of studies up to the early 1980s).

Structural variables have also continued to play a role in word recognition models, whether based on statistical properties (e.g., Mason, 1975) or linguistic ones (e.g., Massaro, Venezky, and Taylor, 1979). Spelling patterns, grapheme-phoneme patterns, orthographic structure, statistical structure, and rule-governed structure represent the more prominent of the orthography-related variables postulated for the word recognition process. What these variables are, how they differ, and what role they might play in word recognition for both the beginning and the experienced reader are the concerns of this chapter. The first section is didactic, intending to unravel the mysteries of English spelling and, in particular, to distinguish the grapheme-phoneme patterning of English from statistical and rule-governed orthographic structure. The second section attends to word recognition theories, centering primarily on the notion of phonological mediation. Although interesting work on word recognition and phonological mediation has been done on other orthographies, including Serbo-Croatian (Feldman, Lukatela, and Turvey, 1985; Lukatela and Turvey, 1990), Hebrew (Navon and Shimron, 1984) and Japanese (Morton and Sasanuma, 1984) the discussion here is restricted to English.

Lurking behind the discussion here is the apparent anomaly that as readers become more and more proficient at translating from spelling to sound, they find less and less use for this knowledge in ordinary reading. For the experienced reader, reading is usually silent. Furthermore, no matter what role might be posited for grapheme-phoneme translation, word recognition in reading is initiated primarily by visual patterns and requires, somewhere within its final stages, a match against a representation in long term memory of the spelling of the word. Important uses for orthographic knowledge remain nevertheless, for both the beginning and experienced reader, as will be pointed out in the concluding section. First, however, the various types of information that could be assembled from sustained experience with English print will be defined and chewed over; then will come speculations on how and when this knowledge might be marshaled in reading.

AN ORTHOGRAPHIC PASTICHE

Grapheme-phoneme Regularity

English spelling is frequently cursed (e.g., Lounsbury, 1909; Pitman, 1961), much less frequently blessed (e.g., Chomsky and Halle, 1968), but seldom studied seriously. The relationship of spelling to sound in English is neither the primordial chaos of the spelling reformers, nor (except in a perverse manner) the ideal underlying structure of the generative phonologists. It has at its core, patterns which originated from Latin orthography of the sixth and seventh centuries, but were heavily modified over a thousand year period, primarily through the influence of sound change. Intermixed with this core, like the swirls of chocolate in a marble cake, are a host of sub-patterns and singularities created through borrowings, spelling reform, and scribal caprice. Nevertheless, by the beginning of the sixteenth century, the counterpoint of morphological and etymological representation with that of the phonological base was firmly established and has undergone little alteration since. The underlying structure and specific patterns in this system described here are those features of grapheme-phoneme regularity that are relevant for the notions of *spelling patterns* (Gibson, Pick, Osser, and Hammond, 1962) and *phonological mediation.*

As a first approximation, we can class the grapheme-phoneme patterns of English as *invariant, variant-predictable* and *variant-unpredictable.* In the first class are a small group of consonants (f, j, ph, q, rh, sh, v, wh, z) that have single mappings into sound, with either no or relatively few exceptions. (It is interesting to note that with the exception of *f,* these are spellings that either did not exist or were rarely used in Old English.)

In the second group, variant-predictable, are most of the remaining consonants and, depending upon one's criterion for predictability, a few of the vowels. However, to claim that the various pronunciations for a spelling are predictable is to assert that there exists a set of features $f_1, \ldots f_n$ such that each pronunciation can be uniquely characterized by a distinct combination of these features. An example is the set of features {initial position; non-initial, pre-stress; non-initial, post-stress} which uniquely characterize the pronunciations for *x.* In initial position it is /z/ (e.g., *xylophone*); in medial position but before the main word stress, it is /gz/ (e.g., *example*); and in any position after the main word stress, it is /ks/ (e.g., *taxi, fox*).

The central issue in establishing the class of variant-predictable pronunciations is in deciding what qualifies as a feature. Position within a word, adjacent letters and sounds, and position relative to the main word stress are all detectable by native speakers. So are morphemic identification and form class. But etymology is not, in that except for a small percentage of the vocabulary, no clues are available within words or the contexts in which they occur to reflect etymology. Furthermore, etymology in the sense of *origin* is often insufficient for predicting grapheme-phoneme correspondences. *Chef* and *chief*, for example, are both from the same French root, yet have different mappings for initial *ch*. This results from *chief* being borrowed before initial /tš/ in French was leveled to /š/ and *chef* being borrowed afterwards. Similarly, *machine* and *chorus* are both from Greek, yet also have different correspondences for *ch*.

A deeper issue in identifying features is reflected in the forms *Indian* and *cordial*. Viewed only in relation to *d, Indian* appears to have the most expected pronunciation, while *cordial, educate*, and a few other words have a less common correspondent. Viewed, however, in relation to the other prepalatal consonants that palatalize before a glide or high front vowel (s, z, t), *cordial* contains the predictable mapping and *Indian*, the unpredictable one (cf. *issue, pleasure, bastion*).

From a linguistic standpoint, there is no simple metric for determining features upon which pronunciation mappings can be made. Therefore, the psychological reality upon which E.J. Gibson originally attempted to base the notion of spelling pattern or upon which Baron and Strawson (1976) and others have attempted to derive *regular* and *irregular* pronunciations remains to be determined.

Consider, as a further example, the vowel mappings in *con* and *cone*. They are both predictable from their graphemic environments and therefore tend to be classed as *regular*. However, exceptions exist; e.g., *ton, glove*. How many such exceptions are required to invalidate the *regular* classification? Compare this example to that of *g* which, like *c*, tends to have one mapping (/ǰ/) before mid and high front vowels (e.g., *giraffe, gem*) and another (/g/) elsewhere. But many exceptions to this pattern exist (e.g., *girl, get, give, gift, gear*) and the majority of these exceptions are high frequency words. From a linguistic standpoint, we would probably establish the *g* and *c* patterns in parallel, and treat *girl, give*, etc., as exceptions. Studies of grapheme-phoneme learning with pseudowords (Venezky, 1976) show, in contrast, that although readers acquire the *c* pattern by the end of elementary school, *g* continues even with college students to be treated as having a single, invariant mapping /g/. Thus; while grapheme-phoneme translation may play a role in word recognition, the concepts of *regular* and *irregular* cannot be completely adduced from linguistic evidence alone.

Orthographic Structure

A second type of orthographic information that has been incorporated into word recognition models has centered not on regularity of grapheme to phoneme mapping, but in the regularity of the letter sequences themselves relative to what occurs most commonly in English words (e.g., Mason, 1975; Massaro, Venezky, and Taylor, 1979). Two types of structure or redundancy have been identified; statistical and rule-governed. *Statistical redundancy* applies to those measures that can be derived solely from the frequency with which letters, letter sequences, and words occur in natural texts. Such measures might be based upon word types or word tokens and might apply to letters, letter sequences, or to any classification of these entities (e.g., vowel, consonant, spirant). *Rule-governed regularity* applies to those properties of letters and letter sequences that can be generalized from either the phonological constraints of English words or the scribal conventions which control the selection of letters for either representing sounds or marking graphemic, graphotactic, or morphological functions. Rule-governed regularity is usually considered to be dichotomous, although through the specification of rules for generating legal pseudowords, levels of legality can be defined.

Statistical Redundancy

Ordered approximations to English, based on algorithms proposed by Shannon (1948), were the first descriptions of orthographic structure utilized by psychologists. Although Miller, Bruner, and Postman (1954) were primarily concerned with information load, later experimenters (e.g., Lefton, Spragins, and Byrnes, 1973; Mewhort and Beal, 1977) have advocated ordered approximations as psychologically relevant descriptions of orthographic structure. A major shortcoming of ordered approximation descriptions is their inability to control structural variations within approximation levels. Although any large group of stimuli generated by this technique will approximate the frequencies of occurrence of English letter sequences, there is no metric incorporated into the method for assessing the relative degree of orthographic structure of strings within order classes.

A second shortcoming of a strict psychological application of this approach is its total reliance on left-to-right generation of letters during word recognition. For example, given bl___ and bl_st as partially resolved strings, the probabilities of identifying the third letter in each on partial (or no) featural information would be the same in that information to the left but not to the right of any letter position is relevant for processing according to Shannon's procedure.

To overcome the first difficulty, summed bigram and trigram counts have been proposed as metrics. Underwood and Schulz (1960) tabulated the bigrams and trigrams in 2,090 words sampled from the Thorndike and Lorge (1944) word list, ignoring word length and letter position within the word. Mayzner and Tresselt (1965) and Mayzner, Tresselt, and Wolin (1965a, 1965b) tabulated bigram, trigram, and tetragram counts by word position and by word length for words from three to seven characters in length, sampled from a corpus of 20,000 words. Mayzner and Tresselt (1965) also give single-letter positional frequencies, which have been used by Mason (1975) to explore differences between good and poor readers in a target search task. Although Mason (1975) confounds rule-governed orthographic structure with positional frequency, a small but significant positional frequency effect remains when these variables are separated (Massaro, Venezky, and Taylor, 1979).

The relationships among single-letter positional frequency, bigram positional frequency, and trigram positional frequency have yet to be explored. Experimenters who use single-letter or bigram frequency tend not to control for differences in the next higher order unit, thus confounding cannot be ruled out. It is possible, however, to generate pseudowords while independently varying summed single-letter positional frequency and summed bigram positional frequency counts. With some straining, the same can be done for summed bigram and summed trigram counts. A further issue that needs to be resolved is the relative importance of token measures and type measures. That the two are not equivalent can be seen from the tabulation of summed token and type counts in Table 1, based on counts generated from Kucera and Francis (1967).

TABLE 1
Summed token and type counts

Pseudo word	Summed counts	
	Tokens	Types
STAP	722	40
TOLT	3271	55
WIFY	11340	26
THET	34517	31

Type-based measures could be derived from an internal lexicon; token measures require not only a lexicon but also frequency of occurrence data for each entry in this lexicon. Although it is reasonable to assume that some forms of both token and type information have psychological reality, it has been argued that the direct application of raw token measures in word recognition is implausible (Savin, 1963). However, some interesting approaches to using token measures embedded within type measures have been proposed by Solomon and Postman (1952), Savin (1963), and Landauer and Streeter (1973).

A further drawback to summed single-letter, bigram, and trigram positional counts, particularly where token counts are utilized, is the dominating role which a small group of high frequency words play. For the four-letter words, as an example, the 37 most frequent words of this length account for approximately one-half of all tokens of four-letter words. This guarantees, on the average, a high, positive correlation between different statistical measures. However, low summed single-letter positional frequency strings will usually be low in summed positional bigram and trigram frequency, but strings high in summed single-letter positional frequency might not be high in the other two measures. Furthermore, since the extremely high frequency words in English are mostly three, four, and (to a lesser degree) five letters in length, the influence of the highest frequency words necessarily decreases with increasing word length. Thus, we would expect a lower correlation between bigram and trigram counts in seven-letter strings than in four-letter strings.

Rule-Governed Regularity

Sequential schemes, even when position and word length are observed, can generate pseudowords which violate English phonological and spelling conventions. For example, *thrsm, sthse*, and *whrst* are unpronounceable pseudowords which have relatively high summed, position-sensitive bigram counts. These can be contrasted with *bipon, slevy*, and *dufip*, which have relatively low summed bigram counts, but are legal from a rule-governed standpoint. Violations can be avoided, for the most part, by using position sensitive, fourth-order approximations which are also high in summed trigram counts. But this seems psychologically unrealistic. An alternative is to utilize pronounceability, as described above. Yet for classifying pseudowords, pronounceability alone is not sufficient in that English orthography is constrained by both phonological and scribal conventions.

Phonological constraints. The most important constraint on English orthography derives from the allowable sequences of sounds in English words. Thus, /sk/ is an allowable initial consonant cluster and therefore spellings for it exist (e.g., *sk, sc, sch*); on the other hand, /tl/ and /dl/ do not occur and never did occur initially in English words and therefore no spellings for these sequences occur in English words (but they do in Tlingit and several other languages in which initial /tl/ and /dl/ are legal). Complicating this relationship between phoneme and grapheme, however, are several factors, including scribal pedantry, which leave us with spellings for (1) sound sequences which once occurred, but have since been dropped from the language (e.g., wr-, kn-, gn-), or for (2) sound sequences that were presumed to have occurred in the language from which a word was borrowed (e.g., *psychology, ptarmigan, debt*).

A further complication is the deviation in serial order of several spellings from the order of sounds which they represent. Chief among these is *wh*, a spelling which at least some English speakers have retained as /hw/, and *-le* as in *bottle*, etc., which spells (in deliberate speech) /ə l/. (*wh-* and *-le* are scribal reversals of earlier *hw-* and *-el*.) But even with these deviations from expected practice, most English sounds are represented in a moderately rational fashion in the orthography (Venezky, 1970). However, since English possesses more than one potential spelling for almost every sound, a second set of constraints, here called scribal constraints, enter into rule-governed orthographic structure.

Scribal constraints. The scribal constraints in English orthography represent distributional patterns for graphemes that are independent of grapheme-phoneme mappings or of sound constraints. For example, unlike Spanish, English resists doubled letters in word-initial position. Only a handful of exceptions to this constraint exists, most involving the form *oo* (e.g., *oodles*, *ooze*, *aardvark*). In other positions, only 15 letters can double; those that don't (or rarely do) are *a*, *h*, *i*, *j*, *k*, *q*, *u*, *v*, *w*, *x*, *y*. But there are further restrictions. With few exceptions, doubled consonants do not occur after secondary vowels (e.g., *ai*, *ou*, *ey*) and digraph units are not allowed to double. For one, *ch*, a pseudogeminate (*tch*) was adopted in early Modern English, at about the same time that *dg* was adopted to represent doubled *g* when it stood for /ǰ/, and *ck* was invented for doubled *k*, which now occurs only in inflected forms of *trek* (e.g., *trekking*) and a few rare borrowings.

Other graphemic constraints control the distribution of *u* – *v* and *i* – *y* (cf. *pout-cow*, *maid-may*) and limit the two-letter words in English to a small set of mostly function words (e.g., *in*, *at*, *of*). Since no English language academy ever existed to impose a grand design on English spelling, what general principles there are result from the confluence of various scribal traditions with the periodic ravages of sound change unaccompanied by spelling change. Yet a principle of sorts does emerge from the current system; viz., "Accede to all visual interests up to, but not beyond the point where passage from spelling to sound is impaired."

Psychological assumptions. Rule-governed descriptions of orthographic structure differ from other definitions of orthographic patterning in two aspects. First, in the utilization of word types rather than word tokens, and second, in classing as regular certain spellings that do not occur (yet) in English words and classing as irregular some that do. The first difference is not essential to the definition of orthographic structure, but is probably more a reflection of the differing epistemologies of linguistics and psychology. The second difference, however, is central to the concept of orthographic structure and requires further explication.

The primary assumption behind the orthographic rules presented here is that readers abstract from their experiences with printed words those spellings that are productive in present-day English, and use these to facilitate recognition. For example, silent initial letters, regardless of the frequency of occurrence of the words in which they occur, are classed as irregular since it is unlikely that new words brought into the English language would ever be spelled with them. (Spelling analogies might present an exception to this assumption and cannot be ignored. However, it is unlikely that silent initial spellings would ever be widely extended.)

On the other hand, the initial sequences *voa-* and *woa-* and the final sequences *-eng*, *-erl*, and *-ofe* do not occur in the first 20,000 words in the Thorndike and Lorge (1944) list, yet they are classed as orthographically regular since they do not violate any phonological or scribal pattern. Thus, pseudowords like *voam*, *woach*, *treng*, *derl*, and *strofe* are pronounceable and structurally regular, even though they contain trigrams which do not occur in English words. The recognizability of such strings relative to similar pseudowords with higher summed trigram counts is an issue that remains to be investigated.

The dichotomy issue. A second issue which merits empirical investigation concerns the assumed dichotomous nature of orthographic regularity. Given the different constraints on orthographic structure discussed above, we should question whether or not the visual and phonological elements are separated psychologically. Are, for example, irregular strings like *clav* and *cklib* processed differently from an illegal string like *tprif*? All are illegal and non-occurring, yet they differ in type of illegality. *Tprif* contains an initial consonant cluster that is phonologically illegal and therefore scribally non-occurring. *Clav* and *ckib* are both phonologically acceptable, but contain scribally outlawed features, viz., final *v* in *clav* and initial *ck* in *cklib*. In, for example, a lexical decision task, do subjects reject phonologically illegal strings before visually illegal ones? If so, must we then postulate two different mechanisms for the lexical decision task: a structural screening process followed by a phonological mediation process, a la Rubenstein, Lewis, and Rubenstein (1971)? A partial answer to these questions has been provided by Hart (1980) who has found differential responses in subjective ratings of wordness and in a lexical decision task to different types of structural violations. (Further experimental evidence on this issue is presented in the next section.)

Finally, the processes through which orthographic regularity facilitates recognition in different experimental tasks need to be examined. Consider, for example, the orthographically irregular pseudoword *kclum*. Does the probability of correctly identifying a target letter depend upon whether it is in the initial portion of the string, which is irregular, or the final portion, which is regular? In other words, we might find no differences between orthographically regular and orthographically irregular strings if we restrict our recognition task to operations on the regular sub-strings.

THE QUESTION OF PHONOLOGICAL MEDIATION

Current models for printed word recognition tend to fall into two major classes: mediated and unmediated, where mediation is generally assumed to be phonological. Representative of the mediated class are the models proposed by Gough (1972), Rubenstein, Lewis and Rubenstein (1971) and Coltheart *et al.* (1977). Although evidence against the necessity for phonological mediation in word recognition has been offered (e.g., Kleiman, 1975; Levy, 1978; Massaro, 1977; Tzeng, Hung, and Wang, 1977; Henderson, 1984), the appeal of this model is still quite high. It may be informative, therefore, to inspect both logically and empirically the rationale of phonologically mediated word recognition, particularly in relation to the lexical decision paradigm which has provided the primary support for this position.

The Logical Basis of Phonological Mediation

Phonological mediation, as expressed in the experimental literature of the past two decades, is not a well-defined process for recognition of printed words. Instead, it tends to be an inchoate concept of recognition, centered on searching a phonological lexicon that has been constructed over time in long term memory. Although few attempts have been made to explicate the tasks involved in such a procedure, it is possible to define the range of possible stages that would be required for phonological mediation (P.M.) to be consistent with the empirical data on printed word recognition. As will be shown below, it is also possible, through appeal to common sense, to narrow this range of possible procedures.

In its purest form, P.M. requires that a fully resolved string of letters be recoded into a phonological form and this form then be matched against entries in a listening lexicon. Recoding from visual to phonological forms is often assumed to be done via grapheme-phoneme rules which have been abstracted from prior reading experience. It seems reasonable to assume that actual rules, in some abstracted form, are utilized, rather than an organized search of the lexicon for words with similar letter patterns (cf. Glushko, 1979; Henderson, 1984). If the latter could be done for letters in their various intraword positions, including medial and final, then phonological recoding would be unnecessary. That is, if a procedure were available for rapid location and matching of letter strings within words, then it is reasonable to assume that this same system could match entire strings also. Therefore, we assume that generalized grapheme-phoneme relationships of some form are utilized. On the nature of such generalizations, more will be said below.

At this point I am assuming that the means by which the visual input is resolved is unimportant for testing the P.M. hypothesis. Furthermore, I am avoiding speculation at this point on the relative times required by the various stages. Notice, however, that the steps suggested above must be supplemented with several additional stages to account for the homophone effect that has been found in a number of lexical decision studies (e.g., Coltheart *et al.*, 1977). In brief, pseudowords that are generally pronounced identically to real English words (i.e., pseudohomophones) take longer to reject in the lexical decision task than pseudowords that are not. Although this effect is considerably more complex than is assumed in most studies, the only aspects of it that are important for now are (a) the effect has been replicated on a number of occasions, and (b) error rates on pseudohomophones are typically low (2–8% range).

Although I will offer later a different hypothesis for the origin of the homophone effect, the low error rate is what is of immediate interest. This implies that if a match is made between a pseudohomophone and an entry in the listening lexicon, the subject does not simply respond *yes*. Instead, a visual match must be made between the input string and the spelling for the matched entry in the listening lexicon. To account for this low error rate, we must assume the first, spellings are readily accessible from phonological entries in the lexicon, and second that the subject has the ability to compare such spellings to the input strings.

These assumptions make the model sketched above consistent with the empirical data for certain classes of pseudowords, but this model does not yet handle real words that have irregular grapheme-phoneme correspondences. Consider what happens, for example, when the first phonological recoding of a real word does not produce the correct pronunciation for that word. If the incorrect pronunciation does not match any entry in the listening lexicon, the subjects cannot respond *no*; if they did, they would have abnormally high error rates on such common words as *who, whole, glove*, and *was*.

Consequently, for the P.M. model to work, a *no* response must not be made on the first lexicon search failure for a stimulus string. Instead, a new pronunciation has to be assigned to the string, and the search repeated. How often to recycle on search failure is a difficult problem to resolve. Consider, for example, a short (and highly frequent) word like *whom*. If pronunciations are initially assigned based on the most frequent correspondences for the letters involved, then the first pronunciation generated for this string would be /hwam/, which will not match any entry in the listening lexicon of a Midwestern English speaker. How the pronunciation would be altered for recycling is a matter of speculation. If we work left to right, and from most frequent to least frequent correspondences, the initial sequence of phonological strings to be tested after /hwam/ would be /ham/, /hwom/, /hom/, /hwʌm/, and /hʌm/. Exactly when (or how) the pronunciation /hum/ would be assigned is difficult to predict, given that *whom* is one of a small number of words in English where *o* is pronounced /u/. But assuming that /hum/ would eventually be assigned, the model shown in Figure 1 would apply.

At this point it is informative to consider several alternatives to Figure 1. On one hand, the search system might not require an exact phonological match. It could, for example, test the spelling of every phonological

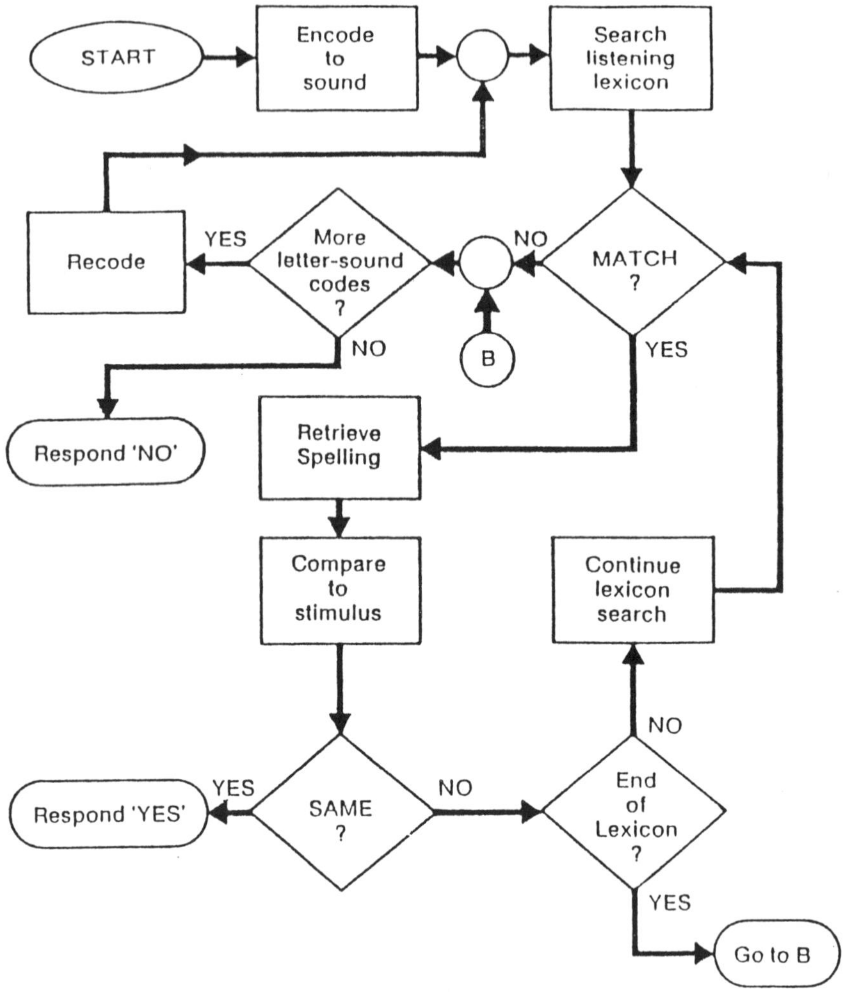

Fig. 1. A processing model for phonological mediation.

string that was within a specified distance of the recoded input, where *distance* was defined by some as yet unspecified phonological metric. If this were practicable, then we might eliminate the need for much of the recycling. It is not immediately obvious how such a metric would be derived, but it is clear that any approximation algorithm would lengthen rejection times for non-words as well as shorten acceptance times for real words.

Furthermore, for multisyllabic pseudowords, large numbers of alternatives would need to be tested. Consider, for example a pseudoword with eight graphemic units, three of which are vowels (e.g., *plesipom*). If each vowel grapheme, on the average, were assumed to have three phonemic mappings that should be tested and each consonant, one, then the total number of pronunciations to test would be 3^3 or 27. To test half of these alternatives (on the average) seems to be beyond what might be achieved in the 600–900 milliseconds that most studies report for rejection times.

An Alternative Hypothesis

According to the argument that lead to the recycling procedure represented in Figure 1, the lengthened rejection time for pseudohomophones should occur not only for the most expected pronunciation of a pseudoword, but also for other plausible pronunciations. Thus, a form like *fleak* that would usually be pronounced to rhyme with *beak*, could also be pronounced to rhyme with *deck* (cf. *bread*). Since recycling is required for phonological access to the lexicon regardless of how phonology is generated from spelling, pseudohomophones based upon less common or *secondary* phonological mappings should produce the same lengthening in rejection time as mappings based on the most common or *primary* mappings.

Consider, for example, the processing of the secondary homophone *cheg*. The primary pronunciation of this is /čɛg/, which does not match any entry in the listening lexicon. But the subject cannot respond *no* at this point; if he or she did, abnormally (and consistently) high error rates would occur for *chord, chorus*, and various other forms, in that their primary pronunciations would also yield non-words. Therefore, for phonological mediation to function smoothly, alternative pronunciations would need to be generated and tested against the listening lexicon. At some point *cheg* will be assigned the pronunciation /kɛg/ which will match the representation for *keg* in the listening lexicon.

Therefore, whatever delay in responding occurs from the *build* representation of *bild* (a primary pseudohomophone) must occur from the *keg* representation of *cheg*. Failure to find a pseudohomophone effect for secondary pseudohomophones would cast further doubt on prelexical phonological mediation. To probe this issue, along with the role of structural regularity, two experiments on word recognition were designed, both using a lexical decision task with college undergraduates as subjects.

Experiment 1

Stimuli

In experiment 1, real words were selected to give two levels of word frequency (high and low), based on Kucera and Francis (1967), and two levels of grapheme-phoneme correspondence (GPC) regularity (high and low).

Pseudowords were generated for the following four classes:

1. Primary homophones: words whose most common pronunciations yielded homophones of English words (e.g., *bild*, *mone*, *coave*, *trane*).
2. Secondary homophones: words whose most common pronunciations would not yield homophones, but whose alternate pronunciations would (e.g., *cheg* (= keg), *sise* (= size), *fleak* (= fleck), *swort* (= sort)).
3. Structurally regular, non-homophones (e.g., *drin*, *rish*, *hamit*, *slaft*).
4. Structurally irregular but pronounceable non-homophones (e.g., *ckif*, *trav*, *hwoty*, *tyroi*).

The real words were designed to contrast a GPC effect with a frequency effect. If phonological mediation occurred, then words with regular GPCs should be accepted faster than words with irregular correspondences. But since GPC regularity might interact with word frequency, these two factors were crossed in the design.

The first two pseudoword groups were constructed to test the primary-secondary pseudohomophone effect just described. The remaining two pseudoword groups were included as controls. According to the phonological mediation hypothesis, groups 1 and 2 should take significantly longer to reject than groups 3 and 4, while groups 3 and 4 should not differ significantly in rejection times. If, on the other hand, the lexical decision task incorporated purely visual matching, group 4 should be rejected most rapidly since it contained the most irregular forms, while groups 1, 2, and 3 should not differ in rejection times.

Results

The results for real words showed a large, significant frequency effect but no GPC regularity effect and no interaction of GPC with frequency. For the pseudowords, primary pseudohomophones required significantly more time to reject than secondary pseudohomophones, while structurally irregular pseudowords were rejected significantly faster than all other types of pseudowords.

Experiment 2

Stimuli

The real words in experiment two were nearly identical to those in experiment 1 and were included as a replication of the experiment 1 real word results. The pseudowords, however, incorporated two modifications. Secondary homophones were replaced by structurally irregular homophones (e.g., *brij*, *ckuf*, *bbaik*, *glovv*), and the two non-homophone lists were replaced by structurally irregular lists in which initial position irregularities (e.g., *aarp*, *kwig*) were contrasted with final position irregularities (e.g., *tecc*, *parnu*, *wealg*).

Results

As in experiment 1, real words showed a large, significant frequency effect but no GPC regularity effect and no interaction of GPC regularity with frequency. For the pseudowords, structurally regular pseudohomophones required significantly more time to reject than any of the other three classes of pseudowords. As predicted, structurally irregular pseudohomophones did not differ significantly from non-pseudohomophones. In addition, pseudowords with initial irregularities did not differ from pseudowords with final position irregularities.

Discussion

These results add further complications for the phonological mediation hypothesis, in that neither secondary pseudohomophones nor structurally irregular homophones showed a pseudohomophone effect. The latter failure can be accounted for only by a visual screening process whereby structurally irregular strings are rejected visually before they are recoded to sound. This does not eliminate the possibility of recoding for those strings that pass the screening, but it does eliminate the possibility of phonological recoding prior to a spelling test. But the failure to find a pseudohomophone effect for secondary pseudohomophones presents a more serious challenge to the phonological mediation hypothesis. If the only phonological representation of a grapheme string that upsets lexical decisions is the one based upon the most common GPCs, then the phonological code cannot be utilized as the primary route to the lexicon.

Rapid rejection of structurally irregular pseudohomophones demonstrates the importance of orthographic structure information in the lexical decision task. Although such information appears to play no role in lexical access in ordinary reading where nearly all input is structurally regular, the availability of such information makes more plausible theories of visual processing that tap such structure for primary resolution of letters (e.g., Massaro, Venezky, and Taylor, 1979). The lower levels of processing, however, appear to contribute little to the overall time required for reading words. The perceptibilities of common English typefaces, for example, differ dramatically, but reading speeds across these same faces are only marginally different (Tinker, 1963).

Although these results complicate the standard phonological mediation hypothesis, they do not eliminate the need for a processing model that includes phonological recoding at some stage. Shulman, Hornak, and Sanders (1978), using a version of the lexical decision task that differs from the one employed here, have also found conditions under which phonological recoding appears not to occur. They hypothesize that the phonological code, when it is generated, is used to retain the stimulus string in short term memory while an exhaustive (visual) search is made. Thus, even when recoding occurs, it does not mediate lexical access. If we assume that *all* strings are recoded phonologically for retention in STM while visual search proceeds, then we can attribute the primary pseudohomophone effect to interference. That is, while the visual search is reaching a *no* conclusion, the phonological form inadvertently makes contact with its homophonic representation in long term memory. The resulting conflict between *matched* and *not matched* indicators then requires extra time to resolve.

The key to fitting this model to the data is the assumption that the simplest phonological representation for a string is generated, strictly as an aid to STM retention and not as a mediator for recognition. Therefore, no phonological recycling occurs and the homophonic nature of secondary homophones is (in general) not discovered. This hypothesis suggests the existence of a basic set of grapheme-phoneme correspondences that are invoked for STM recoding. This set probably has very limited representation for the more complex variant patterns; nevertheless, some variant patterns can probably be stored (e.g., the final e – final consonant patterns for vowels).

Notice that this model differs from the strictly post-lexical phonological generation assumed for non-mediated lexical access. In these models, no phonological representation occurs until after a match is made in the lexicon; then, the complete phonological representation of the word can be retrieved, thereby obviating the need for grapheme-phoneme translation (e.g., Henderson, 1984; Humphreys and Evett, 1985).

CONCLUSIONS

The two experiments just discussed rely upon the lexical decision task which, though reading-like, is clearly not reading. What can we assume about normal reading from all of this? First, the lack of even a hint of a grapheme-phoneme regularity effect with real words leaves phonological mediation in the same class as the chimera, the unicorn, and the succubus. On the other hand, the robust frequency effect ensures that statistical regularity measures will show a strong correlation with response times, even though these relationships might be strictly artifactual. This leaves open the possibility that orthographic factors, whether phonologically related or structural, play a minimal role in the word recognition habits of experienced readers. Structural features might, as suggested by Massaro (1977), facilitate primary recognition of letters, but this probably accounts for little of the variance in total recognition time.

This argument, however, does not rule out the use of GPCs for recognition of words that may be in one's listening lexicon, but not recognized rapidly from print. Similarly, GPCs may be used when visual input is degraded or when semantic processing is slowed by text complexity. The latter case, however, probably does not involve prelexical phonology and therefore most likely represents retrieval of holistic phonological representations or of articulatory programs. The continual improvement of grapheme-phoneme translation that is observed, even into college (e.g., Venezky, 1976) probably results not only from an expanded token store, but also from improved access to this store. If, for example, word recognition involves assembly of information from different cortical areas, then improvement in word recognition could also bring improved ability to access different components of words, including the relationships of particular graphemes and grapheme strings to their pronunciations.

For learning to read, however, both orthography in the general sense and grapheme-phoneme translation specifically appear to play a major role. Recent work on phonological awareness in children (e.g., Fowler, 1990; Liberman, Shankweiler, and Liberman, 1990) gives strong support to the centrality of phonology in the early acquisition of literacy. Ehri (1985) also supports this view, hypothesizing a shift in early acquisition from visual cue processing to phonetic cue processing. Nevertheless, phonetic cue processing still requires processing of visual features as input and matching of spellings after phonological access to validate recognitions. How inexperienced readers shift from phonological access to visual access remains a mystery. Metamorphosis from laborious sounding out of words to fluid, silent reading might involve a number of intermediate stages where orthographic and phonological cues are integrated. Whatever the development sequence (or sequences), large research programs can still be built on the unresolved issues surrounding the types of orthographic and phonological information which readers acquire from exposure to print and how and when this information figures into reading tasks at different stages of literacy acquisition.

NOTES

[1] This chapter is a revision and updating of a paper originally presented at the National Reading Conference in 1980 and published as a chapter in the conference proceedings (Venezky, 1981).

[2] See Venezky (1981) for more detailed descriptions of the studies.

REFERENCES

Baron, J.M. and Strawson, C.: 1976, 'Use of orthographic and word specific knowledge in reading words aloud', *Journal of Experimental Psychology: Human Perception and Performance* **2**, 286–393.

Bauer, D.W. and Stanovich, K.E.: 1980, 'Lexical access and the spelling-to-sound regularity effect', *Memory and Cognition* **8**: 424–432.

Chomsky, N. and Halle, M.: 1968, *The sound pattern of English*, Harper and Row, New York.

Coltheart, M.: 1978, 'Lexical access in simple reading tasks', in G. Underwood (ed.) *Strategies of information processing*, Academic Press, London and New York.

Coltheart, M., Davelaar, E., Jonasson, J.T., and Besner, D.: 1977, 'Access to the internal lexicon', in S. Dornic (ed.) *Attention and performance VI*, Erlbaum, Hillsdale, NJ.

Ehri, L.C. and Wilce, L.S.: 1985, 'Movement into reading: Is the first stage of printed word learning visual or phonetic?' *Reading Research Quarterly* **20**(2): 163–179.

Feldman, L.B., Lukatela, G., and Turvey, M.T.: 1985, 'Effects of phonological ambiguity on beginning readers of Serbo-Croatian', *Journal of Experimental Child Psychology* **39**: 492–510.

Fowler, A.E.: 1990, 'Factors contributing to performance on phoneme awareness tasks in school-age children', *Haskins Laboratories Status Report on Speech Research 1990*, SR-103/104, 137–152.

Gibson, E.J., Pick, A., Osser, H., and Hammond, M.: 1962, 'The role of grapheme-phoneme correspondence in the perception of words', *American Journal of Psychology* **75**: 554–570.

Gibson, E.J., Shurcliff, A., and Yonas, A.: 1970, 'Utilization of spelling patterns by deaf and hearing subjects', in H. Levin and J.P. Williams (eds.) *Basic studies on reading*, Basic Books, New York.

Glushko, R.J.: 1979, 'The organization and activation of orthographic knowledge in reading aloud', *Journal of Experimental Psychology: Human Perception and Performance* **5**: 674–691.

Gough, P.B.: 1972, 'One second of reading', in J.F. Kavanagh and I.G. Mattingly (eds.) *Language by ear and by eye*, MIT Press, Cambridge, MA.

Hart, J.T.: 1980, *The psychological validity of different spelling patterns*. Unpublished doctoral dissertation, University of Delaware, Newark, Delaware.

Henderson, L.: 1984, *Orthography and word recognition in reading*, Academic Press, London.

Humphreys, G.W. and Evett, L.J.: 1985, 'Are there independent lexical and nonlexical routes in word processing? An evaluation of the dual-route theory of reading', *The Behavioral and Brain Sciences* **8**: 689–740.

Kleiman, G.M.: 1975, 'Speech recoding in reading', *Journal of Verbal Learning and Verbal Behavior* **14**: 323–339.

Kucera, H. and Francis, N.W.: 1967, *Computational analysis of present-day American English*, Brown University Press, Providence.

Landauer, T.K. and Streeter, L.A.: 1973, 'Structural differences between common and rare words: Failure of equivalence assumptions for theories of word recognition', *Journal of Verbal Learning and Verbal Behavior* **12**: 119–131.

Lefton, L.A., Spragins, A.B., and Brynes, J.: 1973, 'English orthography: Relation to reading experience', *Bulletin of the Psychonomic Society* **2**: 281–282.

Levy, B.A.: 1978, 'Speech analysis during sentence processing: Reading and listening', *Visible Language* **12**: 81–101.

Liberman, I.Y., Shankweiler, D., and Liberman, A.M.: 1990, 'The alphabetic principle and learning to read', *Haskins Laboratories Status Report on Speech Research 1990*, SR-101/102, 1–13.

Lounsbury, T.R.: 1909, *English spelling and spelling reform*, Harper and Brothers, New York.

Lukatela, G. and Turvey, M.T.: 1990, 'Automatic and prelexical computation of phonology in visual word identification', *Haskins Laboratories Status Report on Speech Research 1990*, SR-101/102, 74–84.

Mason, M.: 1975, 'Reading ability and letter search time: Effects of orthographic structure defined by single-letter positional frequency', *Journal of Experimental Psychology* **104**: 146–166.

Massaro, D.W.: 1977, *Reading and listening* (Technical Report No. 423), Wisconsin Research and Development Center for Individualized Schooling, Madison.

Massaro, D.W., Venezky, R.L., and Taylor, G.A.: 1979, 'Orthographic regularity, positional frequency, and visual processing of letter strings', *Journal of Experimental Psychology: General* **108**: 107–124.

Mayzner, M.S. and Tresselt, M.E.: 1965, 'Tables of single-letter and bigram frequency counts for various word-length and letter-position combinations', *Psychonomic Monograph Supplements* **1**: 13–32.

Mayzner, M.S., Tresselt, M.E., and Wolin, B.R.: 1965a, 'Tables of tetragram frequency counts for various word-length and letter-position combinations', *Psychonomic Monograph Supplements* **1**: 79–143.

Mayzner, M.S., Tresselt, M.E., and Wolin, B.R.: 1965b, 'Tables of trigram frequency counts for various word-length and letter-position combinations', *Psychonomic Monograph Supplements* **1**: 33–78.

Mewhort, D.J.K. and Beal, A.L.: 1977, 'Mechanisms of word identification', *Journal of Experimental Psychology: Human Perception and Performance* **3**: 629–640.

Meyer, D.E., Schwaneveldt, R.W., and Ruddy, M.G.: 1974, 'Functions of graphemic and phonemic codes in visual word recognition', *Memory and Cognition* **2**: 309–321.

Miller, G.A., Bruner, J.S., and Postman, N.: 1954, 'Familiarity of letter sequences and tachistoscopic identification', *Journal of General Psychology* **50**: 129–139.

Morton, J. and Sasanuma, S.: 1984, 'Lexical access in Japanese', in L. Henderson (ed.) *Orthographies and reading*, Erlbaum, London.

Navon, D. and Shimron, J.: 1984, 'Reading Hebrew: How necessary is the graphemic representation of vowels?' in L. Henderson (ed.), *Orthographies and reading*, Erlbaum, London.

Pitman, I.: 1961, 'Learning to read: An experiment', *Journal of Royal Society of Arts* **109**: 149–180.

Rubenstein, H., Lewis, S.S., and Rubenstein, M.A.: 1971, 'Evidence for phonemic recoding in visual word recognition', *Journal of Verbal Learning and Verbal Behavior* **10**: 645–657.

Savin, H.B.: 1963, 'Word-frequency effects and errors in the perception of speech', *Journal of the Acoustical Society of America* **35**: 200–206.

Shannon, C.E.: 1948, 'A mathematical theory of communication', *Bell System Technical Journal* **27**: 379–423; 622–656.

Shulman, H.G., Hornak, R., and Sanders, E.: 1978, 'The effects of graphemic, phonetic, and semantic relationships on access to lexical structures', *Memory and Cognition* **6**: 115–123.

Smith, E.E. and Spoehr, K.T.: 1974, 'The perception of printed English: A theoretical perspective', in B.H. Kantowitz (ed.) *Human information processing: Tutorials in performance and cognition*, Erlbaum, Hillsdale, NJ.

Solomon, R.L. and Postman, N.: 1952, 'Frequency of usage as a determinant of recognition thresholds for words', *Journal of Experimental Psychology* **43**: 195–201.

Solso, R.L. and King, J.F.: 1976, 'Frequency and versatility of letters in the English language', *Behavior Research Methods and Instrumentation* **8**: 283–286.

Thorndike, E.L. and Lorge, I.: 1944, *The teacher's word book of 30,000 words*, Teachers College, New York.

Tinker, M.: 1963, *Legibility of print*. Iowa State University Press, Ames, Iowa.

Tzeng, O.J.L., Hung, D.L., and Wang, S.Y.: 1977, 'Speech recoding in reading Chinese characters', *Journal of Experimental Psychology: Human Learning and Memory* **3**: 621–630.

Underwood, B.J. and Schulz, R.W.: 1960, *Meaningfulness and verbal learning*, Lippincott, New York.

Venezky, R.L.: 1970, *The structure of English orthography*, Mouton, The Hague.

Venezky, R.L.: 1976, 'Theoretical and experimental bases for teaching reading', in T.A. Sebeok (ed.) *Current trends in linguistics* (Vol. 12. Linguistics and adjacent arts and sciences), Mouton, The Hague.

Venezky, R.L.: 1981, 'Letter-sound regularity and orthographic structure', in M.L. Kamil and M.M. Boswick (eds.) *Directions in reading: Research and instruction*, The National Reading Conference, Washington.

Wallach, M.A.: 1963, 'Perceptual recognition of approximations to English in relation to spelling achievement', *Journal of Educational Psychology* **54**: 57–62.

RUMJAHN HOOSAIN

9. GETTING AT THE SOUND AND MEANING OF LOGOGRAPHIC AND ALPHABETIC SCRIPTS

There are three elements involved in written language, namely script, sound, and meaning. Differences between ideographic and alphabetic languages can be expressed in terms of relationships between these elements. This paper will review some such differences with particular reference to Chinese and English. Most of the studies referred to are made in laboratory conditions and their immediate applied implications may not be obvious, but there are indications of differences in the areas of reading and aphasia.

In alphabetic languages, the written symbols primarily represent sounds. Pronunciations are governed by grapheme-phoneme conversions rules that can be of varying degrees of regularity in different languages. It is through their representation of sounds that configurations of letters come to refer to meanings. In Chinese, on the other hand, each written character simultaneously represent a morpheme, the unit of meaning in language, as well as a syllable.[1] Its representation of sound is not spelt out, as in English, but on a character-as-a-whole to syllable-as-a-whole, one to one basis. It is this characteristic that allows written Chinese to be pronounced differently in different dialects, and, while dialects can be mutually unintelligible, the same written language can be shared by all Chinese through the ages ensuring, for example, a common literary heritage. This would be impossible if written characters represent pronunciations according to grapheme-phoneme conversion rules. In an alphabetic (or indeed syllabic) language with dialects as diverse as those of Chinese, written versions of the dialects would be correspondingly mutually incomprehensible (and this has been one drawback of various proposals to alphabetize written Chinese).

One implication of a script which does not represent meaning through the mediation of sound symbols could be that getting at the meaning of such ideographic symbols is more direct. There are now quite a lot of converging experimental evidence to show this. But getting at the sound of ideographic symbols is another matter. There is no indication of any particular facilitation of getting at the sound of ideographic symbols, but direct association of each character with its own pronunciation entails a different pattern of learning.

STROOP AND SIZE INCONGRUITY EFFECTS

In the Stroop test (Stroop, 1935) color words are printed in ink that is congruent or incongruent with the meaning of the words (e.g., the word

I. Taylor and D.R. Olson (eds.), Scripts and Literacy, 131–144.

red can be printed in red ink or in some other color ink). When subjects are asked to name the color of the ink of the printed words, responses times are slower if the ink color is incongruent with the meaning of the words. This effect is taken to mean that although the task is one of identifying ink color, some processing of the meaning of the printed word is unavoidable, and interference results if the meaning is incongruent with the ink color, slowing down response time. Biederman and Tsao (1979) reported that the Stroop effect is bigger for Chinese than for English, implying that avoiding to notice the meaning of color words is more difficult in Chinese than in English.

Corresponding with the Stroop effect, there is a size incongruity effect. When meaning of number names and their physical size are incongruous, such as when *three* is printed physically larger than *nine*, subjects take more time to report which is physically larger. This size incongruity effect is greater for Chinese number names or Arabic numerals which are also ideographic symbols, when compared with English (Besner and Coltheart, 1979; Tzeng and Wang, 1983; Foltz, Poltrock, and Potts, 1984). Thus, again, it is more difficult to avoid noticing the meaning of ideographic symbols than that of alphabetic symbols.

TIME TO PROCESS AFFECTIVE MEANING

Other aspects of the greater ease of getting at the meaning of Chinese characters have also been demonstrated. Hoosain and Osgood (1984) compared the processing times for English by a group of native speakers in the U.S. and processing times for their translation equivalents in Chinese by a group of native Cantonese dialect speakers.[2] Subjects were asked to judge the affective meaning of a diverse group of 60 nouns, verbs, and adjectives, such as *heaven*, and simply say "positive" or "negative" to indicate their subjective affective polarity, as soon as possible after the presentation each word on a screen. A timer was stopped when subjects pronounced their response to each word. Osgood's cross-cultural work (e.g., Osgood, May, and Miron, 1975) has shown very clearly that affective meaning, with the underlying dimensions of evaluation, potency, and activity, is a human universal, and subjects had no difficulty in deciding on affective meaning when they saw the presented words.

Table 1 shows that it took an average of less than half a second to get at the meaning of the words, decide on their affective polarity, and announce the judgement. Both the American and Chinese subjects showed faster times for positive words than negative words, indicating another human universal in a greater readiness to handle and talk about positive things (cf. Boucher and Osgood, 1969; Osgood and Hoosain, 1983). The response times for Chinese words were significantly faster than those for English words. Although such composite response times included stages other than getting

TABLE 1
Reading and meaning response times (in milliseconds) for positive and negative words

	Pronouncing		Processing	
	"Positive"	"Negative"	Positive words	Negative words
Chinese	498	479	964	1045
English	486	503	806	923

at the meaning of the words, comparison of these times with simple reading times suggested that the difference between Chinese and English was due to meaning processes. In simple reading, subjects were asked to pronounce the words "positive" or "negative", or their Chinese equivalents, as quickly as possible when these were shown repeatedly in random order, and latency to vocalization was measured. No processing of meaning was required in pronouncing the words in such a situation. No significant difference in such straightforward reading times for Chinese and English was found. This provided a baseline to contrast the meaning response times, which therefore indicate that the difference between the two languages lies in getting at the meaning of Chinese words and deciding on their affective polarity.

While "positive" and "negative" each has three syllables, their Chinese translations are both single monosyllabic characters. The failure to find any advantage in latency to vocalization for the Chinese words might have to do with the existence of grapheme-to-phoneme conversion rules for English. The reader can get at the sound of English (or any other alphabetic or syllabic script) either through specific association of a word with its pronunciation or through phonographic principles, while only the former is available for Chinese. In a similar comparison, Feldman and Turvey (1980) contrasted the speed of Japanese subjects in naming color words written in the kanji (borrowed Chinese) and kana (syllabic) scripts. Six color names were repeatedly presented to subjects in random order for many times to obtain the latencies to vocalization. Japanese color names are more often written in kanji than the kana, but latency to vocalization was faster for kana.

The average sound duration for the sixty experimental words in the study by Hoosain and Osgood (1984), pronounced by respective native speakers, and measured from the beginning of the first syllable to the end of the last syllable of each word, is longer for Chinese than for English. This fact, together with the finding that meaning judgement times were faster for Chinese, indicate that phonological recoding was less involved for Chinese when subjects performed their meaning judgement tasks. The Chinese subjects did not find it necessary to get at the meaning of presented words through some sound code, or at least not as much as English speaking subjects. Otherwise, since the sound codes in Chinese should bear some relation to their actual pronunciation durations, we would expect meaning response times for Chinese to be longer than the corresponding times for English.

TRANSLATION ASYMMETRY

Translation asymmetry here refers to the phenomenon that the speed of translating from one language to the other is different from that in the reverse direction. This can be due to a difference in the level of achievement in the respective languages, and it is often assumed that translating into the native or stronger language is easier than translating into the non-native or weaker language. In the present case, an unexpected phenomenon reveals the relative speed of getting at the meaning of different languages. This contrasts with the lack of difference in getting at the sound of the respective words.

Hoosain (1986) asked Chinese-English bilinguals to read a list of 200 random Arabic numerals, varying from 1 to 9, as quickly as possible in Cantonese and also in English. Table 2 shows that the mean pronunciation time was 91 milliseconds faster for Chinese than for English. There are two possible reasons for this difference. The subjects could be Chinese language dominant, having started to learn English only in school, although all would have used English as the medium of instruction for at least the last six years. What is more, it has been shown that the sound duration for digits pronounced in Chinese is shorter than in English, Welsh, Spanish, German, Japanese, Hebrew, or Arabic (cf. Ellis and Hennely, 1980; Hoosain, 1984; Naveh-Benjamin and Ayers, 1986; Stigler and Stevenson, 1986). All digits are pronounced as monosyllables in Chinese, although syllabic length is not the sole determiner of sound duration (*six* in English, for example, has a longer pronunciation duration than *seven*). The Arabic numeral reading times served as a baseline for the following comparisons.

TABLE 2
Reading and translation times (in milliseconds) for Chinese and English number names and Arabic numerals

	Stimulus	Response	Time
Reading:	Arabic	Chinese	267
	Arabic	English	358
	Chinese	Chinese	273
	English	English	370
Translation:	Chinese	English	399
	English	Chinese	454

Subjects were asked to read a list of two hundred digit names in English, varying from *one, two,* . . . to *nine* in random order, and also a corresponding list in Chinese. Table 2 shows that reading Chinese number names was faster than reading English number names by 97 milliseconds, which was about the same as the 91 milliseconds difference for reading the Arabic numerals in Chinese and in English. Identical motor responses were being made when the subjects read, for example, *seven* or "7" in English. The difference between reading number names printed in Chinese or in English and reading Arabic numerals lies in the decoding of the stimulus and not in the encoding or production of the response. It is between having to get at the sounds of number names written in the two languages and getting at the sounds of the neutral Arabic numerals. Since the magnitude of difference in pronouncing in Chinese and pronouncing in English was comparable in both sets of tasks, it means that getting at the sound of Chinese number names was about as fast as getting at the sound of English number names.

Subjects were also asked to perform translation tasks. They were given the original list of 200 Chinese number names and asked to translate them aloud as quickly as possible, starting with the first number name and proceeding non-stop until they reached the last number name. They were also asked to do the reverse translation with the list of English number names. Table 2 shows that Chinese-to-English translation was faster than English-to-Chinese translation by 55 milliseconds which was significant. The faster Chinese-to-English translation involved producing motor responses in English, which had been shown to take more time in the reading trials. It also meant translating into the bilingual subjects' non-native language. The explanation for the faster Chinese-to-English times would appear to be that getting at the meaning of the Chinese number names, which was the first stage of translation, was faster than the corresponding task of getting at the meaning of English number names in the English-to-Chinese translation. In the latter case, the faster eventual motor response of pronouncing Chinese answers was not enough to overcome the initial slower access to the meaning of English number names. In this manner, translating into the native language was not faster.

CROSS-LANGUAGE PRIMING

Another indication of the faster speed of getting at the meaning of Chinese words comes from a study of cross-language semantic priming. Keatley (1988) started with over 700 high frequency English words and was eventually able to use about a quarter of them, with Chinese translation equivalents that had primary associate words that were in turn equivalents of the associates of the original English words. Subjects were shown a single-character Chinese word or an English word as a prime, followed by a word or non-word in the other language as a target. Non-words were created by substituting a constituent letter of a word with another letter, or portion of a character with other strokes. The task was to push a button as quickly as possible to indicate if the target was a word or a non-word. Semantic priming occurs if response time for a target is faster with a related prime (e.g., *doctor* as prime and *pain* as target) when compared with an unrelated prime (*doctor* as prime and *pear* as target). Cross-language priming occurs when this effect applies while the prime and target are in different languages. Keatley found cross-language priming effect, but only when Chinese words were the primes and English words were the targets, and not when they were in reversed roles. In each case, the prime was shown for 250 milliseconds.

Subjects in this study were bilinguals who were native Chinese speakers. Their English language skills were screened, and they all had English reading speed and comprehension comparable to native English speakers. The superior Chinese-to-English priming could be owing to the greater ease of getting at the meaning of Chinese words. With the short time that each prime was shown, the greater speed of arriving at the meaning of Chinese means that there was better opportunity for the semantic priming process to operate. This could proceed along the lines of spreading activation (cf. Anderson, 1983), for example, although the actual manner in which cross-language priming operates depends on the interconnection of the two lexicons involved.

The priming effect obtained in this study was not the result of any deliberate reasoning that required relatively longer durations. The effect was actually not significant when the interval between presentation of the prime and the target became longer, two seconds instead of a quarter of a second, indicating that the priming effect involved was automatic rather than strategic. This significance of shorter interval time points to why speed of getting at the meaning of the prime was crucial; getting at the meaning should have been completed in time for spreading activation to take place before the impending presentation of the target.

PHONOLOGICAL RECODING AND READING

Reading models usually postulate two distinct routes for getting at the meaning of what is written. One is a phonological route in which some form of speech recoding, deriving some sound related code from the written symbol, is carried out according to grapheme-phoneme conversion rules, or by direct association, as a preliminary to arriving at the meaning. The other is the visual route in which some form of internal visual representation mediates meaning. It is also often assumed that the visual route is more direct and hence results in faster reading (cf. McCusker, Hillinger, and Bias, 1981). Depending on the circumstance and purpose of the reading task, there could be a greater tendency to rely more on one route or the other, and indeed the two can proceed in a "horse racing" model (cf. Hung *et al.*, 1984).

There is no denying that phonological recoding can and does occur in reading Chinese. Tzeng, Hung, and Wang (1977), for example, showed that in a sentence judgement task (deciding on whether presented sentences were normal or anomalous) phonemic similarity in the constituent characters of sentences, such as when most characters had the same vowel ending, required longer processing time. This showed that some kind of phonological recoding was involved in the sentence judgement, allowing phonemic confusion to interfere. The crucial question, however, concerns the relative involvement of such a process in comparable tasks in Chinese and English. Treiman, Baron, and Luk (1981), designed a sentence verification task, such as deciding whether *Coal/Lead is a kind of plant* is true or false. Some sentences contained homophone words such that when read aloud, they sounded true although the actual meaning was false. These "homophone sentences" in Chinese created less problem when compared with similar sentences in English. The implication is that speech recoding is used less in Chinese, enabling the Chinese subjects to better avoid being misled by the homophone words.

If the need for phonological recoding in reading Chinese text is different we would expect eye-movements in reading Chinese to reveal some distinctive pattern. There are very few eye-movement studies of Chinese, but there are a couple of intriguing findings suggesting that something might be different. In the earliest study of eye-movement in reading Chinese, Shen (Miles and Shen, 1925; Shen, 1926) compared reading of horizontal and vertical texts (with the latter being more common in those days before modern written Chinese) and noted some tendency of eye movement "gliding into a continuous curve" for reading vertical text. More than fifty years later, Stern (1978) reported that the eyes of one of his Chinese subjects tracked smoothly along the line of text (now written left to right) with infrequent saccades and fixations. This was attributed to the speed of access to meaning. Possibly, such smooth eye-movements are obtained under the combination of (a) proficient readers reading for meaning and bypassing the phonological route, and (b) an ideographic orthography which does not represent meanings through primary representation of sounds, which would entail uneven word lengths to reflect sounds, resulting in irregular saccadic movements covering the words. Unfortunately, no systematic effort has been made by investigators with the means and the interest to pursue this phenomenon further.

Other studies of eye-movements found that fixation time as well as the average number of words covered by each saccade are comparable for Chinese and for English (Peng, Orchard, and Stern, 1983; Sun and Stark, 1986). This means that, overall, the reading of Chinese text is not faster than that of English. These studies found that the time spent at each eye fixation pause for both languages was around a quarter of a second. There were more fixations per physical length of Chinese text, although this was compensated for by the greater compactness of written or printed Chinese. (For example, over a range of bilingual publications, such as magazines with Chinese and English equivalent passages, the physical length of the Chinese text is only 60% to 70% of the length of the English.) The net result is that roughly the same number of words (as distinct from characters, in the case of Chinese), about one and three quarters, was covered in each saccade when respective native speakers read in the two languages. It would seem that there are cognitive limits to the speed of processing Chinese text, so that the coverage of a bigger proportion of the the text with each fixation (due to the greater physical compactness of the written language) and quicker getting at the meaning of individual characters do not seem to matter ultimately.

It has been suggested that some form of central feedback control might impose a limit on the possibility of faster movement of the eyes when reading Chinese (cf. Sun and Stark, 1986). One aspect of the Chinese script that might influence feedback control is the absence of distinctive spacing between words over and above that between characters. Word boundaries are not perceptually distinct in Chinese, unlike English or other alphabetic languages. Thus, while the perceptual input is in morphemic units, some higher mechanism has to sort these into words. Furthermore, alphabetic languages have individual variations in word shape, with different word lengths as well as the ups and downs of letters like *l, h, g*, and *j*. With all strokes written within the confines of an allocated square space, Chinese characters do not have the same variation in word shape that provides valuable information for pre-attentive processing in reading continuous text. When the eyes are fixated at any point, peripheral vision of oncoming words provides more visual clues for English than for Chinese, although the exploitation of this information depends on the reader's knowledge of the redundancies of the language. Therefore, eye movement involves a real time control process making use of peripheral as well as focal vision. In the absence of such peripheral information, the eyes of a Chinese reader have to make more frequent fixations to go through the same physical length of text.

There is a another factor which could slow down eye movement in reading Chinese. Reading aloud is traditionally popular. Classes of children reading texts aloud in unison can be quite commonly found in schools. In the absence of grapheme-phoneme conversion rules such as in alphabetic and syllabic languages, the ability to pronounce individual characters is a distinctive mark that one has learned specific words. The habit to make a note of the sound code for each character would result in more frequent eye fixations than required for reading for meaning of texts, since meanings of characters can be fused into chunks but monosyllables have to be coded one by one.

The tendency for noting the sound of each and every character could be further aggravated by the layout of characters. Most Chinese characters are phonetic compounds, with part of each character (the radical) providing some clue to its meaning and another part (the phonetic) providing some clue to its sound, although particularly in the latter case clues are not rule governed. Furthermore, the radicals tend to be located at the top or the left of characters. I have checked the location of the major Chinese radicals (being a component of at least twenty different characters) listed in a small dictionary. Of the 67 radicals so identified, most tend to be located on the left half of characters they occur in, and there are also more occurrences on top than at the bottom (see Table 3). Strokes of Chinese characters are generally written in the order of top-to-down and left-to-right, and the top-left quadrant tends to be locus of semantic information for phonetic compounds. The corollary is that phonetic information tends to be located on the right and in the bottom. The preferred direction of scanning for Chinese subjects is similar to that of most readers of alphabetic languages, that is, top to bottom and left to right (Chen, 1981). This means that the usual location of the phonetic element in phonetic compounds is not conducive to the detection of pronunciation clues.

TABLE 3
Frequency of location of radicals within a character[1]

Top	Bottom	Left	Right	Peripheral	Total
11	3	41	10	2	67

[1] For each of the 67 radicals, only one location is indicated, which is the most frequently found location for that character.

READING PROBLEMS

With a different tripartite script-sound-meaning relationship, would the nature of reading problems in Chinese be different from that of English? For a long time, it was believed that the incidence of reading disability for Chinese was lower than that for English (e.g. Kuo, 1978). Rozin, Poritzky, and Sotsky (1970) even reported that it was easier for native English speakers with reading problems to learn to read English words represented by Chinese characters. It appears that one crucial difference in the requirement for learning to read Chinese is that no grapheme-phoneme conversion rules need be learned. Instead, children simply learn the individual pronunciation of each character. Since the phonetics in characters do not function with regularity, there is no real substitute for one-to-one pairing of the individual character and its own pronunciation. The phonetics themselves, afterall, are not spelt out and have to be learned one by one.

Since the need for figuring out grapheme-phoneme regularities is substituted with memorization of individual pronunciations, it is easy to see how a diagnosis of reading difficulty can be replaced with a verdict of lack of effort. When there are no rules to be mastered, failure to read or write becomes a simple failure of carrying out a mechanical task, which is seen as a motivational or disciplinary rather than cognitive problem.

Some revelation of the nature of reading problems in Chinese is provided by the careful study of Stevenson, Stigler, Lucker, and Lee (1982). The incidences of reading disability in Taiwan, Japan, and the U.S. were found to be comparable. However, when the reasons for the children to have to go back to a prior grade in their reading performance was analysed, an interesting pattern emerged. A much greater percentage of the Chinese children failed to read at their own grade because of comprehension failures, when compared with American children. On the other hand, a much smaller percentage of the Chinese children failed because of sight-reading of isolated single words. Thus, the Chinese children had less problem with one-to-one memorization of individual character sounds which did not require grasping grapheme-phoneme rules.

There is a traditional emphasis on rote learning of Chinese, to the extent that memorization of extended texts is taken as a sign of having learned them (the reading aloud in unison in class is part of this tradition), and Chinese scholars have long accepted this. Chen, Braithwaite, and Huang (1982), for example, noted that Chinese subjects reported memorization to be an easier task, when compared with Australians. Thus, reading tests that assess only sight-reading, or testing only memorization of script-sound correspondence, may not reveal the true picture of reading problems.

NEUROLINGUISTICS AND APHASIA

Given the differences in the manner of getting at the sound and meaning of Chinese, are there indications that neural specialization of language functions as well as language behaviors in aphasia in Chinese have different manifestations? In this regard we find that some earlier views have been challenged. One is that the right hemisphere might be more involved in handling Chinese, particularly single characters, because of the ideographic nature of the script. The distinction of single characters could be due to their simultaneously being perceptual wholes, syllabic units, and units of meaning. This script-sound-meaning convergence provides them with a salience that is absent in units of other languages. Two-character words, on the other hand, involve two perceptual wholes, two syllables, and some interaction of meanings of constituent characters to provide the emergent meanings. But Hasuike, Tzeng, and Hung (1986) argued that findings of right hemisphere advantage for single characters and left hemisphere advantage for two-character words are due to incidental visual conditions of many experiments. Ho and Hoosain (1989) showed that it is possible to obtain right hemisphere advantage for two-character words under extreme visual conditions. Just as for English, the nature of the visual input influences hemispheric asymmetries (cf. Sergent, 1983).

There is also the question of the dissociation of comprehension and pronunciation in some Chinese aphasics, which is taken to be related to greater right hemisphere involvement in the comprehension of Chinese characters (Huang, 1984). The dissociation is manifested in the inability to pronounce characters coupled with good ability to comprehend their meanings, as shown in tasks like picture-word matching. But, dissociation of comprehension and pronunciation is also found in the English aphasia literature (e.g. Benson and Geschwind, 1969), and precise cross-language difference in its incidence or manner of manifestation has yet to be established.

In two large scale surveys, the incidence of crossed aphasia amongst Chinese is not any more common than amongst speakers of alphabetic languages. Li, Hu, Zhu, Song, and Li (1986) reported on 57 cases of cortical lesions. Out of the 40 with non-aphasic language disorders due to attentional and memory impairments, 17 had right hemisphere lesions. But of the 17 with aphasic disorders, all had left hemisphere lesions. Similarly, Zhu, Song, Li, Li, and Hu (1986) reported on 66 cases with sub-cortical lesions and found that of the 56 cases with non-aphasic language disorders, 25 had right hemisphere lesions. But only one of the 10 cases with aphasic disorders had right hemisphere lesion (and the patient was ambidexterous). It thus appears that the left hemisphere is as involved in language functions of the Chinese as with speakers of alphabetic languages.

But, apart from the possibility of differential lateralization, there is also the suggestion that occipito-parietal lobes might be more involved in processing Chinese characters, due to the visual nature of the script, with each individual configuration of strokes being associated with a sound and a meaning. This visual nature applies to both the kanji script of Japanese (as contrasted with the kana script, cf. Paradis, Hagiwara, and Hildebrandt, 1985) and Chinese itself. Tzeng, Hung, Chen, Wu, and Hsi (1986), for example, found that patients with more posterior lesions performed worse than those with anterior lesions, in a visual gluing task in which they had to mentally glue together parts of characters presented sequentially in order to amalgamate them into characters.

Parallel with the significance of visual aspects for Chinese characters, there are suggestions that the motor engram could also play a distinctive role. Many Chinese have the experience of using finger tracing to assist in recall of characters. In the earliest aphasia report, the patient of Lyman, Kwan, and Chao (1938) used finger tracing of the strokes of presented characters to help in reading. It appears that finger tracing provided some proprioceptive cues which assisted in the retrieval of other aspects of

Chinese characters. The patient of Naeser and Chan (1980) would initially write characters in the wrong stroke sequence, but then rewrite them in the correct sequence after the initial completion. It was as if that there was a certain gestalt with individual characters that needed to be maintained, with their individual integrity indicated in stroke composition. It should be noted though that the use of finger tracing has also been found with aphabetic languages (cf. Benson and Geschwind, 1969). Again, what is required is a more careful comparison of the incidence of this behaviour in respective languages, and the role it plays in retrieval of sounds and meanings, beyond impressions gained from incidental reports.

To conclude, we do have indications that the distinctive Chinese script produces differences in the facility to get at the sound as well as the meaning of individual Chinese words. In particular, getting at the meaning of individual words, whether single ideographic characters or two-character words, is faster than that of alphabetic symbols. However, this difference is not directly translated into faster reading of Chinese text, due to other factors involved in reading as well as in reading habits. In neurolinguistics and aphasia, although initial studies suggested differential patterns for Chinese, more recent reports increasingly indicate similarity in lateralization. But the possibility that there could be different locus within the left hemisphere remains to be explored.

NOTES

[1] There are a handful of exceptions in both regards: there are a few characters that have no meaning on their own and each has to be used in conjunction with another character, and there are a couple of sub-syllabic characters.

[2] It should be noted that for the purpose of this study, respective native speakers are more preferable subjects than balanced bilinguals. With the latter, if differential response times are obtained for the two languages, it would not be possible to distinguish whether the subjects are not balanced after all or if there is a genuine language difference.

REFERENCES

Anderson, J.R.: 1983, 'A spreading activation theory of memory', *Journal of Verbal Learning and Verbal Behavior* **22**: 261–295.

Benson, F. and Geschwing, N.: 1969, 'The alexias', in P.J. Vinken and G.W. Bruyn (eds.) *Handbook of Clinical Neurology* (*Volume 4: Disorders of Speech, Perception, and Symbolic Behaviour*), North Holland, Amsterdam.

Besner, D. and Colheart, M.: 1979, 'Ideographic and alphabetic processing in skilled reading of English', *Neuropsychologia* **17**: 467–472.

Biederman, I. and Tsao, Y.C.: 1979, 'On processing Chinese ideographs and English words: Some implications from Stroop-test results', *Cognitive Psychology* **11**: 125–132.

Boucher and Osgood, C.E.: 1969, 'The Pollyyanna hypothesis', *Journal of Verbal Learning and Verbal Behavior* **8**: 1–8.

Chen, M.J.: 1981, 'Directional scanning of visual displays: a study with Chinese subjects', *Journal of Cross-Cultural Psychology* **12**: 252–271.

Chen, M.J., Braithwaite, V., and Huang, J.T.: 1982, 'Attributes of intelligent behaviour: Perceived relevance and difficulty by Australian and Chinese students', *Journal of Cross-Cultural Psychology* **13**: 139–156.
Ellis, N.C. and Hennelly, R.A.: 1980, 'A bilingual word-length effect: Implications for intelligence testing and the relative ease of mental calculation in Welsh and English', *British Journal of Psychology* **71**: 43–51.
Feldman, L.B. and Turvey, M.T.: 1980, 'Words written in kana are named faster than the same words written in kani', *Language and Speech* **23**: 141–147.
Foltz, G.S., Poltrock, S.E., and Potts, G.R.: 1984, 'Mental comparison of size and magnitude: Size congruity effects', *Journal of Experimental Psychology: Learning, Memory, and Cognition* **10**: 442–453.
Hasuike, R., Tzeng, O.J.L., and Hung, D.L.: 1986, 'Script effects and cerebral lateralization: The case of Chinese characters', in J. Vaid (ed.) *Language Processing in Bilinguals: Psycholinguistic and Neurolinguistic Perspectives*, Erlbaum, Hillsdale, N.J.
Ho, S.K. and Hoosain, R.: 1989, 'Right hemisphere advantage in lexical decision with two-character Chinese words', *Brain and Language* **37**: 606–615.
Hoosain, R.: 1984, 'Experiments on digit spans in the Chinese and English languages', in H.S.R. Kao and R. Hoosain (eds.) *Psychological Studies of the Chinese Language*, Chinese Language Society of Hong Kong, Hong Kong.
Hoosain, R.: 1986, 'Psychological and orthographic variables for translation asymmetry', in H.S.R. Kao and R. Hoosain (eds.) *Linguistics, Psychology, and the Chinese Language*, University of Hong Kong Centre of Asian Studies, Hong Kong.
Hoosain, R. and Osgood, C.E.: 1983, 'Processing times for Chinese and English words', *Perception and Psychophysics* **34**: 573–577.
Huang, C.Y.: 1984, 'Reading and writing disorders in Chinese – Some theoretical issues', in H.S.R. Kao and R. Hoosain (eds.) *Psychological Studies of the Chinese Language*, Chinese Language Society of Hong Kong, Hong Kong.
Hung, D.L. and Tzeng, O.J.L.: 1981, 'Orthographic variations and visual information processing', *Psychological Bulletin* **90**: 377–414.
Hung, D.L., Tzeng, O.J.L., Salzman, B., and Dreher, J.: 1984, 'A critical evaluation of the horse-racing model of skilled reading', in H.S.R. Kao and R. Hoosain (eds.) *Psychological Studies of the Chinese Language*, Chinese Language Society of Hong Kong, Hong Kong.
Keatley, C.W.: 1988, 'Facilitation effects in the primed lexical decision task within and across language. Unpublished Ph.D. thesis, University of Hong Kong.
Kuo, W.F.: 1978, 'A preliminary study of reading disability in the Republic in China', *Collected Papers* (National Taiwan Normal University), **20**: 57–78.
Li, X.T., Hu, C.Q., Zhu, Y.L., Song, Z.W., and Li, Y.: 1986, 'Language disorders in patients with cerebral vascular accidents', in H.S.R. Kao and R. Hoosain (eds.) *Linguistics, Psychology, and the Chinese Language*, Hong Kong University Centre of Asian Studies, Hong Kong.
Liu, I.M.: 1983, 'Cueing function of fragments of Chinese characters in reading', *Acta Psychologica Taiwanica* **2**: 85–90.
Lyman, R.S., Kwan, S.T., and Chao, W.H.: 1938, 'Left occipital-parietal brain tumour with observations on alexia and agraphia in Chinese and in English', *The Chinese Medical Journal* **54**: 491–515.
McCusker, L.X., Hillinger, M.L., and Bias, R.G.: 1981, 'Phonological recoding and reading', *Psychological Bulletin* **89**: 214–245.
Miles, W.R. and Shen, E.: 1925, 'Photographic recoding of eye movements in the reading of Chinese in vertical and horizontal axes: Method and preliminary results', *Journal of Experimental Psychology* **8**: 344–362.
Naeser, M.A. and Chan, S.W.C.: 1980, 'Case study of Chinese aphasia with the Boston Diagnostic Aphasia Examination', *Neuropsychologia* **18**: 389–410.

Naveh-Benjamin, M. and Ayers, T.J.: 1986, 'Digit span, reading rate, and linguistic relativity', *The Quarterly Journal of Experimental Psychology* **38**: 739–751.

Osgood, C.E. and Hoosain, R.: 1983, 'Pollyanna II: Two types of negativity', *The Journal of Psychology*, 151–160.

Osgood, C.E., May, W.H., and Miron, M.S.: 1975, *Cross-cultural Universals of Affective Meaning*, University of Illinois Press, Urbana.

Paradis, M., Hagiwara, H., and Hildebrandt, N.: 1985, *Neurolinguistic Aspects of the Japanese Writing System*, Academic Press, New York.

Peng, D.L., Orchard, L.N., and Stern, J.A.: 1983, 'Evaluation of eye movement variables of Chinese and American readers', *Pavlovian Journal of Biological Sciences* **18**: 94–102.

Rozin, P., Poritzky, S., and Sotsky, R.: 1971, 'American children with reading problems can easily learn to read English represented in Chinese characters', *Science* **171**: 1264–1267.

Sergent, J.: 1983, 'Role of input in visual hemispheric asymmetries', *Psychological Bulletin* **93**: 481–512.

Shen, E.C.: 1927, 'An analysis of eye movements in the reading of Chinese', *Journal of Experimental Psychology* **20**: 158–183.

Stern, J.A.: 1978, 'Eye movements, reading, and cognition', in J.W. Senders, D.F. Fisher, and R.A. Monty (eds.) *Eye Movements and the Higher Psychological Functions*, Erlbaum, Hillsdale, N.J.

Stevenson, H.W., Stigler, J.W., Lucker, G.W., and Lee, S.Y.: 1982, 'Reading disabilities: The case of Chinese, Japanese, and English', *Child Development* **53**: 1164–1181.

Stigler, J.W., Lee, S.Y., and Stevenson, H.W.: 1986, 'Digit memory in Chinese and English: Evidence for a temporally limited store', *Cognition* **24**: 1–20.

Stroop, J.R.: 1935, 'Studies of interference in serial verbal reactions', *Journal of Experimental Psychology* **18**: 643–662.

Sun, F. C. and Stark, L.: 1986, 'The analysis of reading eye movements in Chinese and English – an approach to study visual information processing in the central nervous system'. Paper presented at the Shanghai Symposium on Neuroscience. Shanghai, April.

Treiman, R.A., Baron, J., and Luk, K.: 1981, 'Speech recoding in silent reading: A comparison of Chinese and English', *Journal of Chinese Linguistics* **9**: 116–125.

Tzeng, O.J.L., Hung, D.L., Chen, S., Wu, J., and Hsi, M.S.: 1986, 'Processing Chinese logographs by Chinese brain damaged patients', in H.S.R. Kao, G.P. van Galen, and R. Hoosain (eds.) *Graphonomics: Contemporary Research in Handwriting*, North Holland, Amsterdam.

Tzeng, O.J.L., Hung, D.L., and Wang, W.S.-Y.: 1977, 'Speech recoding in reading Chinese characters', *Journal of Experimental Psychology: Human Learning and Memory* **3**: 621–630.

Tzeng, O.J.L. and Wang, W.S.-Y.: 1983, 'The first two R's', *American Scientist* **71**: 238–243.

Zhu, Y.L., Song, Z.W., Li,Y., Li, X.T., and Hu, C.Q.: 1986, 'Language functions of subcortical structures', in H.S.R. Kao and R. Hoosain (eds.) *Linguistics, Psychology, and the Chinese Language*, Hong Kong University Centre of Asian Studies, Hong Kong.

10. SCRIPT FACTORS THAT AFFECT LITERACY: ALPHABETIC VS. LOGOGRAPHIC LANGUAGES

Literacy means the abilities to read and write. Because people learn to read and write simultaneously, the word literacy is usually used to refer to the ability to read alone. The ability to read itself has two components: decoding spelling into sound and decoding spelling into meaning. As Taylor (1987) pointed out recently, there are many factors that can affect our ability to decode spelling into sound and our ability to decode spelling into meaning. In the following, only those script factors that have been studied in our laboratory will be presented with an aim at elucidating their differential effects on the processing of English as an alphabetic language and the processing of Chinese as a logographic language. The first section dealt with the processes of decoding symbols into meanings; and the second, with the processes of decoding symbols into sounds.

FROM WORD/CHARACTER TO MEANING

It is widely held that Chinese logographs map more directly onto meaning than alphabetic words, that the former are visually more unique than the latter, and that the former are interrelated with one another with respect to their graphic features so as to facilitate their memory. Let us consider these three assumptions in turn.

Direct-Image Hypothesis and Experimental Findings

A passage from Wang (1973) reads as follows: "To a Chinese the character for 'horse' means horse with no mediation through the sound ma. The image is so vivid that one can almost sense an abstract figure galloping across the page." This passage has been frequently cited to support theories (e.g., Biederman and Tsao, 1979) without receiving rigorous empirical tests.

Wang's (1973) view is shared by Aaronson and Ferres (1986) among many others. According to this view, Chinese characters are directly encoded as abstract images that are themselves representations of meanings. An opposing hypothesis is the indirect-image hypothesis which asserts that word/character meanings are computed.

There are two types of Chinese characters: phonograms, which contain a phonetic component as a clue to the sound of characters, and pictograms, which are pictographic in origin. Aaronson and Ferres' (1986) and Wang's (1973) claim may apply primarily to pictograms. Therefore, both phono-

I. Taylor and D.R. Olson (eds.), Scripts and Literacy, 145–162.

grams and pictograms were chosen, and the subject's task was to judge as fast as possible whether a Chinese character or English word contains a meaning component specified in advance. If the indirect-image hypothesis is correct, then it would be predicted that Chinese phonograms should be responded as fast as Chinese pictograms and that English words should be responded as fast as Chinese characters.

Study 1. In this study, 32 characters were chosen from Tung Lai (1978). Half the characters were pictograms and half were phonograms. Each character can be used as a "word" and was translated into English. For each character and each English translation, a dominant meaning component was obtained in a preliminary study by testing with 80 high school students. When asked to write down meanings to a stimulus word within a 10-seconds period, a dominant meaning component is defined as the most frequently given response. For example, *water* is a dominant meaning component obtained for the stimulus word *river*.

Sixty college students were timed for judging whether a target item (Chinese pictogram, phonogram, or English word) contained a dominant meaning component that was presented as a prime two seconds prior to the target. It was found that reaction times were faster for English primes than for Chinese primes. Pictograms were not responded faster than phonograms. Chinese characters used as targets were not responded faster than English words used as targets. The finding that reaction times were faster for English primes than for Chinese primes is consistent with the observation that when words are used more frequently, they tend to acquire more meanings (Johnson-Laird, 1983; Miller, 1951). For the Chinese subjects, a Chinese word tends to arouse more meanings than its English translation because the former has been used more frequently, resulting in longer reaction times when Chinese primes were used.

In a further experiment, 21 college students were not only timed for judging whether Chinese pictograms or phonograms contained a dominant meaning component, but also timed for judging whether pictures drawn for the pictograms and phonograms contained the same dominant meaning component. The results showed that reaction times were faster to pictures than to Chinese characters. Reaction times were not faster to pictograms than to phonograms.

The results obtained from these two experiments present strong evidence that the direct-image hypothesis should be rejected. Chinese pictograms do not give rise to images directly as pictures.

Discriminability Hypothesis and Experimental Test

Many psycholinguists who write about Chinese logographs posit that Chinese characters are more unique in shape and will leave unique traces (e.g., Tzeng and Hung, 1988). If Chinese characters have more unique shapes than English words, then it follows that Chinese characters are more discriminable from one another than English words. One of the simplest ways to find out whether such differential discriminability exists between the two languages is to make use of triadic judgments. On each trial a triangular array of three words (two of which are identical) is presented. The subject's task is to indicate, by pressing a right or a left key, which of the bottom words, the left one or the right one, is identical to the top word. In this kind of triadic judgment, it is a well-known fact that the more similar are two comparison stimuli the slower is the reaction time. If Chinese characters are visually more unique than English words, the subject's triadic judgments would be faster when any two Chinese characters are used for comparison than when any two English words are used.

An important variable that affects stimulus discriminability is stimulus complexity. Stimulus complexity for English words can be identified as number of letters in a word. Number of letters in an English word is comparable to number of strokes in a Chinese character. In Study 3, the variable of stimulus complexity was also manipulated to see whether it has comparable effects on the two languages.

Study 3. The subjects were 26 freshmen enrolled in an introductory psychology course at the Chinese University. Their English might be nearly as good as their Chinese.

It was conjectured that Chinese characters with numbers of strokes from 5 to 6 are comparable to English words with three letters in terms of stimulus complexity (A category). Similarly, numbers of strokes from 7 to 8 are comparable to four letters (B category), and numbers of strokes from 9 to 10 comparable to five letters (C category). One hundred characters/words each of A, B, and C categories were randomly selected from high-frequency items (above 50 per million) in Cheng (1981) and Thorndike and Lorge (1944).

There were three degrees of discriminability: 0, 1, 2 to indicate the distance between two comparison items belonging to two categories. If two items were from the same category, the distance was 0. If two items were from two adjacent categories, the distance was 1. Finally, if two items were from categories A and C, then the distance was 2.

It is a surprise to find that Chinese characters were discriminated from each other no better than English words by the Chinese subjects. The only significant source of variation was discriminability. The concept of familiarity cannot be invoked to explain the present finding, because it only favors discriminability of a more familiar language (e.g., Ambler and Proctor, 1976; Egeth and Becker, 1971). This means that Chinese characters should be more discirminable to the Chinese subjects than English words.

Graphical-Feature Hypothesis and Experimental Test

According to this hypothesis, the memorial advantage of Chinese characters over alphabetic words obtained by Park and Arbuckle (1977) and Turnage and McGinnies (1973) is due to meaning components being frequently associated with graphical features in Chinese characters.

That most Chinese characters contain an explicit meaning-conveying component called a radical is well known. This hypothesis, then, asserts that inter-character visual relatedness is responsible for the memorial superiority of Chinese logographs. A second version of the graphical-feature hypothesis is as follows. There are many two-character words with the same second characters to indicate that a set of words belongs to the same category, such as *orchid-flower, peach-flower*, etc. At the level of characters, this second version of the graphical-feature hypothesis claims that the memorial superiority of logographs over alphabetic words is explained by an abundance of Chinese words with the same character endings.

Studies 3 and 4. Study 3 investigated the effect of clustering sets of words with the same radicals on recall. It is impossible to find a sufficient number of two-character words with both characters of each word composed of the same radicals. The only requirement was, therefore, the first characters of a set of two-character words being composed of the same radical. Four lists of seven sets of two-character words each were selected from a dictionary, such that each set consisted of four words with the same radical. A word was randomly selected from each set of four words with the same radical to obtain four control lists each of which consisted of 28 words with distinct radicals. Input mode was either visual or auditory.

Using a free-recall procedure with 150 students of National Taiwan University, it was found that recall was higher in the experimental than in the control condition. However, modality was significant and did not interact with condition, indicating that the memorial advantage was obtained whenever the input mode was visual. Higher recall in the experimental condition can be explained simply by the effect of category clustering.

Study 4 tested the second version of the graphical-feature hypothesis that the memorial superiority of logographs is due to many Chinese words characterized by their sharing the same ending characters. For this purpose, two sets of lists were obtained as in Study 3. For one set of experimental lists, each list consisted of seven groups of four two-character words each, each group having the same ending character. Using the same free-recall procedure as in Study 3, 240 students enrolled at Beijing University participated in the experiment. Although recall was higher in the experimental than in the control condition, input mode was again significant and did not interact with condition.

Since the interaction was not significant, the results can be accounted for by the effects of input modality and category clustering alone. This means that graphic features do not contributed to the visual presentation superiority.

Frequency Hypothesis and Supporting Findings

In two preliminary studies using 84 students enrolled at the Chinese University of Hong Kong, it was found that the visual presentation superiority was obtained for primacy items in short lists of English words as well as for recall of long lists of English words. These findings effectively rule out any explanation of the visual presentation superiority of logographs over alphabetic words in terms of physical script differences.

According to the frequency hypothesis, whether visually presented items are more recallable than auditorially presented materials depends on the differential availabilities of visual versus auditory traces. If some Korean words are more frequently written in Chinese logographs than in Han'gŭl, then the visual traces for these Chinese logographs become more available than those for Hungul, as was obtained by Park and Arbuckle (1977). If a set of words is encountered more frequently in readings than in speech, then their visual traces will become more available than their auditory traces, giving rise to a memorial superiority of visually presented items over auditorially presented items, as was found by Turnage and McGinnies (1973) from their Chinese subjects but not from their American subjects.

The frequency hypothesis assumes that there are two types of frequency: (a) frequency of a verbal item as it appears in print and (b) frequency of a verbal item as it appears in speech. Visual frequency is responsible for the availability of visual traces and auditory frequency for the availability of auditory traces. According to the differential-availability hypothesis, then, whenever there is a large discrepency between visual and auditory frequencies in favor of the former, the visual presentation superiority will obtain. It is perhaps because of this reason that availability was found to be an important predictor of recall but that the classically important variable of word frequency was not (Rubin, 1980; 1983; Rubin and Friendly, 1986).

Study 5. The frequency hypothesis can account for the visual presentation superiority of Chinese logographs over alphabetic words (Turnage and McGinnies, 1973) by noting that there is a discrepancy in kinds of speech many Chinese people use in school and at home. The type of speech (Mandarin) used in formal occasions is different from a dialect used at home for many Chinese people, Moreover, although there is evidence for speech recoding of Chinese logographs in reading (e.g., Tzeng, Hung, and Wang, 1977), it may be less prevalent in Chinese readers than English readers because the former are often not confident about how to pronounce low-frequency characters correctly. For instance, Zhou (1978) estimated that the relationship between graphic cues and sounds in actual characters is very low (30%).

The Chinese people in Hong Kong speak a type of dialect called Cantonese which differs from the standard Chinese (Mandarin) with respect to some most commonly used words not only in speech sound but also in writing. Such dialectic words appear neither in dictionaries not in readings. They appear only in local newspapers and magazines. Therefore, there are two types of words: (a) one type of word that can be written in both dialectic and standard forms and (b) another type of word that can be written only in a standard form.

With a group of 60 Hong Kong college students serving as the subjects, it was found that the visual superiority effect was obtained only for those words that can be written only in a standard form. This type of word is experienced more frequently in print than in speech, producing the visual presentation superiority.

FROM WORD/CHARACTER TO SOUND

Several strategies have been proposed to study spelling-sound correspondences (Henderson, 1982). According to a nonlexical strategy, prelexical translation takes place according to grapheme-phoneme correspondence rules (e.g., Venezky, 1970; Wijk, 1966) or rules determined by "vocalic center groups" (Hansen and Rogers, 1973). According to the second strategy that may be applied to the translation of print into sound, word-specific phonology is directly accessed, as evidenced in the studies of Forster and Chambers (1973) and Frederiksen and Kroll (1976). The third strategy is to use lexical analogies, as early suggested by Venezky and Calfee (1970) and later investigated by Brooks (1977), Glushko (1979), Marcel (1980), and Rosson (1983). The final strategy is a parallel-distributed-processing (PDP) approach (e.g., Seidenberg and McClelland, 1989). The PDP models generally assume interconnecting modules consisting of orthographic, phonological, and hidden units. Weights on connections between units are modified during training. Pronunciation of exception words and nonwords can be accomplished by a single mechanism using weighted connection between units.

A traditional dual-process view that incorporates the first two strategies (e.g., Coltheart, 1978) posits that, separate from the routine for "addressing" the pronunciation of a known word, a person uses a non-lexical routine for assembling the pronunciation of any letter string through a set of spelling-sound correspondence rules. Many models originated from this traditional view assume different spelling units for applying spelling-sound correspondences. The spelling units range from smallest graphemes to submorphemic units to morphemic units or "multi-level" units (e.g.,

Brown, 1987; Seidenberg, Waters, Barnes, and Tanenhaus, 1984; Shallice, Wallington, and McCarthy, 1983; Shallice and McCarthy, 1985).

There are, however, a number of problems for proponents of dual-process models. A major problem comes from demonstrations that lexical information can contribute to the pronunciation of nonwords as well as words (Baron, 1977; Brooks, 1977; Glushko, 1979; Marcel, 1980; Rosson, 1983, 1985), because this certainly weakens the claim that a separate set of correspondence rules is needed to account for the pronunciation of nonwords. Both Glushko and Marcel dismissed the notion of a rule-based pronunciation process and proposed analogy models in which pronunciations are assigned by analogy with and by specific reference to known lexical items.

Although analogy models seem to be an economical solution to the new evidence accumulating, there is as yet no mechanism worked out for how one actually computes a pronunciation for a novel word in such a model. According to a PDP model proposed by Seidenberg and McClelland (1989), pronunciation latencies are obtained first by computing phonological error scores and then by transforming the latter into the former through some arbitrary function. In the following, a component-decidability model that directly computes pronunciation latencies is proposed.

Component Decidability Model

The component decidability model of spelling-sound correspondences basically assumes the following steps in arriving at a word pronunciation. First, the subject starts to extract any detectable pronunciation cues from some smallest component or components. Second, if the pronunciation of such component is uniquely determined as this component is contained in all words in his or her vocabulary, then that unique pronunciation is a correct pronunciation for that component. Third, if the pronunciation of such component is not uniquely determined as this component is pronounced differently when it is contained in different words, then the component in question is combined with an adjacent component to obtain a larger component. The subject makes the same test with this larger component until a unique pronunciation is obtained. Fourth, the same testing procedure is serially applied to all components from the beginning to the final component, and the pronunciation of a word is obtained by blending the component pronunciations. Of course, the pronunciation latency is proportional to the total number of tests applied to determine a correct pronunciation for each component. Parenthetically, in applying the testing procedure, if the obtained pronunciation of a given word is still not unique as in the case of homographs, then the subject goes beyond the word boundary to make a semantic test to decide a unique pronunciation for a given word. For the sake of simplicity, only nonhomographs will be considered in the following. However, the proposed model readily applies to the case of homographs.

Component decidability index. In the following, the model will be applied to English words to determine how many adjacent letters one has to inspect in order to decide a correct pronunciation for any letter in a word. It can be readily seen that the model can be also applied to any language. In English, smallest components of words that provide pronunciation information are letters (denoted by l_i or r_i). Let $w_i = l_1 l_2 - l_n$ stand for any word in the subject's vocabulary and $/w_i/$ for its length or the number of letters in w_i. Furthermore, we need the following notations:

- l-: a beginning letter of a letter string with at least one letter on the right.
- -l: a final letter of a letter string with at least one letter on the left.
- -l-: an inside letter of a letter string with at least one letter on the left and one letter on the right.

We are now in a position to compute the component decidability (CD) index for a letter in a target word, $w_0 = r_1 r_2 \ldots r_m$. Here, $/w_0/ = m$. The CD index for a letter computes how large a segment (C_i) including the letter should be in order to give a unique pronunciation for the letter.

Let us start with r_1 in w_0 which has a right neighbor. Therefore its correct notation should be r_1-, if $m > 1$. For r_1- (C_1), let us form a set of words S_1 as follows:

(1) $S_1 = \{w_i | r_1\text{-} = l_1\text{-}, /w_i/ \leq m\}$.

The set S_1 is a collection of all words which begin with r_1 and are at least of length 2. If r_1 is pronounced uniquely for all w_i's in S_1, then the CD index for r_1 in w_0 is 1. Otherwise, the second set S_2 is formed as follows:

(2) $S_2 = \{w_i | r_1 r_2\text{-} = l_1 l_2\text{-}, /w_i/ \leq m\}$.

Here, it is assumed that $m > 2$. The set S_2 is a collection of all words which begin with $r_1 r_2$ and are at least of length 3. If r_1 is pronounced uniquely for all w_i's in S_2, then the CD index for r_1 in w_0 is 2. Otherwise, S_3, S_4, . . . , S_k can be formed such that for some S_k,

(3) $S_k = \{w_i | r_1 r_2 \ldots r_k = l_1 l_2 \ldots l_k, /w_i/ \leq m, k < m\}$,

r_1 is uniquely pronounced for all w_i in S_k. The sequence $\{S_i\}$ is not vacuous, because w_0 is contained in each S_i, $1 \leq i \leq k$. The obtained k is the CD index for r_1 in w_0.

The CD index for a final letter in w_0 can be similarly obtained. The CD index for an inside letter (-r_i-) poses a problem, because there are often two neighbors to choose for a further test if one test fails. It is assumed that whether r_{i-1} or r_{i+1} is chosen for the S_2 test depends on which $\{S_i\}$

sequence gives a smaller CD index. This assures the uniqueness of a CD index for a letter in a word. If it is further assumed that for each i a letter string (C_i) is chosen in such a way that S_i that contains the letter string contains a smaller number of words, then $\{S_i\}$ sequence is also uniquely determined.

As an example, let us compute CD indices for the component letters in TAPE. Since "T" is not uniquely pronounced when it is used as a beginning letter of any words whose length is larger than or equal to 2 (consider, for example, THIN or TSAR), but is uniquely pronounced for those words beginning with "TA-", the CD indexed for "T" in TAPE is 2. Similarly, the CD index for "-P-" should be 1 because "P" is an inside letter. The CD index for "-A-" will be clearly 4, because its pronunciation is uniquely determined only after all the letter environments are known. Supposed that "E" in "-PE" is always not pronounced. Then, the CD index for "E" in TAPE is 2. Therefore, the CD indices for the component letters in TAPE are {2, 4, 1, 2}.

In the computation of CD indices, S_i is assumed to consist of all words with the properties that they contain C_i and that their lengths are equal to or smaller than m (length of the word in question). The last assumption is only for convenience. If the restriction of word lengths is removed, only minor modifications are required.

As Saffran (1985) pointed out, there is a problem with any lexical analogy model because a person is assumed to store pronunciations of all words in an analogy set in the first place. Instead of computing a pronunciation of a word from an analogy set, then, isn't it easier to retrieve a word pronunciation from the analogy set? The same problem seems to apply to the present model. However, this problem arises because it is assumed that the subject recognizes a word and accesses its sound representation instantaneously. It is known, however, that this will not happen for most words.

In the course of computing pronunciations for new words, it is assumed that children gradually shift from an independent processing mode to a parallel processing mode by computing pronunciations of two or three adjacent letters in parallel. It is through parallel processing that children start to respond to larger spelling units.

Latencies of Voicing Isolated Words/Characters

Suppose that words are pronounced according to *independent serial processing and final blending*. Suppose further that words are m letters long. Then, the naming latency should consist of (a) time of encoding letters (T_E), (b) time of executing tests for each letter to determine its pronunciation, and (c) time of blending individual letter pronunciations and their motor output ($T_{B\ \&\ M}$):

$$(4) \qquad RT = T_E + \sum_{i=1}^{m} (k_i a) + T_{B\,\&\,M}$$

Here k_i is the CD index (= number of tests executed to find a unique pronunciation) for letter i and a stands for the processing time for each test. The basic idea is that for a larger CD index more tests are required and hence a longer pronunciation time obtains. Although some exponential function of k_i seems more appropriate, a linear function of k_i is assumed for the sake of simplicity.

The effect of reading practice is hypothesized to take place in the way of processing a word in terms of larger and larger spelling units. For skilled readers most monosyllabic words are then pronounced by processing initial consonants (their CD index, k_1) and ending strings or "bodies" (their CD index, k_2) as follows:

$$(5) \qquad RT = T_E + (k_1 + k_2)a + T_M$$

Here, $T_{B\,\&\,M}$ is replaced by T_M, because the time of blending component pronunciations now takes place simultaneously with the time of computing component pronunciations. For extremely high frequency words, they are responded as constituting a unit component. In this case we have

$$(6) \qquad RT = T_E + a + T_M$$

Of course T_E in each equation depends on word frequency, and the three time components in Equation 6 may proceed in cascade or partially in parallel.

English words. Ten four-letter exception words and their regular controls were randomly selected mainly from Brown (1987), Seidenbeerg (1985), and Seidenberg *et al.* (1984). They were considered as low-frequency words according to the classification of the latter studies. In Table 1, a CD index was calculated for each constituent letter and Σk_i obtained for each word. Also listed in Table 1 are $k_1 + k_2$ computed from initial consonants and ending strings. It is clear from the table that the mean of Σk_i for exception words is larger than that for regular controls, $t(9) = 4.36$, $p < 0.01$. Only one exception appears for the pair, NUDE and NAIL. In this case the regular control NAIL has two vowel letters which tend to give larger CD indices. When both the exception words and regular controls are considered on the basis of initial consonants and ending strings, $k_1 + k_2$ was uniformly larger for each exception word than for its regular control ($t(9) = 1.3 \times 10^{19}$, $p < 0.01$). In conclusion, number of tests required for arriving at a correct pronunciation for a constituent letter is a good measure for accounting for a difference in the pronunciation latencies between exception and regular words. Number of tests required for arriving at correct pronunciations for initial consonants and ending strings seems a better measure. It will be

TABLE 1
CD indices for low-frequency exception and regular words

Exception	k_i	$k_1 + k_2$	Regular	k_i	$k_1 + k_2$
BOWL	8	3	BELT	6	2
COMB	9	4	COKE	8	3
DEAF	11	3	DICE	8	2
LOSE	11	3	LIFT	7	2
NUDE	7	3	NAIL	8	2
PINT	8	4	PILL	7	3
SOUL	10	4	SICK	8	3
TOUR	9	4	TRAP	7	3
VASE	10	3	VENT	6	2
WOOL	10	3	WING	7	2
Mean	9.3	3.4	Mean	7.2	2.4

seen that this measure is suitable for use in comparing the pronunciations of English words with Chinese characters.

When initial strings ({BOW-} from BOWL, {BOW-} stands for a *set* of four-letter words whose three beginning letters are BOW) and ending strings ({-OWL} from BOWL) were both analyzed for exception words and regular controls, there are more words with the same ending strings than with the same initial strings for regular words, {-xyz} = 7.4 (mean) and {xyz-} = 1.9 (mean), $t(9) = 3.95$, $p < 0.01$. The tendency is much smaller and not significant for exception words, {-xyz} = 4.2 versus {xyz-} = 2.7, $t(9) = 2.04$, $p > 0.05$. In other words, ending strings are more common for regular words than for exception words.

Chinese characters. Zhou (1978) estimated that there are 81% of Chinese characters formed by compounding sound-cuing phonetics and meaning-conveying radicals. He further estimated that the relationship between phonetics and sounds in actual characters are very low (30%).

Although calculation of the mean of CD indices for all Chinese characters is not impossible, it is instructive to find the mean CD indices for part of Chinese characters. For this purpose, all Chinese characters whose initial consonants are unaspirated [p^o] were chosen. The unaspirated [p^o] is the first phonetic symbol in the *zhuyin fuhao*, a Chinese system of phonetic symbols used by Chinese children before they start to read Chinese characters in Taiwan. There are altogether 351 such characters. Excluding 35 singletons, the pronunciations of only 35 out of 313 phonograms can be exactly predicted from their phonetic components. The mean of $k_1 + k_2$ is easily calculated as follows:

$$\text{Mean} = \frac{(2 + 2)\ 278 + (2 + 1)\ 35}{313} = 3.89$$

This mean is higher than that for a sample of 10 randomly selected English exception words. When those Chinese characters whose pronunciation can be exactly predicted from their phonetic components are defined as regular characters and the other phonograms defined as exception characters, then the means of $k_1 + k_2$ are calculated to be 3.0 and 4.0, respectively.

Although those characters beginning with a particular consonant are only part of all Chinese characters, it is clear that most Chinese characters are exception characters. On the other hand, most English words are regular. It is no wonder that most Chinese are not consciously aware that some part of a Chinese character gives a clue to its pronunciation. When students were explained about this fact, it was found that they learned to read new characters must faster than when they were not explained (Ai, 1924; Liu, 1978).

Comparison. A large difference in CD indices between English words and Chinese characters is expected to produce a difference in their voicing latencies. Thus, Seidenberg (1985) observed from his experiments that, in comparison to low- and high-frequency English words, low-frequency Chinese characters took much longer to read aloud than high-frequency characters. These data are presented in Table 2. In Table 2 are also shown the data obtained by Hue (1992) and Liu, Chou, and Wu (1993).

Although the voicing latencies of extremely high-frequency words (or characters used as words) should tend to converge to some low values for all languages, the pronunciations of low-frequency words more faithfully reflect their CD indices. Therefore, the difference in naming latencies between high-frequency and low-frequency words (called the frequency

TABLE 2
Naming latencies in seconds

Target Item	English			Chinese		
	Low	High	Diff	Low	High	Diff
(from Seidenberg, 1985)						
Regular/Phonogram	0.56	0.54	0.02	0.88	0.74	0.14
Exception/Non-Phonogram	0.58	0.54	0.04	0.98	0.73	0.25
(from Hue, 1992)						
Regular	–	–	–	0.90	0.68	0.22
Irregular	–	–	–	1.10	0.71	0.39
(from Liu *et al.*, 1993)						
Regular	–	–	–	0.59	0.47	0.12
Irregular	–	–	–	0.79	0.47	0.32

Note: Low = low frequency items, High = high frequency items.

effect) for each language is a good measure to test the effect of differential CD indices for different languages. As Table 2 shows, these differences are uniformly larger for Chinese characters than for English words. This is in agreement with generally higher CD indices for Chinese characters than for English words.

Pronouncing Words/Characters in Context

It is natural to assume that pronunciations of words/characters demand more resources when they have to be computed through entire configurations than when they can be computed through constituents. This will produce important processing differences especially when words/characters are to be pronounced in the context of some other words/characters. This section considers this type of phenomenon as it follows from the CD model.

It was mentioned that Chinese characters generally have larger CD indices than English words. This means that in order to pronounce a character its entire configuration has to be considered simultaneously. Baron (1977) called those subjects who were relatively good at the word-specific mechanism (responding to entire configurations) Chinese and those subjects who were relatively good at the orthographic mechanism Phonecians. Suppose that a character is to be pronounced in the context of some other character. Then, in order to produce a facilitative effect, two entire configurations have to be processed simultaneously. The excessive demand for additional resources may counteract a possible facilitative effect of context. A study (Liu, 1988) has been conducted to demonstrate this prediction.

Before presenting this study, it should be noted that Chinese characters represent morphemes. Many *words* are formed by combining two characters or three to create meanings that are distinct from the meanings of the original characters. For instance, character *fire* can be combined with character *vehicle* to form a two-character word which stands for *train*. *Nonwords* can be formed by re-pairing characters.

Study 6. Two-character words and nonwords were used. Forty-one students at National Taiwan University served as the subjects. The task was to name a designated character, located at the first or second position of two-character strings, or in isolation. The obtained mean naming times are presented in Table 3. It was found that, for two-character words, characters were voiced slower in the second position than in the first position. This tendency was more marked for nonwords than for words. It was also found that first (second) characters were voiced slower in nonwords than in isolation or in words, while characters in isolation were not voiced significantly faster than first (second) characters in words. As was expected, then, there was no facilitative effect from word contexts, but was inhibitory effect from nonword contexts.

TABLE 3
Teaction times in seconds and error rates (Study 6)

Target	Alone	Word	Nonword
First Character	0.529 (4.8%)	0.560 (4.2%)	0.607 (2.4%)
Second Character	0.524 (5.4%)	0.585 (2.4%)	0.699 (7.1%)

Study 7. The same subjects of Study 6 participated in Study 7. In this study, three-character words or nonwords were used, and the subjects were to name a designated character, located at the first or second or third position of three-character words or nonwords or in isolation. The obtained results are presented in Table 4. The major findings are as follows. First, the mean reaction time to first characters was slower in nonwords than in words or in isolation, while first characters were voiced in words not significantly slower than in isolation. Second, the subjects responded to second characters slower in nonwords or words than in isolation, while it was not significantly faster in the word condition than in the nonword condition. Finally, third characters were responded slower in nonwords or words than in isolation, while the difference between the word and nonword conditions was not significant.

When the results of Studies 6 and 7 are combined, through the systematic manipulations of string length and character position, an orderly change in voicing latencies was observed from first to second to third positions and from two-character to three-character string lengths. Therefore, an explanation based on masking through flanking characters can be excluded. Perhaps, sound activation is more efficiently cued by preceding sounds than guided by the spelling-sound relationship in logographic languages.

TABLE 4
Reaction times in seconds and error rates (Study 7)

Target	Alone	Word	Nonword
First Character	0.570 (5.6%)	0.584 (1.6%)	0.669 (7.1%)
Second Character	0.538 (5.6%)	0.642 (6.3%)	0.682 (5.6%)
Third Character	0.525 (4.8%)	0.604 (2.4%)	0.637 (4.0%)

Study 8. Instead of presenting two-character Chinese words of Study 6, English "compound" words such as *life-boat, like-wise* were used. Thirty-four Hong Kong college students named constituent words (boat or life) in compound words (life-*boat* or *life*-boat) or compound nonwords (like-*boat* or *life*-wise) or in isolation (*boat* or *life*). The obtained results are summarized in Table 5. It is evident from the table that, irrespective of first or second constituents, they were pronounced faster in compound words than in isolation or compound nonwords, while there was no appreciable difference in latencies between naming constituents in isolation and in compound nonwords.

TABLE 5
Reaction times in second and error rates (Study 8)

Target	Alone	Word	Nonword
First Constituent	0.526 (2.7%)	0.482 (1.9%)	0.538 (2.4%)
Second Constituent	0.532 (1.6%)	0.486 (1.9%)	0.532 (1.6%)

The results from Study 6 to 8 taken together, therefore, demonstrate that different spelling-sound relationships for different languages as can be specified by their CD indices also have an important effect on pronouncing words/characters in the context of some other words/characters.

CONCLUSION

When diversified findings from the literature are combined with the present results, a unified view on the memorial superiority of Chinese logographs over English words emerges. Frequently, the memorial superiority of Chinese logographs refers to the visual presentation superiority. That Chinese logographs do not directly give rise to images and are no more visually unique than English words is compatible with the observation that, when words are used more frequently, they tend to acquire more meanings (Miller, 1951; Johnson-Laird, 1983). This means that meanings of words/characters are acquired and come to be dissociated from the way in which words/characters were originally created. To Chinese linguistics who are well aware of the origins of characters, the character for "horse" triggers a vivid image of an abstract figure galloping across the page. However, to most Chinese such a vivid image will not be aroused.

That the visual superiority effect can be demonstrated for English words with Chinese subjects effectively rules out any interpretation of the effect as attributable to physical script differences between Chinese logographs and alphabetic words. The results of Study 5 naturally lead to a view that it is because of a discrepancy in frequencies of visually and auditorially experiencing verbal items what produces the observed visual superiority effect. Later studies confirmed this view (e.g., Liu, Zhu, and Wu, 1992; Zhu, Liu, Shieh, and Fan, 1992).

With respect to the process of decoding spelling into sound, because of the relatively poor decidability of character components in pronouncing Chinese characters, it takes longer to voice low-frequency Chinese characters than low-frequency English words. Moreover, it was found that there is no facilitative effect of context on the pronunciation of Chinese characters.

ACKNOWLEDGMENT

Portions of the research reported here were supported by a grant from the Center for Hong Kong Studies, Chinese University of Hong Kong and Grant NSC 75-0301-H002-09 from National Science Council, Republic of China.

REFERENCES

Aaronson, D. and Ferres, S.: 1986, 'Sentence processing in Chinese-American bilinguals', *Journal of Memory and Language* **25**: 136–162.

Ai, W.: 1924, 'A study of frequently used characters and their form, sound, and meaning', *Teaching and Learning* **3**, No. 5.

Ambler, B.A. and Proctor, J.D.: 1976, 'The familiarity effect for single-letter pairs', *Journal of Experimental Psychology: Human Perception and Performance* **2**: 222–234.

Baron, J.: 1977, 'Mechanisms for pronouncing printed words: Use and acquisition', in D. LaBerge and S. J. Samuels (eds.) *Basic processes in reading: Perception and comprehension*, Erlbaum, New York, pp. 175–216.

Biederman, I. and Tsao, Y.-C.: 1979, 'On processing Chinese ideographs and English words: Some implications for Stroop-test results', *Cognitive Psychology* **11**: 125–132.

Brooks, L.: 1977, 'Visual pattern in fluent word identification', in A.S. Reber and D.L. Scarborough (eds.) *Toward a Psychology of Reading*, Erlbaum, Hillsdale, NJ.

Brown, G.D.A.: 1987, 'Resolving inconsistency: A computational model of word naming', *Journal of Memory and Language* **26**: 1–23.

Cheng, C.M.: 1982, 'Analysis of present-day Mandarin', *Journal of Chinese Linguistics* **10**: 281–358.

Coltheart, M.: 1978, 'Lexical access in simple reading tasks', in G. Underwood (ed.) *Strategies in information processing*, Academic Press, London, pp. 151–216.

Egeth, H. and Becker, D.: 1971, 'Differential effects of familiarity on judgments of sameness and differences', *Perception and Psychophysics* **9**: 321–326.

Forster, K.I. and Chambers, S.M.: 1973, 'Lexical access and naming time', *Journal of Verbal Learning and Verbal Behavior* **12**: 627–635.

Frederiksen, J.R. and Kroll, J.F.: 1976, 'Spelling and sound: approaches to the internal lexicon', *Journal of Experimental Psychology: Human Perception and Performance* **2**: 361–379.

Gluskho, R.: 1979, 'The organization and activation of othographic knowledge in reading aloud', *Journal of Experimental Psychology: Human Perception and Performance* **5**: 674–691.

Hansen, D. and Rogers, T.S.: 1973, 'An exploration of psycholinguistic units in initial reading', in K.S. Good (ed.) *The Psycholinguistic Nature of the Reading Process*, Wayne State University Press, Detroit.

Henderson, L.: 1982, *Orthography and visual word recognition in reading*, Academic Press, New York.

Hue, C.W.: 1992, 'Recognition processes in character naming', in H.C. Chen and O.J.L. Tzeng (eds.) *Language processing in Chinese*, Elsevier Science Publishers, Amsterdam.

Jeng, C.I., Lai, M.W., and Liu, I.M.: 1973, 'Category norms in Chinese and English from bilingual subjects', *Acta Psychologica Taiwanica* **15**: 81–153.

Johnson-Laird, P.N.: 1983, *Mental models: Towards a cognitive science of language, inference, and consciousness*, Harvard University Press, Cambridge, MA.

Liu, I.-M.: 1988, 'Context effects on word/character naming: Alphabetic versus logographics languages', in I.-M. Liu, H.-C. Chen, and M.-J. Chen (eds.) *Cognitive aspects of the Chinese Language (Vol. 1)*, Asian Research Service, Hong Kong.

Liu, I.-M., Chou, T.-L., and Wu, J.-T.: 1993, *Encoding operation and transcoding as the major loci of the frequency effect*, National Chung-Cheng University.

Liu, I.-M., Chuang, C.-J., and Wang, S.-C.: 1975, *Frequency count of 40,000 Chinese words*, Lucky Books, Taipei, Taiwan.

Liu, I.-M., Zhu, Y., and Wu, J.-T.: 1992, 'The long-term modality effect: In search of differences in processing logographs and alphabetic words', *Cognition* **43**: 31–66.

Marcel, T.: 1980, 'Surface dyslexia and beginning reading: A revised hypothesis of the pronunciation of print and its impairments', in M. Coltheart, K. Patterson, and J.C. Marshall (eds.) *Deep dyslexia*, Routledge and Kegan Paul, London.

McClelland, J.L. and Rumelhart, D.E.: 1985, 'Distributed memory and the representation of general and specific information', *Journal of Experimental Psychology: General* **114**: 159–188.

Miller, G.A.: 1951, *Language and communication*, McGraw-Hill, New York.

Park, S. and Arbuckle, T.Y.: 1977, 'Ideograms versus alphabets Effect of script on memory in "biscriptural" Korean subjects', *Journal of Experimental Psychology: Human Learning and Memory* **3**: 631–642.

Rosson, M.B.: 1983, 'From SOFA to LOUCH: Lexical contributions to pseudoword pronunciation', *Memory and Cognition* **11**: 152–160.

Rosson, M.B.: 1985, 'The interaction of pronunciation rules and lexical representations in reading aloud', *Memory and Cognition* **13**: 90–99.

Rubin, D.C.: 1980, '51 properties of 125 words: A unit analysis of verbal behavior', *Journal of Verbal Learning and Verbal Behavior* **23**: 23–38.

Rubin, D.C.: 1983, 'Associative asymmetry, availability, and retrieval', *Memory and Cognition* **11**: 83–92.

Rubin, D.C. and Friendly, M.: 1986, 'Predicting which words get recalled: Measures of free recall, availability, goodness, emotionality, and pronunciability for 925 nouns', *Memory and Cognition* **14**: 79–94.

Saffran, E.M.: 1985, 'Acquired dyslexia: Implications for models of reading', in G.E. MacKinnon and T.G. Waller (eds.) *Reading research: Advances in Theory and Practice (Vol. 1)*, Academic Press, London, pp. 231–258.

Seidenberg, M.S.: 1985, 'The time course of phonological code activation in two writing systems', *Cognition* **19**: 1–30.

Seidenberg, M.S. and McClelland, J.L.: 1989, 'A distributed, developmental model of word recognition and naming', *Psychological Review* **96**: 523–568.

Seidenberg, M.S., Waters, G.D., Barnes, M.A., and Tanenhause, M.K.: 1983, 'When does irregular spelling or pronunciation influence word recognition?', *Journal of Verbal Learning and Verbal Behavior* **23**: 383–404.

Shallice, T., Warrington, K.E., and McCarthy, R.: 1983, 'Reading without semantics', *Quarterly Journal of Experimental Psychology* **35A**: 111–138.

Shallice, T. and McCarthy, R.: 1985, 'The operation of the phonological route: Evidence from "phonologic reading" in acquired dyslexic patients', in K. Patterson, J. Marshall, and M. Coltheart (eds.) *Surface dyslexia*, Erlbaum, London.

Taylor, I.: 1987, 'Psychology of literacy: East and west', in D. de Kerckhove and C. Lumsden (eds.) *The alphabet and the brain: Relateralization of writing*, Springer-Verlag, New York.

Thorndike, E.L. and Lorge, I.: 1944, *The teacher's wordbook of 30,000 words*, Teachers College Press, New York.

Tung Lai: 1978, *Recognizing Chinese Characters*, Mingjen, Taipei.

Turnage, T.W. and McGinnies, E.: 1973, 'A cross-cultural comparison of the effects of presentation mode and meaningfulness in short-term recall', *American Journal of Psychology* **86**: 369–381.

Tzeng, O.J.L. and Hung D.L.: 1988, 'Cerebral organization: Clues from scriptal effects on lateralization', in I. M. Liu, H.C. Chen, and M.J. Chen (eds.) *Cognitive aspects of the Chinese language* (*Vol. 1*), Asian Research Service, Hong Kong.

Tzeng, O.J.L., Hung, D.L., and Wang, W.S.Y.: 1977, Speech recoding in reading Chinese characters', *Journal of Experimental Psychology: Human Learning and Memory* **3**: 621–630.

Venezky, R.L.: 1970, *The Structure of English Orthography*, Mouton, The Hague.

Venezky, R.L. and Calfee, R.C.: 1970, 'The reading competency model', in H. Singer and R.B. Ruddell (eds.) *Theoretical Models and Processes of Reading*, International Reading Association, Newark.

Wijk, A.: 1966, *Rules of Pronunciation for the English Language*, Oxford University Press, Oxford.

Zhou, Y.-G.: 1978, 'To what degree are the "phonetics" of present-day Chinese characters still phonetic?', *Zhongguo Yuwen* **146**: 172–177.

Zhu, Y., Liu, I.-M., Shieh, Y.-T., and Fan, C.: 1992, 'Differences in visual and auditory word frequencies and the visual superiority effect in Chinese', in P.-Z. Kuang and C.-T. Chang (eds.) *Proceedings of the 5th international conference on cognitive aspects of the Chinese language*, Science, Beijing.

CHE KAN LEONG

11. ORTHOGRAPHIC AND PSYCHOLINGUISTIC CONSIDERATIONS IN DEVELOPING LITERACY IN CHINESE*

It is not without significance that this symposium on "Scripts and Literacy" takes place at the McLuhan Centre on Culture and Technology. McLuhan's publications have done much to alert us to the role of the medium of representation and the psychological consequences of literacy.

For the purpose of this article, the terms script and orthography are used interchangeably to refer to a system of writing or visible language whereby writers could encode their linguistic messages so that readers could decode these symbols or codes to interpret their meaning (Jensen, 1970). Literacy is recognized as ranging on a continuum (from fully literate through semi-literate to functionally illiterate), is context-dependent (school literacy may differ from work force literacy), and encompasses more than reading and writing (Leong, 1989; Olson, 1987). Further more, "What matters is what people do with literacy, not what literacy does to people" (Olson, Torrance, and Hildyard, 1985: 15).

Rather than taking such a comprehensive view of literacy, I will restrict my discussion to what is termed analytic reading (Mattingly, 1972) with emphasis on accessing the abstract, internal lexicon of a morphemic writing system (Chinese) in Chinese readers to enable them to derive meaning from words and from discourse. I will begin by discussing briefly if orthographies evolve from picture-writing through semasiography to logographic and then alphabetic writing and if the last-named system could be assumed to be more advanced in the hierarchy of linguistic derivation. Extending the argument of Mattingly (1985; 1987), I will attempt to show that Chinese as a morphemic script could be just as *productive* linguistically as an alphabetic orthography. This argument has a bearing on the acquisition and development of reading conceived as part of the literacy continuum. In particular, I will show the commonality in the component process of lexical access of Chinese and English. I will then examine some of the linguistic variables that might impinge on the development of literacy in Chinese in light of our advances in computer technology. Throughout this paper, the term Chinese refers mainly to modern standard Chinese (Kratochvil, 1968) or the vernacular written style (Baihuawen), which is contrasted with the highly formalized classical style or Wenyan.

I. Taylor and D.R. Olson (eds.), Scripts and Literacy, 163–183.

'EVOLUTION' OF WRITING SYSTEMS REVISITED

In the study of the history of writing systems there have been considerable discussions of the role of pictures and objects as symbols of writing. Gelb (1963: 190) would exclude "objects of art resulting from an artistic-aesthetic urge" but traced the origin of writing to simple pictures. Jensen (1970: 24), however, would include objects in an object-writing system if the production is "by the act of drawing, painting or scratching on a durable writing-material" and if the production is for "the purpose of communicating." Thus the Yoruba man in jail sending his wife a stone, a piece of charcoal, some shrivelled grains of maize, and some pepper , all wrapped in a rag is accepted as object-writing. This encoded "written" message was decoded as "my body is healthy" (the hard stone), "my prospects are bleak or black" (the black charcoal), "my clothing is in tatters" (the rag), "my body is gaunt with sufferings" (the shrivelled grain), but "my spirit is roused" (the hot pepper). There are other instances of object-writing among Iroquois and Algonquin Indians and other tribes.

Closer to our current thinking of writing are the *semasiographic systems* which represent thoughts and feelings only loosely connected with speech. A message in semasiography has only one meaning to the encoder and decoder of the message, but its actual form if spoken is not fixed. Jensen calls this idea-writing and contrasts it with word-picture-script. In idea-writing, the pictures are "linked only loosely to the corresponding form of expression" (Jensen, 1970: 50), whereas a word-picture-script is a code for a specific spoken word. Whether semasiography is taken as marginal writing is seen as "ultimately a personal choice about how to use words" (Sampson, 1985: 30).

The general trend in the development of writing systems is for the pictures to become more stylized and conventionalized. The result is that

> the bond linking form and meaning could break completely, and instead the phonetic equivalent of the picture gained the upper hand: the picture was no longer, or no longer solely, the representation of an object or of the *meaning* of the word naming it, but at the same time, or even solely, a colourless and meaningless fixing of a certain *sound* or *sound-complex*. This transition is known as "PHONETICIZATION" (Jensen, 1970: 51, author's italics).

This phoneticization stage is also recognized by Gelb (1963: 12): "From then on writing gradually lost its character as an independent mode of expressing ideas and became a tool of speech, a vehicle through which exact forms of speech could be recorded in permanent form." Chao (1968) is more explicit in his seminal work *Language and Symbolic Systems*. He states: "Visual symbols do not begin to be writing until they have a close correspondence to language" and, "if a sign represents a specific part of language, it is writing; if it represents things directly, it is not." (p. 101). Thus the keynote of writing is an expression of language with all its ramifications and not merely a transcription of speech (Olson, 1988).

In all these discussions it should not be assumed uncritically that writing systems evolve from picture-writing to logographies, then syllabaries and alphabets. Nor should it be assumed that the alphabetic orthography as the latest invention in the history of writing is the best system to transcribe all languages. What should be noted is that different writing systems develop different ways of mapping phones, morphemes and syllables onto the symbols for similar communicative purposes, and that the implied hierarchical ordering of scripts may not follow. The further suggestion that a logographic script such as Chinese militates against logical considerations (Goody and Watt, 1963) simply cannot stand up to scrutiny.

The traditional view that writing "evolves" from picture-writing through logographic, syllabic to alphabetic writing has been critically re-examined by Mattingly (1985, 1987). Reviewing historical development, he suggests that alphabets could "evolve" from logographies without an intervening syllabic stage as with Egyptian and that

> no alphabets have developed from syllabic or word-syllabic systems, for apart from the Ugaritic cuneiform alphabet . . . all other alphabets are derived directly or indirectly from the West Semitic consonantal alphabets (Mattingly, 1985: 21).

Further more, there are either "logographic traditions (Mesopotamian, Hittite, Cretan, and Sino-Japanese) or alphabetic traditions (Egyptian and West Semitic)" (Mattingly, 1985: 21). Mattingly emphasizes the importance of *productivity* in an orthography. A productive orthographic pattern is one which can be freely generalized to new forms to accommodate possible utterances of the language. A productive orthographic system is also one which enables the transcriptions of all the words in the language with some form of phoneticization. Because there are many ways and many levels in which linguistic utterances can be represented, it is not to the point to say that the alphabet is the most productive orthographic system or is necessarily the best way to write all languages. To answer this question, we would need to examine the principles by which orthographies represent language.

PRODUCTIVITY OF THE CHINESE ORTHOGRAPHY

The principles by which orthographies represent language vary along a continuum of linguistic transparency and opaqueness. The phonologically shallow or regular Serbo-Croatian does not encourage the kind of flexible coding processes as the phonologically deep English orthography (Feldman and Turvey, 1983). This assertion should not be taken to mean that access to the internal lexicon in the more transparent Serbo-Croatian is exclusively phonological. Empirical findings from Turvey and his colleagues suggest that it is much more efficient to automatize the general, transparent and productive relation between the bivalent Roman and Cyrillic letter patterns and phonetic forms of the phonologically shallow Serbo-Croatian orthography. In comparison, the 65 graphemic units in a corpus of 20,000 English words as analyzed by Venezky (1967) "are not related directly to sound, but to an intermediate morphophonemic level first and then to sound" (p. 84).

In this connection, the notion of a *practical orthography* can help us to understand both the productivity and learnability of such a system. Practical orthographies are presumed to be based on semantic representation of lexical content and not on phonetic renderings and that lexical items are transcribed morphemically because morphemes carry both semantic and phonological values. It is this abstract phonological knowledge that enables language learners to differentiate phonetic realizations of [s], [z], [ez] as in seat*s*, pay*s*, and judge*s*. Similarly, internal morphological representation of inflection and derivation helps learners to be aware of morphemic boundary rules in such words as MIS#HAP.

The question of interest is the way in which Chinese as a practical orthography contributes to productivity. It bears repeating that the equivalent of a WORD in Chinese is polymorphemic and consists of a combination of two or more characters. Chinese characters are linguistic units associated with morphemics rather than language-independent ideas and that they have an intricate internal structure encompassing both meaning ("morpho") and sound ("phonemics"). These characteristics are discussed in some details elsewhere (Leong, 1973; 1986). An example is shown in the formation of the character 江 (river). There the radical 氵 corresponds to "hydro" or water, and the phonetic 工, which means "work", provides the phonemic component. The phonetic component here, as in other instances, has a sense-discriminative function in discriminating the composite character from others with similar components. It also serves a sense-determinative function of denoting a morpheme or a word (the equivalent of "work"). Other examples from the signific radical 氵in 江 are 泳 (swim), 湖 (lake), and a number of other lexical items.

From this kind of combination and permutation within acceptable linguistic rules, it is estimated that a corpus of between 4,000 to 7,000 characters is reasonably adequate for practical purposes (Leong, 1973: Wang, 1973). While these characters do not map regularly or directly onto the phonological forms of the morphemes they stand for, they share certain features of the spoken language without representing it. This is achieved through the *double articulation* outlined above (see also Coulmas, 1984). In this sense, Vachek's (1973) proposal in his functionalist theory of written language that read or written language is an alternative form of spoken language with structural properties of its own may apply well to Chinese.

Principles of Phonology of Chinese

Traditionally, Chinese language is described as monosyllabic, isolating (compared with inflectional language), and analytic (with few bound forms).

Most of the characters (in excess of 80% of the corpus) are formed on the "phonetic compounds" principle, while the remainders are derived from the principles of pictographs, ideographs, "loan" and "analogous" characters (Leong, 1973, 1986; Wang, 1973). It is helpful to outline the principles of phonology in Chinese, as there is a lack of understanding of how Chinese characters are "pronounced".

In Chinese phonology, the Chinese character is traditionally divided into an initial and a final. The initial is the way a character (syllable) begins, usually with a consonant (e.g., [K] in [kən] 根 or "root"). The final of a syllable is the syllable minus the initial (e.g., [-ən] in the above example. There are a number of syllables (e.g., 安 [ən] or "calm") which do not begin with a consonant. These syllables are said to begin with the "zero initial". The initial and final of a character and a system of suprasegmental features known as tones play an important role in reading words and sentences.

In essence, the tone is primarily the pitch contour or pattern of the voiced part of the character, such that if the initial is voiced, the tone begins with the initial and spreads over the whole syllable; and if the initial is voiceless, the tone is spread over the final only. The classical tones of the Chinese language are: high level or even tone (꜀平), low rising tone (‘上), low falling or going tone (去’), and high rising or entering tone (入,), with the last-named tone generally having a shorter time duration. It should be noted that the actual pitch, the pitch range, and the time intervals of the syllables are relative to the voice of the individual and the mood at the time of the utterance.

There are some slight variations of the classical tones in Putonghua or the common (national) language, but the general principles are invariant. Putonghua is the language of the common people with pronunciation based on the Beijing dialect, the grammar of the northern dialects and the lexicon of modern literate Chinese. The arrangement of the four tones is shown schematically in Figure 1a. These four classical tones are subdivided into the higher and lower series with a middle series for the entering tone in the predominant southern dialect Cantonese, which is spoken by a considerable number of southern Chinese (Wong, 1968).

The nine variant Cantonese tones are portrayed in the musical scale in Figures 1b, 1c and 1d. Figure 1e illustrates the application of these principles of tones to read the /fu/ sound in Cantonese. In this connection, the characters classified under the entering tone in Cantonese typically end with the final stops /p, t, k/. In Putonghua, these final stops are glottalized and then truncated. This general process of the loss or truncation of final consonants is an indication of the progression of the different dialects in the direction of the common language (Wang and Cheng, 1970). The system of tones is important in distinguishing the considerable number of homophones which result from the dominance of vowel sounds over

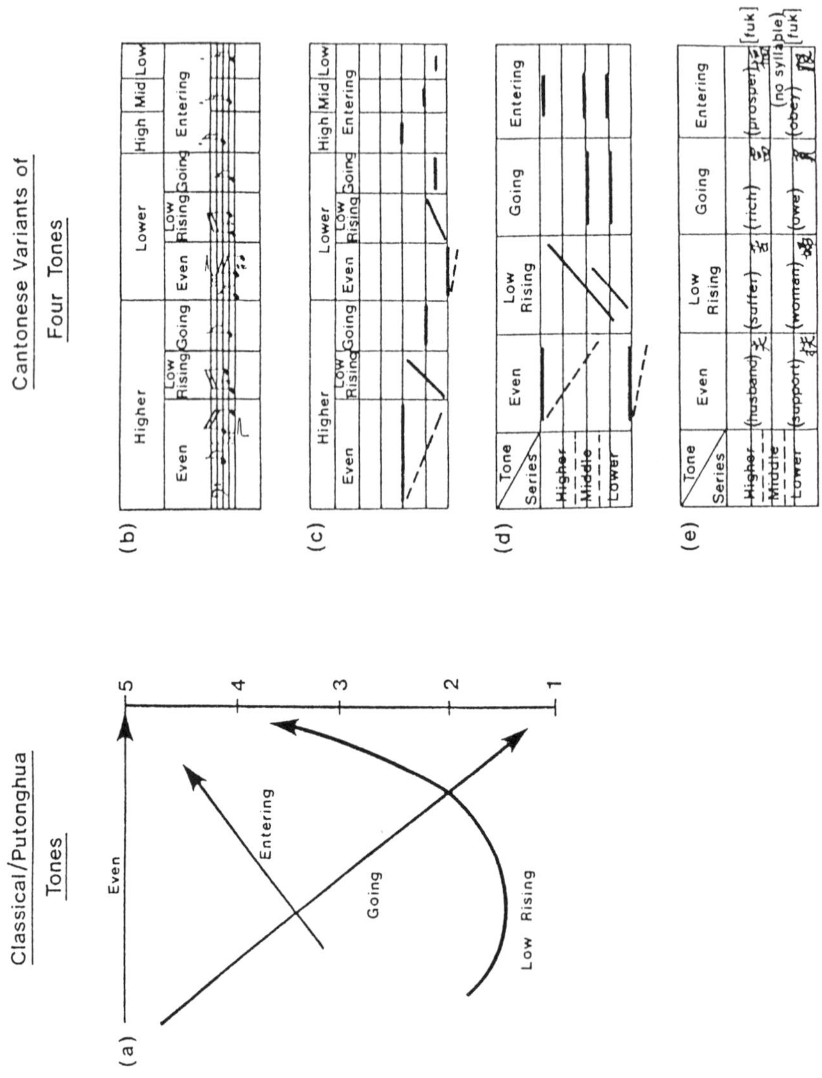

Fig. 1. Classical/Putonghua tones and Cantonese variants of four tones. (After Leong, 1986: Fig. 2.)

consonant sounds. The different tones must also be accommodated to avoid homophone collision in any word-unit phonetic conversion in computerizing Chinese, as will be discussed later.

Phonological Transcription of Chinese Characters

The "pronunciation" of individual Chinese characters is achieved by utilizing the principles of tones in general and the homonymous or rhyming characteristics of phonetic compounds sharing the same constituent phonetics in particular. One approach know as *direct pronunciation* uses the principles of (heterographic) homophones or characters identical in pronunciation but different in orthographic pattern. An example is 拾 (to pick up) read as the heterographic homophone 十 (ten). The disadvantage of this approach is that quite often there are no homophones to serve as the exemplars for pronouncing other characters or the exemplary homophones could be orthographically more complex and of lower frequency in usage than the character to be pronounced.

Another approach is to rely on *heterographic homophones* with variations in the tone. An example is 刀 (knife) which is pronounced on the basis of 到 (to arrive) by changing the going tone of the latter exemplar to the even tone to derive the correct pronunciation of the character "knife." This approach overcomes the shortcomings of the direct pronunciation, but the tone transformation presents its problems. Not the least is the conflict between the Putonghua system and the local dialects (e.g., Cantonese) leading to the degradation of tones.

A much more effective principle in pronunciation in use since about 600 A.D. is that of 反切 */fanqie/* [fantsi] (/q/ being an alveolo-palatal, aspirated affricate). This principle involves the combination of two and only two characters in such a way that the final of the first character and the initial of the second character are elided and that the tone of the to-be-pronounced character is the same as that of the second character. In other words, the initial of the first character and the final of the second character are "blended" after the elison of their respective final and initial. An example is the pronunciation of 條 or 条 (branch or strip), which is given as 徒聊 within the fanqie principle thus:

徒 [t'u] + 聊 [l'iau] = [t'] + [iau] = [t'iau] 條 or 条

The fanqie principle provides a powerful means of pronouncing Chinese characters, but is not immune from the drawback of the non-equivalence of tones of the to-be-pronounced character and of the exemplar because of vicissitudes of the sound system over thousands of years.

From the above discussion of several main principles in pronouncing Chinese it is clear there are generative possibilities in the phonology of Chinese as a practical orthography. For those not steeped in the writing system it is often thought that the productive procedure in pronouncing new characters is by recovering their sound directly from component phonetic radicals resembling known ones. While to some extent this approach via the phonetic radicals may work, it is the fanqie principle in the last analysis and historical antecedents that are more helpful in the productive aspect of pronouncing Chinese characters.

Lack of understanding of the fanqie principle and incomplete knowledge of etymological distinctions and separateness are the main reasons for misreading in Chinese (L. Wang, 1973). An example of misreading of the former kind is that of 吼 (to roar) which is pronounced by blending /fu/ and /hau/ and not by direct recovery of the phonetic radical 孔 as in the first syllable in Confucius. An example of misreading of the latter is the pair of characters 眼 /yen/ and 目 /mu/, both meaning eye, if /yen/ is pronounced according to the sound of the /mu/ radical. Etymologically, the derivation is from 限 /hsien/ (limit), which has a different meaning, and this derivation is the basis for the pronunciation.

It should be borne in mind that in the course of evolution over the millennia the phonology of the Chinese script has undergone considerable changes and that phonetic compounds may have lost their original characteristics. Despite these changes in the sound system, the meaning of the symbols remain relatively static. This can be illustrated from an excerpt in the classic *Book of Songs*:

風雨如晦，雞鳴不已

既見君子，雲胡不喜？

Wind and rain, dark as night,
The cock crowed and would not stop.
Now that I have seen my lord,
How can I any more be sad?
Arthur Waley: *Book of Songs*

Confucius or Mencius might have read the above in archaic pronunciation and we may read it in Putonghua or Cantonese. The pronunciation of the characters may vary, but there is little problem in understanding the poem. This stability in structure is one of the distinguishing features of the Chinese orthography.

Morphological Transcription of Chinese Characters

If the principle of phonology is not always invariant in the pronunciation of Chinese, the morphological characteristics of the orthography are much more productive (Chao, 1968). The richness of the recovery of new words in the orthography to make contact with the language is discussed in relation to morphological reduplication and affixation (both prefixes and suffixes).

Morphological reduplication is involved when a repetition or a partial repetition of a morpheme is directly related to a grammatical function. Reduplication may focus on the same or on different syllables and may take on different forms as follows: XYXY 叮噹叮噹 ("ding dong"), XXYY 家家戶戶 ("every home and house"), XXY 濛濛雨 ("drizzling [rain]"), XYXZ 大天大亮 ("in broad daylight"), XZYZ 買空賣空 ("buying empty, selling empty" or speculation). From the point of view of function, morphological reduplication is used for terms of address as in 媽媽 (mama); for miscellaneous compound nouns as in 娃娃 (baby), 洋娃娃 (foreign baby), 毛毛虫 (hairy insect); for distributive purposes as in 一人一塊 (one person one piece); and for emphasis of tone and stress as in 他漸漸了解了 (He gradually understands) with the same morpheme (third and last) undergoing a tonal change.

It is in *morphological affixation* or derivation that the Chinese orthography is most productive in mapping onto the meaning aspect of the language (Chao, 1968). Here the concepts of 實字 *full character* or full morpheme (analogous to the sense-determinative aspect) and of 虛字 *empty character* or empty morpheme (analogous to the sense-discriminative aspect) are useful, although the fullness or otherwise of meaning is a matter of degree, and not of kind.

Typically, productivity in affixation in Chinese is more concerned with empty characters or words. Some samples will be cited to show the versatility in prefixes and suffixes. In *prefixes* 禁 (prohibits) used before verbs can generate 禁用 (prohibit from using), 禁煙 (prohibit from smoking) . . . ; 可 (-able) can generate 可愛 (lovely), 可惡 (detestable), 可憐 (pitiable), 可笑 (laughable), 可靠 (reliable), 可口 (palatable), 可口可樂 (palatable, enjoyable as a translation for Coca Cola) . . . ; 好 (good) can generate 好吃 (good to eat), 好看 (good to look at or pretty), 好聽 (sounds good), 好做 (easy to do) . . . ; 自 (self or auto) can generate 自由 (freedom), 自動 (automatic), 自治 (self-rule), 自殺 (kills self or commits suicide), and others. Then there are many "foreign prefixes" to accommodate scientific words, new words or other loan words. These foreign prefixes are characterized by their departure from their usual grammatical functions to form new loan words. A good example is 準 which is normally an adverb as in 準時 (arriving in time), but is used adjectively as in 準學者 (quasi-scholar). Some other examples of foreign prefixes are: 單 (mono- or single) can generate 單細胞 (unicellular) . . . ; 多 (many or multi-) can generate 多音節 (polysyllabic), 多元論 (pluralism) . . . ; 汎 (pan-) can generate 汎美 (Pan-American) . . . ; 親 (pro-) as in 親美 (pro-American), 親共 (pro-Communist) . . . ; 反 (anti-) as in 反革命 (counter-revolutionary) . . .

In the Chinese orthography *suffixes* are more numerous than prefixes and are usually empty morphemes with neutral tone. These versatile end morphemes generate a considerable number of new words. Some examples are: 者 (-er) can generate 學者 (learner), 跑者 (runner), 筆者 (writer) . . . ; 然 (-ly) can generate 忽然 (suddenly), 自然 (naturally), 當然 (of course) . . . ; 人 (person or -er) can generate 工人 (workman), 証人 ("proof man" or witness), 媒人 (go-between), 夫人 (lady or Mrs.) . . . ; 心 (heart) can generate 良心 (conscience), 耐心 (patience), 同情心 (sympathy), 信心 (confidence). The so-called modern suffixes are usually translations from foreign suffixes. Some examples are: 論 (-ism) as in 唯物論 (materialism), 相對論 (relativism) . . . ; 率 (rate) as in 速率 (velocity), 效率 (efficiency), 生產率 (productivity) . . . ; 學 (-ology) as in 哲學 (philosophy), 心理學 (psychology) . . . ; 性 (-ty, -ness) as in 彈性 (elasticity), 伸縮性 (flexibility), 片面性 (one-sideness). Then there are miscellaneous suffixes to generate different grammatical categories. All in all, affixation in Chinese plays an important part in the way in which the morphemic script can be read productively.

PSYCHOLINGUISTIC ASPECTS OF LEARNING CHINESE

The above discussion of the characteristics of the Chinese orthography makes clear that while Chinese is morphemically based there are also phonological properties that help to recover the language. From a different perspective, while the English orthography is phonemically based, morphemic and morphological principles are needed in the productive use of the language. The interactions between languages and their orthographies have some bearing in the acquisition and development of literacy.

In the case of Japanese with its bi-scriptal kanji and kana the earlier suggestion that this system may explain the very small prevalence rate of reading disabilities in Japanese is found to be over-stated. The more recent postulate of Tsunoda (1985) linking the Japanese orthography with the Japanese brain dominance pattern and, by implication, with cognition is provocative. Tsunoda's putative finding of the "co-existence" of emotional and logical processes in the language-oriented left hemisphere as an explanation of the Japanese sensitivity to the world and his claim that Japanese are Japanese because they speak Japanese seem to remind us of the Whorfian hypothesis. These proposals need the support of a strong theoretical framework and vigorous experimental verification.

To return to Chinese, the assertion by Mattingly (1984: 19) that

> Logographic systems are the least demanding in this respect (language access), since access only to morphological and not to the morphophonemic aspects of the representation is required, but the obvious price paid is that a large set of characters must be remembered. Alphabetic systems, on the other hand, are the most demanding . . .

will need some modification. The suggestion that the initial advantage in learning to read might go to the Chinese, who would transcribe the morphemes in their script, as compared with the English, who would need to make contact with the language from acoustic and articulatory segments of phones and syllables, will need to be further investigated.

Morphemic Processing in Accessing Chinese

There is now considerable evidence that the rapid, automatic access of words as lexical items from the abstract, internal lexicon is necessary, though not sufficient, for reading comprehension (Downing and Leong, 1982; Leong, 1987; Perfetti, 1985). The psychological question of interest in learning the Chinese orthography is the role of visual processing in accessing the Chinese lexicon and if phonetic recoding also plays a part, at least at the working memory stage.

Some answers to the first question may be found from a series of experiments using the Stroop (1935) interference paradigm in reading Chinese (Biederman and Tsao, 1979; Fang, Tzeng, and Alva, 1981; Tsao, Wu, and Feustel, 1981). The general finding of the Stroop task is that subjects are much slower in naming colors when the colored ink spells the name of an incongruous or conflicting color. The explanation is that in performing the Stroop task subjects are aware of reading the print (even though instructed not to do so) and some mental effort and time are expended in suppressing what has been read in favor of naming the color. This interference effect has been shown in many languages (Bierderman and Tsao, 1979). The pertinent question is whether the magnitude of interference (the time taken to name the color with the incongruous or conflicting word minus the time needed to name the color of the unmarked patch) differs across scripts. This differential latency should provide some insight into the encoding of Chinese.

The several studies indicate that there are considerable difference in the magnitude of the Stroop interference effect and that the morphemic script produces much greater interference than either alphabetic or syllabary scripts. This was shown by Biederman and Tsao (1979) in comparing adult English and Chinese readers. These researchers also found consistently *smaller* Stroop interference times for the different comparisons (Spanish-English, Hungarian-English, French-English, German-English) and the overall mean times as well as smaller overall mean times for bilinguals than monolingual English controls. Results from these control tasks suggest that whatever retards the Stroop performance of the Chinese bilinguals is not due to their bilingualism. They are actually slower in naming the colors of the print when the incongruous words are in Chinese. Findings from Fang, Tzeng, and Alva (1981) extend this line of research and are strongly suggestive of a systematic relationship between the magnitude of Stroop interference and the degree of similarity between the scripts used. In a study to investigate between language and within language interference for

Chinese-English bilinguals, Chen and Ho (1986) found that language proficiency of the subjects and the compatibility between stimuli and responses affected response reaction time. When the source of interference is compatible with the response language (using Chinese to name Chinese items) there is greater interference than when the stimulus and response languages are not compatible.

The different Stroop studies indicate that readers of English generally cannot refrain from using the phonological system inherent in a phonemic script whereas readers of Chinese may not be able to refrain from the advantage of the configural morphemic script (Chen and Juola, 1982). It is likely that readers of different scripts will use the strategy which is the most appropriate or the most efficient for that script. For Japanese who use both the phonetic kana and the morphemic kanji there have been clinical observations about the dissociation of these processes in Japanese aphasic patients (Sasanuma, 1980). These clinical findings point to the application of specific strategies most suitable for the efficient processing of a particular script. The Japanese kanji is most likely processed through the orthographic code to gain access to the abstract internal lexicon, whereas in the Japanese kana access to the abstract internal lexicon is likely gained through the phonological code.

Phonetic Recoding in Accessing Chinese

The psycholinguistic analyses of the Chinese orthography and the findings from the Stroop interference paradigm should not be taken to mean that the access to the abstract, internal Chinese lexicon is *exclusively* via the visual or meaning route. The principle of etymology and the systems of tones cast some doubt on the oft-held belief that Chinese as a morphemic writing system maps onto speech at the level of words rather than phonemes and that Chinese readers can bypass the phonological route in reading. There is also psychological evidence from the work of Tzeng and his colleagues (see, Hung and Tzeng, 1981; Tzeng and Wang, 1983; for representative works) to suggest that phonetic recoding in reading Chinese may be needed some of the times at the working memory stage to aid text comprehension.

In Experiment 1 of Tzeng, Hung and Wang (1977) Chinese subjects were visually presented with 4 characters randomly selected, followed immediately by an oral interference task and were then asked to recall the previously presented 4 characters in order. The interference task was either phonemically similar or dissimilar to the target characters. The hypothesis was that if phonetic recoding occurred, then the interference characters would disrupt the memory for the to-be-recalled items. The results confirmed this hypothesis. The second experiment of Tzeng *et al.* using sentences (normal version and anomalous version) with phonemically similar words and phonemically dissimilar words provided further support for the hypothesis. Phonemic similarity was found to affect not only short-term retention of unrelated character but also the reading of meaningful sentences. The interpretation of these results is that the dual phonological and visual coding processes typically used in processing English could also apply to a morphemic script, but that the two processes are differentially utilized.

Recently, Seidenberg (1985) examined the issue of phonological and visual coding in reading both English and Chinese. The results show that in each script a large corpus of higher frequency words is recognized visually without phonological mediation and that phonological mediation applies only to processing of lower frequency words. The possible reason for this is that lower frequency words allow for or demand more time to use phonological information, to enable the lexical items in a cohort of linguistic candidates (Glushko, 1979) to activate their phonological representations. An alternative explanation is suggested by Liu (1988) in that phonological representations could be triggered by smaller word fragments for high frequency words so as to make the effect of the phonological variable not significant. The corollary is that the vocalization of a set of words could be *equally* phonologically mediated and this concept includes "not phonologically mediated" as a special case. Quite aside from Liu's logical explication, it is important to note that the Seidenberg findings stress the interactive process of word recognition in a chronometric or time-course framework.

Automatic Word Processing as Necessary for Reading Comprehension in Chinese

From a different perspective within the time-course information processing framework, Leong and his colleagues have found some evidence for the role of the rapid, automatic processing of Chinese characters and words (double characters) in reading comprehension in children (Chung, Cheng, and Leong, 1988) and in adult Chinese readers (Leong, Cheng, and Mulcahy, 1987).

In the Chung, Cheng, and Leong (1988) study, the subjects consisted of a total of 108 Chinese children with 36 children dichotomized as skilled and less skilled comprehenders in each of grades 4, 5 and 6. Experiment 1 involving lexical decision of 40 real Chinese characters selected according to printed frequency (high or low) and matched with 40 pseudo characters. A 3 (grade) × 2 (reading level) × 2 (lexicality) × 2 (frequency) ANOVA of reaction time measures (RTs) of the correct responses with repeated measures on the last two factors shows significant main effects for grade ($F(2, 102) = 4.09$, $p < 0.05$), lexicality ($F(1, 102) = 178.33$, $p < 0.001$), and frequency ($F(1, 102) = 59.81$, $p < 0.001$). Experiment 2 was another lexical decision task with 40 real Chinese words similarly selected and matched with 40 pseudo Chinese words. A 3 (grade) × 2 (reading level)

× 2 (lexicality) × 2 (frequency) ANOVA of the correct RT scores with repeated measures for the last two factors shows significant main effects for grade ($F(2, 102) = 4.06$, $p < 0.05$), lexicality ($F(1, 102) = 257.46$, $p < 0.001$), and frequency ($F(1, 102) = 145.54$, $p < 0.001$). These results are displayed in Figure 2, which shows the mean latency scores by grade, reading ability, lexicality and frequency for the Chinese characters (upper panel) and words (lower panel). Experiment 3 testing the utilization of sentential contexts in priming "congruous", "related", and "unrelated" target lexical items provides a further verification of the notion of automaticity in terms of one concept activating another concept as necessary for reading proficiency in children.

The results of Experiments 1 and 2 cannot be attributed to the more, or less, efficient use of the feature code in the global analysis of the characters and words because this will not show the lexicality effect. The three experiments taken as a whole suggest that older and more skilled readers have a more efficient lexical code to extricate more *relevant* information inherent in Chinese characters and words. In this sense, the findings support the general notion of verbal efficiency put forward by

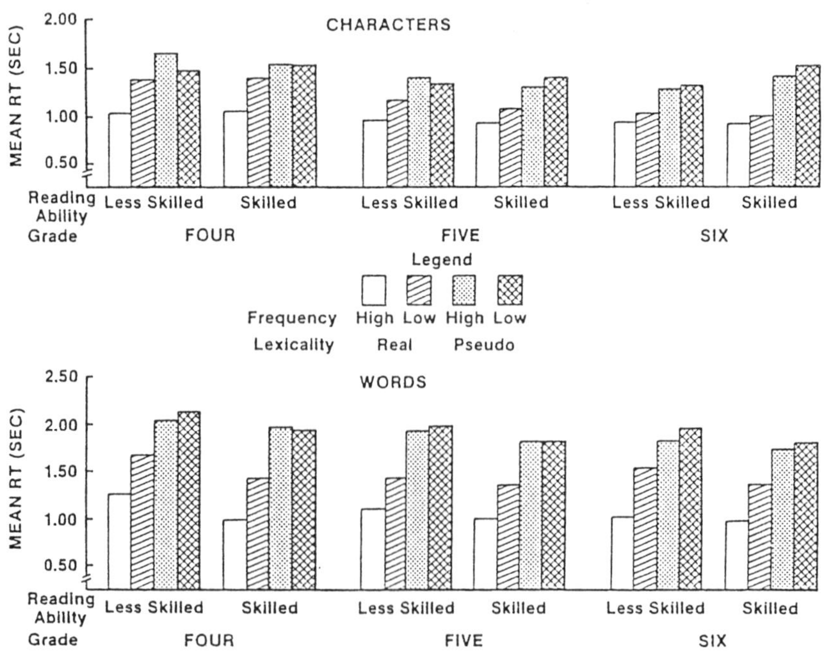

Fig. 2. Mean latency scores (sec) by grade, reading level, lexicality and frequency for Chinese characters (upper panel) and words (lower panel). (From Experiments 1 and 2 of Chung, Cheng, and Leong, 1988.)

Perfetti (1985) to explain the necessary role played by word processing in reading comprehension in English.

The Chung *et al.* study with Chinese children finds support in a parallel study by Leong, Cheng, and Mulcahy (1987) involving mature Chinese readers in vocalization and lexical decision experiments with single Chinese characters. The hypothesis tested was that rapid, automatic processing of lexical items in a morphemic orthography (Chinese) is necessary, though not sufficient, for reading comprehension. The subjects consisted of 23 skilled adult comprehenders contrasted with 23 less skilled adult comprehenders from a large subject pool of 166 subjects on the basis of a Chinese reading comprehension test with 12 passages and 50 comprehension questions.

Experiment 1 was a vocalization latency task with 80 open class Chinese characters selected according to printed frequency (high or low) and orthographic structure (simple or complex). Analyses of variance of the vocalization latencies of the correct scores show significant main effects of reader ability ($F(1, 44) = 17.79$, $p < 0.001$), printed frequency ($F(1, 44) = 308.20$, $p < 0.0001$), and orthographic structure ($F(1, 44) = 13.23$, $p < 0.001$); and the greater contribution to the variance of low frequency, complex characters. Experiment 2 was a lexical decision task with another 40 open class Chinese characters. Analyses of variance of the lexical decision latencies of the correct scores show significant main effects of reader ability ($F(1, 44) = 11.31$, $p < 0.01$), lexicality ($F(1, 44) = 88.10$, $p < 0.0001$), and orthographic structure ($F(1, 44) = 58.20$,

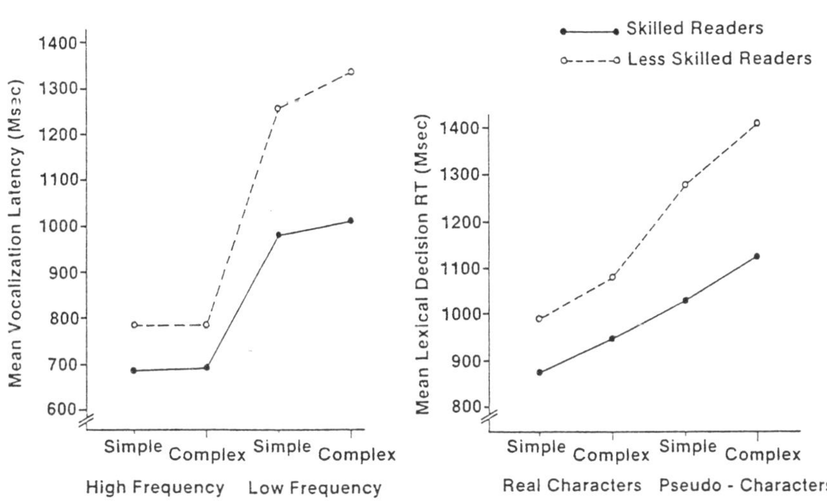

Fig. 3. Mean latency (msec) for vocalization and lexical decision tasks for skilled and less skilled readers. (Adapted from Leong, Cheng, and Mulcahy, 1987: Figs. 1 and 3.)

$p < 0.0001$); and the greater contribution to the variance by pseudo characters. The mean vocalization latency and mean lexical decision reaction time for the skilled and less skilled comprehenders are displayed in Figure 3. These results uphold the automaticity hypothesis and are generally confirmed by treating the items as random effects. The interaction of the various factors in the two experiments suggest their conjoint effects on the response or retrieval of access to the Chinese lexicon.

Commentary

The above results taken together suggest that skilled comprehenders have a more efficient lexical code to extract more *relevant* information inherent in Chinese characters and words. These findings from a different script parallel similar studies in English and support the verbal efficiency postulate of Perfetti (1985) as an explanation for one source of reading proficiency and reading difficulties. The extraction of relevant information in lexical access in Chinese is affected in the main by printed frequency, orthographic structure, and lexicality. The interaction of these factors also suggests their influence on the same stage of processing and it is likely that the response or retrieval stage of processing is most affected. In lexical decision experiments much depends on the discriminability of the characters or words and pseudo characters or pseudo words and the subjects' response criterion. These arguments have been proposed in accessing the English lexicon and could possibly apply to the access of Chinese lexical items (Seidenberg, 1985). In vocalization experiments with Chinese (e.g., Leong *et al.*, 1987, Experiment 1) it is likely that the Chinese characters are processed post-lexically in that lexical entries are first located, parsed and phonetic recoding used if necessary (see also, Hung and Tzeng, 1981; Tzeng *et al.*, 1977).

That phonetic recoding is used in accessing the English lexicon is generally supported in the literature (see Wagner and Torgesen, 1987, for review). The covariance theory of van Orden (1987) suggests that phonological coding has a much more protracted development than hitherto thought and that the effect of spelling-to-sound correspondence or, alternatively, the conflict of spelling and sound patterns is of critical importance, particularly to poor readers. These various findings should not preclude the use of the visual or graphemic code in processing English, at least some of the time; just as phonetic recoding would need to be utilized at times in the processing of Chinese.

Hung, Tzeng, Salzman, and Dreher (1984) presented further evidence on this question of the interplay of phonological and visual coding in general. With three experiments across two different writing systems (Chinese and English) they found that only good readers are able to use the phonological route as a support or backup system when the visual route is disturbed by mixed-case distortion. They also suggested that good readers may not need to bypass the phonological route as for such readers word recoding would be rapid and automatic. From a different perspective, Besner and Hildebrandt (1987) have shown that for Japanese subjects orthographically familiar words printed in the Japanese katakana are named faster than orthographically unfamiliar words and nonwords all printed in katakana because the visual or orthographic route is generally faster than the phonological route. These results are taken to mean that as in English lexical access of words written in the phonetic katakana could be achieved, under certain circumstance, without reference to phonology. Reviewing evidence on lexical access from pathological and intact subjects in selected cross-linguistic studies, Besner (1987) raises the question of the extent of similarity between the different visual and phonological codes across orthographies. He suggests that the phonological code involved in reading kana would be more related to articulatory mechanisms than would phonological processing in English.

From the literature it would seem that there are some common psychological processes in lexical access in different orthographies, but the nature of the representation may differ (Besner, 1987).

Computerization of Chinese

The computer technology has an important role to play in the development of literacy. It is often argued, and quite rightly, that the morphemic script such as Chinese and the Japanese syllabary with its kanji script may not be conducive to such a technology (Unger, 1984; 1987). Nevertheless, there are advances and that computerized typing and editing are now available in many orthographies, including Japanese and Chinese (Becker, 1984; Chu, 1985). According to Becker, a flexible encoding system of superalphabets enables the computer to deal with some 16 million characters including Chinese and a phonetic conversion system (with the use of romaji conversion in some systems) facilitates the conversion from hiragana to kanji with considerable success.

In the computerization of Chinese four main input systems have been reported (Becker, 1984; 1985; Hu, Chang, and Huang, 1977; Huang, 1985). These are the whole character system, arrangement by radicals, the Three Corner Coding Method and the word-unit phonetic conversion system. In the whole character method, each character is given a two-byte code and the user has to make a visual search of the characters from a large keyboard. This is time-consuming and makes considerable cognitive demand on the user. The arrangement by radicals (a corpus of 214 radicals) is an improvement, except that there are no hard and fast rules on the demarcation of radicals and fairly complex computer softwares are needed. The third approach, the Three Corner Coding Method is favored by Huang and his colleagues as a "good candidate for use on a worldwide scale" (Huang, 1985: 23). This method basically sorts patterns of strokes of characters into a logical system of 99 major and 201 minor symbols and uses a horizontal and a vertical format in its architecture. The code for any character according to this method is determined by the six digits for the major or minor symbols.

The fourth approach, that of the word-unit phonetic conversion system, is also discussed by Huang and is particularly advocated as "merely superior to any of the alternatives" by Becker (1985: 32). In essence, this system makes use of these psycholinguistic principles: (a) phonetic conversion of word units rather than Chinese characters, (b) morphological and grammatical parser, and (c) disambiguation of rare and bound homophones. An example to illustrate these principles is from the Japanese kana "kuruma-de" (by car) and "ku-ru-made" (until coming). Both lexical items are grammatically derived from roots of "kuruma" (car) and "ku" (come) and the computer will need to parse the input by using a morphological grammar of the language. Similar systems of phonological and morphological parsing are needed in the computerization of Chinese and Becker suggests that the time spent on learning Putonghua and systems of phonetic conversion of Chinese characters and words is more worthwhile than that spent on learning some coding schemes.

In general, there are two main phonetic conversion systems in Chinese. One is 注音符號 the system of *phonetic symbols*, which is sometimes known as "bopomofo" to designate the first four letters ㄅㄆㄇㄈ. The other system is 拼音 *pinyin* or Chinese language spelling (e.g., "gongzuo" for 工作 or work). Whichever system is adopted , the input mechanism to the computer is similar. Becker (1985) gives an example of the Chinese word 漢字 (hanzi or Chinese word) which is homophonous with 漢子 (fine man) and the two words differ only in their tones. The user first enters the phonetic spelling either in bopomofo or through pinyin and presses the lookup key. With homophones such as shown, the user has to press a further key designated as "1, 2, 3, 4" for the four tones and zero for unstressed syllables to disambiguate the tones. Thus "hanzi" can be encoded as "han4zi4" and "fine man" as "han4zi0". This system of computerization making use of word-unit phonetic conversion, grammatical parsing and accommodation for variant tones has much to recommend itself. The difficulty is with the mastery of either the bopomofo phonetic symbols or the pinyin systems. In particular, the tonal variations are not always easily demarcated by the users. This new learning for many Chinese may be a reasonable price to pay if the ease in computerization brings much benefit in literacy development. In the 1980s and the years ahead, knowledge acquisition extends beyond what Popper (1972: 238–239) envisages as accruing from the use of "papers, pens, pencils, typewriters, dictaphones, the printing press and libraries" to include the mainframe, mini- and micro-computer technology.

SUMMARY

Writing systems differ in the way in which they transcribe the possible words in the abstract internal lexicon and as expressions of different languages. As a practical orthography Chinese may be as *productive* as many other writing systems. "Pronunciation" of Chinese characters is achieved with some measures of success through several linguistic principles, particularly that of fanqie. It is in derivational morphology that Chinese is the most productive. Morphological principles of reduplication, affixation are utilized to write the large number of possible utterances of the Chinese language.

From the psychological perspective, access to the Chinese lexicon is most efficient via the visual or orthographic route, but phonetic recoding is also needed at times, particularly at the working memory stage to aid text comprehension. Experimental studies in Chinese both parallel and support the verbal efficiency postulate as a source of variation for reading comprehension in English. Though there are common psychological processes in the access of the internal lexicon in different orthographies the precise nature of visual and phonological coding and the underlying representation will need to be further delineated. In the computerization of the Chinese orthography for literacy development there are now sophisticated hardware and software input systems based on the internal structure of the characters or phonetic conversion through the use of phonetic symbols of bopomofo or pinyin. It seems clear what the noted linguist Chao (1968) called the operational efficiency in terms of information per chunk in Chinese could with advantage be combined with some phonetic transmission system for computerization. All these technological advances will have considerable social, cognitive and linguistic consequences.

NOTE

* This is an expanded version of a paper read at the Invitational Symposium on "Scripts and Literacy: East and West" held at the McLuhan Centre on Culture and Technology, University of Toronto, June 1–4, 1988. Part of this paper is based on Leong: 1986, *Annals of Dyslexia*, 36, 82–102.

REFERENCES

Becker, J.D.: 1984, 'Multilingual word processing', *Scientific American* **251**: 96–107.

Becker, J.D.: 1985, 'Typing Chinese, Japanese, and Korean', *Computer* **18**: 27–34.

Besner, D.: 1987, 'On the relationship between orthographies and phonologies in visual word recognition', in A. Allport, D. Mackay, W. Prinz, and E. Scheerer (eds.) *Language perception and production*, Academic Press, London, pp. 211–226.

Besner, D. and Hildebrandt, N.: 1987, 'Orthographic and phonological codes in the oral reading of Japanese Kana, *Journal of Experimental Psychology: Learning, Memory, and Cognition* **13**: 335–343.

Biederman, I. and Tsao, Y.-C.: 1979, 'On processing Chinese ideographs and English words: Some implications from Stroop test results', *Cognitive Psychology* **11**: 125–132.

Chao, Y.R.: 1968, *Language and symbolic systems*, Cambridge University Press, London.

Chen, H.-C. and Ho, C.: 1986, 'Development of Stroop interference in Chinese-English bilinguals', *Journal of Experimental Psychology: Learning, Memory, and Cognition* **12**: 397–401.

Chen, H.-C. and Juola, J.F.: 1982, 'Dimensions of lexical coding in Chinese and English', *Memory and Cognition* **10**: 216–224.

Chu, Y. (ed.): 1985, 'Chinese/Kanji text and data processing' [Special Issue], *Computer* **18**(1): 11–66.

Chung, C.M., Cheng, S.C., and Leong, C.K.: 1988, 'Interaction of reader and stimulus characteristics in children's recognition of Chinese', in I.M. Liu, H.-C. Chen, and M.J. Chen (eds.) *Cognitive aspects of the Chinese language (Vol. 1)*, Asian Research Services, Hong Kong, pp. 41–56.

Coulmas, F.: 1984, 'Arbitrariness and double articulation in writing', in L. Henderson (ed.) *Orthographies and reading*, Hillsdale, NJ, pp. 57–66.

Downing, J. and Leong, C.K.: 1982, *Psychology of reading*, Macmillan, New York.

Fang, S.P., Tzeng, O.J.L., and Alva, L.: 1981, 'Intralanguage vs. interlanguage Stroop effects in two types of writing systems', *Memory and Cognition* **6**: 609–617.

Feldman, L.B. and Turvey, M.T.: 1983, 'Word recognition in Serbo-Croatian is phonologically analytic', *Journal of Experimental Psychology: Human Perception and Performance* **9**: 288–298.

Gelb, I.J.: 1963, *A study of writing*, University of Chicago Press, Chicago.

Glushko, R.: 1979, 'The organization and activation of orthographic knowledge in reading aloud', *Journal of Experimental Psychology: Human Perception and Performance* **5**: 674–691.

Goody, J. and Watt, I.: 1963, 'The consequences of literacy', *Comparative Studies in Society and History* **5**, 304–345.

Hu, L.R., Chang, Y.W., and Huang, J. K.-T.: 1977, *The Three-Corner Coding Method: The digitalized Chinese dictionary*, Northern Gate Book, Taipei.

Huang, J. K.-T.: 1985, 'The input and output of Chinese and Japanese characters', *Computer*, 18, 19–24.

Hung, D.L. and Tzeng, O.J.L.: 1981, 'Orthographic variation and visual information processing', *Psychological Bulletin* **90**: 377–414.

Hung, D.L., Tzeng, O.J.L., Salzman, B., and Dreher, J.: 1984, 'A critical evaluation of the horse-racing model of skilled reading', in H.S.R. Kao and R. Hoosain (eds.) *Psychological studies of the Chinese language*, Chinese Language Society of Hong Kong, Hong Kong, pp. 75–101.

Jensen, H.: 1970, *Sign, symbol, and script* (3rd ed.), George Allen and Unwin, London.

Kratochvil, P.: 1968, *The Chinese language today*, Hutchinson, London.

Leong, C.K.: 1973, 'Hong Kong', in J. Downing (ed.) *Comparative reading*, Macmillan, New York, pp. 383–402.

Leong, C.K.: 1986, 'What does accessing a morphemic script tell us about reading and reading disorders in an alphabetic script?' *Annals of Dyslexia* **36**: 82–102.

Leong, C.K.: 1987, *Children with specific reading disabilities*, Swets and Zeitlinger, Lisse, The Netherlands.

Leong, C.K.: 1989, 'A schoolman's "Doubtfulness" – Metaphors on literacy and cognition', in C.K. Leong and B.S. Randhawa (eds.) *Literacy and cognition: Theory, research, and application*, Plenum, New York, pp. 17–31.

Leong, C.K., P.-W. Cheng, and Mulcahy, R.: 1987, 'Automatic processing of morphemic orthography by mature readers', *Language and Speech* **30**: 181–197.

Liu, I. M.: 1988, 'Context effects on word naming: Alphabetic versus logographic languages', in I.M. Liu, H.-C. Chen, and M.J. Chen (eds.) *Cognitive aspects of the Chinese language, (Vol. 1)*, Asian Research Service, Hong Kong, pp. 81–92.

Mattingly, I.G.: 1972, 'Reading, the linguistic process, and linguistic awareness', in J.F. Kavanagh and I.G. Mattingly (eds.) *Language by ear and by eye*, MIT Press, Cambridge, MA, pp. 133–147.

Mattingly, I.G.: 1984, 'Reading, linguistic awareness, and language acquisition', in J. Downing and R. Valtin (eds.) *Language awareness and learning to read*, Springer-Verlag, New York, pp. 9–25.

Mattingly, I.G.: 1985, 'Did orthographies evolve?' *Remedial and Special Education* **6**(6): 18–23.

Mattingly, I.G.: 1987, 'Morphological structure and segmental awareness', *Haskins Laboratories Status Report on Speech Research SR-92*, 107–111.

Olson, D.R. (ed.): 1987, 'Understanding literacy' [Special Issue], *Interchange* **18**(1/2): 1–173.

Olson, D.R.: 1988, 'Writing', in P.W. Goetz (ed.) *The New Encyclopedia Britannica, (Vol. 29)*, Encyclopedia Britannica, Inc., Chicago, pp. 982–1006.

Olson, D.R., Torrance, N., and Hildyard, A. (eds.): 1985, *Literacy, language and learning: The nature and consequences of reading and writing*, Cambridge University Press, New York.

Perfetti, C.A.: 1985, *Reading ability*, Oxford University Press, New York.

Popper, K.: 1972, *Objective knowledge: An evolutionary approach*, Clarendon Press, Oxford.

Sampson, J.: 1985, *Writing systems: A linguistic introduction*, Stanford University Press, Stanford, CA.

Sasanuma, S.: 1980, 'Acquired dyslexia in Japanese: Clinical features and underlying mechanisms', in M. Coltheart, K.E. Patterson, and J.C. Marshall (eds.) *Deep dyslexia*, Routledge and Kegan Paul, London, pp. 48–90.

Seidenberg, M.S.: 1985, 'The time course of phonological code activation in two writing systems', *Cognition* **19**: 1–30.

Stroop, J.R.: 1935, 'Studies of interference in serial verbal reactions', *Journal of Experimental Psychology* **18**: 643–661.

Tsao, Y.-C., Wu, M.-F., and Feustel, T.: 1981, 'Stroop interference: Hemisphere difference in Chinese speakers', *Brain and Language* **13**: 372–378.

Tzeng, O.J.L., Hung, D.L., and Wang, W. S.-Y.: 1977, 'Speech recoding in reading Chinese characters', *Journal of Experimental Psychology: Human Learning and Memory* **3**: 621–630.

Tzeng, O.J.L. and Wang, W.S.-Y.: 1983, 'The first two R's', *American Scientist* **71**: 238–243.

Tsunoda, T.: 1985, *The Japanese brain: Uniqueness and universality* (Y. Oiwa, Trans.), Taishukan Publishing, Tokyo.

Unger, J.M.: 1984, 'Japanese orthography in the computer age', *Visible Language* **XVIII**: 238–253.

Unger, J.M.: 1987, *The fifth generation fallacy: Why Japan is betting its future on artificial intelligence*, Oxford University Press, New York.

Vachek, J.: 1973, *Written language: General problems and problems of English*, Mouton, The Hague.

van Orden, G.C.: 1987, 'A rows is a rose: Spelling, sound, and reading', *Memory and Cognition* **15**: 181–198.

Venezky, R.L.: 1967, 'English orthography: Its graphical structure and its relation to sound', *Reading Research Quarterly* **2**: 75–105.

Wagner, R.K., and Torgesen, J.K.: 1987, 'The nature of phonological processing and its causal role in the acquisition of reading skills', *Psychological Bulletin* **101**: 192–212.

Wang, L.: 1973, *Chinese phonology*, Chung Hwa Publishing, Hong Kong (in Chinese).

Wang, W. S.-Y.: 1973, 'The Chinese language', *Scientific American* **228**: 50–63.

Wang, W. S.-Y. and Cheng, C.C.: 1970, 'Implementation of phonological change: The Shuangfeng Chinese case', *Papers for the Sixth Regional Meeting of the Chicago Linguistic Society*.

Wong, S.L.: 1968, *A Chinese syllabary pronounced according to the dialect of Canton*, Chung Hwa Publishing, Hong Kong (in Chinese).

INSUP TAYLOR AND KWONSAENG PARK

12. DIFFERENTIAL PROCESSING OF CONTENT WORDS AND FUNCTION WORDS: CHINESE CHARACTERS VS. PHONETIC SCRIPTS

INTRODUCTION

This study explores two issues related to scripts and reading. First, any language has two kinds of words, content words and grammatical morphemes, and readers develop the strategy of processing the former more carefully than the latter. Second, this strategy is easier to develop in Korean and Japanese texts where content words are written in logographic, and visually complex, Chinese characters, while grammatical morphemes are written in visually simple phonetic scripts.

Since Chinese characters are discussed in several chapters in this volume, especially in "Introduction" by the editors, here we will make only a few observations on them.

Chinese characters are used by about one quarter of the world population, by Chinese, Koreans, and Japanese. Characters in a comprehensive dictionary can number as many as 50,000, of which a few thousand are designated for common use. For such numerous characters to be discriminable, they have to be complex in shape, with their strokes ranging from 1 to 64. Up to a few hundred common and simple characters are easily learned, even by preschoolers (see Tanaka, this volume). But it requires time and effort to master a few thousand of them, especially when each character has multiple readings, as in Japanese (see Yamada, in this volume). One is driven to ask, Why are characters not given up in favor of a simpler script? Gaur (in this volume) suggests that they are kept for national unity in China or prestige in Japan and not for any linguistic reasons.

Contrary to Guar, there are many good linguistic reasons for keeping Chinese characters, as explored in detail elsewhere (Taylor and Olson, and also Hoosain, in this volume). The Chinese language is full of homophones, which are differentiated in Chinese characters. The Korean and Japanese languages contain numerous Sino-Korean and Sino-Japanese words (words borrowed from Chinese hundreds of years ago). The meanings of such words are grasped faster and more accurately when written in logographic characters than in phonetic scripts.

Of many experiments that show processing differences between logographic characters and phonetic letters, we will cite only one. Typically a Japanese word that can be written in two Kanji (Chinese characters used in Japan) can be written in 2-to-5 Hiragana or Katakana (two forms of the Japanese syllabary). In Saito's experiment (1981) on comprehension,

I. Taylor and D.R. Olson (eds.), Scripts and Literacy, 185–195.

sentences containing Kanji words were responded to faster than those containing Kana words. Two-morpheme Sino-Japanese compound words are customarily written in Kanji, and not in a Kanji-Kana mixture. Saito's test words included uncustomary Kanji-Kana words as well as Kana-Kanji words. The subjects comprehended the sentences containing the former faster than the latter.

Why are sentences containing Kanji words comprehended faster than those containing Kana words? In Japanese and Korean texts logographic characters tend to be used to write content words, while phonetic scripts tend to be used to write native grammatical morphemes. Such differential uses of Chinese characters and a phonetic script in a text has important implications on reading processes. Specifically, important words tend to be written in darker, more complex characters and less important words in lighter, simpler phonetic scripts. The different appearances of two types of words should promote their differential processing.

In processing any object or event, an efficient processor will differentiate important components from unimportant ones and process the former more deeply than the latter, thus using limited cognitive resources to the best advantage. The differential processing of important and unimportant information has been amply demonstrated in reading or listening to stories and passages (e.g., Johnson, 1970; Shebilske and Fisher, 1981).

Consider P.G. Hamerton's sentence

The art *of* reading *is to* skip judiciously.

The content words (in plain font) in Hamerton's sentence convey semantic contents, and hence are considered important, while the function words (in italics) have little semantic contents of their own (though they relate or modify the content words), and hence are considered less important. A reader can recover almost no meaning of Hamerton's sentence from a sequence of its four function words,

the, of, is, to,

while she can do so from a sequence of its four content words

art, reading, skip, judiciously.

Content words (CWs) in most languages include nouns, verbs, adjectives, and some adverbs. But grammatical morphemes (GMs) tend to differ among unrelated languages: articles and prepositions in English; particles in Chinese; and postpositions and verb and adjective inflectional endings in Korean and Japanese.

Among English FWs, some (*the*, *of*, *is*, *to*) are short, frequent, have little semantic content, unstressed, and so on, and are called prototypical FWs. When college students were asked to delete from a passage as many words as possible but without impairing comprehension by readers (as in composing a telegram), they deleted prototypical functions words leaving undeleted content words (cited in Taylor and Taylor, 1990: 89).

That a skilled reader differentially processes CWs and prototypical FWs has been shown in eye-movement studies. Figure 1 shows that fixation durations roughly reflect the relative importance of words in a sentence. Note that the prototypical FWs are not even fixated.

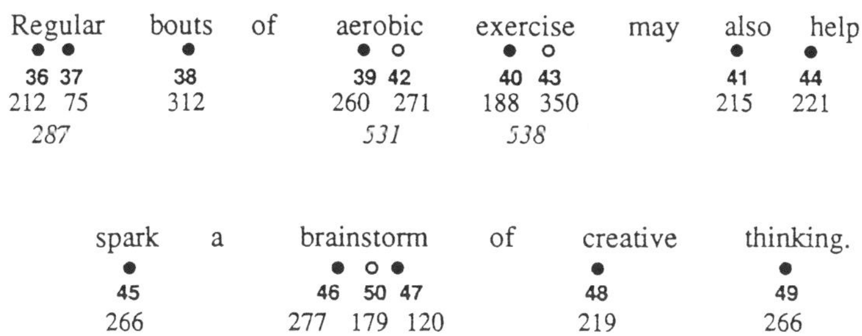

Fig. 1. Eye movements during reading. Solid dots indicate the loci of fixations; open dots indicate regressive fixations. Numbers indicate: in boldface, the order of fixations; in plain font, fixation durations in msec; and in italics, gaze durations (Taylor and Taylor, 1990, Fig. 5-1, adapted from Rayner and Pollatsek, 1989, Fig. 4-1; by permission of Prentice Hall, Inc., Englewood Cliffs, NJ).

Once more, the questions asked in this chapter are: First, any language has two kinds of words, content words and grammatical morphemes, and readers develop the strategy of processing the former more carefully than the latter. Second, this strategy is easier to develop in Korean and Japanese texts where content words are written in logographic, and visually complex, Chinese characters while grammatical morphemes are written in visually simple phonetic scripts. But first we will study differential processing of CWs and FWs in English text.

The chapter reports five experiments: simple Experiment 1 on English script and reading as a warm up for, and comparison with, the main study, i.e., Experiments 2, 3, 4, and 5 on Korean scripts and reading.

ENGLISH CONTENT WORDS AND FUNCTION WORDS

In English text, visual distinction between CWs and prototypical FWs is provided, roughly, by word length: CWs tend to be long (an average 5 letters) compared to prototypical FWs (on average 2 letters). This visual distinction can be enhanced by manipulations such as printing CWs in boldface or printing FWs in small size.

Experiment 1: English CWs and FWs in Different Fonts

Materials and Procedures. Three passages were taken from three different chapters of Gail Sheehy's *Passage: Predictable Crises in Adult Life* (1974/76). The three were same in length (923 words after slight adjustment) and were assumed to be similar in readability and style. Each of the three passages was divided into nine paragraphs, which, along with a page of instructions, were stapled together to form a booklet.

Each of the three passage was assigned to one of three experimental conditions: I. CWs in boldface; II. prototypical FWs in small print; III. plain font. A sentence in condition I looks like,

The **art** of **reading** is to **skip judiciously**.

The first page of each booklet was instructions to subjects, printed in the condition in which the subjects would read. The instructions read:

Read silently this passage, one paragraph per page. When you finish reading each paragraph, raise your head; I will record your reading time and ask comprehension questions.

Comprehension questions were three-item multiple questions on contents, one question per paragraph.

Subjects and Design. Subjects were nine graduate students, who were paid $5 for the task that took about 50 min. Each subject read all the three passage/conditions, one at a time, and answered comprehension questions. The order in which the nine subjects read the three passages/conditions is systematically varied, as shown in Table 1.

TABLE 1
Order of reading three passage/conditions (English).

Subject	Passage/Conditions		
1,4,7	I	II	III
2,5,8	II	III	I
3,6,9	III	I	II

I. CWs in boldface; II. FWs in small print; III. plain font.

Results. The subjects's comprehension was satisfactory and is not discussed further. For each subject, the three passage/conditions were rank ordered in terms of reading speed. For most subjects, the ranks from the fastest to the slowest were: CWs in boldface, FWs in small print, and plain font. The three conditions differed significantly. So, enhancing visual distinction between CWs and prototypical FWs did speed reading. Between two ways to enhance visual distinction, CWs in boldface was more effective than FWs in small prints.

KOREAN HANCHA AND HAN'GŬL

In Korean writing, CWs and GMs tend to be written in two different types of scripts, Hancha (Chinese character or characters) and Han'gŭl (alphabetic syllabary), respectively. The Korean grammatical morphemes include postpositions that come after nouns to indicate the grammatical roles of the nouns and verb or adjective endings. Visually, Hancha (1 to 26 strokes) tend to be more complex than Han'gŭl syllable blocks (2 to 8 strokes) (see Figure 2, below). GMs are native Korean and are written in Han'gŭl, whereas the majority of CWs are Sino-Korean and can be, though need not be, written in Hancha.

Four experiments, one in Canada and three in South Korea, were carried out to see whether (1) a passage that expresses CWs in Hancha is read faster than a passage that expresses both CWs and GMs in Han'gŭl, and (2) if so, what proportion of CWs-in-Hancha is optimal.

Experiment 2: Reading Passages in Three Proportions of Hancha Words (Canada)

Test Materials. Three editorials from one Korean newspaper, the *Korea Times*, were selected as reading materials. The three editorials were assumed to be similar in readability and style, having been written for the same newspaper on similar topics (political-economic) perhaps by the same editor.

For the experiment the three editorials were re-written in such a way that one editorial contained 0% Hancha, the second 10% Hancha, and the third 50% Hancha. The editorials remained the same in contents and structure, regardless of their proportions of Hancha. Figure 2 shows the same sentence with 0% and 50% Hancha (selected from the passages used in Experiment 3 to be reported below).

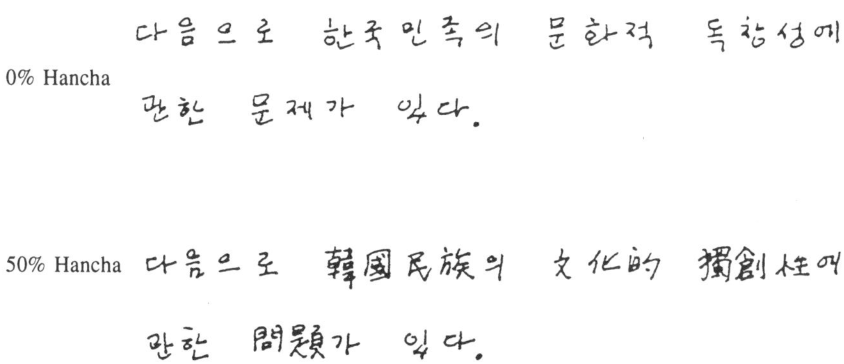

Fig. 2. The same sentence with 0% Hancha (or all-Han'gŭl) and 50% Hancha. The sentence says, "Next, there is a problem concerning the Korean people's cultural originality."

Each passage (973 words after minor adjustments) was divided into seven segments, each segment containing one to two paragraphs. The seven segments were stapled into one booklet.

Subjects were nine (four female and five male) adult Korean immigrants (aged between 30 and 49) in Toronto, Canada. Eight of them have college education and one has high-school education; all read Korean newspapers. Each subject was paid $5 for the experimental task that lasted for about 50 min.

Hancha Recognition. The first part of the experiment was Hancha recognition as tested on three-item multiple-choice questions. For this test, 30 words that can be written in two Hancha were selected from the test materials, and each Hancha word was written on one index card. Out of 30 Hancha words, 10 were randomly selected for each subject, who had to recognize minimum 8 out of 10 Hancha words to qualify for the main experiment.

Passage Reading. For the main experiment of passage reading, the subjects were numbered 1 to 9 in the order of their appearance, and the passages were numbered I (0% Hancha), II (10% Hancha), and III (50% Hancha). The design ensured that each subject read all the three passage/Hancha proportions whose order of presentation varied systematically, as shown in Table 1 for the English passages.

The instructions to the subjects were similar to those given to the English-speaking subjects in the Experiment 1. Comprehension questions were as follows.

1. (After reading each page) List three key words.
2. What is the main point of this page?
3. (After reading the whole passage) What is the title of this editorial?

Results and Discussion. All subjects passed the Hancha recognition test. They also answered the comprehension questions satisfactorily. To see whether subjects' reading times varied for the three proportions of Hancha, the data were analyzed in the same manner as for the English data in Experiment I. The totals of rank orders were: 12 for 0% Hancha, 22 for 10% Hancha, and 20 for 50% Hancha; 0% Hancha passage was read faster than either 10%- or 50%-Hancha passage. An analysis of variance using repeated measure was significant at $p < 0.001$ ($F2, 34 = 51.19$).

The passage with CWs-in-Hancha was expected to be read faster than the one with no Hancha, but the results are opposite from what was expected. How are the negative results explained? Today, most Korean reading materials in South Korea as well as Canada tend to be written in Han'gŭl only. Most likely, because of their unfamiliarity, Hancha words are recognized slower than the equivalent Han'gŭl words. In an earlier experiment in which a subject read a Hancha-Han'gŭl mixed (53%–47%) passage and a Han'gŭl-only passage on a computer screen, exposing each word at his or her own pace, the same words took longer to read in Hancha than in Han'gŭl (Kang *et al.* cited in Taylor and Taylor, 1983, p. 89). Furthermore, on the Hancha recognition test of Experiment 2, the average correct recognition score was 8 out of 10; thus the subjects' knowledge of the Hancha words in the passages was less than perfect.

Experiment 3: Reading Passages in Three Proportions of Hancha Words (Korea)

Experiment 3 repeated Experiment 2 with different sets of passages and subjects. Subjects were university students in Korea whose textbooks tend to contain some Hancha.

Procedures. Reading materials were 15 paragraphs taken from a university textbook used in Korea. The 15 paragraphs were divided into three sets according to the proportions of Hancha, as in Experiment 2: I. 0% Hancha; II. 10% Hancha; and III. 50% Hancha (see Figure 2, above). The order of presentation of the three sets was systematically varied for the subjects, as in Experiments 1 and 2 (see Table 1, above). Unlike in Experiment 2, the reading materials were displayed on a computer screen, one paragraph at a time.

Subjects were 18 female and male sophomores in a Korean university. They were instructed to read each paragraph as fast as they could and then to answer comprehension questions, which consisted of listing keywords and the topic sentence of the paragraph. When a subjects finished reading, he or she pressed a response key that stopped a timer and erased the paragraph from the computer screen.

Results and Discussion. All subjects answered the comprehension questions satisfactorily. For all subjects, without an exception, the reading speed was the fastest for "I. 0% Hancha," intermediate for "II. 10% Hancha," and slowest for "III. 50% Hancha." The differences in reading times between the three conditions is significant in an analysis of variance (p < 001; F2, 24 = 10.05).

Experiment 4: Naming Han'gŭl or Hancha Words

In an earlier experiment, Korean-Canadian subjects took longer to silently read Hancha words than Han'gŭl words (Kang *et al.*, cited in Taylor and Taylor, 1983: 89). In Experiments 2 and 3, the Hancha-Han'gŭl mixed passages may have been read slower than the Han'gŭl-only passage because individual Hancha words were read slower than Han'gŭl words. Experiment

4 attempted to equate naming (reading aloud) times of Hancha words with those of their Han'gŭl equivalents by providing practice for the former.

Procedures. From the Experiment 3 materials 85 CWs written in Hancha were taken, and these words were made into Han'gŭl words in one list and were left in Hancha in the other list.

Subjects were 13 female and male juniors at a university in Korea. They were asked to read aloud each word presented in the center of a computer screen. Presenting a word triggered a timer, which stopped when a subject named the word. The list of Han'gŭl words was presented twice, to obtain each subject's mean naming time. But the list of Hancha words was presented repeatedly, between 9 and 15 times over two to three days, until its naming time became faster and similar to that for the list of Han'gŭl words.

Results. After practice on Hancha naming, the naming time per word per subject was 0.56 sec for Han'gŭl words and 0.58 sec for Hancha words. The reading times of the two lists of words are similar, though they are slightly faster for Han'gŭl words.

Experiment 5: Reading Passages in Three Proportions of Hancha Words: after Practice

The subjects of Experiment 5 were the same 13 juniors who practised in naming Hancha words in Experiment 4. And the test materials and procedures were the same as those used in Experiment 3.

Figure 3 shows the effect of practice, by comparing the times to read the same materials by two groups of subjects, one without practice with Hancha words in Experiment 3 and the other with practice in Experiment 5. The practice dramatically reduced the reading times for all the three sets of materials. The effect of practice was largest for the 50% Hancha, intermediate for the 10% Hancha, and smallest for the 0% Hancha. The difference between 0% and 10% almost disappeared after practice.

If only a few days of practice with Hancha makes such a difference, how much more effective would a few months or few years of practice be? Chinese characters are difficult to master, but once enough of them are learned, they can be useful in reading.

GENERAL DISCUSSION

The set of five experiments investigated whether enhancing visual distinction between important CWs and unimportant FWs/GMs will speed passage reading. The results were positive in the English experiment but negative in the Korean experiments. Why? English words in different fonts

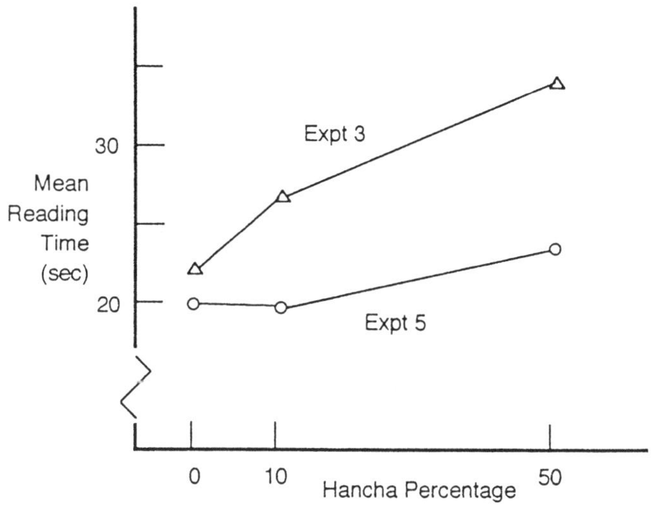

Fig. 3. Effect of practice on Hancha words: the times to read the same passages by two groups of subjects, one without practice in Experiment 3 and the other with practice in Experiment 5.

are still the same words in the same scripts. By contrast, Korean words in Han'gŭl and Hancha are the same words in two quite different scripts. And Korean readers, even university students, are more practiced in reading Han'gŭl words than Hancha words. In Experiment 5, several hours of practice in reading aloud Hancha words narrowed, though did not eliminate, the differences in reading times between the all-Han'gŭl passages and the passages containing the practised Hancha words.

In discussing the Korean results, it is instructive to consider the Japanese language and its scripts. Korean and Japanese are similar in their GMs, in having Sino-Korean/Japanese words, in using Chinese characters, along with a native phonetic script. But there are some differences in details.

Japanese content words tend to be written in Chinese characters, whether they are of Chinese or Japanese origin, more than do Korean content words. Consider the word *hana*, a Japanese native word with two meanings, "flower" and "nose," which are usually written in Kanji, 花 for "flower" and 鼻 for "nose." By contrast, the Korean native words for "flower" and "nose" do not have Hancha for them and are written in Han'gŭl syllable blocks. (The Hancha for "flower" may be used for a Sino-Korean word, such as *hwa-byŏng* "flower vase.") Thus, Japanese readers can develop the strategy, "Spot and process Kanji words at the expense of Hiragana words." Korean readers too develop the equivalent strategy but with much less confidence, for they cannot ignore Han'gŭl words, which might be important content words.

In Japan Sakamoto photographed the eye movements of college students reading the same short sentences written once in Hiragana (syllabary) only and once in Hiragana mixed with Kanji. The all-Hiragana sentences required twice as much time and showed a shorter perceptual span, more frequent fixations, longer fixations, and more regressions (cited in Sakamoto and Makita, 1973). A Hiragana-Kanji mixed text was read faster than an all-Hiragana text, perhaps because the former is familiar than the latter, and/or because the mixed text, but not the pure Hiragana text, allows differential processing of content words and grammatical morphemes. Even when the familiarity is controlled, still words are comprehended faster in Kanji than in Kana (see Saito, 1981, cited earlier).

In Japan, Kanji are indispensable, and are taught from grade 1 in primary schools. All reading materials, except those intended for preschoolers, contain many Kanji. By contrast, in South Korea, Hancha are taught not in primary schools but in middle and high schools. And Hancha tend to be used sparingly in newspapers, magazines, and books. Perhaps because Hancha are not taught and used extensively, even sophomores and juniors are not well practised with Hancha reading. Consequently, Hancha in a passage may slow down the reading of that passage, just as was found in the present study. Hancha should be taught thoroughly and used extensively, as in Japan, for them to serve useful functions; otherwise, they should not be taught at all, thus saving time and energy expended in learning and using Hancha.

There may be yet another reason why the Korean results differ from the Japanese results. In visual appearance, difference in complexity between Hancha (1 to 26 strokes) and Han'gŭl syllable blocks (2 to 8 strokes) is smaller than between Kanji (1 to 24 strokes) and Hiragana (1 to 6 strokes). In other words, CWs in Hancha do not stand out from GMs in Han'gŭl syllable blocks in a Korean text as much as do CWs in Kanji from GMs in Hiragana in a Japanese text.

A reviewer of this research suggested that the Korean study should repeat the English one (boldface for CWs and plain font for GMs). Such a study may be worth doing in the future, but it will not address one of the questions asked in this research, namely, the role of Chinese characters in Korean texts.

In conclusion, visual distinction between important CWs and less important GMs facilitates differential processing of the two types of words, and hence text processing. The differential processing has been demonstrated with English reading and Japanese reading but not with Korean reading, perhaps because Chinese characters (in which CWs are written) are not well practised in Korea as are in Japan. Chinese characters are useful only when they are well practised.

Today, wherever Chinese characters are used – the People's Republic of China, the Republic of China (Taiwan), Singapore, Japan, South Korea

– there is a great debate on whether to abolish or keep Chinese characters. Toward resolving the debate, one must consider various factors, such as the availability of an efficient script that can replace Chinese characters and the role Chinese characters play in reading.

ACKNOWLEDGMENTS

Taylor thanks Helena Fivi Chitiri and Yong-Gon Kim for carrying out Experiments 1 and 2, respectively, in Toronto, Canada. These two experiments were supported by a Connaught Foundation grant to the McLuhan Program. Park thanks Seung-Eun Choi for carrying out Experiments 3, 4, and 5, in Daegu, South Korea.

REFERENCES

Johnson, R.E.: 1979, 'Recall of prose as a function of the structural importance of the linguistic units', *Journal of Verbal Learning and Verbal Behavior* **9**: 12–20.

Kang, J., Chong, J., and Taylor I.: 1983, 'Reading in all-Hangul or Hangul-Kanji mixed scripts', in I. Taylor and M.M. Taylor, *The psychology of reading*, Academic Press, New York.

Saito, Hirofumi: 1981, 'Use of graphemic and phonemic encoding in reading Kanji and Kana', *The Japanese Journal of Psychology* **52**: 266–273.

Shebilske, W.L. and Fisher, D.F.: 1981, 'Eye movements reveal components of flexible reading strategies', in M.L. Kamil (ed.) *Directions in reading: Research and instruction*, National Reading Conference, Washington, DC.

Sheehy, G.: 1974/76, *Passages: Predictable crises of adult life*, Bantam Books, New York.

Rayner, K. and Pollatsek, A.: 1989, *The psychology of reading*, Prentice Hall, Englewood Cliffs, NJ.

Sakamoto, T. and Makita K.: 1973, 'Japan', in J. Downing (ed.) *Comparative reading*, Macmillan, New York.

Taylor, I. and Taylor, M.M.: 1990, *Psycholinguistics: Learning and using language*, Prentice Hall, Englewood Cliffs, NJ.

PART III

EARLY STAGES OF LEARNING TO READ

MIHO T. STEINBERG

13. TEACHING JAPANESE TODDLERS TO READ KANJI AND KANA

> When I have explained everything and they still ask me, all over again, "Why do you start them so young?" I say, "Why would you deprive a child of such great joy for so long?"
>
> Shinichi Suzuki
> (Originator of the method to teach violin to young children)

I. EIGHT COMMON MISCONCEPTIONS

There are a number of misconceptions that most Japanese have regarding reading fundamentals. Eight of these fundamental conceptions are:

1. The ability to speak and to speak clearly is necessary for learning to read and to be a good reader.
2. The ability to write, to form kanji and kana, is necessary for learning to read.
3. Kanji (Chinese style characters) such as 自動車 (*jidosha* car), 橋 (*hashi* bridge), 薬 (*kusuri* medicine), and 乾電池 (*kandenchi* battery) are more difficult for a child to learn to read than single kana (Japanese syllabic script (such as い (i), ク (ku) ら (ra).
4. Single kana such as イ (i), く (ku), and ラ (ra) are easier for a child to read than whole kana words such as テレビ(*terebi* television set), うどん (*udon* noodles) パンダ (*panda*).
5. Single kana should be taught first so that children will then be able to read kana words.
6. Children should be taught to read words in kana before they learn to read words in kanji.
7. Two year old children do not know enough language to be taught to read.
8. Two year old children are intellectually too young to learn to read, especially kanji and books written in kanji.

It is because most people, including reading educators, hold such misconceptions that there has been little progress in teaching reading to young children in Japan. Until such fundamental misconceptions are corrected, there will be no progress.

I. Taylor and D.R. Olson (eds.), Scripts and Literacy, 199–214.

II. THE TRUE CONCEPTIONS

1. False: The Ability To Speak And To Speak Clearly Is Necessary For Learning To Read And To Be A Good Reader.

   True: Speaking Is Irrelevant For Reading.

Even children who are too young to speak can begin to learn to read. For example, our own son, Kimio, who was slow in speaking, nevertheless was able at 24 months of age to identify 48 written words, phrases and sentences, even though he could say only 15 of them (This was in Hawaii and the language was English). For example, if we would call out a word such as "dog", which he could not say, he still could search through his stack of written cards on which words were written and find the right one. Or, if we gave him the card on which was written *Open the door*, he would look at the card and go open the door (Steinberg and Steinberg, 1965).

It is important to realize that even if children never acquire the ability to speak, they can still learn to read. In this regard, our colleagues and we were able to teach a three-year-old girl to read kanji and kana words even though she had been unable to speak since birth (Steinberg and Chen, 1980). She was, however, able to hear and understand speech (what others said) without difficulty. But, even if she had been deaf, as some of our other research subjects were, she could have been taught to read (Steinberg, 1982; Steinberg, 1984; Steinberg, Harada, Tashiro, and Yamada, 1982; Steinberg, Harada, Tashiro, and Yamada, 1982).

It should be kept in mind that reading involves the ability to understand the meaning of what is written. Whether or not what is written can be pronounced is irrelevant to the reading process. Thus, in teaching children, one need not require that they speak. And, if they can speak, one should not worry about their pronunciation. Trying to correct their pronunciation when teaching reading can frustrate and distracts them from the true purpose of reading, which is getting meaning from the written forms.

2. False: The Ability To Write, To Form Kanji and Kana, Is Necessary For Learning To Read.

   True: Writing Is Irrelevant For Reading.

Children can learn to read, and read well, without being able to write. Research with colleagues shows that by four years of age, children can be reading books which Japanese children in Grade 2 and beyond read, even though they have little writing ability (Steinberg, Yoshida, and Yagi, 1985). As we all know, young children have little of the physical control of the fingers and hand that is necessary for making the fine coordinated movements (Steinberg and Yamada, 1980). Making reading dependent on the ability to write, as is generally done in school, slows down the potential of readers. If reading and writing are to be connected, it is writing which should follow reading.

Reading essentially involves the visual processing of written forms. Whether a person can create those forms is irrelevant for reading. The situation is similar to our being able to identify the faces of people and other things in our environment. We can recognize faces easily, but it is only with great difficulty that we can draw those faces, if at all.

3. False: Kanji Are More Difficult For A Child To Learn Than Single Kana.
   True: Kanji Are Easier To Learn Than Single Kana.

Research with colleagues shows that children have *less* trouble learning to read kanji words than they do single kana. (Learning to write kanji is, of course, more difficult than writing single kana.) We have found that children will learn complicated kanji such as 乾電池 (*kandenchi* battery) and 薬 (*kusuri* medicine) faster than single kana forms such as イ (*i*) and く (*ku*) (Steinberg and Oka, 1978; Steinberg and Yamada, 1977). This is because the sounds which are said when the kanji are seen are more interesting and meaningful than those which are said with kana. Kana generally are just syllables and not words for the child. They are less meaningful and of less interest. What is meaningful is learned more quickly regardless of how complex the written form may be. Actually, we find that children learn meaningful kanji at least *twice* as fast as single kana! Often, children will remember a kanji on just being shown it once or twice, providing that the kanji involves a word that they know. The memory of young children for retaining complex kanji is amazingly good in this regard.

4. False: Single Kana Are Easier For A Child To Read Than Whole Kana Words.
   True: Kana Words Are Easier To Learn Than Single Kana.

When the learning of single kana, イ (*i*), く (*ku*), ら (*ra*), etc. is compared with that of whole kana words, テレビ (*terebi* television), こたつ (*kotatsu* a kind of foot warmer), アイスクリーム (*aisukurimu* ice cream), etc., we find that it is the words that are learned faster (Steinberg and Yamada, 1977). In fact, the kana words, whether in hiragana (cursive syllabic script) or katakana (simplified syllabic script), are learned at the same rate as kanji words. This again indicates that children are mainly responding to meaning. They do not care how long or how complex a written word is, nor do they care whether it is written in kanji or kana. What they are interested in is the meaningfulness or content of what they are reading.

5. False: Single Kana Must Be Taught First So That Children Will Then Be Able To Read Kana Words.
   True: Single Kana Need Never Be Taught, Only Kana Words.

People generally assume that the only way that children will be able to read kana words is by teaching them single kana first, by some sort of rote method. However, there is a better way. Children should be taught whole kana words right from the start. (The words, of course, must be ones that they already know from hearing in speech, otherwise the words will not be meaningful. This also applies to kanji words, too.) While learning to read kana words, children will notice, *on their own*, that certain kana always occur with certain speech sounds (Steinberg, 1981). They notice, for example, the ビ in テレビ (*terebi* television) and in ビール (*biiru* beer) and as a result form a connection between the written form ビ (*bi*) and the speech sound of "bi".

By the time the children have learned about 50 katakana or 50 hiragana words, they will have learned by induction to identify most of the individual component kana symbols on their own (Steinberg, Yoshida, and Yagi, 1985). Thus, children only need to be taught written forms which interest them, that is, meaningful words.

Children need never be given single kana to learn, something that generally proves boring to them since much more practice is required in their learning. Furthermore, children who are not taught by the single kana method will be more fluent readers. They will not read in a slow unnatural syllable by syllable fashion but will read quickly to recover words and their meaning by sight. Any new words, however, will be read by them in the syllable by syllable fashion.

6. False: Children Should Learn To Read Words In Kana Before They Learn To Read Words In Kanji.
   True: Kana Should Not Be Taught Before Kanji.

Nowadays, children in school are generally taught to read hiragana, the cursive syllabic script, before kanji. And, prior to World War II, katakana, the simplified syllabic script, was taught first (Shuto, 1977). There is no sound basis for either of these practices. Instead of wasting children's (and teachers') time in learning to read a multitude of words in hiragana which they will rarely ever read again いぬ (*inu* dog), やま (*yama* mountain), てれび (*terebi* television set), etc., children should be taught the regular forms of words right from the start, that is 犬 (dog), 山 (mountain), テレビ (television set). After all, in order to be good readers they must be able to read these words in kanji and katakana (the proper kana form for television set) anyway. Learning all the words first in hiragana does not make it significantly easier for the child later.

Thus, one should not select written words for teaching on the basis of whether they are written in kana or kanji, as is usually the case. Actually, *any* order is good. The only consideration should be whether the word is a meaningful or interesting one for the child. Since the child will learn to read words more or less equally fast whatever system of writing is used, one may as well use the proper writing form to begin with.

7. False: Two Year Old Children Do Not Know Enough Language To Be Taught To Read.
True: Language Knowledge Need Not Be Well Developed.

A partial knowledge of language is all that is needed for the children to learn to read without difficulty. Actually, the ordinary two year old can understand many vocabulary items (dog, cat, milk, boy, girl, run, walk, drink, eat, big, small, red, etc.) and a large number of phrases and sentences composed of those items (The boy is big, small cat, Drink the milk, etc.) (The 1, 2 and 3 year olds mentioned in the following section, #8, demonstrate this point very dramatically.)

There is, therefore, more than enough language knowledge that the child has with which to begin the teaching of reading. We teach the child to read the language (in speech) that the child can understand. We do not teach language items that the child does not know. As the child's knowledge of language expands, then, too, can the complexity of the reading materials be expanded.

8. False: Two Year Old Children Are Intellectually Too Young To Learn To Read, Especially Kanji And Books Written In Kanji.
True: Two Year Olds Can Learn To Read, Even Books Written In Kanji.

Two year olds can learn to read and can enjoy doing so, according to our two long term research studies. The first involves teaching 2 and 3 year olds in a Hiroshima preschool (Steinberg and Sakoda, 1982). The second involves three 1 and 2 year old Hiroshima children who were taught to read at home by their parents (Steinberg, Yoshida, and Yagi, 1985). The results of these studies will be presented in detail in the following section.

There is a widespread belief that children are not sufficiently intelligent to be able to learn to read at such ages as 2 or 3 years, or even 4 years. What people fail to appreciate is that such young children have *already* succeeded in a much greater intellectual achievement. That achievement concerns their learning of language. Child language acquisition research shows that the speech understanding of a 2 year old is rather well developed, with a great complexity in terms of form and meaning, even if their ability to speak is at a lower level. Since when children learn to read they are essentially only learning visual labels for words which they already know through hearing speech, it is clear that reading is much less of an accomplishment than that of language learning.

Furthermore, the memory of young children is truly remarkable. Younger children can remember a very complex word form with just one or two showings, as long as those words are ones that are meaningful form to them (Steinberg and Oka, 1978; Steinberg and Yamada, 1977).

III. LONG TERM RESULTS

1. *The Preschool Research*

In the preschool study, there were 21 children, all from an ordinary working class neighborhood in Hiroshima. They ranged in age from 20 months to 38 months when the teaching (in accord with our program) began, with most children being around $2^1/_2$ years old. After 8 months of instruction, about 15 minutes daily, the children learned an average of 101 words, phrases and sentences. After another 8 months, that figure just about doubled, with the number of phrases and sentences greatly increased. Most of the single words were kanji, many being the names of other children in the class. Table 1 shows sample items learned by one typical 2 year old after receiving 16 months of classroom teaching, by which time she was a little older than 3 years. She learned a total of 185 words (138 kanji and 47 kana) and 29 phrases and sentences.

TABLE 1
Sample items learned by a 2-year old girl

kanji	机	desk
(total 135)	椅子	chair
	洗う	to wash
kana	みかん	tangerine
(total 47)	テレビ	T.V.
phrases and sentences	ごめんなさい	I'm sorry
(total 29)	顔を洗いましょう	Let's wash our faces

2. *The Home Research*

While such results may appear impressive, they pale beside those of the three children who were taught to read at home. These children were taught to read by their parents in accord with our program. After only 12 months, with only 15 minutes or less of instruction daily, the one boy (Yutaka) and the two girls (Hitoko and Tomoko), (both of whom were sisters) were able to read simple books on their own! During this period, Yutaka learned at least 561 words and 198 phrases and sentences. Of the 561 words learned by Yutaka, 284 were kanji. For Hitoko and Tomoko, 170 of the 304 words were kanji. A large number of the kanji which the children learned were ones which the Japanese Ministry of Education reserves for teaching in Grades 4, 5, and 6 of elementary school. A general reading test, the Sakamoto Reading Diagnostic Test, was given to the children. You can see in Table 2, at ages of 3 and 4 years, the children

TABLE 2
Results of Sakamoto Standard Reading Test

	Yutaka 4 yr 2 mo		Hitoko 3 yr 11 mo		Tomoko 4 yr 10 mo	
	Grade		Grade		Grade	
	Year	Semester	Year	Semester	Year	Semester
Word recognition	1	2	1	3	2	2
Understanding sentences	2	2	2	1	3	2
Understanding phrases	1	3	2	2	3	1
Reading Kanji	3	2	2	2	3	1
Total	2	2	2	2	3	1
Reading age	8 yr 0 mo		7 yr 11 mo		8 yr 6 mo	
Reading index (100 = Average)	192.0		202.1		175.9	

Note: In each school year there are three semesters.

are between Grades 2 and 3 of elementary school in their overall achievement.

According to the test, the children have a reading Age of around 8 years. Actually, their true reading ability is greater than the test results show, because the test was designed for children about twice their age. The instructions and the way the test is given is very hard for little 3 and 4 year olds to follow.

By the time the children were entering elementary school, their kanji vocabulary was quite impressive, especially in the case of Yutaka. Testing by an independent tester showed that Yutaka knew almost all of the Grades 1, 2, and 3 Ministry of Education required kanji; most of the Grade 4 ones and a good proportion of the Grade 5 and 6 ones. All this when he was only 6 years 3 months old! (Steinberg, Yoshida, and Yagi, 1985)

The children, now in elementary school, are at a reading level two or more grades beyond that of their school mates. For all three, reading is one of the greatest sources of pleasure. They follow their own interests and use reading as a means for satisfying their curiosity and furthering their knowledge.

The fact that the children at home were able to learn so much more than the children in the preschool, even though they had been taught on the basis of the same reading program and had received about the same amount of instruction time daily (15 minutes) is likely due to differences in teaching individuals and groups. Fifteen minutes spent with a group of children is not as effective as fifteen minutes spent with one or two children. A teacher with many children in a classroom simply cannot do as much for the individual child as can the parent with just one or two children at home. A parent can discover exactly what the child does or does not know and then make adjustments to fit the needs of the child.

IV. THE TEACHING PROGRAM

1. *The Program Steps*

The reading program which had been developed to teach reading to the researchers' son in the past, was modified and used for this program. Using word as the minimal unit, the procedure which was used in teaching to read English worked similarly well with Japanese.

The reading program consists of four steps: 1. *Word Familiarization*, 2. *Word Reading*, 3. *Phrases and Sentence Reading*, and 4. *Book Reading*. Each step involves essential ideas and knowledge which the child must acquire. By the completion of the last step, the child will have learned all of the basics of reading that are necessary for fluent reading at his or her language and intellectual level.

The steps are ordered so that each preceding step serves as the basis for the one which follows. Thus, Step 1 Word Familiarization is the basis for Step 2 Word Reading, Step 2 is the basis for Step 3, and so on. It is important to note, however, that a prior step may be continued along with the ones that follow. For example, Step 2 Word Reading may be continued even though the child has proceeded on to Step 3 or even Step 4. Continuation is beneficial for the child because there is almost no end to learning vocabulary. There are always new words to learn.

2. *The Basic Ideas of the Steps*

The ideas involved in each of the steps are briefly described below.

Step 1: Word Familiarization. The purpose of this step is to acquaint children with the shapes of written forms and to make them aware of the idea that these forms are related to objects and spoken words of the language. With respect to written forms, when the child first looks at them, they have no meaning for them. All that he or she sees is a jumble of lines with little distinguishing features. What the child must learn is to notice how written forms are different from one another; that they have different shapes and different patterns. The child will do this as long as he or she is exposed repeatedly to written forms and is encouraged to inspect them for similarities and differences. In this step, the child does *not* have to remember particular written forms; that comes later in Step 2.

That written forms can symbolize words (or objects) is the key to learning to read. The child must come to realize that written forms are not meaningless lines but that each has a different meaning. Once the child gets this idea, the child is ready to word. That is what is learned in the second step, that of Word Reading.

Step 2: Word Reading. In this step, children must learn which particular written form is connected with which particular spoken word (or object). They must learn, for example, that パンダ (panda) is associated with the spoken word パンダ ("panda") while the form of 猫 (cat) is associated with the spoken word of 猫 ("neko"). It is not enough that the child knows, as in Step 1 Word Familiarization, that the form of パンダ and of 猫 represent some spoken words. Now, they must learn which particular written form goes with which particular spoken word (or object).

Grammatical function items like *desu* (be) and the various grammatical particles (*wa*, *ga*, *de*, *no*, etc.) should not be taught as separate items. They should only be taught indirectly in the context of phrases and sentences, as in Mary *no* inu (*no*'s; *inu* dog) independent items, they lack interest and are low in meaningfulness. Children who are given such items to learn will quickly get bored.

The child will be ready to go on to the next step, that of learning to read phrases and sentences, when about 50 or so individual words have been learned. With a variety of nouns, verbs and adjectives, the child will have little trouble in learning phrases and sentences which are made out of these words.

Step 3: Phrase and Sentence Reading. This step is similar to the preceding one except that larger written units, the phrase and sentence, are dealt with. Its goal is for the child to read phrases and sentences with ease and understanding. It is not necessary that phrase teaching be done before sentence teaching. Whatever unit is of interest in a particular situation is what should be taught, e.g., '*a black dog* or '*The dog is black*'.

It is in phrase and sentence teaching that the child becomes exposed to various function words and a variety of particles and learns to read them through context. Children will have no difficulty in learning such items when those items are contained in phrases and sentences that interest them.

Step 4: Book Reading. Learning to read books is probably the most interesting of all reading activities for children, since there is an excitement that a story can generate which the reading of isolated words, phrases and sentences cannot. The purpose of this step is to provide children with the knowledge and experience that will enable them to read books on their own.

The reading of books involves something more than just the reading of sentences. It special feature is that it consists of sentences that are meaningfully related to one another. Since books range widely in the number and length of sentences which they contain, the best strategy is to select the shorter ones first. Further, the stories should be simple, ones that the child can easily understand. Actually, books can also be made at home. For example, a series of photographs or pictures involving the life of the child can be pasted on a page along with some written sentences. A trip to the zoo which the child has taken would make a good little enjoyable story book. Such personal books hold great interest for children.

It should be emphasized that although the child is systematically taught to read books at this last step of the reading program, this is not to imply that books should not be introduced before this time. On the contrary, books should be read to children just as soon as they can follow a story. Reading books to the child at as early an age as possible will make the child familiar with the nature of books and stimulate interest in them. In this way, the child will be well prepared when he or she is taught book reading in this final step.

3. *Summary of the Four Steps*

The essentials of the four steps are summarized in Table 3. The goals and nature of each step is noted.

TABLE 3
Summary of the four steps of the reading program

Step 1: Word familiarization
- Children become familiar with the shapes and patterns of written words.
- Children become aware that written words are meaningful and are related to spoken words and objects.

Step 2: Word reading
- Children learn which particular written word is connected with which particular spoken word or object. For example, the written word of *neko* is connected with the spoken word "neko" or the animal cat.
- Children learn to read a variety of meaningful words. These are mainly nouns, verbs and adjectives. Function words such as *ga* (subject marker), *no* (possessive marker), *wa* (topic marker) are not taught.

Step 3: Phrase and sentence reading
- Children learn to read larger units, phrases and sentences. These phrases and sentences will contain many of the single words which they have previously learned.
- Children learn to read function words in the course of learning phrases and sentences – *watashi no hon* (my book) and *Hana wa kiree desu* (Flowers are pretty), for example.

Step 4: Book reading
- Children learn to read a sequence of sentences which are meaningfully related to one another, that is to say, stories.
- Children become independent readers.

V. GUIDING TEACHING PRINCIPLES

The approach which we believe should be taken toward the teaching of reading may be expressed in terms of four guiding principles: 1. Teach Meaningful Words, Phrases and Sentences in a Natural Situation, 2. Teach Only Items the Child Understands in Speech, 3. Teach Through Play, and 4. Expose the Child to Written Items. Each of these principles will now be discussed.

1. *Teach Meaningful Items in a Natural Situation*

The words, phrases and sentences that are interesting for the child, that are part of the child's everyday life, are the kind of written items which should be selected for teaching. The more the written items are concerned with the objects and events in the child's everyday life, the more the child will be eager to learn them. For example, if the child wants to eat noodles or play with a toy car, then the words, *udon* (noodles) and *jidosha* (car) can be written and taught. Similarly, phrases and sentences with those words like *oishii udon* (delicious noodles), *akai jidosha* (a red car) and *Jidosha ga hoshii* (I want a car), can be introduced.

Since there are more than enough naturally occuring items in the home environment to teach, one never has to worry about a lack of items to write down. However, the items which are selected for teaching should be ones that the child *already* can understand when one says them. In this way, one will always be sure that the child knows the meaning of the item which one has decided to teach.

2. *Teach Only Items the Child Understands in Speech*

One should avoid teaching new words, phrases and sentences to the child when teaching reading. If the child does not know the word "eraser" or the phrase "tall building" in speech, then such items should not be taught as part of the reading program. Learning new speech items places an additional burden on the child. We do not want the child to experience frustration or develop any sort of bad attitude towards reading as a result. As long as the teaching of reading is based on speech which the child is familiar with, there will be no danger of the child being strained by being given reading materials beyond his or her intellectual level.

We estimate that 24 months of age is when all ordinary children can begin to learn to read based on the results of a number of research studies. By then, children will have developed sufficient understanding of speech and also sufficient knowledge of how to participate in play activities and games. Because the reading program uses various play activities for the purpose of teaching, the child must be mature enough to be able to do these activities, even though they may appear to be utterly simple to adults.

Thus, while reading can be taught earlier than 24 months of age (as our own research shows), we believe that given the wide range of differences in children a later age is a safer choice. A younger child who is slow to learn language and to get the ideas involved in playing simple games may experience some frustration and parents and teachers may become disappointed and give up on the reading program.

3. *Teach Through Play*

The teaching of reading to young children should always be done through play. The reading activities and games that are given to the child must be ones that the child enjoys and regards as play, and not some tedious boring task. The child should never be forced to participate.

When the child does participate in some activity or game, one should expect that the child will be soon become bored and tired of it. That being so, one should be ready to change an activity or game just as soon as the child begins to lose interest. Forcing the child to continue will only create a negative attitude toward reading, and this should be avoided at all costs. If all of the child's learning experiences are enjoyable, he or she will naturally develop a good attitude and a strong motivation toward reading.

To teach a young child to read, a total of 15 minutes or so per day is all that is necessary. However, one should not expect to complete the entire 15 minutes in a single encounter. A child's attention span can be very short. That being so, a few minutes here and there during the course of the day is the best way to fulfill the time requirement. And, any place – the classroom, the kitchen in the home, and even the toilet – can be used for the purposes of teaching.

4. *Expose the Child to Written Items*

The child can learn much more than you can teach directly, simply by being exposed to written items. Once the child gets the idea that written forms represent words or objects, the child can begin to learn those forms by himself or herself. What is necessary, though, is that the child be exposed to written words along with some indication as to their meaning.

For example, in train stations and elsewhere, the child might notice that the word for woman appears over the women's washroom while that for man appears over the men's washroom. One might point this out to the child if the child does not notice. Or while walking along the street, one might point out some store signs, such as *udon* (noodles), *okashiya* (sweet shop), *sakanaya* (fish market), etc.

The more the child is exposed to written words along with an idea as to their meaning, the more the child will be attracted to do some learning on his or her own. It is surprising how much a child can learn in this way.

VI. BENEFITS OF EARLY READING

Why teach a young child to read? After all, one can just wait and let the child learn to read when he or she goes to elementary school. Actually, the answer to this question is basically a simple one. By teaching a child to read at an early age, you will be enriching the child's life, both emotionally and intellectually. At the same time you will be helping to establish a close and intimate relationship between the child and the parent or teacher.

1. *Brings Pleasure and Enrichment*

A child who can read has a means for acquiring pleasure, for books are one of the finest sources for providing a child with emotional satisfaction. The earlier a child is able to read, the earlier such pleasure becomes available to the child. Of course, children enjoy having their parents or others read books to them. But other people's time is limited, and they cannot always be spending their time reading to the child. The child who knows how to read, however, has a degree of independence. Whenever he or she wants to read, he or she can do so.

Besides emotional pleasure, reading provides enjoyment since it serves both to stimulate and satisfy the curiosity of the child. Reading provides new ideas and new knowledge. As such, it enriches the intellectual development of the child. The earlier the child can learn to read, the earlier this source of enrichment can contribute to the intellectual development of the child.

There are other benefits, too, in a child's learning to read at an early age. Four others will be considered here.

2. *Love of Reading Established*

A love of reading will be firmly established. This has been true not only of our son, to whom we taught English, but also of the Japanese children in Hiroshima to whom Japanese was taught. The Hiroshima children began to learn to read at 1 and 2 years of age on the basis of our program and years later are now in elementary school. They find great enjoyment in reading materials of all sorts, especially books and magazines (Steinberg, Yoshida, and Yagi, 1985; Steinberg and Steinberg, 1975; Steinberg and Steinberg, 1980).

When children learn to read at school, they may not always develop a good feeling for and a positive attitude toward reading. Some children at elementary school even develop a hatred for reading. Needles to say, this negatively affects these children's level of achievement in most school subjects. However, by having children reading and enjoyment what they read, even before going to elementary school, would ensure that such disasters would be avoided.

3. *The Child will be a Superior Reader*

Children will be good readers and even superior readers. The children in our Hiroshima study read much faster, more accurately, with more comprehension and had a greater knowledge of kanji than did other children of their age group. Our own son, too, was many grades ahead of his classmates. He was reading at a high school level while still in elementary school! (Steinberg and Steinberg, 1980) Thus, one may reasonably expect that children will be superior readers both in terms of speed and accuracy.

4. *The Child will be More Knowledgeable*

Children who can read at an advanced level at an early age can acquire knowledge from books and other sources on their own more readily than children who do not have such a reading ability. Then, too, when they start to go to school, they may be able to read and learn what children in more advanced grades are generally given. At the very least, they should be able to do well at their grade level in all subjects which involve the use of reading.

5. *The Educational Level of the Entire Nation can be Raised*

The fact that children can read at a younger age has important implications for society as a whole. For if a nation adopted an early reading program, the educational level of that nation could be significantly raised. Teachers would not have to spend as much time as they do at present on teaching reading and there would be more time for them to devote to teaching other subjects. Since the children would already be able to read, they would be able to progress much faster in these other subjects than they ordinarily would.

VII. A FINAL NOTE ON EARLY READING

Most early reading programs have been severely criticized, both in Japan, America and elsewhere, and rightfully so. Such programs indicate a great lack of understanding of the nature of reading. Furthermore, they use methods and techniques that are inappropriate for the interests and needs of young children.

As an example of justifiable criticism, it is worth considering a portion of the recent report published by the Japan Ministry of Education (July 15, 1986) from the Committee for Survey and Research on Preschool Curriculums (Japan Ministry of Education, 1986). The report states,

> It is detrimental to give non-individualized instruction to a class and to make children memorize written forms and numbers mechanically at a time when children differ widely in their development; it nips the children's spontaneous interest and curiosity as well as their thinking process in the bud.

We could not agree more with the views of the committee. Children *do* learn at different rates and instruction should be designed to fit the needs of the individual child. And this can also be done at a class level. Most certainly mechanical memorization is *not* the way to teach reading. Reading instruction should be designed so that it stimulates the child's interest and thinking. It is precisely these sorts of things that our reading program takes into account and is reflected in the reading program that we offer.

ACKNOWLEDGEMENT

The author wishes to express her thanks to Dr. Danny D. Steinberg for his contribution to an earlier draft of the paper.

REFERENCES

Steinberg, Danny D.: 1981, 'Learning kana by induction', *Dokusyo Kagaku* [Science of Reading] **25**(2): 59–69.

Steinberg, Danny D.: 1982, 'Overcoming linguistic limitations of hearing-impaired children', *Topics in Language Disorders* **2**(3): 17–28.

Steinberg, Danny D.: 1984, 'Psycholinguistics: Application. The writing system as a native language for the deaf', in *Annual Review of Applied Linguistics*, Cambridge University Press, London.

Steinberg, Danny D., Harada, Michie, Tashiro, Michiko, and Yamada, Akiko: 1982, 'A one year old congenitally deaf child learns Japanese written language', *Chokaku Shogai* [Auditory Disorders] **376**(7): 22–46.

Steinberg, Danny D., Harada, Michie, Tashiro, Michiko, and Yamada, Akiko: 1982, 'A one year old congenitally deaf child learns Japanese written language', *Chokaku Shogai* [Auditory Disorders] **377**(8): 16–29.

Steinberg, Danny D. and Oka, Naoki: 1978, 'Learning to read kanji is easier than learning individual kana', *Shinrigaku Kenkyu* [Japanese Journal of Psychology] **49**(1): 15–21.

Steinberg, Danny D. and Sakoda, Kumiko: 1982, 'Teaching reading to two year olds in a preschool', *Dokusyo Kagaku* [Science of Reading] **26**(3): 115–130.

Steinberg, Danny D. and Chen, Shing-ren: 1980, 'A three year old mute-hearing child learns to read: the illustration of fundamental reading principles', *Dokusyo Kagaku* [Science of Reading] **24**(4): 134–141.

Steinberg, Danny D. and Steinberg, Miho T.: 1975, 'Reading before speaking', *Visible Language* **9**(3): 197–224.

Steinberg, Danny D. and Steinberg, Miho T.: 1980, 'Early reading from infancy: a case study', *Working Papers in Linguistics* [University of Hawaii] **12**: 41–83.

Steinberg, Danny D. and Yamada, Jun: 1977, 'Theory and method for teaching reading', *Shinrigaku Hyoron* [Psychological Review] **20**: 61–81.
Steinberg, Danny D. and Yamada, Jun: 1980, 'When are children ready to write?' *Kyoiku Shinrigaku Kenkyu* [Japanese Journal of Educational Psychology] **28**(4): 46–54.
Steinberg, Danny D., Yoshida, Kyoko, and Yagi, Reiko: 1985, 'Teaching reading to one and two year olds at home', *Dokusyo Kagaku* [Science of Reading] **29**(1): 1–17.
Suto, Hisayoshi: 1977, 'Nyumonki kanamoji shidoho ryakushi oyobi bunken kaisetsu' [A brief history and commentary on the teaching of kanji in early grades], *Kyoiku Chosa Kenkyusho Kiyo* [Proceedings of the Committee for Survey and Research] **13**: 65–70.
Yonen Kokugo Kyoiku Kai [Association of Elementary Japanese Education]. Newsletter of Association of Elementary Japanese Education, 1986.

JUN YAMADA

14. ASYMMETRIES BETWEEN READING AND WRITING FOR JAPANESE CHILDREN

Recent research suggests that learning to read and spell in English is more or less asymmetrical, i.e., can be unrelated to one another. Spelling disability exists along with apparently normal reading ability (Nelson and Warrington, 1974; Frith, 1980; Jorm, 1983; Waters, Bruck, and Seidenberg, 1985; Joshi and Aaron, 1988). The existence of children and adults with spelling problems, i.e., a one-way asymmetry, seems to be explained at least in part by the use of a partial cues strategy, which works relatively well in reading but fails in spelling (Frith, 1980). Recently, however, a peculiar one-way asymmetry has been discovered with children who can spell a few words which they cannot read (Bradley and Bryant, 1980; Bradley, 1985). In the early stages of learning written words, children using a visual strategy for reading and a phonological strategy for spelling develop unexpected reading problems (Bradley, 1985).

One general question we might raise here is whether asymmetries as found among English-speaking people occur in other scripts. This question could be addressed by examining reading and spelling in different scripts. Japanese kanji, a logographic type of writing using Chinese-origin characters, could be an interesting script to use in this regard (see Taylor and Taylor, 1983; Sampson, 1985; and Unger, 1987, for characteristics of kanji).

For an asymmetry to emerge, there must be a variable or variables which differentially influence the learner's reading and spelling performance. Thus our question is now whether such variables operate to affect the reading and spelling of kanji. Actually, it is not hard to pick out a number of possible variables. I shall list five.

(1) The presence of homophonous kanji might hinder spelling but not reading. Selecting the appropriate kanji from among a pool of plausible alternatives could be a first hurdle in spelling (selecting the appropriate kanji is defined here as part of spelling).

(2) A partial cues strategy as proposed by Frith (1980) might also be used by Japanese children in reading graphically complex kanji, and thereby enlarge the gap between reading and spelling achievement.

(3) The dual- or multiple-reading (interpretation) system of kanji with one or more *kun*-readings (Japanese origin) and one or more *on*-readings (Chinese origin) might contribute to difficulty in reading but not in spelling.

(4) While graphically complex kanji are not necessarily difficult to learn to read (Steinberg and Yamada, 1978–79; Kaiho and Nomura, 1983), they would be difficult to learn to spell.

(5) The lack of sound-grapheme correspondence in kanji might cause

I. Taylor and D.R. Olson (eds.), Scripts and Literacy, 215–230.

asymmetries. A learner must learn to associate a kanji as a whole to its speech sound as a whole. Such a holistic association (especially at the beginning stages of learning new kanji) may result in asymmetries, because for one reason or another the association from a kanji to its sound may be stronger (or weaker) than the association from the sound to the kanji. (To the extent that English-speaking children make use of grapheme-sound correspondences, the asymmetry between reading and spelling should be at a minimum even though the grapheme-to-sound and sound-to-grapheme correspondences are not entirely symmetrical. See Waters *et al.*, 1985.)

The variables above, if taken individually, should operate in the expected directions, but what the end-product would be with those variables interacting with one another is a different question. Moreover, simply identifying those variables does not explain why there are good readers who are poor spellers, and poor readers who are good spellers. We have to directly examine the learners' behavior. The present study attempts to investigate such asymmetries in children. Such a study is important, too, from an educational viewpoint. As Bradley (1985) noted, if various types of asymmetries do occur, then teaching methods should take into account the particular asymmetry and attempt to remedy the deficiency.

METHOD

Subjects

The sample consisted of one class of 39 4th graders (age range: 9;01 (9 years/1 month)–10;00), one class of 39 5th graders (age range: 10;01–11;00), and one class of 37 6th grades (age range: 11;01–12;00) who were randomly selected from a larger population of an average elementary school in Hiroshima. Approximately half the children were boys and half girls. All were Japanese monolingual from average income families.

Materials and procedure

On-reading kanji (Chinese) rather than *kun*-reading kanji (Japanese) were used as the test material, since they are used 4.6 times more frequently than are *kun*-reading kanji (Hayashi, 1982). Twenty-four Grade 3 kanji and 24 Grade 4 kanji were selected almost randomly from the Kaiho and Nomura (1983) list (see Table 1, and see Kaiho and Nomura for linguistic characteristics of the items such as number of strokes, graphic regularity, frequency, etc.). On the reading test, the kanji were presented in isolation although most kanji were bound morphemes. With no contextual cue presented, this test can measure the true ability of children to read the target kanji. The instructions were "Give the *on*-reading of each kanji writing it in hiragana." (Hiragana is a Japanese syllabic script which all of the

TABLE 1
The Test Kanji

G3 kanji	幸	歯	根	号	習	階	究	軽	暑
	感	細	祭	指	次	商	族	守	悪
	曲	洛	屋	飲	湖	*者/植			
G4 kanji	司	菜	臣	史	給	漁	唱	旗	功
	停	令	票	節	貯	極	囲	毒	副
	産	席	説	想	熱	察			

* By mistake 者 was used only in the reading test and 植 only in the spelling test.

children had learned.) On the other hand, on the spelling test, where the same kanji items were used, a simple unambiguous context written in hiragana and kanji for each test item was so arranged that the subjects were able to decide which one of the several homophonous kanji to spell (Table 2). The subjects were asked to fill in each blank with the appro-

TABLE 2
Examples of the Spelling Test

1. びわ（こ）
2. （いん）りょう水
3. （おく）上（じょう）にあがる
4. 毎日の生（せい）（かつ）
5. 作（さっ）（きょく）家（か）になりたい
6. （あく）人（にん）をつかまえる
7. 野（や）球（きゅう）の（しゅ）び

priate kanji. The testing order was fixed: the reading test was first given on one occasion, and the spelling test on another occasion. Testing was done in a classroom setting.

Four Categories of the Stimulus Kanji

Following the Bradley (1985) procedure, stimulus kanji were classified into four categories: 1) kanji which were read and spelled (designated as RS), 2) kanji which were read but not spelled (R𝕊), 3) kanji which were not read but spelled (ℝS), and 4) kanji which were neither read nor spelled (ℝ𝕊). (Following E. B. Coleman, ℝ and 𝕊 are used here instead of Bradley's $\bar{R}$ and $\bar{S}$.) If substantial numbers of kanji fall into the R𝕊 and ℝS categories, kanji can be said to be double asymmetrical.

Subgroups of Subjects

Subjects in each grade group were classified into five subgroups according to their reading scores on the one hand, and their spelling scores on the other. A total of 25 (5 by 5) subgroups were thus formed. The five subgroups were designated as R^5, R^4, R^3, R^2, and R^1 for reading, as S^5, S^4, S^3, S^2, and S^1 for spelling, and 25 subgroups as R^5S^5, R^5S^4, . . . , and R^1S^1 for reading and spelling combined. Each "5" subgroup was composed of subjects whose test scores fell above the group mean + 1 *SD*, each "4" subgroup between the group mean + 0.5 *SD* and + 1 *SD*, each "3" subgroup between the group mean – 0.5 *SD* and + 0.5 *SD*, each "2" subgroup between the group mean – 1 *SD* and – 0.5 *SD*, and each "1" subgroup below the group mean – 1 *SD*. The existence of a prominent double asymmetry would be established if subgroups such as R^5S^1, R^5S^2, R^4S^1, and R^4S^2 on the one hand, and R^1S^5, R^1S^4, R^2S^5, and R^2S^4 on the other were observed.

Scoring and Error Classification

Each correct response was given a score of 1 and each error response a score of 0. For the Grade 4 group, the Grade 3 kanji were scored but not the Grade 4 kanji because most of the Grade 4 kanji had not been taught at the time of testing.

To uncover possible sources of asymmetries errors were classified separately for reading and spelling.

Reading Errors

Three categories of errors (together with no responses) accounted for 96% (Grade 5 group) to 97% (Grade 4 group) of total reading errors.

(1) *Kun-reading.* The dual-reading system was difficult for some subjects; they read some kanji with a *kun*-reading (Japanese) instead of an *on*-reading (Chinese), e.g., 菜 /sai/ → /na/ ("→" means "was incorrectly read as"). These errors are often serious in reading a text because they result in incomprehension of the meaning of the kanji words.

(2) *Graphic Similarity Error.* Some kanji are so similar to other kanji that some children found it difficult to distinguish between them, e.g., 央 /ou/ → /ei/ (英). Errors were classified as graphic similarity errors if at least one radical (a special meaning part of a kanji) in the child's response kanji was present in the stimulus kanji. A subjective "somewhat similar" criterion was also used to classify those errors.

(3) *Mismatching in a Compound.* Given an *on*-reading kanji that is a bound morpheme, some children were able to retrieve a two-kanji (sometimes three- or four-kanji) compound in which the bound morpheme kanji was embedded, but they read (wrote in hiragana) the other constituent of the compound, e.g., 説 /setsu/ → /mei/ (明) because they had retrieved 説明 /setsu-mei/.

Few errors were classified into more than one category. Some errors were sequential. For example, 湖 /mizuumi/ "lake" was incorrectly read as /mizu/ "water" or /mi/ or /umi/ "ocean." This was regarded as a *kun*-reading error followed by a mismatching error, but was included only in the *kun*-reading error since the mismatching error ensued from the *kun*-reading error. Sequential errors did not arise frequently. Semantic errors, e.g., 毒 /doku/ "poison" → /kona/ (粉) "powder," characteristic of deep dyslexic errors, were rare. So were phonological errors, e.g., 曲 /kyoku/ → /kyaku/.

Spelling Errors

Four categories of errors (together with no responses) accounted for 95% (Grade 6 group) to 96% (Grade 4 group) of total spelling errors.

(1) *Invented Kanji.* Because of the graphic complexity of kanji, some subjects invented their own kanji, some being products of new combination of familiar radicals, e.g., ⿰亻享 for 停, and others being omissions, additions, and inversions of part of the target kanji, e.g., 族 → 族 (for spelling, the arrow means "was incorrectly written as").

(2) *Homophonous Kanji.* Some subjects failed to give the appropriate kanji from among several homophonous kanji, e.g., 10 階 "10th story" → 10 回 "10 times" (both are pronounced /jikkai/).

(3) *Graphic Similarity Errors.* Graphic similarity errors were made, e.g., 臣 → 巨 for /jin/ or /shin/. The criteria for identifying this type of error were the same as those for reading.

(4) *Mismatching in a Compound.* Mismatching errors also occurred where the other constituent of a compound was presented in hiragana, e.g., 想 (/sou/) → 像 (想像 for /sou/zou/).

Some errors were sequentially made as in reading. A few subjects spelled /shi/ (指) as 可 , which was an invented kanji for 司 /shi/. This could have been called a "homophonous-*then*-invented-kanji" error, but because the invented kanji error ensued from the homophonous error, it was included only in the homophonous category. An error such as 祭 /sai/ for 際 /sai/ could have been named a "homophonous-*and*-graphic-similarity" error; instead it was classified both as a homophonous error and as a graphic similarity error. The sequential and simultaneous errors actually occurred but rarely. Semantic errors. e.g., 祭日 /saijitsu/ "national holiday" → 休日 /kyuujitsu/ "holiday" and 祝日 /shukujitsu/ "national holiday" were also rare, and no phonological errors were found.

RESULTS

Several Findings

The reading and spelling scores were generally not very high. To compare the three grade groups, the mean percentages of correct responses and classified errors for Grade 3 kanji were summarized as shown in Table 3. The effects of Grade on correct response were significant both for reading [$F_1(2, 112) = 20.16$, $p < 0.01$ and $F_2(2, 66) = 5.81$, $p < 0.01$] and spelling [$F_1(2, 112) = 19.89$, $p < 0.01$ and $F_2(2, 66) = 5.89$, $p < 0.01$] thus suggesting, not surprisingly, that the children's performance in kanji improves as they get older. However, achievement was poor for the Grade 6 group, who reached only the 61% correct level for reading and the 68% correct level for spelling.

Table 3 indicates three main sources which could have brought about asymmetries between reading and spelling: Failure to distinguish *on-* and *kun-*reading kanji in reading, graphic complexity reflected in invented kanji and visual similarity errors in spelling, and homophonous errors in spelling.

Failure to distinguish kanji reading *on-* and *kun-*readings accounted for 53% to 60% of the total reading errors in the three grade groups. Related to this was the finding that kanji with single-readings (i.e., only one *on-*reading) were far easier than kanji with multiple-readings. The mean percentage correct scores of the Grade 3 single-reading kanji (No. items = 7) were 73.4, 77.7, and 79.9, respectively, for Grades 4, 5, and 6; whereas

TABLE 3
Mean proportion of response types of reading and spelling (13 Kanji)

Group (No. subjects)	Correct	Kun-reading	Invented Kanji	Homophone	Visual similarity	Mismatch	No response	Other
4	32.2	41.4	–	–	2.7	4.4	19.3	2.7
(n = 39)	39.2	–	7.4	15.1	1.0	1.1	35.6	2.4
5	50.5	26.6	–	–	1.4	1.4	18.7	1.9
(n = 39)	55.9	–	4.2	8.8	1.7	1.0	26.8	3.2
6	60.9	23.3	–	–	1.7	1.5	10.7	1.9
(n = 37)	67.9	–	9.9	6.0	3.2	0.1	12.0	4.2

Note: Numbers above the bar are reading scores and numbers under the bar are spelling scores.

those of the multiple-readings (No. items = 16) were 17.1, 38.6, and 52.5, respectively. Single-reading kanji were also easier to spell than multiple-reading kanji; spelling scores for single-reading-kanji were 67.4, 72.3, and 72.6; spelling scores for multiple-reading kanji were 27.1, 48.7, and 65.8. It is incorrect, therefore, to assume that the multiple-reading factor has no effect on spelling even though that factor may seem irrelevant in spelling. However, the result that reading scores for the multiple-reading kanji were consistently lower than the spelling scores does suggest that one-way asymmetry of kanji spelled but not read occurs.

In spelling, invented kanji and homophonous errors accounted for 29% to 49% of the total errors in the grades. Invented kanji errors might be expected to reflect visual complexity of kanji as assessed by the number of strokes. However, no significant correlations were obtained, since there were a few outliers such as 号 and 幸, which have a smaller number of strokes but were easy to misspell. However, the number of strokes was significantly correlated with the spelling scores for the oldest group although not for the youngest group: –0.27 (*n.s.*) for the Grade 4 group, –0.37 ($p < 0.10$) for the Grade 5 group, and –0.50 ($p < 0.05$) for the Grade 6 group. Since the number of strokes did not correlate with the reading scores, graphic complexity should be a variable which produces a one-way or a two-way asymmetry between reading and spelling, i.e., kanji which are read but not spelled correctly or, conversely, kanji which are spelled but not read correctly. Kanji with many strokes could be a candidate for the former, while kanji with fewer strokes could be a candidate for the latter.

No correlations were obtained between the number of homophonous kanji taught by the end of the previous grade and the spelling score. It appears that occurrence of homophonous errors depends on how familiar the alternative kanji are to the subject when the target kanji is not a familiar one: If alternative were so familiar that he or she knew that they were inappropriate to select, then no response rather than homophonous errors would be made. Notwithstanding the non-significant correlations, it does not seem unreasonable to expect a one-way asymmetry, i.e., kanji which are read but not spelled, that would arise from homophony.

Four Categories of Kanji

The item-based correlations between reading and spelling were 0.88 (N = 23), 0.61 (N = 47), and 0.31 (N = 47) for Grades 4, 5 and 6, respectively. A marked double asymmetry between reading and spelling was exhibited for kanji as a whole. Table 4 presents the mean percentages of four categories of kanji together with Bradley's (1985) data for English children as a comparison. Bradley's data show that while the R~~S~~ words always outnumber the ~~R~~S words, the ~~R~~S words drastically decrease from the younger to the older group such that they almost disappear in the older

TABLE 4
Mean proportion of English words and Kanji in four categories

	RS	R$\mathbb{S}$	$\mathbb{R}$S	$\mathbb{R}\mathbb{S}$
Bradley's study				
6$^{1}/_{2}$–7-yr.-olds (n = 30)	42	21	13	24
7–7$^{3}/_{4}$-yr.-olds (n = 20)	62	18	2	18
Present study				
9-yr.-olds (n = 39)	24	9	15	52
10-yr.-olds (n = 39)	43	14	17	25
11-yr.-olds (n = 37)	50	16	20	15

group. In contrast, the mean $\mathbb{R}$S kanji was consistently greater than the mean R$\mathbb{S}$ kanji in each grade although the difference was not significant ($p > 0.05$), and both the R$\mathbb{S}$ and the $\mathbb{R}$S kanji somewhat increased slightly as the grade advanced.

While there were four categories for kanji as defined above, it was possible to divide many of kanji into five types in terms of the relative frequency of RS, R$\mathbb{S}$, $\mathbb{R}$S, and $\mathbb{R}\mathbb{S}$ responses. These kanji were named RS-type, R$\mathbb{S}$-type, $\mathbb{R}$S-type, R$\mathbb{S}$&$\mathbb{R}$S-type, and $\mathbb{R}\mathbb{S}$-type. The criteria used for categorization were as follows. To be an RS-type kanji, it was required that RS responses made for the kanji be 70% or more; to be an R$\mathbb{S}$-type kanji, it was required that R$\mathbb{S}$ responses made for the kanji be 20% or more and that $\mathbb{R}$S responses made for the same kanji be 10% or less; to be an $\mathbb{R}$S-type kanji, it was required that $\mathbb{R}$S responses made for the kanji be 20% or more and that R$\mathbb{S}$ responses made for the same kanji be 10% or less; to be an R$\mathbb{S}$&$\mathbb{R}$S-type kanji, it was required that R$\mathbb{S}$ responses made for the kanji be 15% or more and that $\mathbb{R}$S responses made for the same kanji be 15% or more; and to be an $\mathbb{R}\mathbb{S}$-type kanji, it was required that $\mathbb{R}\mathbb{S}$ responses made for the kanji be 70% or more. More than 50% of the kanji tested were put in one (or sometimes two) of the five types; the rest fell in between the types. The results are summarized in Table 5.

The R$\mathbb{S}$-type kanji were relatively easy to read but difficult to spell. Most of them are easier to read because they are single-reading kanji, but they were difficult to spell because the visual complexity factor overrides the single-reading effect. Indeed the mean number of strokes of the eight single-reading kanji in Table 5 was significantly greater than that of the remaining 15 single-reading kanji [12.1 for the R$\mathbb{S}$-type kanji and 9.4 for the non-

TABLE 5
Five types of Kanji

Grade	RS	R$	ℝS	R$&ℝS	ℝ$
4	号 習 究	感	宇 曲 活	商 階 族	根 軽 暑 細 祭 指 守 屋 飲
5	号 習 副 商	階 漁 貯 停 祭	幸 菜 臣 央 功 囲 熱	感 票 節 席 次 活	根 暑
6	習 究 副 産 曲 令 給 活	旗 席 貯 停 族	根 習 感 細 菜 臣 央 漁 囲 唱 指 守 曲 屋	功 票 熱 極 察 湖	—

R$-type kanji, $t(21) = 2.37$, $p < 0.05$]. The mean graphic regularity index (Kaiho and Nomura, 1983) of the eight single-reading kanji was also significantly lower than that of the remaining 15 single-reading kanji [3.4 for the R$-type kanji and 3.9 for the non-R$-type kanji, $t(21) = 2.33$, $p < 0.05$]. Thus, it may well be that the R$-type kanji arose as a result of the interaction of visual complexity and multiple-reading.

The ℝS-type kanji were relatively difficult to read but easy to spell. Most of these kanji were homographs, which lowered their reading scores. However, since 活 (R$ responses = 8%; ℝS responses = 31%) for the Grade 4 group, and 臣 (3; 33) and 央 (0; 31) for the Grade 5 group are single-reading kanji, some explanation is needed. These kanji are easy to spell because of their simple configurations, but seem difficult to read probably because of the low concreteness of these kanji (see Kaiho and Nomura, 1983). The concreteness index of these kanji was low (43, 36, and 31 for 活, 央, and 臣, respectively; the mean index of the remaining single-reading kanji was 51). (It should be noted that when spelling, the degree of concreteness of these kanji was heightened because a meaningful context was presented.)

The R$&ℝS-type kanji were kanji whose reading and spelling are most doubly asymmetrical. These kanji differentially had homographic, homophonous, and visual complexity effects, which varied depending on the subjects. For 族, which is neither homographic nor homophonous at the stage of Grade 4, the visual complexity factor worked toward the R$\mathbb{S}$-type direction for some subjects, whereas the visual similarity factor (放 and 旅 bearing visual similarity to this kanji) toward the $\mathbb{R}$S-type direction for other subjects.

In connection with the R$\mathbb{S}$&$\mathbb{R}$S-type, or double asymmetrical kanji, there was no kanji that exhibited no asymmetry (e.g., kanji with the percent of R$\mathbb{S}$ and $\mathbb{R}$S responses being both below 10 and the percent of RS and $\mathbb{R}\mathbb{S}$ being both above 20 were not observed). It is thus concluded that kanji are more or less asymmetrical.

Finally it is noticed that some kanji did not always fall into the same type across the grade. For example, 漁 (69; 0) fell into the R$\mathbb{S}$-type at Grade 5 but into the $\mathbb{R}\mathbb{S}$-type (3; 24) at Grade 6. This would be surprising, were it not for the fact that many G5 subjects made a homophonous error, 料 or 量, in spelling, presumably because these homophonous kanji had been introduced toward the end of Grade 4.

Subgroups of Children

The distribution of R^iS^j subgroups is shown in Table 6, in which a clear-cut double asymmetry is observed in each grade group even though extreme cases such as R^5S^1, R^4S^1, and R^1S^5 did not occur. (The subject-based correlations between reading and spelling were 0.58 (N = 39), 0.66 (N = 39), and 0.49 (N = 37) for Grades 4, 5, and 6, respectively.) Thus, there were R$\mathbb{S}$ subjects such as the R^5S^2, R^5S^3, R^4S^2, and R^3S^1 subjects, and there were surprising $\mathbb{R}$S subjects such as the R^1S^4, R^1S^3, R^2S^4, and R^3S^5 subjects

The R$\mathbb{S}$ subjects, who comprised 6 to 14% of the groups in the present study, are analogous to the good readers but poor spellers in Frith (1980), although the R^5S^3 and R^5S^2 subjects may be somewhat better readers than Frith's subjects. The existence of R$\mathbb{S}$ subjects can be explained not only

TABLE 6
Distribution of R^iS^j subjects (%)

	R^1	R^2	R^3	R^4	R^5
S^1	3–8–5	8–5–5	3–5–11	0–0–0	0–0–0
S^2	8–3–0	3–0–0	10–8–8	0–3–3	3–0–0
S^3	3–5–3	3–0–5	21–18–14	3–3–11	3–3–0
S^4	0–0–3	3–3–0	13–8–8	3–10–3	3–3–11
S^5	0–0–0	0–3–0	5–3–3	0–5–3	8–8–11

Note. These numbers indicate the percentage of subjects in G4, G5, and G6 groups, respectively, according to subgroup.

by the partial cues strategy but also by linguistic properties of kanji. Thus, for example, in addition to a partial cues strategy, the use of which was suggested by a high rate of invented kanji (n = 7) in spelling, the R^5S^2 subject in the Grade 4 group demonstrated an inability to select the appropriate kanji from among several homophonous kanji, thereby making as many as 9 homophonous errors in spelling. The RS̸ subjects were those who had many more RS̸ responses than R̸S responses. Their means of RS̸ and R̸S responses were 20.4% and 2.9%, 28.2% and 7.4%, and 31.1% and 9.8% for the Grade 4, 5, and 6 subgroups, respectively. A one-way asymmetry was very clear in these children.

The discovery of R̸S subjects was rather surprising. (It should be noted that the existence of many R̸S kanji itself does not presuppose the existence of R̸S subjects although the reverse is true.) The R̸S subjects, who comprised 9 to 14% of the groups, were those who produced many more R̸S than RS̸ responses. These subjects' means of RS̸ and R̸S responses were 1.1% and 29.3%, 5.3% and 43.4%, and 4.3% and 48.9% for the Grade 4, 5, and 6 subgroups, respectively. Again a one-way asymmetry, but in the opposite direction this time. This was very clear in these children. Most of their incorrect responses in reading were no responses and/or *kun*-reading errors.

A question concerning whether double asymmetry occurs within individual subjects could be asked here. If, for example, subjects are identified as "double asymmetry" subjects by producing more RS̸ and R̸S responses than the group means, are there then double asymmetry subjects? The answer is that such subjects gradually developed for no double asymmetry subjects were found in the Grade 4 group, while four (10%) and two (5%) occurred in the Grade 5 and 6 groups. There were two R^3S^3, one R^3S^2, and one R^2S^1 subjects in the Grade 5 group, and one R^3S^3 and one R^1S^1 in the Grade 6 group. To a great extent, their reading and spelling were independent of one another.

DISCUSSION

Several characteristics of learning kanji by Japanese children were revealed in this study. The first feature is that there are a variety of asymmetries for kanji. All of the test kanji were more or less doubly asymmetrical, i.e., for each of the kanji there were at least one RS̸ response and one R̸S response in each grade group. Moreover, in addition to the two types of singly asymmetries kanji (RS̸ and R̸S kanji), there were doubly asymmetry kanji (RS̸&R̸S kanji). If a set of kanji were 100% doubly or singly asymmetric, it would mean the learning burden would become doubled. Although that did not occur, the results showed that learning to read kanji takes place more or less independently or learning to spell them.

The existence of the RS̸ and R̸S kanji may seem in line with the existence of the RS̶ and R̶S English words found by Bradley (1985). But the reason for the existence is different for English and kanji. Bradley proposed that in the earliest stages of learning to read and spell English words, young children use a visual strategy for reading and a phonological strategy for spelling. By contrast, although Japanese children seem to use a visual strategy for reading kanji, they do not use a phonological strategy for spelling them. The presence of the RS̶ and R̶S kanji should be ascribed to psycholinguistic properties such as the multiple-reading principle, homophony, graphic complexity, etc., which interact and differentially affect reading and spelling performance. The effects of such variables appear to be intensified in the process of learning many kanji so that the number of the R̶S kanji, for example, did not decrease as the learners got older as was the case with the English-speaking children (Table 4).

Parallel to the above feature was a second feature, i.e., the occurrence of asymmetries in individual children. An expected RS̶ subgroup of children, who read better than they spelled was found, and whose counterpart had been found among English-speaking children by Nelson and Warrington (1974), Frith (1980), and others. The use of a partial cues strategy in reading would certainly lead to RS̶ children, but it is not the only way to explain them. Some children appeared to have more difficulty in choosing the appropriate kanji from several homophones in spelling than in choosing the appropriate reading from alternative readings of the kanji in reading. This asymmetrical difficulty in selection is not necessarily unique to kanji reading, however. In everyday life, we have a similar experience in learning a person-name association. Although we can tell the name of a lady we know when seeing her on one occasion, we may not be able to recall her when hearing her name on another occasion. (This could happen not only when we know many Marys but also when we know only one Mary.) We may call this the "I-can't-remember-the-lady-though-I-know-her-name" phenomenon. In learning kanji, the kanji is substituted for the "lady". This occurs because there are no (or little) analytic correspondence between grapheme and sound in kanji.

On the other hand, an unexpected R̶S subgroup of children was discovered. These children appear unique in Japanese since many of them were found to have more difficulty in correctly reading the kanji than in spelling it. Again, this asymmetrical difficulty is not necessarily specific to kanji learning. We sometimes experience the opposite of the above phenomenon. That is the "I-can't-remember-her-name-though-I-know-the-lady" phenomenon, in which it happens that although we can visualize the features of the lady upon hearing her name, we may not be able to recall her name upon seeing her. Kanji function in the same way as the "lady" because of the lack of correspondence between grapheme and sound.

Finally, the children's performance was far from perfect both in reading and in spelling. Even Grade 6 children averaged only 61% for reading and 68% for spelling Grade 3 kanji. One of the main difficulties lies in the many-to-many correspondence system of kanji. One-to-one kanji are relatively easier to learn, as was shown by the finding that single-reading kanji were much easier than multiple-reading kanji. In the early stages of learning kanji in school, children have to learn only single reading kanji, whereas in the later stages inevitably many-to-many correspond kanji are introduced. And it is in those later stages that the learning burden greatly increases.

Consequently, learning kanji is no simple task, and the kanji learned or half-learned seem to be stored in a complicated way. How complicated is suggested by the network of errors which occur in reading (Figure 1) and in spelling (Figure 2). Moreover, if a graphically similar kanji, 旗 , for example, is added in Figure 1, the network becomes far more complicated.

The many-to-many relation explains not only some asymmetries, but also difficulty of learning kanji, i.e., asymmetry is associated with learnability. Thus, for example, more asymmetrical learners tend to be poor learners of reading and/or spelling, although some very poor learners exhibited little asymmetry simply because they made no response. Likewise kanji with more asymmetry tend to be difficult kanji for reading and/or spelling. The many-to-many relation system is thus a key concept for kanji. Some writers, e.g., Umesao (1988) and Nomura (1988), have recently abandoned *kun-*

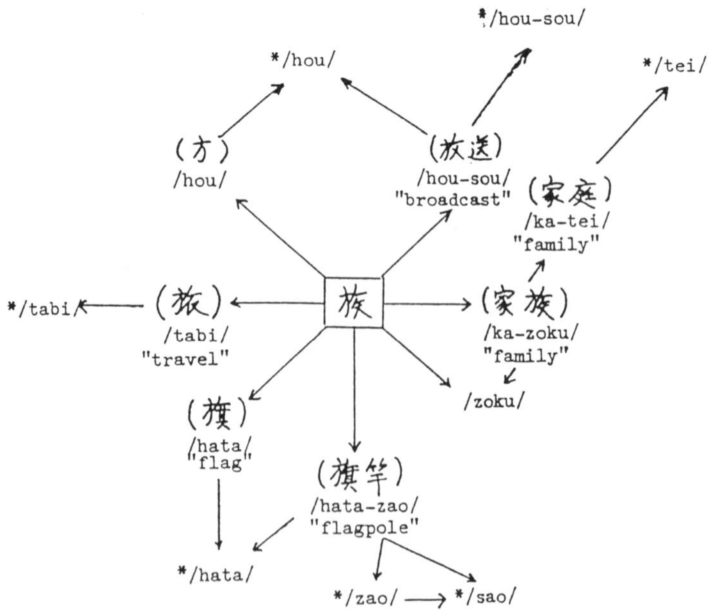

Fig. 1. Associative network of errors in reading. The kanji in parentheses is a covert response and the reading with an asterisk is an overt incorrect response.

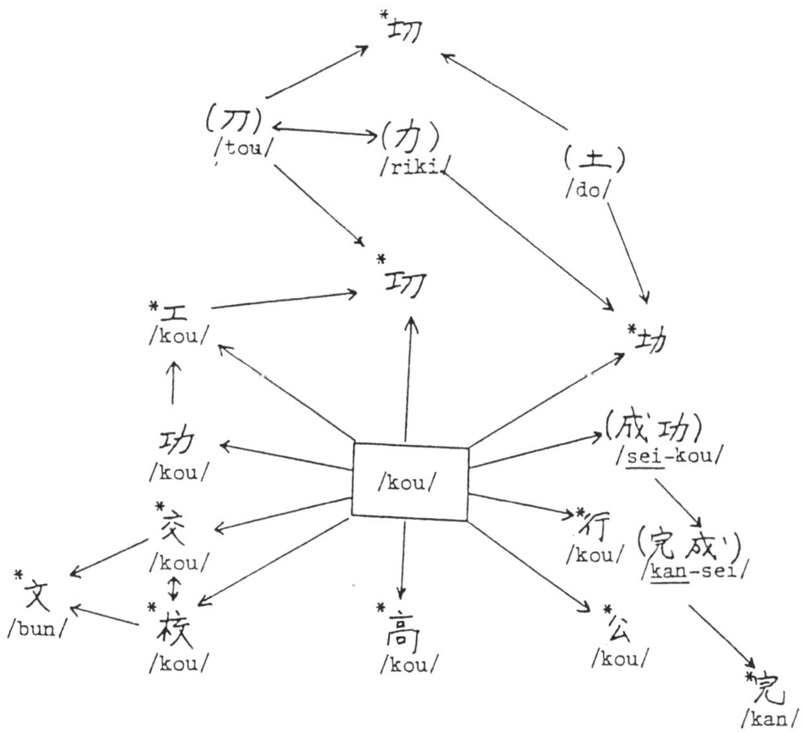

Fig. 2. Associative network of errors in spelling. The kanji in parentheses is a covert response and the kanji with an asterisk is an incorrect overt response.

reading kanji for hiragana. If this new way of writing pervades the Japanese society, then the effect it would bring about on learners of kanji could be enormous. For the abandonment of *kun*-reading kanji means modification of the many-to-many relation, which would reduce the learning burden, and thus asymmetries (Cf. Unger, 1978).

In summary, the nature of the script exerts great influence on asymmetry between reading and spelling. To be more specific, homophony, homography, graphic complexity, the degree of the transparency of a script, etc., determine the degree of asymmetry. For example, the more phonologically opaque, the more asymmetrical between reading and spelling. Furthermore, asymmetry is related with the learnability of the script, i.e., the more asymmetrical, the less learnable. If kanji is a more asymmetrical script than is English for example, it would suggest that kanji is a more difficult script to learn and use. Sasanuma (1980: 53) states in passing that by the end of high school most children can read and write the minimal set of 1850 kanji that has been adopted for standard use by the Ministry of Education. This statement is simply incorrect. It may be easy to learn to recognize 1850 fair ladies in our daily life in 12 years, but it is certainly not easy for children to have to learn 1850 multi-faceted and peculiarly shaped kanji in a two-dimensional space in that period.

ACKNOWLEDGEMENTS

The cooperation of F. Torigoshi and T. Kuramoto, and the invaluable comments of E. B. Coleman are greatly acknowledged. A slightly different version of this chapter appeared in *Journal of Psycholinguistic Research*, 1992, 21, pp. 563–580.

REFERENCES

Bradley, L.: 1985, 'Dissociation of reading and spelling behavior', in D.D. Duane and C.K. Leong (eds.) *Understanding learning disabilities: International and multidisciplinary views*, Plenum Press, New York.

Bryant, P.E. and Bradley, L.: 1980, 'Why children sometimes write words which they do not read', in U. Frith (ed.) *Cognitive processes in spelling*, Academic Press, London.

Frith, U.: 1980, 'Unexpected spelling problems', in U. Frith (ed.) *Cognitive processes in spelling*, Academic Press, London.

Hayashi, O.: 1982, *Zusetsu nihongo* [Graphic Japanese], Kadokawa Shoten, Tokyo.

Jorm, A.F.: 1983, *The psychology of reading and spelling disabilities*, Routledge and Kegan Paul, London.

Joshi, R.M. and Aaron, P.G.: 1988, 'Specific reading disability and spelling disability: Are these dissociable', in R.M. Joshi (ed.) *Written language disorders*, Kluwer, Dordrecht.

Kaiho, H. and Nomura, Y.: 1983, *Kanji-johoshori no shinrigaku* [A psychology of information processing in kanji], Kyoiku Shuppan, Tokyo.

Nelson, H.E. and Warrington, E.K.: 1974, 'Development spelling retardation', *British Journal of Psychology* **65**: 265–274.

Nomura, M.: 1988, *Kanji no mirai* [The future of kanji], Chikuma-shobo, Tokyo.

Sampson, G.: 1985, *Writing systems: A linguistic introduction*, Stanford University Press, Stanford, Cal.

Sasanuma, S.: 1980, 'Acquired dyslexia in Japanese: Clinical features and underlying mechanisms', in M. Colheart, K. Patterson, and J.C. Marshall (eds.) *Deep dyslexia*, Routledge and Kegan Paul, London.

Steinberg, D.D. and Yamada, J.: 1978–79, 'Are whole word kanji easier to learn than syllable kana? *Reading Research Quarterly* **14**: 88–99.

Taylor, I. and Taylor, M.M.: 1983, *The psychology of reading*. Academic Press, New York.

Unger, J.M.: 1987, *The fifth generation fallacy*, Oxford University Press, New York.

Umesao, T.: 1988, *Nihongo to nihon-bunmei* [The Japanese language and civilization], Kumon-shuppan, Tokyo.

Waters, G.S., Bruck, M., and Seidenberg, M.: 1985, 'Do children use similar processes to read and spell words?' *Journal of Experimental Child Psychology* **39**: 511–530.

TAKESHI HATTA AND TAKEHIKO HIROSE

15. READING DISABILITIES IN JAPAN: IMPLICATIONS FROM THE STUDY OF HEMISPHERE FUNCTIONING

In the present study, we would like to introduce reading disabilities (RD) in Japanese children and several experiments, which might shed some light on the relationships between reading ability and hemisphere functions.

1. READING DISABILITIES IN JAPAN

Since the first English written article about RD by Japanese psychiatrist Dr. Makita (1968), the view prevails that RD is extremely rare among children in Japan compared to Western countries. Dr. Makita reported the incidence rate of RD in Japan was 0.98%. It is generally believed that the incidence rate of RD in Western countries ranges from 10–20%. If the claim of rarity is true, the orthography, writing and/or reading systems of Japanese can be regarded as superior to the other language writing systems and the main factor of RD incidence is due to the characteristics of orthography.

However, the claim of rarity does not correspond to the common sense in recent Japanese society. It is said that 70, 50, 30% of the children are "left behind" or "are going to be left behind" in high, junior high and primary schools, respectively (Kitao, 1984). Many educational psychologists and school teachers regard that the primary reason for the ones "left behind" is poor reading abilities.

The primary reason why Dr. Makita estimated so low an incidence rate seems to us that the simply asked school teachers to report to him the number of children with reading difficulties. The teachers could have regarded a child as RD only when he/she could not pronounced a written word, and the child who could pronounce but did not understand the meaning could have been classified as normal reader. As you may know, unlike English, two writing systems, Kanji and Kana, are employed in Japanese. Kanji is a logograph that represents meaning and Kana is a syllabic script that has a regular letter to syllable correspondence. The beginning readers learn oral reading and writing of all Kana letters (41 Hiragana and 41 Katakana) in their elementary school. Until the end of the first grade, most of the children can pronounce written Kana words and can write spoken words in Kana letters. As Kana have a one-to-one correspondence between letter and pronunciation, mastering such a skill is not so difficult. But children learn about 1000 Kanji in elementary school. As Kanji do not correspond to syllables and their structure is generally complex, some children fail to master Kanji.

I. Taylor and D.R. Olson (eds.), Scripts and Literacy, 231–246.

The purpose of the first experiment was to find real incidence rate of RD in Japan and to examine the characteristics of RD and good readers.

Experiment 1

Method

Subjects were 871 (443 males and 428 females) Japanese children aged 11. Low intelligence children (below IQ = 85) were not included in the analyses of the data. Four hundred and thirty eight were from three urban area schools and 443 were from three rural area schools. The Kitao's Reading Ability Test (KRAF) and Kyoken Intelligence Test were administered at each school following the instruction in the manual. The KRAT is developed for 8–13 years old children based upon modern cognitive psychology. The KRAT consists of five subscales: word discrimination I (target word finding in a list of meaningful words); word discrimination II (discrimination of words from nonsense words); sentence comprehension; sentence memory; and reasoning.

Results

The incidence rate of RD is shown in Table 1. RD refer to the children who show 2 years or more behind in reading ability and have over 85 IQ, and GR refer to the children who show 2 years or more ahead in reading ability and have over 85 IQ. Our data show that the incidence rate of RD is about 11%.

TABLE 1
Incident rate of reading disabilities

Definition	Incident rate
One or more years behind	29.62%
Two or more years behind	10.91%
Three or more years behind	1.61%

The incidence rate of RD shows gender difference: More boys show RD than girls and more girls are GR than boys. Table 2 shows the IQ distribution for children with RD and for GR. GR's IQ are generally high compared to that of RD's. However, 3.6% of RD have superior IQs of over 120.

Table 3 shows the profile scores for RD on the reading ability test. The analysis of variance revealed that the subscale scores of the sentence memory and the reasoning were inferior compared to the other subscales and there is no significant difference between male and female RD.

TABLE 2
IQ distribution of reading disabilities and good readers

	IQ – 90	90 – 100	100 – 110	110 – 120	120 – 130	130 –
Reading disabilities	38.2%	25.4%	25.5%	7.3%	3.6%	0.0%
Good readers	0.0%	3.9%	15.6%	50.6%	16.9%	13.0%

TABLE 3
Mean deviation values (1–10) of reading disabilities between male and female

Subscales	Values: Male	Female
Word discrimination I	3.60	3.52
Word discrimination II	3.32	3.76
Sentence comprehension	3.63	3.52
Sentence memory	3.06	2.91
Reasoning	2.98	3.27

Discussion

The results show that RD in Japan are not so rare as has been believed but appear to be as prevalent as in many Western countries. Our results cast doubts on the claim of crucial significance of orthography, that is, the use of logograph or the mixed use of Kanji and Kana scripts as a major factor determining the incidence of RD. Recently, Stevenson *et al.* (1982) conducted a cross-cultural study where they compared reading ability between Asian countries and the U.S.A. They found that 3% of the children in the U.S.A. and 2% of the children in Taiwan were two years behind. On the other hand, 8% of the Japanese children were 2 years behind. They claimed that RD in Japan is more prevalent than in the other countries. Although the reason why Japanese show more RD than the others is not clear, both Stevenson *et al.*'s studies and our own studies cast doubts on the claim of rarity by Makita (1968).

We also found a sex difference in incident rate of RD. This finding agrees with other studies e.g. Downing and Leong (1982).

Our findings indicate that RD is strongly associated with an inferior sentence memory and reasoning but not with the word discrimination abilities. In other words, RD are inferior in deep levels of reading processes but are not inferior in shallow levels of reading processes. The crucial factor of RD incidence should be sought in the characteristics of hemisphere function rather than in orthography system itself. RD may have some different characters in hemisphere function from non-RD.

In the following three experiments, we will try to get some information about this problem using primary school and preschool children.

2. HEMISPHERE FUNCTIONS OF THE READING DISABILITIES: IMPLICATIONS FROM THE RESULTS OF DICHOTIC LISTENING TEST

Inter-relationships between hemisphere specialization and intellectual abilities including reading ability have been suggested for a long time, but the systematic examination has just begun. Recently, Bryden (1986) administered dichotic listening tests and psychometric tests to 120 university students and revealed that a right ear advantage (REA) in the verbal dichotic listening test correlated with the psychometric measures of verbal ability but a left ear advantage (LEA) in musical dichotic listening tests do not correlate with psychometric measures of spatial ability. Kraft (1983) reported that only right-handed and right-eyed subjects with familial dextrality showed a strong correlation between REA for verbal stimuli and verbal intelligence.

However, several studies have found that a large REA was shown in patients of psychopathological disease (Lerner *et al.*, 1977; Lishman *et al.*, 1978). So it seems rather too hasty to agree with simple linear correlation between REA in verbal stimuli and intellectual abilities.

The purpose of this experiment was to examine the relationships between REA and verbal intellectual abilities such as reading ability. As recent studies concerning to hemisphere specialization has begun to point out the importance of hemispheric load-sharing and collaboration or synergy of the left and right hemispheres (Best, 1985; Dimond, 1974; Hatta, 1986), we introduced new index bilateral recall ratio (BRL), in dichotic listening tests.

Experiment 2

Method

Subjects. Thirty-two right-handed subjects, half males and half females, between ages 10 to 11 (mean 10.6) participated in this experiment. All subjects were 5th graders in the urban area. The criteria of subjects selection included right handedness and no history of neurological or hearing problems.

Apparatus and Procedure. The Kitao's reading ability test, Kanji reading test, Kanji writing test, Kyoto University NX intelligence test and dichotic listening test were administered to each subject. A Dichotic listening test

(DLT) was given in a quiet room individually. The used DLT tape was the same as the one used in Hatta (1987) and consisted of 56 vowel-consonant-vowel (VCV) pairs spoken by females. ORO-OPO and UPA-UKA were the examples of the used DLT tape. In this tape, subjects can hear vowels perfectly because they are presented from both ears, so the performances to detect consonants are compared between both ears.

Subjects were instructed to attend to both ears evenly and were requested to recall what they heard during 5 seconds intertrial intervals. Following practice with tape of digit pairs in 10 trials, the VCV pairs were presented. The earphone channel order was counterbalanced across subjects.

Results

The means and SDs of scores on reading ability test, Kanji writing test, Kanji reading test, IQ, REA, BLR, and DLT recall score (DLTR) are shown in Table 4. REA and BLR are calculated by the following formula: REA = 100 × (right ear recall – left ear recall)/(right ear recall + left ear recall), BLR = 100 × (number of simultaneous recall from both ears)/(right ear recall + left ear recall). DLTR is the total number of correct recalls irrespective to the side of ears.

To examine the relationships between reading ability and other variable, a multiple regression analysis (Tanaka *et al.*, 1984), where reading ability was a dependent (or criterion) variable and others were independent (or explanatory) variables, was conducted. The multiple correlation coefficient was 0.854 and R-square was 0.730. This multiple correlation coefficient was significant ($F(6, 25) = 11.25$, $p < 0.01$) by an analysis of variance. Table 5 shows the simple correlations between all variables. As

TABLE 4
Mean scores and SDs of reading ability test, Kanji writing test, Kanji reading test, IQ, REA, BLR, and DLT recall (DLTR)

	Mean	SD
Reading ability test*1	0.77	1.43
Kanji writing test*2	67.34	19.39
Kanji reading test*2	76.88	19.71
IQ	105.00	17.55
REA*3	8.37	20.79
BLR*4	20.08	10.17
DLTR*5	51.66	11.96

*1 (Reading ability age) – (Clonical age)
*2 distributes from 0 to 100%
*3 distributes from –100 to 100%
*4 distributes from 0 to 50
*5 distributes from 0 to 100%

TABLE 5
Simple correlation between all variables

	RAT	KWT	KRT	IQ	REA	BLR	DLTR
Reading ability test		0.638*	0.746*	0.739*	–0.023	0.527*	0.361
Kanji writing test			0.725*	0.563*	–0.197	0.477*	0.725*
Kanji reading test				0.659*	–0.112	0.482*	0.495*
IQ					–0.057	0.446*	0.449*
REA						–0.226	–0.125
BLR							0.727*
DLTR							

* $p < 0.01$

apparent from the Table 5, reading ability correlated with the variables of Kanji writing, BLR, IQ, and Kanji reading but not REA and DLTR.

Table 6 shows the standard partial regression coefficients (beta) or the unique contributions (or usefulness) of the independent variables in the regression equation. The unique contribution was estimated by the drop in R-square if each independent variable was employed from the regression equation and the remaining variables appropriately reweighed. Table 6 shows that the subjects' reading ability is explained by BLR, IQ, DLTR and Kanji reading but the reading ability is not explained by REA.

TABLE 6
Standardized partial regression coefficients (beta) in multiple regression analyses where reading ability was dependent variable

Independent variables	Beta	SE of Beta	F
Kanji writing test	0.002	0.012	0.033
Kanji reading test	0.032	0.013	6.099*
IQ	0.034	0.012	8.299*
REA	0.007	0.007	0.851
BLR	0.050	0.023	4.577*
DLTR	–0.036	0.020	3.301*

* $p < 0.01$

Discussion

The results indicate that reading ability did not correlate with REA, DLTR, or writing abilities. Reading ability correlates with BLR, IQ, and Kanji reading. For more than 20 years, it has been believed that the majority of normal subjects exhibit a REA on verbal DLT (Kimura, 1967). Strong relationships are thought to exist between REA and cognitive abilities such as reading or writing, though only a few studies attempt to link these relationships systematically with normal children. Recently, Bryden (1986) reported a strong correlation between REA in verbal DLT and psychometric measures of verbal abilities such as word encoding, and vocabulary. These results differ from his previous findings and common sense.

We suspect that the discrepancy between Bryden's study and ours may come from the subject population. For example, Bryden employed university students as subjects but we used primary school pupils as subjects. It is clear that the uniformity of cognitive ability in university students is high because they, unlike our subjects, have passed several selection procedures. Our subjects have wide variability, as can be seen in IQ scores ranging from 82 to 134. Thus, a strong correlation between REA and cognitive ability may fit the limited sample population but not general population. The result of non-significant relation between reading ability and DLTR suggest that memory component, in this case short term memory, may not have such an important role in reading ability. Reading ability may reflect more complex or deeper levels of cognitive abilities. Further, Kanji writing has no significant relation to reading ability. This finding seems to suggest dissociation between Kanji writing from Kanji reading (see Yamada, in this volume). When Japanese cannot remember how to write Kanji, they use Kana scripts instead of using Kanji. Both educated and uneducated people show this phenomenon.

We employed BLR as a measure which reflects hemisphere collaboration. The high BLR score reflects the fact that a subject succeeded to recall stimuli simultaneously from both ears and low BLR score reflects the fact that a subject failed to recall stimuli from both ears. The failure to recall bilaterally seems to reflect the failure, first to share attention to both ears simultaneously and second to access the information transferred across the corpus callosum.

Figure 1 shows the model of BLR success. Suppose that a subject succeeds bilateral recall in one (A) trial, not only he/she succeeds VCV transfer from the right ear – left temporoparietal lobe – left frontal lobe, but also he/she succeeds to transfer VCV from the left ear – right temporoparietal lobe – left temporoparietal lobe – left frontal lobe. In (B) trial, he/she succeeds to recall VCV only from one ear (presumably from the right ear) where he/she succeeds only access VCV from the right ear – left temporoparietal lobe – left frontal lobe. More concretely, subject succeeds both intra- and inter-hemispheric transfers in (A) trial, but in (B) trial subject fails inter-hemispheric transfer. This model suggests therefore the importance of bihemispheric collaboration for high BLR score.

In short, high correlation between BLR and reading ability and low correlation between REA and reading ability indicates the importance of hemispheric collaboration in cognitive performance, as several studies have proposed (Dimond, 1974; Levy, 1985; Best, 1985; Hatta, 1986).

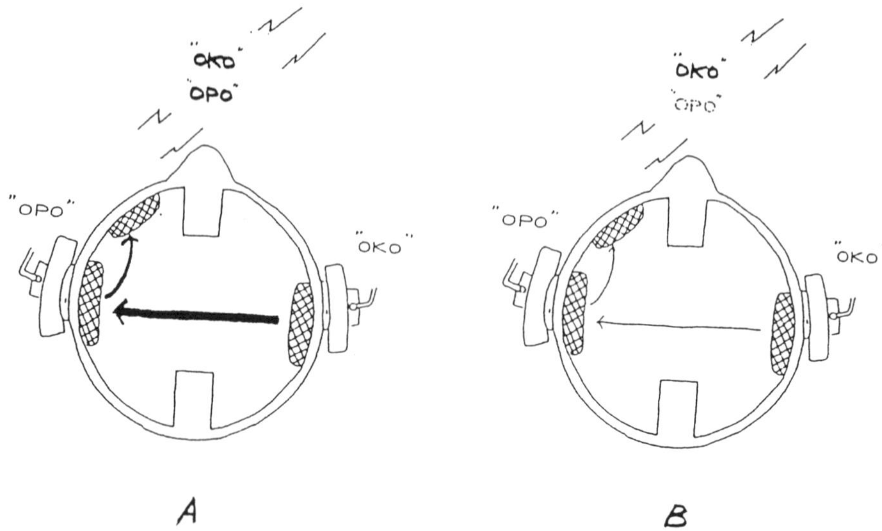

Fig. 1. Mechanisms of BLR success and failed trials.

3. HEMISPHERE FUNCTION AND READING ABILITY; IMPLICATIONS FROM THE RESULTS OF TACTILE TEMPORAL RESOLUTION TEST

The purpose of this study was to examine the relationships between reading ability and the ability of tactile temporal resolution using 5th graders of the primary school. Several studies have suggested that the ability of temporal resolution is one of the crucial factors in development of language acquisition (Gates and Bradshaw, 1977; Schwartz and Tallal, 1980). Further, it is said that children who have delay in language development show poor ability in temporal resolution which include analyses of spatial factor and sequential factors (Nakatuka, 1986). Recent study by Hatta and Moriya (1988) revealed that the development of tactile temporal resolution in 10-year old children (5th graders) does not reach the adults' level. Their study showed that although the efficiency of the intra-hemispheric transfer in 10-year old children became comparable to that of adults, the efficiency of inter-hemispheric transfer is inferior to that of adults. This finding seems to support the view that inter-hemispheric communication or collaboration is very important in normal development of cognitive and intellectual abilities (Dimond, 1974; Dennis, 1976; Best, 1985; Hutchington, 1983).

Although the importance of relation between the ability of temporal resolution and cognitive abilities have been stressed, few has examined this relationship systematically. No information about the development of temporal resolution in tactile, visual, and auditory function and about their relations to children's cognitive abilities have been presented. We wish to begin this examination in the following experiment. At first, we aimed to examine the relationship between the ability of tactile temporal resolution and cognitive ability in school age children.

Experiment 3

Method

Subjects. Forty primary school children (aged between 10.5 and 11.6) participated in this experiment. Twenty two were female and 18 were males and they had no known history of neurological and academic problems.

Apparatus and Procedure. A tactile stimulator (HO-84, Sanwa) was employed to deliver stimuli through stainless-steel rods (dia. 2 mm). This stimulator presents tactile stimuli (40 g force for 200 ms by means of a magnet) to selected fingers of the hands in an order and at intervals which are programmed beforehand.

Subjects were tested individually in a quiet room of the school. Each stimulus trial consisted of three or four upward strikes on each of three or four fingertips (the subject was placing the hands palm down on the apparatus) through pre-programmed presentation schedules. The inter-trial interval was set to 2 s. Repeated stimuli were applied to the same finger in some trials. The subject indicated orally the fingers which have been stimulated, and order of the stimulation. Each subject was given 24 trials for each hand after 8 practice trials, therefore, 56 trials were given in total. The order of the left and the right hand conditions was counter-balanced across subjects and the right hand first for the other half subjects.

The Kitao's reading ability test and Kyoto University NX intelligence test were administered to all the subjects one week before the tactile stimulation experiment.

Results

Linear regression equation and Peason's correlation coefficients were calculated (1) between reading ability and intelligence test, (2) between reading test and accuracy score of the left hand condition, and (3) between reading ability and accuracy score of the right hand condition.

Table 7 shows the results of the analyses. The results show that the reading ability correlates with both intelligence test and the accuracy score of the left hand condition, but not with the accuracy score of the right hand condition.

TABLE 7
Linear regression equations and Peson's correlation coefficients

	Linear regression equation	Peason's correlation coefficiet
Reading ability test and IQ	Y = 53.90 + 7.69X	0.799
Reading ability test and accuracy of left hand	Y = 31.52 + 3.18X	0.492
Reading ability test and accuracy of right hand	Y = 47.59 + 0.71X	0.108

Discussion

As many studies suggest, functional components in neocortical commissures mature at different times, completing at around puberty (Quinn and Geffen, 1986: Salamy, 1978; Yakovlev and Lecours, 1967). It is hypothesized that some differences might exist in hemisphere connection efficiency according to subjects' cognitive ability development. That is, as our subjects were before puberty, there must be some individual differences in their maturation of hemisphere function, especially in hemisphere collaboration systems. If the hemisphere collaboration is important for good reading ability as Experiment 2 suggested, some relation between reading ability and hemisphere collaboration in tactile temporal resolution must have emerged.

The results indicated (1) children who showed high reading ability have high IQ and high score in tactile sequential information processing in the left hand condition; and (2) there is no correlation between reading ability and the score in the right hand condition. It is hypothesized that the verbal response in the left hand stimulation requires the inter- and intra-hemispheric transfers of information (probably from right parietal lobe – left parietal lobe – left temporal lobe), whereas verbal right hand stimulation requires no inter-hemispheric transfer of information, requiring only intra-hemispheric transfer of information (see Figure 2). Therefore, the comparison of the performances between the left and the right hand verbal response conditions seem to offer some information about the efficiency of intra- and inter-hemispheric transfers of information.

The result of high correlation between reading ability and left hand performance means the following; children's ability in reading correlates with their efficiency of hemisphere connection, that is, collaboration of both hemispheres. The performances of both hands were not significantly different when subjects responded in non-verbal style. This means that the

∞

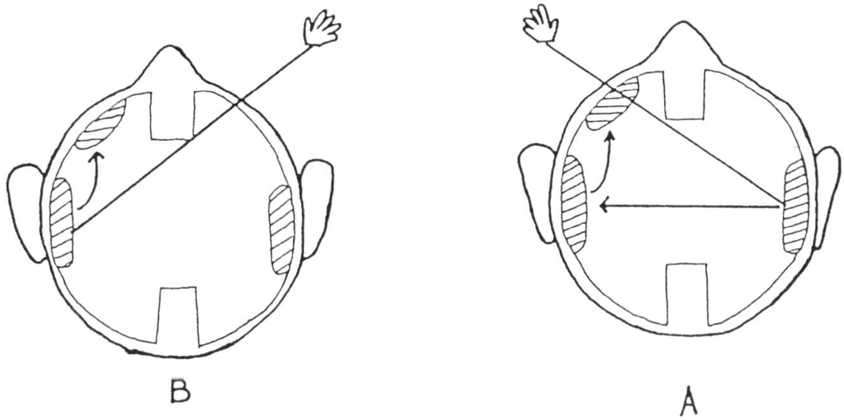

Fig. 2. Mechanisms of verbal response for the left (A) and right (B) hand stimulation conditions.

difference of the left and the right hand conditions was not caused by the perceptual efficiency in processing of tactile stimulation but the efficiency in transcoding the perceived tactile stimuli to verbal responses.

4. HEMISPHERE FUNCTIONS AND VERBAL ABILITY IN PRESCHOOL CHILDREN

Both Experiment 2 and 3 seem to stress the importance of the relation between reading ability and hemisphere collaboration. According to Yamamoto and Hirose (1988), there is a strong correlation between the verbal cognitive abilities (assessed by the selected ITPA subscales) in preschool childhood and reading ability assessed after the children entered primary school. They suggested that children who showed high scores in the verbal cognitive abilities in their kindergarten age acquired high scores in the reading ability at the third grade in their primary school.

Kindergarten children participated in this study and were given verbal ability test, dichotic listening test and other cognitive tests. The relations of verbal ability to hemisphere functioning and other cognitive abilities were examined.

Experiment 4

Method

Subjects. Thirty-nine kindergarten children ranged from 4.7 to 6.6 years old (mean 5.6) participated in this experiment. They were all non-left handers according to the revised H. N. handedness inventory and had no known neurological and psychological problems by the parents and teachers reports (Yamamoto, 1987).

Apparatus and Procedures. A VCV dichotic listening test (DLT), selected ITPA language development test (ITPA), figure discrimination test (DIST), and figure drawing test (DRT) were administered to each subject within two weeks individually at a quiet room of the kindergarten. The used tape of DLT was identical to that of Experiment 2. Each subject was instructed that he/she will hear the spacewomen's speech from both ears and to report what they said to the experimenter. The precise procedure was the same as that of the Experiment 2. ITPA consisted of four subscales of the original test as follows; understanding, inference, expression, and construction of sentence. The DIST was to identify the target figure or letter which located at the left side among four comparison stimuli located at the right side of the sheet. The comparison stimuli consisted of the 0, 90, 180, and 270 degree rotated figures or letters of the target stimulus. The size of each stimulus was approximately 2 × 2 cm large. This identification test consisted of 15 trials. In the DRT, subject was asked to copy the target stimulus (size was 2 × 2 cm large) which was presented at the top in the vacant space of the sheet. Figure 3 shows the used stimuli. This test consisted of 15 trials.

Two postgraduate students who have no knowledge about this study evaluated the subjects' performance separately according to the criteria

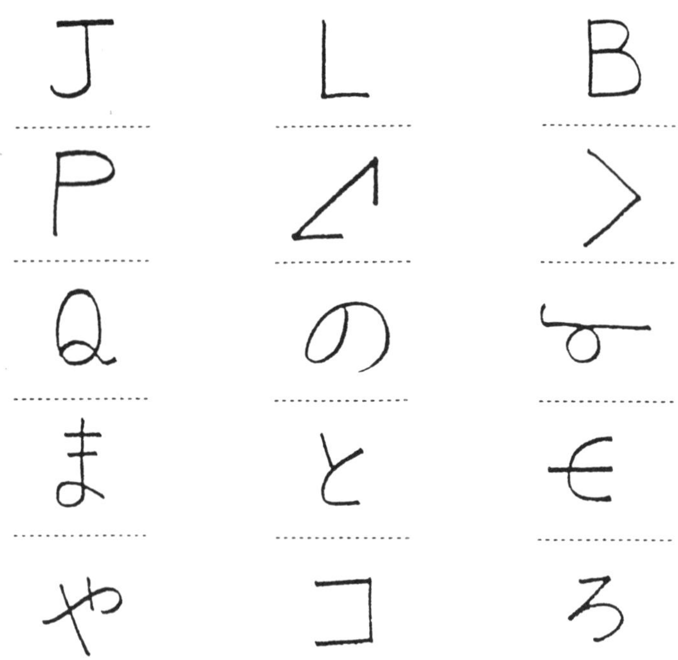

Fig. 3. Samples of the used stimulus in DIST.

informed by the authors. The assessment scorings of the two judges were 98.5 percent identical.

Results

Table 8 shows means and SDs of the results of the right ear advantage (REA) in DLT, ITPA, DIST, and DRT.

To examine the relation of the verbal ability to the hemisphere functioning and other cognitive abilities, a multiple regression analysis (Tanaka *et al.*, 1984) was administered. The verbal ability was a dependent (or criterion) variable and others were independent (or explanatory) variables. The multiple correlation coefficient was 0.690 and R-square was 0.476. This multiple correlation coefficient was significant ($F(3, 35) = 10.601$, $p < 0.01$ by an analysis of variance.

Table 9 represents the simple correlation matrix of the variables. Table 10 shows the standard partial regression coefficient (Beta) or the unique contribution (usefulness) of the independent variables in the regression equation. The method of the estimation of this unique contribution was identical to that of Experiment 2.

As apparent from Table 9 and 10, there was a strong relationship between verbal ability and DRT. The relation between verbal ability and REA was also significant. But the results failed to find significant relation between

TABLE 8
Mean scores and SDs of REA, ITPA, figure discrimination test, and figure drawing test

	Mean	SD
REA*1	–3.928	27.277
ITPA*2	4.566	0.896
DIST*3	13.641	2.560
DRT*4	53.795	16.369

*1 distributes from –100 to 100%
*2 age of vebal ability
*3 distributes from 0 to 15
*4 distributes from 0 to 75

TABLE 9
Simple correlation between all variables

	REA	ITPA	DIST	DRT
REA		0.404	–0.135	0.227
ITPA			0.254	0.636
DIST				0.463
DRT				

TABLE 10
Standardized partial regression coefficient (beta) in multiple regression analyses where the score of IPTA was dependent variables

Independent variables	Beta	SE of Beta	F
REA	0.009	0.004	4.649*
DIST	0.012	0.050	0.056
DRT	0.030	0.008	14.470*

* $p < 0.01$

verbal ability and DIST. The verbal ability can be explained by DRT and REA but not by DIST. This means that the ability of simple discrimination or perception ability is not a crucial contributor to the verbal ability but hemisphere lateralization (REA) and hemisphere collaboration (DRT) contribute strongly to the verbal ability as described later.

Discussion

The results show that there are significant relation both in verbal ability to REA and verbal ability to DRT. However, there is no significant relation between reading ability and DIST. In Experiment 2, we failed to find significant relationship between reading ability and REA. However, as the used measures and subject sample age were different, (in Experiment 2 Kitao's Reading Test and 5th graders were employed, and ITPA and preschool children were employed in this experiment) this discrepancy was not so queer. Rather, if the selected ITPA predicts reading ability in elementary school as described before, the significant relation between verbal ability and REA seems to suggest that the development of hemisphere specialization in preschool children is one of the prerequisites of their good reading ability in their primary school age.

The more prominent relation between verbal ability and DRT than the relation between verbal ability and REA seems to suggest an important fact. Although DIST consisted of the ability of simple perceptual ability, DRT consisted of at least plural functions such as perception of the target stimulus and reconstruction of the stimulus by the aids of both verbal and motor functions. This is apparent from the study of Kirk (1986) where he studied the development of drawing ability of Reys-Osterieth figure longitudinally. He found that though the ability of copying develops with age in general, the ability makes rapid progress in the age between 10 and 14 years old. He interpreted that this phenomenon was due to the fact that subjects learn to let the right hemisphere (spatial understanding) and the left hemisphere collaborate, that is, the sequential components of graphic problems in copying the complex figure is coded in verbal terms. The Kirk's claim seems to be supported by the results of our previous study with learning disabilities. Yamamoto and Hatta (1984) asked learning disabled children and normal children of age 10 to 11 years old to match tactile stimulus which was given to the left and the right hand as the multiple choice recognition stimuli. Normal subjects showed superior performance than learning disabled as expected but showed no hand difference. Learning disabled showed poor performance but showed clear left hand superiority. Normal subjects made involuntary covert and overt verbalization frequently though they were asked not to make verbalization. These verbalization seems to aid working memory vividly. They interpreted that the synergy of the hemispheres brought superior performnce with no hand difference in normal children and deficit of the synergy in learning disabled brought left hand superiority and poor performance.

The findings by Kirk (1986) and Yamamoto and Hatta (1984) seem to suggest that the superior performance of DRT requires hemisphere collaboration or synergy. Therefore, the strong relation between verbal ability and DRT seems to suggest the importance of the collaboration of both hemispheres in verbal ability of the preschool children.

5. CONCLUSION

Based upon the results of four experiments, we may be able to present several tentative conclusions.

First, though we have systems of writing which are different from other countries, we have reading disabilities as the other countries have. Based upon the recently developed standardized reading test, the incidence rate of reading disabilities corresponds to the one in other countries. This fact suggests that the orthography is not a crucial causal factor to reading disabilities.

The three experiments reported here shed light on the relationship between reading ability and hemisphere function. The hemisphere function has a strong relation to the reading ability in children. More concretely, collaboration of both hemispheres seems to have a special role in reading ability. Further, the simple or shallow levels of perceptual ability have no significant relation to the reading ability of primary and pre-school children.

ACKNOWLEDGMENTS

This study was supported in part by a Ministry of Education Grant-in-aid for Science and Culture (No. 62124033).

REFERENCES

Best, C.T.: 1985, *Hemispheric function and collaboration in the child*, Academic Press, Orlando.

Bryden, M.P.: 1986, 'Dichotic listening performance, cognitive ability, and cerebral organization', *Canadian Journal of Psychology* **40**: 445–456.

Dimond, S.J.: 1972, *The double brain*, Churchill Livingstone, London.

Dennis, M. and Whitaker, H.A.: 1976, 'Language acquisition following hemidecortication: Linguistic superiority of the left over right hemisphere', *Brain and Language* **3**: 472–492.

Downing, J. and Leong, C.K.: 1982, *Psychology of reading*, Macmillan, New York.

Gates, A. and Bradshaw, J.L.: 1977, 'Music perception and cerebral asymmetries', *Cortex* **13**: 390–401.

Hatta, T.: 1986, *Hemisphere collaboration mechanisms in children*, Rowdo-keizai-sya, Tokyo.

Hatta, T.: 1988, 'The reliability of dichotic listening performance: Comparison of CVC and VCV tapes', *Psychologia* **31**: 84–90.

Hatta, T. and Moriya, K.: 1988, 'Developmental changes of hemisphere collaboration for tactile sequential information', *International Journal of Behavioral Development* **11**: 451–465.

Hutchington, B.B.: 1983, 'Finger localization and reading ability in three groups of children ages three through twelve', *Brain and Language* **20**: 143–154.

Kimura, D.: 1967, 'Functional asymmetry of the brain in dichotic listening', *Cortex* **3**: 163–178.

Kirk, U.: 1985, 'Hemispheric contributions to the development of graphic skill', in C.T. Best (ed.) *Hemispheric function and collaboration in the child*, Academic Press, Orlando.

Kitao, N.: 1984, *Reading ability test TK-I*, Taken Syuppan, Tokyo.

Kraft, R.H.: 1983, 'The effect of sex, laterality, and familial handedness on intellectual abilities', *Neuropsychologia* **21**: 79–89.

Lerner, J., Nachshon, I., and Carmon, A.: 1977, 'Responses of paranoid and nonparanoid schizophrenics in a dichotic listening test', *Journal of Nervous and Mental Disease* **164**: 247–353.

Lecy, J.: 1969, 'Possible basis for the evolution of lateral specialization of the human brain', *Nature* **224**: 614–615.

Levy, J.: 1985, 'Interhemispheric collaboration: Simple-mindedness in the asymmetric brain', in C.T. Best (ed.) *Hemispheric function and collaboration in the child*, Academic Press, Orlando.

Lishman, W.A., Toore, B.K., Colbourne, C.J., McMeehan, E.R.L., and Mance, R.M.: 1978, 'Dichotic listening in psychotic patient', *British Journal of Psychiatry* **132**: 333–341.

Makita, K.: 1986, 'The rarity of reading disability in Japanese children', *American Journal of Orthopsychiatry* **38**: 599–614.

Nakatsuka, Z.: 1986, Personal communication.

Quinn, K. and Geffen, G.: 1986, 'The development of tactile transfer of information', *Neuropsychologia* **24**: 793–804.

Salamy, A.: 1978, 'A commissural transmission: maturational changes in human', *Science* **200**: 1409–1411.

Schwartz, J. and Tallal, P.: 1980, 'Rate of acoustic change may underlie hemispheric specialization for speech perception', *Science* **207**: 1380–1381.

Stevenson, H.W., Stiegler, J.W., Luckner, G.W., Lee, S., Hsu, C., and Kitamura, S.: 1982, 'Reading disabilities: The case of Chinese, Japanese, and English', *Child Development* **53**: 1164–1181.

Tanaka, Y., Tarumi, T., and Wakimoto, K.: *Handbook of statistical analyses by personal computer*, Kyoritsu Syuppan, Tokyo.

Yakovlov, P.I. and Lecours, A.R.: 1967, 'The myelogenetic cycles of regional maturation of the brain', in A. Minkowski (ed.) *Regional development of the brain in early life*, Davis, Philadelphia.

Yamamoto, M. and Hatta, T.: 1984, 'Cerebral functional asymmetry and MBD children: A synergistic deficit of hemispheres?', *International Journal of Neurosciences* **24**: 142–148.

Yamamoto, M. and Hirose, T.: 1988, Personal communication.

Yamamoto, M.: 1987, 'Checklist for social development of kindergarten children', submitted to journal.

SHIN-YING LEE, DAVID H. UTTAL, AND CHUANSHENG CHEN

16. WRITING SYSTEMS AND ACQUISITION OF READING IN AMERICAN, CHINESE, AND JAPANESE FIRST-GRADERS

As the chapters in this volume indicate, researchers have shown an increasing interest in the relation between orthography, visual information processing, and reading comprehension. These issues are important, for although the study of reading is one of the oldest and most intensely investigated topics in psychology, most research has been conducted with subjects who read an alphabetic language, usually English. Studying similarities and differences in the processes involved in reading non-alphabetic orthographies provides a means of testing the generality of findings in the psychology of reading.

The focus of this chapter is on the comparison of the initial acquisition of literacy among children learning to read Chinese, Japanese, and English. Most research on the relation between the characteristics of writing systems and the acquisition of literacy has relied on theoretical analyses of the cognitive demands of learning to read the different writing systems. There have been few comparative studies of the acquisition of basic reading skills among children learning to read different types of writing systems. Researchers have suggested that some writing systems may be more or less difficult to read than others, but few researchers have actually tested their hypotheses.

A comparative study of the early acquisition of reading in Chinese, Japanese, and English is of interest for several reasons. First, these languages typically have been used as exemplars of three types of orthographies: logographic, syllabic, and alphabetic (Just and Carpenter, 1987). Thus, a comparative study of first-graders learning to read Chinese, Japanese, and English could provide insight into similarities and differences in the reading process of very different writing systems. Second, it has been claimed that the basic acquisition of a logographic writing system such as Chinese, or a syllabic writing system such as Japanese, may be easier than the acquisition of an alphabetic language, such as English. Gleitman and Rozin (1977), for example, suggested that reading a logographic orthography is easy because it does not require mastering an arbitrary system focusing on symbol-sound relations such as the ones in an alphabetic orthography. They also have suggested that a logographic orthography allows the child to focus more on the abstraction of meaning from text; children do not have to go through the intermediate step of deducing the sound of a word. Along these lines, researchers have noted that reading disabilities seem to be virtually unknown in countries that use logography or syllabic writing

I. Taylor and D.R. Olson (eds.), Scripts and Literacy, 247–263.

systems (Makita, 1968; Rozin, Poritsky, and Sotsky, 1971). The arbitrary nature of the alphabetic system is blamed for the relatively high incidence of reading disabilities in the United States.

Empirical research suggests that Gleitman and Rozin's suggestion may not be correct. In a comparative study of elementary-school children's reading ability in Japan, Taiwan, and the U.S., Stevenson, Lee, Lucker, Kitamura, and Hsu (1982) found that the percentage of children with reading disabilities (defined as reading at a level at least two grades behind their current grade level) was comparable in the three countries. However, finding that the percentage of children with reading disabilities is comparable in the three cultures does not necessarily mean that the reading process is similar for children who learn to read Chinese, Japanese and English. Rather than focusing on the worst readers in the cultures, we are interested in the general influence of orthography on the initial acquisition of reading. Thus, in this report we compared the reading achievement patterns in Chinese, Japanese, and American first-grade children.

One other important reason to compare the early acquisition of reading in different writing systems is that children just learning to read may be influenced more by the effect of orthography than skilled readers. Tzeng and Hung (1980) concluded that the major effect of differences in writing systems involve primarily lower-level perceptual processes. Because the beginning reader's performance probably is much more strongly affected by these processes, it is interesting to study the differences in the early acquisition of reading in languages that use the three basic styles of orthography. Tzeng and Hung's work led us to hypothesize that early reading is most likely to show the effects of orthography than fluent reading, in which higher-level processes play a greater role.

One particular way in which Chinese, Japanese, and English differ that may affect the initial acquisition of reading concerns children's attempts to pronounce newly encountered words. In English and other alphabetic systems, it is possible for children to make a reasonable guess at the pronunciation of new words once they have mastered the sound patterns of the alphabet. Even though there is no direct, systematic grapheme-to-phoneme correspondence in English (Venezky, 1970), children can often make accurate guesses about the correct pronunciation of words they have not learned. In Chinese, however, the cues to pronunciation are much less direct and require more extensive knowledge of the characteristics of the language (Tzeng and Hung, 1981). In Japanese, the combination of two different types of writing systems, *kana* and *kanji*, also presents difficulties for the child learning to read. In this chapter we present data that consider the role of ease and use of pronunciation cues as a factor in the early acquisition of literacy in children learning to read Chinese, Japanese, and English.

We begin with a discussion of how children learn to pronounce Chinese and Japanese. Following this, the method for constructing a test to compare the reading achievement of Chinese, Japanese, and American first-graders is outlined. Finally, we present data on Chinese, Japanese, and American first-graders' reading of words they have learned in their texts, and of words they have not yet encountered in the reading curriculum. The results are discussed in terms of the relation between orthographies and early reading achievement.

ORTHOGRAPHY AND PRONUNCIATION IN CHINESE AND JAPANESE

A review of the characteristics of the Chinese and Japanese writing systems is beyond the scope of this paper. [Reviews of Chinese and Japanese are available in Hung and Tzeng (1982), Just and Carpenter (1987), Taylor and Taylor (1983), Stevenson, Lee, and Stigler (1986), and Unger (1987).] Our focus is on how children learn to read and pronounce new words in learning these languages.

It is important to distinguish between the processes used by older children and adults and those used by children just learning to read. Hung and Tzeng (1981) have suggested that competent reading of all orthographies is a highly automatic process. In all languages, once readers become familiar with the majority of words that they encounter, they typically do not focus on the individual parts of the orthography (e.g., letters, radicals, syllabaries). For example, research has indicated that competent English-speaking children achieve a high degree of automaticity by about third grade; low-achieving third-graders continue to rely largely on the decoding of individual words (Perfetti and Hogaboam, 1975). The pronunciation of Chinese characters, which are used both in written Chinese and written Japanese (*kanji*), usually cannot be predicted without some extensive prior knowledge of the writing system. Hung and Tzeng (1980) found that adult Chinese readers had about a 40% chance of correctly pronouncing words they had never seen before. In contrast, even young readers of English have a reasonably high chance of correctly pronouncing words once they have mastered the basics of the grapheme-phoneme correspondence.

How do children learn to read Chinese? At the beginning of the first semester of first-grade, children are taught to read a simple phonetic spelling system. These extra-orthographic systems are needed because without a great deal of prior knowledge, children have very little chance of being able to pronounce new characters correctly. In the People's Republic of China, the *pinyin* system is used. This system is based upon the Roman alphabet. In Taiwan, a syllabary system known as *zhuyin fuhao* is used. In the elementary textbooks, *pinyin* or *zhuyin fuhao* are printed beside all new characters to facilitate the pronunciation of the characters. After learning these systems, Chinese characters are introduced.

In Japan, early reading instruction focuses primarily on *hiragana*, the syllabary. Most mothers attempt to teach their children at least some *hiragana* before the children enter first grade, and indeed most Japanese kindergartners are proficient with all 46 *hiragana* by the time they start first grade. Knowing *hiragana* is important because it provides a means of pronouncing all Japanese words. Although Japanese is written with a combination of Chinese characters (*kanji*) and syllable symbols (*kana*), Japanese can be written and read entirely in *kana*. By the end of first-grade children have learned to read about 76 *kanji*, these *kanji* are presented with *furigana*, which are small versions of the *hiragana* printed beside a *kanji* to provide pronunciation cues. *Furigana* are also used with *kanji* that are difficult or unusual for adults. *Pinyin, zhuyin fuhao*, and *furigana* thus all serve the same basic function: they provide a means of pronouncing Chinese characters that the reader does not know. An example lesson from the Chinese, Taiwanese, Japanese, and American first-grade textbooks is shown in Figure 1.

Method

Outline of the Studies

The findings come from three studies. All studies were conducted as part of a larger project on the influence of cultural factors on children's academic achievement.

Study 1. First grade children from Beijing, China, and Chicago were compared on their reading performance. In Beijing, 11 representative schools were selected. Because of the greater heterogeneity of the population in Chicago, 20 schools were chosen to represent the Chicago metropolitan area. Two classrooms within each school were randomly selected. All children in the Chinese classes were tested, yielding a sample of 1023 children. In Chicago, six children (three boys and three girls) were randomly chosen from each of the 40 classrooms. The Chicago sample thus consisted of 240 children. Every child was individually given both word decoding and comprehension tests.

Study 2. First grade children enrolled in 20 classrooms in Taipei, Taiwan; Sendai, Japan; and Minneapolis participated in the study. In each city, two classrooms were chosen at random from 10 schools selected to be representative of the schools in each of the cities. A total of 2,111 children (912 Chinese, 789 Japanese, and 410 American children) were given an individually administered reading test that included knowledge of alphabet (*zhuyin fuhao* in Chinese and *hiragana* in Japanese), word decoding, text comprehension, and reading of text.

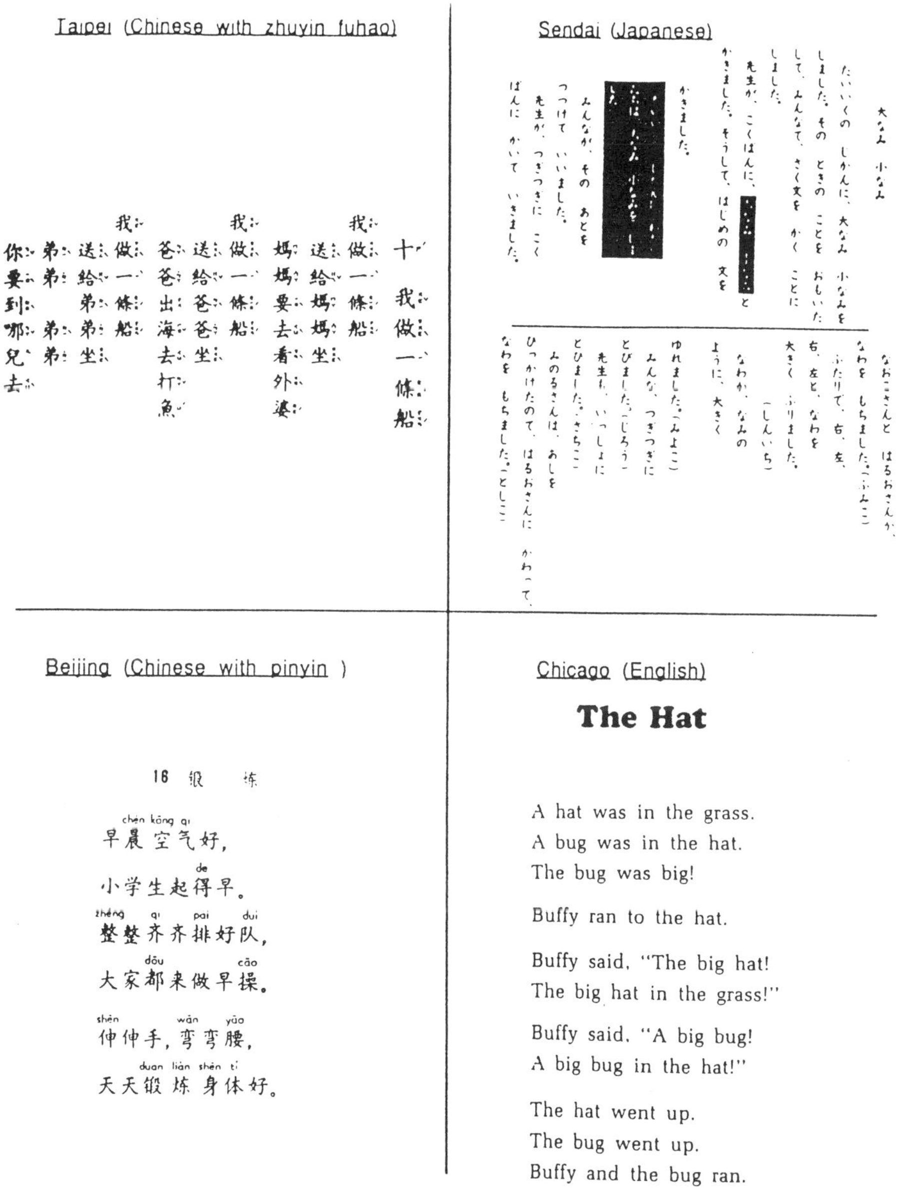

Fig. 1. Examples from first-grade reading texts used in Taipei, Sendai, Beijing, and Chicago. *Zhuyin fuhao* notation is on the right of each of the characters in the Taiwan texts and *pinyin* appears above new or difficult characters in the text from the People's Republic of China. The Chinese text used in Taipei and the Japanese text reads from top to bottom, right to left. The Chinese text used in Beijing, as well as the English text reads from left to right and top to bottom.

Study 3. This study was conducted in Taipei, Taiwan; Sendai, Japan; and Chicago. In Sendai and Taipei, 10 representative schools were selected. The children in Chicago were enrolled in the 20 schools included in Study 1. Within each school, two classrooms were randomly chosen. All 2,763 children in the selected classrooms were given a comprehension test. Six children (three boys and three girls) were randomly chosen from each classroom for an individually administered test of word decoding.

Textbook Analyses, Test Construction and Administration

The construction of culturally fair and appropriate tests is a common problem in comparative research. Translations, even if done assiduously, may be inappropriate because children in one culture may not be familiar with the words used in another culture. Our method of test construction differs from other methods of constructing comparative reading tests in two ways: First, all the tests were constructed simultaneously in two (Study 1) or three (Study 2, 3) languages. Second, we constructed our reading test on the basis of detailed analyses of textbooks used in the cities involved. Two separate analyses of the curricula were conducted: one of the elementary reading textbooks used in Chicago and Beijing, and the other of the textbooks used in Sendai, Taipei, and Minneapolis. We will describe in detail the test construction process for Study 1.

Selecting a textbook was straightforward in Beijing, Taipei, and Sendai because a standardized curriculum is used in each location. In Chicago and Minneapolis, we chose the series used by the largest number of schools in our studies.

Textbook Analyses. The grade and semester level at which each new word was introduced in the textbook was entered into a computer database. Even at this early stage a problem arose that was a function of the different writing systems. The definition of a "word" is straightforward in English, but more difficult in Chinese and Japanese. In Chinese, one character could be a word if it has meaning by itself. The combination of characters becomes a new word on the basis of a derived new meaning. The same character can have different meanings in different words. A word, therefore, is defined as one or more characters that has unique meaning. In English, neither regular forms of the plural of nouns, nor regular conjugations of verbs, such as the past participle, were counted as new words. Irregular plurals (e.g., child to children) or irregular conjugations of verbs (e.g., go to went) were counted as new words.

All words in the English textbooks were entered into a computer database. A dictionary of new words was constructed for Book 1, and each word in the next successive level book of the series was compared to all words in the dictionary. New words thus were defined as those words occurring in a given text that were not in the dictionary previously. As each new word in the text was encountered, its grade and semester level of introduction was noted automatically. In analyzing the Chinese texts, the words were defined, rewritten in *pinyin*, and entered into the computer, along with the English translation of the words and the grade and semester levels when they were first introduced. This method provided us with a listing of when each word was introduced in the curriculum, as well as a tally of the number of words introduced at each semester level.

From these analyses, we obtained data on the number of words taught throughout the elementary school years in the four cities. Figure 2 shows the number of words introduced in the elementary school reading books in Beijing and Chicago (Study 1). Chinese textbooks contained more unique words than American textbooks for Grades 1 to 3. In the last three years of elementary school, however, American children were exposed to many more new words than were Chinese children.

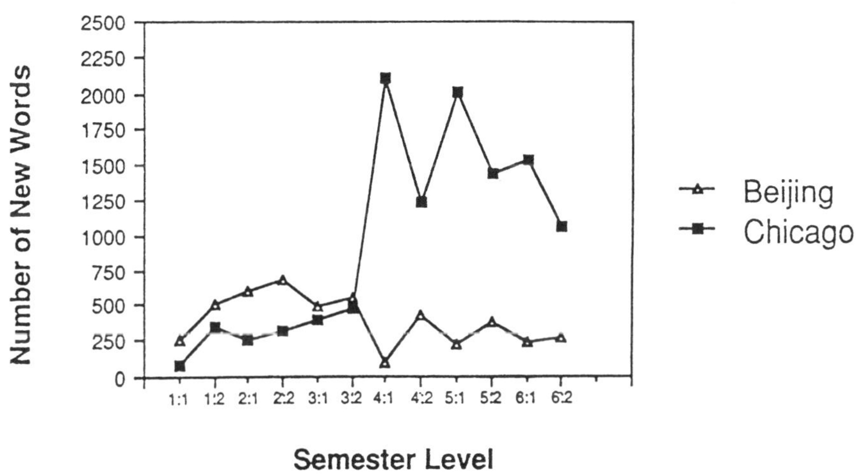

Fig. 2. Number of new words taught every semester in the Beijing and Chicago reading textbooks.

Test Construction. Based on the textbook analyses, we constructed a reading test with two parts: word decoding and comprehension. The analysis of the order of introduction of new words provided the basis for our assessment of words common to the two countries. Our original goal in constructing the decoding portion of the test was to include the same words for all countries at each grade and semester level. This proved to be impossible because there were not enough words common to the curricula used in the two countries. Thus, we included some words that were common and some that were not common to the two curricula. Ten words were chosen on the basis of frequency of usage from the pool of new words available at each semester. The tests progressed successively from first grade, first semester through sixth grade, second semester.

The second portion of the test was comprehension. This portion was divided into two subsections: phrase or sentence comprehension, and paragraph comprehension. The phrase and sentence comprehension subsection was included in grades 1 to 3; the paragraph comprehension subsection was included from grades 4 to 6. The same number of new words had to be introduced in the sentences and paragraphs for both countries. The number of words from previous semesters was also taken into account. Grammatical structures were also checked by a bilingual linguist, to ensure that the complexity of the sentences and paragraphs was comparable. We also tried to match the paragraphs thematically as closely as possible. For example, the paragraph used in the second semester of sixth grade in the United States was about the restoration of the Statue of Liberty, and the Chinese paragraph was about the restoration of the Great Wall.

The procedure for constructing the reading tests for Studies 2 and 3 was very similar except that the curricula in the three languages was considered simultaneously and the design of the tests were matched among the languages at the grade level rather than the semester level.

Test Administration. For Study 1, tests were administered individually to one child at a time. In the word decoding section, children were asked to read aloud the words presented. In the section testing comprehension of phrase and sentences, children were asked to read the phrase or sentence and then choose the picture from a set of alternatives that best represented the idea or action described in the phrase or sentence. Once children started the section for a semester level, they proceeded through all the test items for that semester. If a child missed three out of ten words, testing was discontinued. In the paragraph comprehension portion of the test, the child was asked to read paragraphs at each semester level and then answer several questions about their content. Testing was discontinued if a child missed 2 out of 4 comprehension questions at any semester level.

The test administration procedure for Studies 2 and 3 were basically similar, except that the stopping criteria differed from study to study.

Results

Most of our results involve two comparisons: of items at or below children's grade level, and of items above children's grade level. The pattern of results for these two comparisons varies substantially among the four locations. We believe it is likely that characteristics of the different writing systems are partly responsible for these differences.

Figure 3 shows the results for word-decoding for first-graders from Studies 1 and 3. The two graphs depict the percentage of subjects who

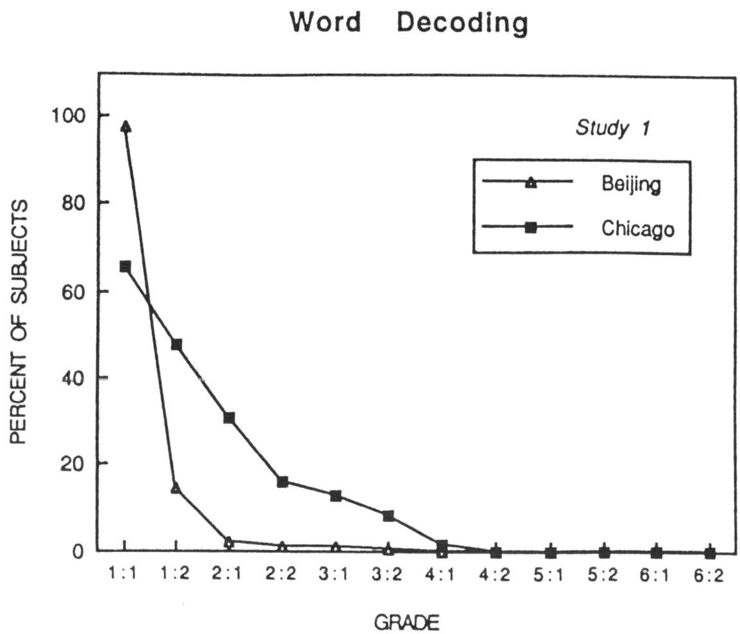

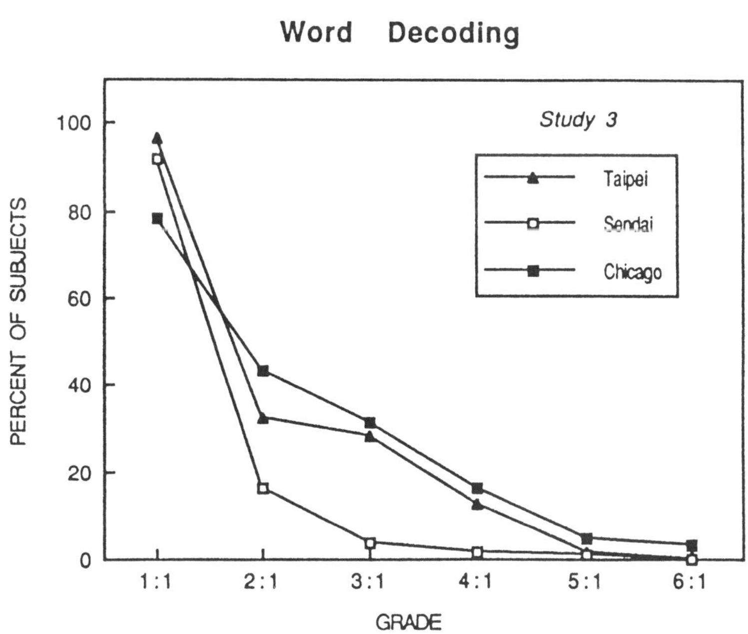

Fig. 3. Percent of subjects completing each level of the word decoding tests for Study 1 and Study 3.

passed each grade level of the tests. The pattern of the results was similar for the two studies. In all cities some children failed to read the words even for the first-semester of the first-grade, and this percentage was substantially higher among the American first-graders than among the Chinese and Japanese first-graders. That is, American children performed worse than children in the other countries when reading words at the first-grade level. Over 90 percent of the children from Sendai, Taipei, and Beijing could read words introduced during the first grade, but less than 80% of the Chicago children could do so. This finding suggests that the commonly held belief that alphabetic languages are more difficult to learn than logographic or syllabic language could be true. However, as the remainder of the graphs show, the pattern of performance was different for decoding words beyond the children's current grade level. In both studies, American children performed much better than the Japanese and Chinese children on words beyond the first-grade level. A higher percentage of American children read words beyond their grade level than did their Chinese and Japanese counterparts.

A similar pattern obtained for the results of the comprehension test (see Figure 4). Almost all of the Chinese children were able to comprehend the first-grade reading material, but only about 80 percent of the American children were able to do so. However, significantly more American than Chinese first-graders were able to comprehend materials beyond their grade level and were able to proceed to later grade levels of the test than were their Chinese counterparts.

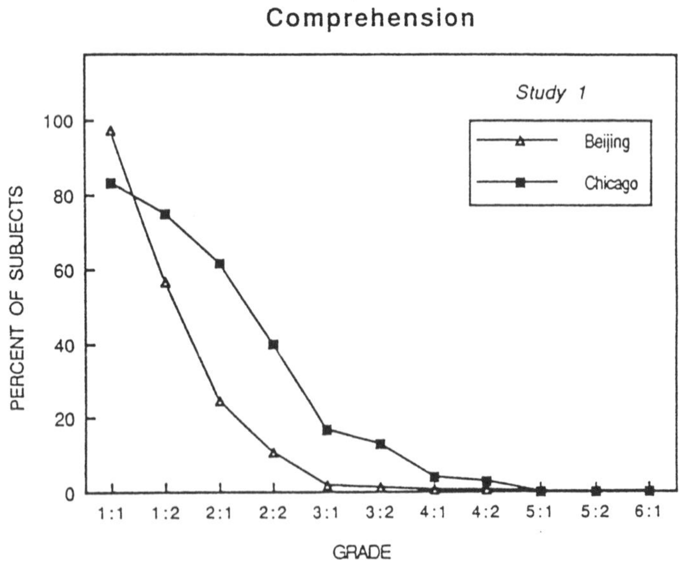

Fig. 4. Percent of subjects completing each level of the comprehension test for Study 1.

Another way to examine these results is to compare the performance of children who actually continued the tests to the higher grade and semester levels. Figure 5 shows the performance of children from Study 2 on the word decoding test at each grade level. American children performed less well than the Chinese and Japanese children on the first-grade level words. However, for reading words beyond their grade level, American children performed significantly better than the Chinese and Japanese children. Similar results are shown in Figure 6 for the comprehension test from Study 1 at each semester and grade level. Chinese children did better than American children on questions at the semester level in which they are enrolled. But beyond their current semester level, American children performed at a higher level than Chinese children.

To assess further the relative pattern of performance on the comprehension tests, we examined children's ability to decode the key words in each paragraph. The key words were those that were introduced in the textbook at the target level for the paragraph. This analysis allowed us to assess whether children's failures in comprehension resulted simply from an inability to read words that were critical to abstracting the meaning of the paragraphs and questions, or from generally poor comprehension skills. As shown in Figure 7, the pattern of results for these key words is very similar to that for the decoding words: American children do less well on the key words at their current semester level, but American children are able to read significantly more key words beyond their grade level than their

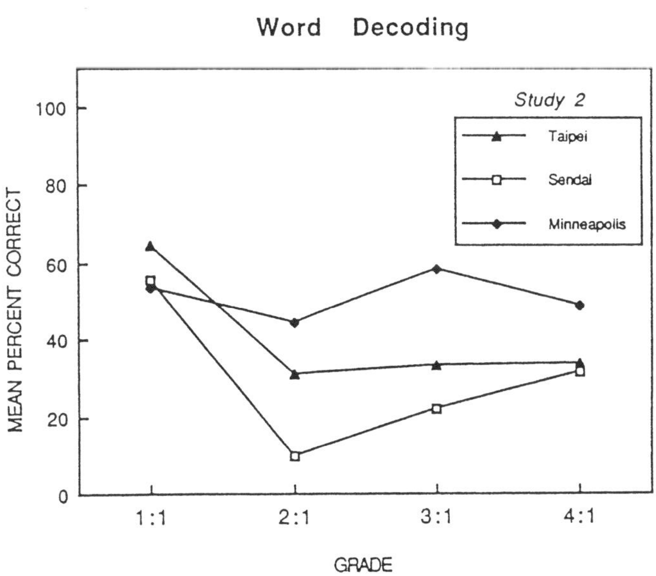

Fig. 5. Average percent of correctness on word decoding test of children at various levels of reading skills.

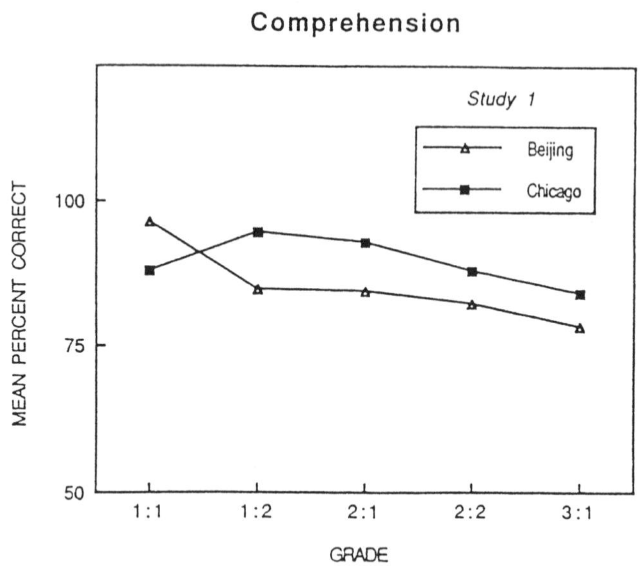

Fig. 6. Average percent of correctness on comprehension test of children at various levels of reading skills.

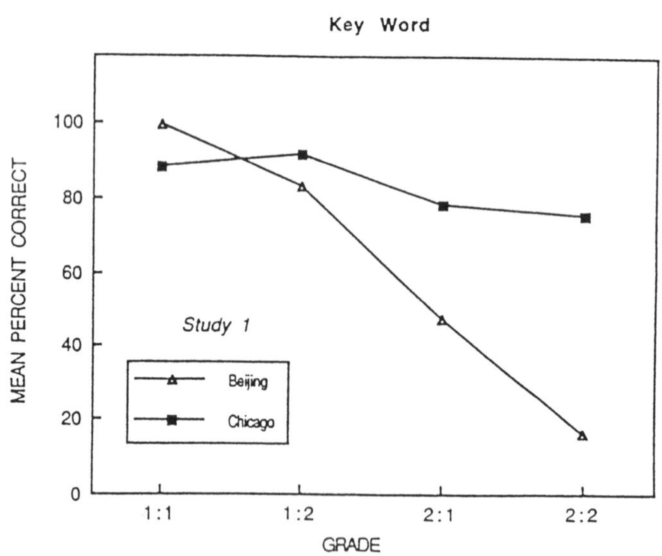

Fig. 7. Average percent of correctness on decoding the key words of children at various levels of reading skills.

Chinese counterparts. American children thus were more likely to be able to answer comprehension questions beyond their grade level.

The pattern of the results cannot be attributed solely to the characteristics of a single test. Our results are based on three different reading tests that were given to large samples of children in five locations. For both word decoding and reading comprehension, consistent findings were shown that American first-graders, on average, did less well on reading material at their current grade level than did the Chinese and Japanese first-graders. But a substantially greater proportion of the American children were able to read materials beyond their current grade or semester level. In addition, those American children who were able to read beyond their grade level were able to read at a higher level than their Chinese and Japanese counterparts.

Explanation of the Cross-Over Interaction. What accounts for the consistent findings that American children were better able to read words beyond their grade level? This could be the direct result of the orthography. Once children have mastered the basic letter-to-sound rules of English orthography, they can make good guesses at the sounds of words they have not previously encountered. Children who learn to read Chinese characters or Japanese *kanji* do not have this advantage.

Another important aspect of the data is the relatively poor performance of American children for words at their current grade level. One could argue that this difference also reflects the characteristics of the English writing system. Perhaps a certain percentage of children learning to read English simply fail to understand the code of grapheme-phoneme correspondence. While this may be true, it seems worthwhile to examine the characteristics of the distribution of the reading scores in the Chicago first-grade sample. As shown in Figure 8, the total range of the mean scores for each classroom in comprehension scores is much wider in Chicago than in Taipei or Sendai for Study 3. A comparable pattern of results was found for comparisons of children in Chicago and Beijing in Study 1.

We believe that the broad distribution of American scores could be related both to the characteristics of the tasks encountered by American children learning to read English, and the educational practices for handling slow and fast readers in the American classrooms. In other words, the American sample contained both more poor readers and more good readers. Poor readers have difficulty reading any words, but the good readers are able to read words even several semesters beyond their current grade level. In contrast, the Chinese and Japanese samples have fewer children at either end of the distribution of reading performance. The distribution of scores from Study 2 supports this contention. We counted the number of children from each city who received the highest and the lowest 100 scores from all three cities and combined the results. If children from the three cities performed equally well in reading, approximately 33 children from each

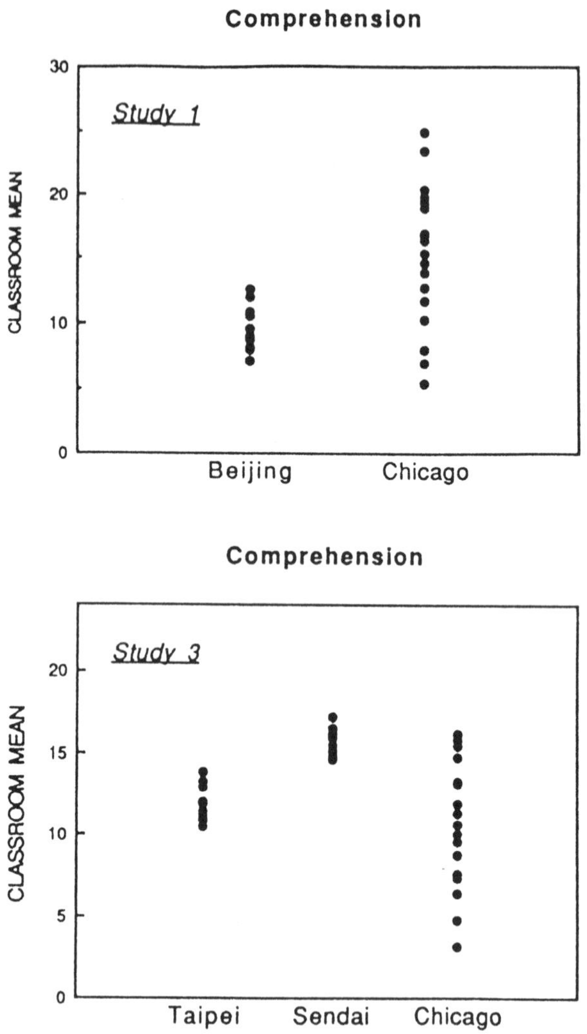

Fig. 8. Mean Scores on the comprehension tests for each school in Beijing and Chicago (Study 1), and Taipei, Sendai, and Chicago (Study 3).

city should be among those obtaining the top and bottom scores. In fact, American children were overrepresented in both groups. Fifty-eight American children were among the 100 first graders with the lowest scores in reading performance and 40 American children were among the top 100 children with the highest scores in reading scores. We believe that the greater number of poor readers in the American sample could be partly responsible for the finding that fewer American children were able to read words at their grade level. Similarly, the greater number of good readers in the American sample could be partly responsible for the finding that more American children were able to read words beyond their grade level.

The results suggest that some American children may have difficulty with the initial stages of reading English. We cannot say for sure if this is an independent effect of orthography, but it is important to consider the characteristics of English per se before generalizing to all alphabetic languages. Several researchers have demonstrated that the initial acquisition of decoding skills is faster in children learning to read highly regular alphabetic systems, such as Turkish (Oney and Goldman, 1984) or Finnish (Kyostio, 1980). Regularity in English orthography is found at the morphophonetic level, not at the phonetic level. Thus, English cannot be learned as a set of simple writing-to-sound rules. It is important not to allow these difficulties to bias our interpretation of the relative difficulty of learning to read all alphabetic languages. English appears to be a relatively difficult language in which to gain an understanding of the grapheme-to-phoneme code. An interesting question for further research is whether the cross-over interaction that we have shown in the patterns of American children's reading achievement patterns would also be found in cultures that use more regular alphabetic orthographies.

Discussion

Our results reveal that the relation between orthography and the acquisition of literacy is more complex than has been assumed previously. The earliest acquisition of reading skills may depend strongly on phonemic awareness and segmentation skills involved in learning an alphabetic languages; these skills may be relatively unimportant when learning to read a logographic language. Once the initial principle of grapheme-to-phoneme correspondence is mastered, however, the alphabetic language may offer a significant advantage. The ability to sound out words allows children reading an alphabetic language to guess the sounds of words they have not encountered before. In contrast to the suggestion of some researchers (e.g., Gleitman and Rozin, 1977), our data provide no indication that learning to read is easier when the child learns to read a non-alphabetic language. In fact, the absence of a means of sounding out characters means that pronunciation of new words is a common problem for the Chinese and the Japanese readers.

An additional advantage of an alphabetic system concerns the acquisition of new word meanings from context. There is evidence (e.g., Nagy, Anderson, and Herman, 1987) that this is an important factor in the acquisition of new vocabulary words once children acquire basic decoding skills. Even if children cannot pronounce a word completely, they still can use the contextual and previous information as cues to deduce the word's meaning. But this is much more difficult or even impossible when reading a logographic writing system. Guessing the meaning of the word from context becomes much more difficult when the possibility of sounding out the word is reduced. Thus, the greater possibility of deriving the meaning of a word from context is another positive advantage of an alphabetic writing system.

The Importance of Instruction. Our results also show that it is important to consider the role of curriculum and instruction when considering differences in achievement patterns in countries that use different orthographies. Children in all Asian countries did better than American children on words at their current grade level. This finding is similar to comparable studies of mathematics achievement (Bartsch and Fang, 1987; Stigler *et al.*, 1982). The probability that children will actually learn the concepts included in the curricula is much higher in Japanese and Chinese than in American schools.

One can, in fact, interpret the results as an interaction between the nature of the orthography and the nature of the curriculum and instructions. For the Chinese first-graders, learning characters is the primary task of learning to read. For American children, however, the task is not simply learning words; they must learn the rules of their orthography. Perhaps it is not surprising, then, to learn that the Chinese curriculum contains more than twice as many words in first grade as the American curriculum. Thus, our results do not constitute a criticism of the Chinese curriculum or teaching methods. The nature of Chinese orthography dictates that instruction is critical in the acquisition of new words, and the design of the Chinese curriculum appears to reflect this fact.

Conclusion. Our results indicate that attempts to characterize different writing systems as easy or difficult to learn may not capture all of the influences of the writing system. Each writing system has both easy and difficult features. The ways that these languages are taught, and the patterns of achievement that we have found, reflect different aspects of the writing systems. Just as early cross-cultural research failed in its attempts to describe cultures as more or less primitive, we believe that attempts to describe writing systems along a simple continuum of difficulty are inadequate. What is needed instead is detailed analyses of the tasks that the child faces in learning a particular language.

ACKNOWLEDGEMENTS

Our collaborators throughout this project are Harold Stevenson and Max Lummis in the United States; Chen-Chin Hsu in Taipei; Siero Kitamura in Sendai; and Tong Lequan, Fang Ge in Beijing. We wish to thank the participants of the conference, and the organizers, Insup Taylor and David Olson, for their helpful comments.

REFERENCES

Bartsch, K. and Fang, G.: 1987, 'Asian and American math textbooks and achievement patterns', Paper presented at the Meetings of the Society for Research in Child Development, Baltimore, Maryland.

Gleitman, L.R. and Rozin, P.: 1977, 'The structure and acquisition of reading I: Relations between orthographies and the structure of language', in A.S. Reber and D.L. Scarborough (eds.) *Toward a Psychology of Reading*, Erlbaum, Hillsdale, NJ.

Hung, D.L. and Tzeng, O.J.L.: 1981, 'Orthographic variation and visual information processing', *Psychological Bulletin* **90**: 377–414.

Just, M.A. and Carpenter, P.A.: 1987, *The Psychology of Reading and Language Comprehension*, Allyn and Bacon, Inc., Boston, MA.

Kyostio, O.K.: 1980, 'Is learning to read easy in a language in which the grapheme-phoneme correspondences are regular?' in J.F. Kavanagh and R.L. Venezky (eds.) *Orthography, Reading, and Dyslexia*, University Park Press, Baltimore.

Liberman, I.Y., Liberman, A.M., Mattingly, I., and Shankweiler, D.: 1980, 'Orthography and the beginning reader', in J.F. Kavanagh and R.L. Venezky (eds.) *Orthography, Reading, and Dyslexia*, University Park Press, Baltimore.

Makita, K.: 1968, 'The rarity of reading disability in Japanese children', *American Journal of Orthopsychiatry* **38**: 599–614.

Nagy, W.E., Anderson, R.C., and Herman, P.A.: 1987, 'Learning word meanings from context during normal reading', *American Education Research Journal* **24**: 237–270.

Oney, B. and Goldman, S. R.: 1984, 'Decoding and comprehension skills in Turkish and English: Effects of the regularity of grapheme-phoneme correspondences', *Journal of Education Psychology* **76**: 557–568.

Perfetti, C.A. and Hogaboam, T.: 1975, 'The relationship between single word decoding and reading comprehension skill', *Journal of Education Psychology* **67**: 461–469.

Rozin, P. and Gleitman, L.R.: 1977, 'The structure and acquisition of reading II: The reading process and the acquisition of the alphabetic principle', in A.S. Reber and D.L. Scarborough (eds.) *Toward a Psychology of Reading*, Erlbaum, Hillsdale, NJ.

Rozin, P., Poritsky, S., and Sotsky, R.: 1971, 'American children with reading problems can easily learn to read English represented by Chinese characters', *Science* **171**: 1264–1267.

Stevenson, H.W., Stigler, J.W., Lucker, G.W., Lee, S.Y., Hsu, C.C., and Kitamura, S.: 1982, 'Reading disabilities: The case of Chinese, Japanese, and English', *Child Development* **53**: 1164–1181.

Stevenson, H.W., Lee, S.Y., and Stigler, J.W.: 1986, 'Learning to read Japanese', in H. W. Stevenson, H. Azuma and K. Hakuta (eds.) *Child Development and Education in Japan*, Freeman, New York.

Stigler, J.W., Lee, S.Y., Lucker, G.W., and Stevenson, H.W.: 1982, 'Curriculum and achievement in mathematics: A study of elementary school children in Japan, Taiwan, and the United States', *Journal of Educational Psychology* **74**: 315–322.

Taylor, I. and Taylor, M. M.: 1983, *The Psychology of Reading*, Academic, New York.

Tzeng, O.J.L. and Hung. D.L.: 1980, 'Reading in the non-alphabetic writing system: Some experimental studies', in J.F. Kavanagh and R.L. Venezky (eds.) *Orthography, Reading, and Dyslexia*, University Park Press, Baltimore.

Tzeng, O.J.L. and Hung, D.L.: 1981, 'Linguistic determinism: A written language perspective', in O.J.L. Tzeng and H. Singer (eds.) *Perception of Print: Reading Research in Experimental Psychology*, Erlbaum, Hillsdale, NJ.

Unger, J.M.: 1987, *The Fifth Generation Fallacy: Why Japanese is Betting its Future on Artificial Intelligence*, Oxford University Press, New York.

Venezky, R.: 1970, *The Structure of English Orthography*, Mouton & Co., The Hague, The Netherlands.

PURUSHOTTAM G. PATEL

17. BRAHMI SCRIPTS, ORTHOGRAPHIC UNITS AND READING ACQUISITION

INTRODUCTION

The different scripts used to represent the Indo-Aryan, Dardic, Dravidian, Austro-Asiatic, and Tibeto-Burman languages in India and in the adjoining Indo-Chinese region are based on a writing system known as Brahmi which evolved in Ancient India (Gelb, 1952; Hale, 1982; Shapiro and Schiffman, 1983; Ruhlen, 1987; Comrie, 1987). The linguistic adaptability of Brahmi to genetically unrelated languages is an interestingly unusual case in the evolutionary history of writing. It seems that the linguistic principle underlying Brahmi is such that it can facilitate reading acquisition, at least, initially. This paper indicates how the Hindu scholars in ancient India formulated the orthographic design of Brahmi and relates it to the current phonological notions of moraic and extrametrical units; it also suggests how Brahmi orthography can be relevant to reading acquisition and presents some observations on how Gujarati children in India learn to use it.

ADAPTABLE DRAVIDIAN AND AUSTROASIATIC LANGUAGES

The script known as "Kharosti", which emerged in India during the reign of Emperor Ashok (272–326 B.C.), was a syllabary related to Proto-Semitic; it was used only in the extreme Northwest of India for six centuries (Das Dupta, 1958); while Brahmi has flourished from the third century B.C. onwards (Buhler, 1963; Upasak, 1960; Verma, 1971). Basham (1967: 394) suggests that the Brahmi script documented in the Ashokan inscriptions represents the Sanskrit sound system so well that it must have had a long developmental history. As Upasak (1960) argues, "Brahmi may have begun as a mercantile alphabet, based either on vague memories of the Harappa script or derived from contact with Semitic traders, indeed it may have owed to both these sources; but by the time of Ashoka, it was the most developed and scientific script of the world" (p. 21).

The Ashokan Brahmi consists of seven vowels, including nasal and 33 consonants, including semi-vowels (Verma, 1971). Following Buhler (1959), Upsak (1960) suggests that "a distinction between the basic and evolved forms is easily traceable, especially in case of the scriptal units for vowels which represent the Sanskrit grammatical rules of Vriddhi and Guna sandhis" (p. 15). Buhler (1959) compared the North Semitic and the Brahmi scripts and noted the direct involvement of the pre-Paninian Hindu phoneticians in the linguistic design of Brahmi, especially in relation to (1)

I. Taylor and D.R. Olson (eds.), Scripts and Literacy, 265–275.

the five nasal letters, (2) a sign for nasalization, and (3) the non-expression of a medial vowel in accordance with the teachings of the Hindu phonologists who considered it inherent in every consonant, etc. Consonant conjuncts are also found in Ashokan Brahmi (Dani, 1986: 44).

Brahmi has not only been the underlying orthographic design in the different scripts for the different language communities in Indo-Aryan and Dravidian India; it has been found adaptable as well in the adjacent Austro-Asiatic and Tibeto-Burman linguistic peninsula. The multitude of the different scripts used in the entire Brahmi linguistic domain involve two prototypic types: Dewanagari and Grantha. The scripts for Dravidian and some Austro-Asiatic languages are based on Grantha, while the other scripts are related to Dewanagari which was developed for the Indo-Aryan classical language Sanskrit (Krishnamurti and Gwynn, 1985; Danvivathana, 1987; Miller, 1956; Haas, 1956; Jones and Khin, 1953; etc.). In his monograph on the Burmese writing system Roop (1972: ix) suggests that "The extent of early India influence in continental Southeast Asia in nowhere more apparent than in the use of Indian writing systems for noncognate languages covering large parts of the latter area." The Sukhothai script of Thailand is derived from the Ancient Khmer Civilization which ruled it from the tenth to thirteenth centuries A.D. (Briggs, 1951; Coedes, 1968). As Danvivanthana (1987: 24) points out, "The Grantha form of the Brahmi script is the origin of the Khmer script. The Grantha came to be used in Indo-China through the spread of the Buddhist religion and contact in trade. In 300 B.C. Ceylon became the first country in South-East Asia which brought the Grantha script into use." The Tibetan and Burmese scripts, which developed about 700 A.D. and 500 A.D., respectively, are based on Dewanagari (Trager, 1974; Jones and Khin, 1953). Brahmi, thus, allowed the growth of different scripts and came to be used for both polysyllabic and tonal monosyllabic languages.

It is generally assumed that it is the nature of linguistic organization that determines the type of writing system that can adapt and survive in a given linguistic community. The Chinese logographic system has extended only eastward, but not westward (Wang, 1981). The linguistic structure of Japanese could not do with the logographic system by itself; it required the addition of the syllabary, which travelled from to Japan via China and Korea (Miller, 1967). In his analysis of the evolutionary process underlying the development of the Greek alphabet, Pedersen (1931: 146) argued that

> The various types of language have all made their own contributions to the development of writing. A language with many simply constructed mono-syllabic words, and also with some words of more than one syllable, was the best foundation for the formation of the first mixed word-and-syllable script: such a language was spoken by the Summerians. The transfer to a language richer in syllables, especially one with simple syllables, necessarily furthered the transformation of the script in such a way that word-characters became rarer, and syllable-characters increased: Assyrian was just such a language. A language with many

complex syllables, like Old Persian and other ancient Indo-European languages, must necessarily provide an incentive for breaking up syllables artificially.

Pedersen's analysis certainly applies to the emergence of the vocalic graphemes in the Greek alphabet, in particular and the alphabetic system in general. Interestingly, Brahmi, which is presumably related historically to Proto-Semetic writing and was developed for an Indo-Aryan classical language, namely, Sanskrit, has adapted to the linguistic patterns of Dravidian languages in India and to those of the Austro-Asiatic and Sino-Tibetan languages in the Indo-Chinese peninsula. The modifications necessary for the scriptal representation of the Dravidian language, Tamil, were made as early as the third to second centuries B.C. (Mahadevan, 1971).

LINGUISTIC ORGANIZATION OF BRAHMI

The classification of the Dewanagari and Grantha scripts has been problematic for many analysts. Gelb (1952) raises the question as to whether the linguistic organization of Brahmi should be considered syllabic or alphabetic. Cohen (1958) labels it "l'écriture syllabo-alphabétique de l'Inde" in his discussion of what he calls "le néosyllabisme". Miller (1967) and Jensen (1970) agree with Cohen (1958) and consider it semi-syllabic. Some consider the system outright syllabic (Lambert, 1953; Mohanan, 1986). Actually, Taylor's (1980) analysis of the Korea "Hangul" as an "alphabetic syllabary" applies to Brahmi in an important way. Regarded in terms of grapho-phonological correspondences, Brahmi and Hangul allow maximum alphabetic representation. When Brahmi is conceived in terms of written representation and processes, it becomes clear that the minimal phonological units are arranged in larger, hierarchical configurations (cf. Henderson, 1984).

The origin of the linguistic design of Brahmi seems to be related to the oral mode of learning in ancient India. Vedic students were obliged to memorize and preserve the verses without any changes and deviations, a task which required knowledge of pronunciation techniques. The pronunciation manuals known as Pratishakhyas give a word-for-word version and provide rules on how to construct from it the text in continuous recitation. The Pratishakyas are phonetic treatises relating to the pronunciation of the four Vedas. As Scharfe (1977: 130) explains, "The Veda reciter had to learn how to constitute the continuous text from the word-for-word text, observing the rules of vowel and consonant sandhi as well as those of accentuation." The Rigveda Pratishakhya ascribed to Vedamitra Shakalya breaks up the text into words and syllables by dissolving sandhi (Scharfe, 1977) to help the Rigveda priests to count syllables so that they could articulate the metrical arrangement accurately. Thieme (1935: 124) aptly describes the different Pratishakhyas as 'reading grammars'. In little known monograph, Mahulkar (1981: 49) suggests that

> The Pratisakhya grammarians observed the natural, articulatory patterns in speech production and worked out the distinction between syllabic and nonsyllabic sounds. . . . the Pratisakhya writers started with *a scaler notion of speech sounds organized within syllables rather than speech sounds as delimitative units following each other sequentially.*

This enabled them to concentrate their attention on the structure of a syllable and to distinguish the sonant (vocalic) and the consonant elements according to the functions they performed within the syllable. When it came to writing a phone they used different signs if it had different functions in the syllable or it had a different attachment. Accordingly, the *r* in *krama* was written differently from that in *karma*: In the former it was the second element of the consonant cluster going with the first sonant (), while in the latter it was the first element of the consonant cluster going with the second sonant ().

Recent developments in phonological theory are specifically relevant to the question of what Brahmi orthographic units represent. Focusing on the "problems arising from the analysis of consonant sequences" in syllable structure, Hyman (1985: 2–3) suggests that ". . . languages group segments into beats or weight units (WU's) which, to some extent, correspond to the traditional notion of the mora in certain of its realizations." Moras are timing units or beats: Heavy syllables are supposed to consist of two moras and light syllables are treated as single moras. Moras operate as timing units in tone languages as well. Hyman (1985: 10) points out that "In most tone and tonal accent languages, it is the mora that is the tone-bearing unit (TBU)."

The other notion which is relevant to the interpretation of Brahmi orthographic units involves "extrametricality" in autosegmental representations. It is suggested that certain constituents on the periphery of a stress domain should be excluded from consideration when applying stress rules; such stress-peripheral constituents are called "extrametrical" (Hayes, 1982). Pulleyblank (1986: 19) argues that the notion of extrametrical constituents is basically "applicable in tone systems": "Tonal constituents that are marked as extratonal lose their extratonality if they cease to be on the periphery of the relevant domain." In what specific ways are the notions of moraic units and extrametrical constituents applicable to Brahmi orthographic units?

The written representational units in Brahmi are moraic, consisting of the onset (initial consonant or consonants) and the vocalic nucleus of the syllable, leaving out the coda (final consonant in syllabic organization). The hierarchical organization of the syllable consists of the onset (consonant or consonant cluster), the nucleus (vowel), and the coda (consonant or consonant cluster). The vocalic nucleus and the onset together form the unit, while the coda, which is mainly extrametrical, is treated as an independent unit which is either made moraic by adding the schwa vowel to it or left alone. In other words, the prevocalic consonants and the vocalic constituents together form spatio-hierarchically arranged units and the extrametrical constituents form independent units, either as moras (when the schwa vowel is added) or as phonemes. This proposal accounts for all the available descriptions of the different scripts based on Brahmi (Lambert, 1953; McGregor, 1972; Krishnamurti and Gwynn, 1985; Miller, 1956; Haas, 1956; Roop, 1972; Danvivathana, 1987; etc.). To look at some of the details briefly, all the vocalic and consonantal segments have their counterparts in graphemic features, which are combined to form spatially delimited hierarchical units. The shapes of the vocalic constituents change in non-initial positions. The vowel "schwa" has no independent graphemic form; it is implicitly present in all independent consonantal written units (unless otherwise indicated with a diacritic under them), which are, in terms of current phonological theory, either moraic or extrametrical. The spatial positions of the non-initial vocalic graphological features have different designated locations around the consonantal graphemic features. In mora-graphic configurations, consonantal constituents remain central and the noninitial vocalic constituents are placed to the left, to the right, above, and below them. (See McGregor, 1972 and Krishnamurti and Gwynn, 1985 for details on how Hindi is written in Dewanagari and Telugu is written in Grantha, respectively.) The topographical organization of the consonantal-vocalic units in the Brahmi scripts is interesting in terms of the models of orthographic processing in cognitive neuroscience (see, Patel, in press, for the linguistic-topographical analysis of Brahmi scripts).

How would this picture accommodate tonal markers, for example, in Thai? Recall Hyman's (1985) suggestion that the moraic units carry the tonal patterns in tone languages. To take the case of Thai, the monosyllables are divided into the "live" and "dead" categories and the consonants arc divided into three tonal classes: middle, high, and low. There are five tones in Standard Thai which have different values depending upon the tonal class of the syllable-initial consonant symbol with which they are being used. Danvivathana (1987: 131–132) suggests that

For each voiceless high consonant, there is a corresponding low consonant which has the same phonetic value except for tone. It is noted by Fang Kuei Li in his *A Handbook of Comparative Tai* (1976), p. 23, that the voiceless low consonants were originally voiced. They have become devoiced, and the distinction of old voiced and voiceless consonants is utilized to mark the different in tones.

Along with the class of the prevocalic consonants, the second conditioning factor for tone marking is the types of the syllable used, whether it is "live" or "dead". All tonal markers are superscripts which are placed over the prevocalic consonants of the moraic units whose tones they mark. When consonants carry noninitial vocalic superscripts over them, the tonal markers are placed on top of them. Without going into the rules of tone selection, it can be seen that the moraic nature of the Brahmi orthographic unit must have been a major factor in the survival of the system since the creation of the ancient Thai script "Sukhothai" which was modelled after the Grantha form of Brahmi under the influence of the Ancient Khmer civilization.

To recapitulate, Brahmi and its two major prototypic scripts, namely, Dewanagari and Grantha, characteristically consist of spatio-hierarchical units called "aksharas" which represent moras and extrametrical consonants. Does the linguistic-orthographic delimitation of units in Brahmi writing have any significance for reading acquisition?

BRAHMI AND READING ACQUISITION

Developmental research now clearly suggests that the ontogenetic process begins with whole patterns and children gradually learn to segment these gestalt like utterances into smaller units (Waterson, 1981; Peters, 1983; Macken, 1979; etc.). Researchers also recognize that the ability to segment speech into different hierarchical units follows a developmental course as reading emerges as a component of language acquisition (Patel, 1983). Children initially perceive utterances as "united semantic wholes" and begin by segmenting them into "intonational-semantic groups of subjects and predicates" (Karpova, 1977). Later during middle childhood, syllables are perceived as segmentable units in phrases, words follow syllables and the phonemes are the last in the development of segmental awareness (Karpova, 1977; Fox and Routh, 1975; Liberman, Shankweiler, Fischer, and Carter, 1974; Mattingly, 1978; Stanovich, Cunningham, and Cramer, 1984). Interestingly, it is specifically in this process that children with developmental dyslexia are weak (Doehring, Trites, Patel, and Fiedorowicz, 1981; Stanovich, 1988; Olson, Wise, Conners, Rack, and Fulker, 1989). Recent work on remediation also indicates that strategies which provided training in segmenting words into syllabic-orthographic units (for example, in German) help children in learning to read regular and nonsense words orally (Scheerer-Neuman, 1981).

Since Brahmi delimits moras and extrametrical consonants by organizing the phonemic-graphemic features into spatial-hierarchical configurations (not in linear sequences as alphabets do), one would expect children learning to read in this system to have a natural beginning. Brahmi helps children to grow into reading as a part of their natural psycholinguistic development, in that it provides intraword structure into delimited units. Operationally, the intervention strategy suggested by Scheerer-Neuman (1981) is integrally built into Brahmi representation, which should facilitate reading acquisition, at least in the early stage.

READING ACQUISITION IN GUJARATI CHILDREN

An exploratory study was conducted in Baroda (Gujarat, India) to see how Gujarati children progress in reading acquisition. This paper focuses only on reading skills; see Patel and Soper (1987) for a complete account of the study which included spelling and segmentation skills also. A total of 120 Gujarati-speaking children from a socioeconomically-culturally homogeneous private school, 40 each in the first month of Grades 2, 3, and 4 (age range 7 to 9 years) were administered tests involving oral word reading, word comprehension (word-picture matching), and paragraph comprehension (paragraph-picture matching). The words and paragraphs were ecologically valid, in that they were taken from Grades 1 to 4 textbooks.

The scores on oral word reading, word comprehension and paragraph comprehension show similar patterns of development; the performances in Grades 2 and 3 are effectively equivalent and there is substantial progress in Grade 4. Performance on paragraph comprehension was generally good, ceiling effects do not appear to have played a role though, for only 3, 2, and 3 subjects obtained the maximal scores in Grades 2, 3, and 4, respectively. As for correlations, oral word reading and word comprehension are related only in Grade 3.

The scores on oral word reading, word comprehension and paragraph comprehension show similar patterns of development; with more than 90% of the children performing correctly on three-quarters or more of the text items.

TABLE 1
Percentage of children scoring at different score-ranges

Score	Grade 2	Grade 3	Grade 4
Oral word reading			
> 16	0	0	0
16–24	0	2.5	0
25–32	65	45	7.5
33–40	35	52.5	92.5
Word comprehension			
> 16	0	0	0
16–24	0	0	0
25–32	10	2.5	0
33–40	90	97.35	100

Even children beginning Grade 2 achieved high scores on oral word reading (both regular and nonsense), suggesting that these children can transform sequences of orthographic units into sound patterns after just one year of classroom time. It should be noted that these children at the beginning of Grade 2 are not just barking at the print; they can also make sense of written words and paragraphs. What is striking is that in the basic reading skills, that is, in oral word reading and word-paragraph comprehension, the improvement is not monotonic; it shows spurts.

Oral word reading and word comprehension are related at the beginning of Grade 2 and in Grade 3, by Grade 4, however, they appear to develop independently perhaps reflecting the fact that by Grade 4 children can read (pronounce) words quite independently of their knowledge of what such words mean. The general reduction in correlation between oral word reading and word-paragraph comprehension (and in other tasks in the study) over Grades 2 to 4 may be related to general differences between subjects or interactions between these differences and training at home prior to formal schooling, special abilities related to "precocious reading acquisition" (Patel and Patterson, 1982), or possibly, differential effects of developing neurocognitive mechanisms at each grade level.

The role of Brahmi in the obtained pattern of reading acquisition has to be inferred. It may be that the orthographic intraword segmentation in terms of moras and word-final extrametrical consonants which can be easily transformed into phonological lexical patterns aids the process of lexical access. Lexical access, at least partially, may involve decoding. The directly available phonological representation "cannot but help processing for comprehension in working memory" (Shankweiler, Liberman, Mark, Fowler, and Fischer, 1979). As Perfetti and McCutchen (1982: 242) suggest, ". . . It remains accurate to characterize short-term memory functioning as heavily relying on speech properties that are acoustic or articulatory analogs or perhaps both". It remains to be seen what specific functions are performed by Brahmi in lexical-semantic processing for comprehension.

Children learning to process the alphabetic system of English "tend to process idiosyncratically and unevenly over the years" (Belmont and Belmont, 1978: 39). Remarkably, the pattern of results in this study on oral word reading, word comprehension, phonemic-graphic segmentation show a similar pattern. There was no difference between Grades 2 and 3, but a "spurt" in Grade 4. Correlations between each of these sets of scores was nil at Grade 4, which may suggest that many relatively independent abilities follow the same uneven developmental course. The developmental time course in learning to read in a syllabo-phonemic Brahmi script calls for no significant revision in the reading acquisition models motivated on the basis of alphabetic scripts (Frith, 1985). The role of prelexical phonological decoding in the initial stage and the a gradual shit towards postlexical phonological decoding in reading acquisition over the early school years (Coltheart, 1983) are also apparent in case of the Brahmi-derived Gujarati script.

CONCLUDING REMARKS

The linguistically sophisticated ancient Hindu scholars formulated an orthographic system which has survived through the ages and allowed the development of a multitude of scripts, Dewanagari and Grantha being prototypic. These scripts have also been adopted by non-Indo-Aryan languages of the Indo-Chinese peninsula. It seems that the adaptability of Brahmi is not due to religion and trade only; it is the nature of the linguistic design underlying Brahmi which appears to have played a significant role in its adaptability. The written units in Dewanagari and Grantha clearly represent moras and extrametrical consonants. The intraword structural segmentation that Dewanagari and Grantha provide to the reader appears to facilitate reading acquisition, at least, in the initial stage.

REFERENCES

Basham, A.L.: 1967, *The Wonder that was India*, (Third Revised Edition), Sidgwick and Jackson, London.

Belmont, I. and Belmont, L.: 1978, 'Stability and change in reading achievement over time: Developmental and educational implications', *Journal of Learning Disabilities* **11**: 8–88.

Buhler, G.: 1963, *On the Origin of the Indian Brahmi Alphabet*, (3rd Ed. First published in 1895), The Chowkhambha Sanskrit Series, Varanasi.

Cohen, M.: 1958, *La grand invention de l'écriture et son évolution*, Imprimerie Nationale, Paris.

Coltheart, M.: 1983, 'Phonological awareness: A preschool precursor of success in reading', *Nature* **301**: 370.

Comrie, B. (ed.): 1987, *The World's Major Languages*, Oxford University Press, New York.

Dani, A.H.: 1986, *Indian Palaeography*, Munshiram Manoharlal Publishers Pvt. Ltd., Delhi.

Danvivathana, N.: 1987, *The Thai Writing System*, Helmut Buske Verlag (Forum Phoneticum), Hamburg.

Doehring, D.G., Trites, R.L., Patel, P.G., and Fiedorowicz, C.A.M.: 1981, *Reading Disabilities: The Interaction of Reading, Languages, and Neuro-psychological Deficits*, Academic Press, New York.

Fox, B. and Routh, D.K.: 1975, 'Analyzing spoken language into words, syllables, and phonemes: A developmental study', *Journal of Psycholinguistic Research* **4**: 331–342.

Frith, U.: 1985, 'Beneath the surface of developmental dyslexia', in K. Patterson, J. Marshall, and M. Coltheart (eds.) *Surface Dyslexia*, Erlbaum, London, pp. 301–330.

Gelb, I.J.: 1952, *A Study of Writing*, University of Chicago Press, Chicago.

Haas, M.R.: 1956, *The Thai System of Writing*, American Council of Learned Societies, Washington, DC.

Hale, A.: 1982, *Research on Tibeto-Burman Languages*, Mouton Publishers, New York.

Hayes, B.: 1982, 'Extrametricality of English stress', *Linguistic Inquiry* **13**: 227–276.

Henderson, L.: 1984, 'Writing systems and reading processes', in L. Henderson (ed.) *Orthographies and Reading: Perspectives from Cognitive Psychology, Neuropsychology, and Linguistics*, Erlbaum, London.

Hyman, L.M.: 1985, *A Theory of Phonological Weight*, Foris Publications, Dordrecht.

Jensen, H.: 1970, *Sign, Symbol, and Script*, Allen and Unwin, London.

Jones, R.B., Jr. and Khin, U.: 1953, *The Burmese Writing System*, American Council of Learned Societies, Washington, DC.

Karpova, S.N.: 1977, *The Realization of Verbal Composition of Speech by Preschool Children*, Mouton, The Hague.

Krishnamurti, Bh. and Gwynn, J.P.L.: 1985, *A Grammar of Modern Telugu*, Oxford University Press, Delhi.

Liberman, I.Y., Shankweiler, D., Fischer, F.W., and Carter, B.: 1974, 'Explicit syllable and phoneme segmentation in the young child', *Journal of Experimental Child Psychology*, **18**: 201–212.
Macken, M.A.: 1979, 'Developmental reorganization of phonology: A hierarchy of basic units of acquisition', *Lingua* **49**: 11–49.
Mahadevan, I.: 1971, 'Tamil Brahmi inscriptions of the Sangam Age', *Proceedings of the Second International Conference-Seminar of Tamil Studies*, IIATR, Madras.
Mahulkar, D.D.: 1981, *The Pratisakhya Tradition and Modern Linguistics*, M. S. University Press, Baroda.
Mattingly, I.G.: 1978, 'The skills of the plodder', *Contemporary Psychology* **23**: 731–732.
McGregor, R.S.: 1972, *Outline of Hindi Grammar*, Clarendon Press, Oxford.
Miller, R. A.: 1956, *The Tibetan System of Writing*, American Council of Learned Societies, Washington, DC.
Miller, R.A.: 1967, *The Japanese Language*, University of Chicago Press, Chicago.
Murti, M.S.: 1984, *An Introduction to Sanskrit Linguistics*, D. K. Publications, Delhi.
Patel, P.G.: 1983, Review article on *Orthography, Reading and Dyslexia* (J.F. Kavanaugh and R.L. Venszky, eds.), *Language* **59**: 636–653.
Patel, P.G.: (in press). 'The two cortical visual pathways and developmental dyslexia: Relevance of the syllabo-phonemic organization and the topographical features of the Brahmi scripts of India', *Journal of the Indian Speech and Hearing Association*,
Patel, P.G. and Patterson, P.: 1982, 'Precocious reading acquisition: Psycholinguistic development, IQ, and home background', *First Language* **3**: 139–153.
Patel, P.G. and Soper, H.V.: 1987, 'Acquisition of reading and spelling in a syllabo-alphabetic writing system', *Language and Speech* **30**: 69–81.
Pedersen, H.: 1931, *The Discovery of Language: Linguistic Science in the Nineteenth Century*, Harvard University Press, Cambridge.
Perfetti, C.A. and McCutchen, D.: 1982, 'Speech processes in reading', *Speech and Language: Advances in Basic Research and Practice* (Vol. 7), Academic Press, New York, pp. 237–269.
Peters, A.M.: 1983, *The Units of Language Acquisition*, Cambridge University Press, Cambridge.
Pulleyblank, D.: 1986, *Tone in Lexical Phonology*, D. Reidel Publishing Company, Dordrecht.
Roop, D.H.: 1972, *An Introduction to the Burmese Writing System*, Yale University Press, New Haven.
Ruhlen, M.: 1987, *A Guide to the World's Languages*. (Vol. 1, Classification), Stanford University Press, Stanford.
Scharfe, H.: 1977, *Grammatical Literature*, Otto Harrassowitz, Wiesbaden.
Scheerer-Neumann, G.: 1981, 'The utilization of intraword structure in poor readers: Experimental evidence and a training program', *Psychological Research* **43**: 155–178.
Shankweiler, D., Liberman, I.Y., Mark, L.S., Fowler, C.A. and Discher, F.W.: 1979, 'The speech code and learning to read', *Journal of Experimental Psychology: Human Learning and Memory* **5**: 531–545.
Shapiro, M.C. and Schiffman, H.: 1983, *Language and Society in South Asia*, Foris Publications, Dordrecht.
Stanovich, K.E., Cunningham, A.E. and Cramer, B.R.: 1984, 'Assessing phonological awareness in kindergarten children: Issues of task comparability', *Journal of Experimental Child Psychology* **38**: 175–190.
Taylor, I.: 1980, 'Korean writing system: An alphabet? a syllabary? a logography?, in P.A. Kolers, M.E. Wrolstad, and H. Bouma (eds.) *Processing of Visible Language* (Vol. 2), Plenum Press, New York.
Thieme, P.: 1935, *Panini and the Veda: Studies in the Early History of Linguistic Science in India*, Globe Press, Allahabad.

Upasak, C.S.: 1960, *The History and Palaeography of Mauryan Brahmi Script*, Nava Nalanda Mahavihara, Nalanda (Patna).

Verma, T.P.: 1971, *The Palaeography of Brahmi Script*, Siddharth Prakashan, Varanasi.

Wang, W.S.-Y.: 1981, 'Language structure and optimal orthography', in O.J.L. Tzeng and H. Singer (eds.) *Perception of Print: Reading Research in Experimental Psychology*, Erlbaum, Hillsdale, NJ.

Waterman, N.: 1981, 'A tentative developmental model of phonological representation', in T. Myers, J. Laver, and J. Anderson (eds.) *The Cognitive Representation of Speech*, North-Holland Publishing, Amsterdam.

ESTHER GEVA

18. ORTHOGRAPHIC AND COGNITIVE PROCESSING IN LEARNING TO READ ENGLISH AND HEBREW

The extent to which disabilities are dependent upon orthographic characteristics has been a controversial issue in the research literature for quite some time (Leong, 1986; Liu, 1988; Stevenson, Lucker, William, and Shin-Yin, 1982; Taylor and Taylor, 1983). On the one hand, it has been argued that logographic languages such as Chinese and Japanese present to readers symbols that are consistent and meaningful, and therefore easy to decode (Libermann, Shankweiler, Fischer, and Carter, 1974; Makita, 1968; Rozin, Poritsky, and Solsky, 1971). Therefore, it was argued, reading disabilities are not prevalent among speakers of these languages (Rozin and Gleitman, 1977). In contrast, alphabetic languages require readers to learn to match phonemes, abstract linguistic units, to graphemes. For this reason, reading disabilities should be more prevalent among those learning to read alphabetic languages than among readers of logographic languages.

A more recent version of this "script dependent hypothesis" emerged with the conceptualization of alphabetic languages as differing in their "orthographic depth" (Frost and Bentin, 1992; Katz and Frost, 1992; Peereman, 1992; Turvey, Feldman, and Lukatela, 1984). Accordingly, alphabetic orthographies differ in how systematically spelling and pronunciations can be mapped onto each other. A shallow orthography allows a simple one-to-one correspondence between letters and sounds. Conversely, a deep orthography, such as English, while still abiding by the alphabetic principle, employs a more complex set of relationships between letters and sounds (Gough, Juel, and Griffith, 1992). The effects of orthographic depth on beginning readers has been recognized by educators for several decades (Gillooly, 1973). However, recently, there has been a growing interest in studying the effects of orthographic depth on the development of reading skills in various languages (see for example, Azzam, 1993; Carlisle, 1993; Cuetos, 1993; Fang-Hu and Catts, 1993; Geva and Clifton, 1994; Geva, Wade-Woolley, and Shany, 1993; Gough, Juel, and Griffith, 1992; Katz and Frost, 1992).

Attempts to relate the orthographic depth hypothesis to the incidence of reading disabilities have not been restricted to comparisons between logographic and alphabetic languages. Proponents of the "script dependent" position maintain that the likelihood of reading disabilities is much lower in "shallow" orthographies such as Italian than in "deep" orthographies such as English. A study by Lindgren, De Renzi and Richman (1985) provides some experimental support for the "script dependent hypothesis". These authors found a higher incidence of reading disabilities among English

I. Taylor and D.R. Olson (eds.), Scripts and Literacy, 277–291.

speaking grade five children in the United States than among a comparable sample of Italian children. It is unfortunate that Lindgren and his colleagues focused on a discrepancy between verbal ability and reading comprehension in order to define dyslexia, a procedure which has been criticized in various publications (see Wong, 1986; Siegel, 1989) as it confounds reading comprehension with difficulties in forming grapheme-phoneme associations. It is the latter skills which underlie severe reading difficulties (Siegel and Ryan, 1988; Stanovich, 1986).

A theoretical perspective highlighting the role of underlying cognitive and linguistic skills in the emergence of reading and language proficiency leads to an opposite hypothesis (See for example, Bialystok and Ryan, 1985; Cummins, 1984; Geva and Ryan, 1993; McLaughlin, Rossman, and McLeod, 1986; Morrison, 1992; Siegel, 1994; Siegel and Ryan, 1984). According to the "central processing" hypothesis, individuals whose underlying cognitive and linguistic skills are deficient should experience difficulties in the development of basic reading skills regardless of the language and the script involved. Some support for this hypothesis comes from Stevenson *et al.* (1982). They found that reading disabilities exist among Japanese, Chinese and English speaking children, and that the incidence of reading disabilities in these three cultures is similar.

One way of examining these two opposing positions is to study reading and linguistic skills of children learning to read simultaneously in two different languages, based on two different scripts. The "script dependent" hypothesis entails that some children may have problems in learning to read English whether it is their first (L1) or second (L2) language, but may have minimal problems in learning to read a shallow orthography such as voweled Hebrew, due to its simple and systematic grapheme-phoneme correspondence rules (see below). The "central processing" hypothesis entails that underlying cognitive and linguistic factors should correlate with reading skills in L1 and L2, and that children who are considered reading disabled or having reading difficulties in their L1 should demonstrate problems in their L2, as well.

So far only a handful of studies examined experimentally the relationships among indices of reading disabilities in bilingual learners. Yet, there is some clinical evidence that supports the "central processing" hypothesis (Obler, 1989; Petrie and Geva, 1991; Wiss, 1987). On the whole, these case studies suggest that individuals who have decoding problems in their L1 have decoding difficulties when decoding in L2, regardless of orthographic depth. Wiss (1987) reports the case study of Jenny, a learning disabled girl who was underachieving significantly in reading and spelling in English and French, and who made similar spelling errors in both languages. Note that English and French are both considered to have deep orthographies. The case studies reported by Obler and by Petire and Geva involved individuals with Hebrew as their L1 and English as their L2. These individuals experienced severe reading problems in both languages. Yet, the authors note that the reading errors observed in these individuals reflected differences in the nature of the orthographies. Such findings suggest that it may be necessary to modify the extreme positions outlined above, and consider the joint contribution of orthographic complexity and underlying central processing mechanisms to a general theory of reading and reading problems in monolingual and bilingual learners (see also Geva and Siegel, 1991).

The purpose of the research reported here was to examine these alternative hypotheses experimentally. Two questions were addressed: (a) the nature of the relationships between children's basic reading skills in L1 and L2, and (b) the role of underlying cognitive factors such as non-verbal ability and memory in understanding children's performance on English and Hebrew linguistic and reading tasks. Before describing the research the short section below provides a brief comparison of Hebrew and English script (For a more detailed comparison of English and Hebrew scripts see Geva, Wade-Woolley, and Shany, 1993).

HEBREW AND ENGLISH ORTHOGRAPHIES – A BRIEF COMPARISON

Hebrew, like English, is an alphabetic orthography, but is read from right to left. Voweled Hebrew may be characterized as a shallow orthography (Frost and Bentin, 1992; Shimron, 1993). There is a direct and invariant correspondence between the twenty two letters and the associated phonemes. Furthermore, the correspondence among graphemes and phonemes applies also to the vowel diacritics. In modern spoken Hebrew certain phonemic distinctions originally made in ancient Hebrew have been reduced. For example, " ט " (tet) and " ת " (tav) are both pronounced as /t/, "א" (alef) and " ע " (ayin) are both pronounced as /a/. Yet, the orthographic realization of these distinctions has been maintained, resulting in many homophones. Five consonants are printed differently when they appear at the end of words, a factor which may contribute to task complexity at the beginning stages of reading and writing (Geva, Wade-Woolley, and Shany, 1993). Additionally, some consonants may be visually confusing to novices due to similar spatial features e.g., " צ " (ts) and " ע " (ã) (Geva and Siegel, 1991).

Hebrew vowels in the form of dots and dashes are placed below, above or to the left of the consonants. These vowels are quite close to the cardinal vowels in their phonetic realization (Berman, 1978). While in ancient Hebrew a distinction was made between tense (long) and lax (short) vowels, in modern Hebrew all vowels tend to be pronounced close to their tense realization (Berman, 1978). For instance, speakers do not distinguish between the diphthong "ei" (tzerei) and the short vowel "e" (segol), both of which are often pronounced as /e/ (as in *yet*). Yet, unlike English, the phonemes associated with Hebrew vowels are invariant.

In English, in order to determine the phonemic value of some graphemes one needs to consider more than one letter. For example, the phonemic value of *b*, *d*, *f*, *l*, *n*, *r*, *v*, *z* can be determined in word-initial positions without considering other letters. For all the other letters, at least one additional letter must be identified before the value of the first phoneme in a word can be determined. Sometimes the reader needs to consider at least four more letters before the first phoneme can be unambiguously determined (e.g., "chord" vs. "chore"). At other times, the addition of one grapheme can radically change the pronunciation of a letter elsewhere in the word, as in the case of the "silent e" long vowel marker. Additionally, there are idiosyncratic words in English, like "yacht", which need to be learned individually since they cannot be pronounced either by rule or analogy on the basis of their spelling.

In sum, unlike English, the pronunciation of words in Hebrew very rarely requires readers to consider exceptions associated with specific letter strings, idiosyncratic spellings, grapheme position in the word and vowel combinations. The formation of letter-sound associations and word decoding requires the learner to master fewer rules, and does not entail the creation of a large repertoire of exception words read on the basis of analogy rather than rule as is the case in English (e.g., *have* vs. *gave*). For this reason, accurate word decoding in voweled Hebrew can be learned easily, and can be executed in a linear and systematic fashion (Geva and Siegel, 1991). Modern Hebrew includes borrowed words, but their orthographic realization is, on the whole, transparent. It is possible to take advantage of Hebrew's regularity and learn to decode without any oral proficiency in or semantic knowledge of the language. This does not mean, of course, that lexical, syntactic and semantic information does not contribute to efficient lexical access and to comprehension (Shimron and Navon, 1982; Verhoeven, 1990).

METHOD

Sample

Results reported here concern grade 2 and grade 5 normally achieving (NA) students and a sample of learning disabled (LD) children. The sample consisted of 46 grade 2 and 45 grade 5 NA students, attending an English-Hebrew bilingual day-school, and 18 grade 1–6 identified learning disabled children, attending a bilingual English-Hebrew day-school catering to the needs of children with learning disabilities. Both schools are private, and may be characterized as primarily middle-class. In both schools, situated in a large metropolitan area in Canada, half of the day is devoted to the instruction of the regular English program, and half of the day to the instruction of the Hebrew language and various cultural subjects taught in Hebrew.

Results reported here are based only on those children for whom English was L1 and Hebrew L2. In both schools reading is taught with a combination of meaning based and skills based techniques.

Instruments

Cognitive Measures

Non-verbal ability. The Raven's coloured Progressive Matrices (Raven, 1965) were used to assess children's non-verbal ability. Percentile scores were used in the analyses.

L1 short term memory. Short term memory in L1 was assessed with a short term memory word span task (hereafter, "E-Span") developed by Geva and Ryan (1993) from frequent nouns in the English lexicon (e.g., "moon", "milk"). Children are to repeat lists of orally presented unrelated words of increasing length. At the lowest level there are 3 words in a trial. In each subsequent level the list length increases by 1. At the highest level there are 9 words in a trial. In each level there are 2 trials. Testing stops when the child misses both trials within a level.

L1 working memory. A sentence working memory (WM) task, developed by Siegel and Ryan (1989) was used to assess working memory in English (hereafter, "E-WM"). The E-WM task is modeled on a task developed by Daneman and Carpenter (1980). Children's ability to process and store information is tested by asking them to (a) complete the last word in sentences taken from everyday contexts (e.g., "on my two hands I have ten? ____ (fingers)"), (b) to store that word in memory as they proceed with subsequent sentence(s), (e.g., "In the winter it is cold, in the summer it is? ____ (hot)"), and (c) to recall the stored words to all the sentences at the end of each trial (e.g., "fingers", "hot").

L2 short term memory. Short term memory in L2 was assessed with a parallel short term memory word span task (Geva and Ryan, 1993) (hereafter "H-Span"). To ensure lexical familiarity, it was developed on the basis of common nouns taught in the bilingual English-Hebrew day schools, e.g., "shabath" (Sabbath), "sefer" (book), "shemesh" (sun). The structure, administration and scoring of the H-Span task are identical to those described above for the E-Span task. Instructions are given in English.

L2 working memory. An opposites working memory task (Geva and Ryan, 1993) was used to assess Hebrew working memory (hereafter "H-WM"). The task is modeled on McKeough (1982), who developed it to test children in their L1 (English). It employs the same storage and processing operations present in other working memory tasks. Children are asked to provide the opposites to a set of orally presented words (e.g., "black", "large"). The set length increases by 1 item from level to level. At the lowest level the child has to provide the opposites to 2 words. At the fifth (and last) level there are 6 items per trial. Within each level there are 3 trials. Testing stops when the child misses all the trials in a level. Instructions are given in English.

Syntactic Skills

L1 syntactic skills. The "E-Cloze" task, developed by Siegel and Ryan (1984) was used to assess children's syntactic knowledge. This cloze-like oral sentence completion task consists of 20 unrelated sentences which are read to the child one at a time. The child is asked to provide the missing word in each sentence. The missing words vary in terms of their syntactic function (e.g., "The three little pigs ate ____ "; "The girl ____ is tall plays basketball well").

L2 syntactic skills. A Hebrew task parallel to the E-Cloze was developed for this study (hereafter "H-Cloze"). It consists of 20 sentences read to the child one at a time. The content and vocabulary are based on the school curriculum. As is the case with the E-Cloze, the syntactic function of the omitted words varies among the sentences (e.g., verbs, adjectives, nouns, conjunctions).

L2 Oral Proficiency

All Hebrew teachers were asked to rate the Hebrew oral proficiency of the students participating in the study on a 1–7 scale developed by Shohamy for assessing the oral proficiency skills of Israeli children learning English as a Foreign language (1984). A rating of 1 is assigned to individuals whose Hebrew oral proficiency is minimal, and who are unable to express themselves beyond a few formulaic phrases (e.g., "my name is . . ."). A rating of 7 is assigned to individuals whose Hebrew oral proficiency is native-like.

Dependent Measures

L1 word recognition. The Word Identification subtest of the Wide Range Achievement Test (WRAT) (Jastak and Jastak, 1978), (hereafter, "E-Words") was used to test out-of-context English word recognition. Testing stops when the child makes 10 consecutive errors. The mean percent correct (out of 75) was used.

L1 pseudoword decoding. It is commonly accepted that reading pseudowords is a purer measure of phonological skills and orthographic knowledge than word recognition. The Word Attack subtest of the Woodcock Reading Mastery Test – Revised (Woodcock, 1987) was used to assess children's ability to decode pseudowords in English. This test (hereafter "E-Non-words") consists of 50 pronounceable "non-words" which comply with English orthographic rules (e.g., "plip", "cigbet"). Testing stops when the child makes 6 consecutive errors. The mean percent correct (out of 50) was used in the analyses.

L2 word recognition. A Hebrew word recognition test was developed by Geva on the basis of the vocabulary taught in the grade 1–5 program in the school. This test (hereafter "H-Words") consists of 60 unrelated words with the vowels intact. Two variables are manipulated in the list: familiarity and word length. Administration procedures are identical to those employed on the E-Words (The Cronbach alpha for this test is 0.92) (For more details see Geva and Siegel, 1991).

L2 pseudoword decoding. To test the ability of children to decode Hebrew pseudowords, a "H-Non-words" task was developed by the author. The test consists of 44, two-syllable voweled pseudowords e.g., "atzen" (עָצֶן) and "xithes" (חִתֶס). Administration procedures are identical to those employed with the "E-Nonwords". Results are reported in terms of percent correct (The Cronbach alpha for this test is 0.95).

Procedures

Children were tested on an individual basis in a quite room in the school. Data collection took place during the spring term, and was divided into three sessions. The first session was devoted to a brief student interview and the administration of the Raven's Matrices. The administration of the memory and reading tasks was done in two blocks: one for the English (L1) tasks, and the other for the Hebrew (L2) tasks. Within a block the order of administration of specific tasks remained constant. Administration of the English and Hebrew blocks was counterbalanced within each grade level. Testing was carried out by 5 English-Hebrew bilingual university students.

RESULTS

Relationships between Reading and Linguistic Skills in L1 and L2

Relationships among basic reading skills in L1 and L2. As can be seen in Table 1, which summarizes the intercorrelations among English and Hebrew measures, there are positive and significant correlations among

TABLE 1
Intercorrelations among English and Hebrew measures

		ENGLISH					
		Words	Non-words	Cloze	Span	WM	Non-verbal
	a. NA Sample (n = 91)						
H	Words	0.40***	0.26**	0.42***	0.37***	0.27**	0.14
E	Non-words	0.44***	0.33**	0.33**	0.27**	0.20*	0.14
B	Cloze	0.01	–0.23*	0.46***	0.20	0.25**	0.14
R	Span	0.01	0.02	0.20*	0.50***	0.20*	0.16
E	WM	0.04	–0.28**	0.41***	0.32**	0.33**	0.12
W	Non-verbal	0.37***	0.30**	0.20*	0.23*	0.32**	–
	b. LD Sample (n = 18)						
H	Words	0.43*	0.59***	0.37*	0.36*	0.37*	–0.04
E	Non-words	0.29*	0.39*	0.19	0.26	0.25	–0.03
B	Cloze	n.a.	n.a.	n.a.	n.a.	n.a.	n.a.
R	Span	0.19	0.31*	0.49**	0.34*	0.50**	–0.14
E	WM	0.15	0.35*	0.67***	0.31*	0.54**	0.19
W	Non-verbal	0.30[a]	0.10	0.34	0.03	0.25	–

[a] $p < 0.06$; * $p < 0.05$; ** $p < 0.01$; *** $p < 0.000$.

the L1 ad L2 measures of basic reading skills in the NA and LD samples, alike. This is true both for the word recognition measures, which require children to read out loud real words in English and Hebrew, as well as for the Nonwords tasks, in which children read pronounceable pseudowords in both languages. These results provide support for the central processing hypothesis: regardless of orthographic complexity, the nature of the alphabet and language proficiency, individual differences seem to underlie L1 and L2 word recognition and word attack skills.

Linguistic knowledge in L1 and L2. Due to their low Hebrew oral proficiency, children in the LD group were not able to deal with the Hebrew oral sentence Cloze task. As a result it was impossible to calculate the correlations between the E-Cloze and H-Cloze for the LD group. Yet, as can be seen in Table 2, in the NA sample the correlation between H-Cloze and the Hebrew oral proficiency measure was extremely high ($r = 0.78$). This high correlation suggests that teachers' rating of Hebrew oral proficiency provide a valid assessment of children's L2 oral proficiency, including syntactic knowledge. Furthermore, as can be seen in the top panel of Table 1, NA children's ability to perform the Cloze task in English and Hebrew was positively and significantly intercorrelated ($r = 0.46, p < 0.001$). In other words, children who were better able to identify the syntactic and semantic function of the missing words in their L1, could also perform this task more successfully in Hebrew, their L2, even though they were clearly less proficient in that language.

TABLE 2
Intercorrelations among measures within each language – NA sample (n = 91)

	Words	Non-words	Cloze	Span	WM	Oral prof.
a. English						
Words	–	0.67***	0.44***	0.33**	0.34***	
Non-words	–	–	0.12	0.33**	0.19*	
Cloze	–	–	–	0.40***	0.49***	
Span	–	–	–	–	0.38***	
WM	–	–	–	–	–	
b. Hebrew						
Words	–	0.74***	0.53***	0.29**	0.43***	0.54***
Non-words	–	–	0.37***	0.16[a]	0.26**	0.39***
Cloze	–	–	–	0.50***	0.81***	0.78***
Span	–	–	–	–	0.57***	0.48***
WM	–	–	–	–	–	0.72***

[a] $p < 0.06$; * $p < 0.05$; ** $p < 0.01$; *** $p < 0.000$.

It is also interesting to note in Table 1 that while the E-Cloze scores correlated positively with measures of basic reading skills in Hebrew (r = 0.42 with H-words, and r = 0.33 with H-Nonwords), the H-Cloze measure did not correlate with the parallel English E-Words and E-Nonwords reading measures.

The Role of Cognitive Factors

Relationships among memory measures in L1 and L2. An examination of parts a and b of Table 1 also reveals that the L1 and L2 span and WM measures were positively and significantly intercorrelated in both the NA and LD samples. For instance, the correlation between the WM measures in English and Hebrew was $r = 0.33$ ($p < 0.01$) in the NA sample, and $r = 0.54$ ($p < 0.01$) in the LD sample. Likewise, the correlation between the English and Hebrew span measures was also positive and significant in these two samples ($r = 0.50$, $p < 0.001$) and $r = 0.34$, $p < 0.05$, respectively.

Relationships among cognitive measures and language skills in L1 and L2. To deal with this topic, let us first examine the relevant correlations. As indicated earlier, in this study the Raven's matrices were treated as a measure of non-verbal ability. It is interesting to note in Table 1 that all the English language and memory measures correlated positively but moderately with non-verbal ability. The correlations range from $r = 0.20$ for that between the Raven's and the E-Cloze, to $r = 0.37$ for the correlation between the Raven's and E-Words. At the same time the Hebrew language and memory measures do not correlate with non-verbal ability. Yet, as can be seen in Table 2, all the Hebrew language and memory measures correlate highly with Hebrew oral proficiency. This pattern of results suggests that underlying non-verbal ability may explain a substantial portion of the variance in basic reading and language skills in English. Yet, when reading in the second language is concerned, memory for verbal materials, measured in either language, and proficiency in the L2 play a more dominant role.

In order to examine the hypothesis that the significant correlations among language and basic reading skills can be explained in terms of basic underlying cognitive factors such as non-verbal ability and memory, two additional sets of analyses were carried out. The first involved partialling out non-verbal ability form the correlations between the L1 and L2 reading and linguistic measures. Results of this analysis are presented separately for the NA and LD samples in Table 3.

An examination of the correlations of interest in Table 3 and a comparison of these correlations with those in Table 2 shed some light on the nature of the interrelationships among English and Hebrew reading, linguistic and memory measures. It is revealing that when non-verbal ability was partialled out the correlations among the English and Hebrew reading and Cloze measures were unaffected. It is important to emphasize that this conclusion applies to the NA as well as to the LD sample. In other words,

TABLE 3
Intercorrelations among English and Hebrew measures with non-verbal ability partialled out

		ENGLISH				
		Words	Non-words	Cloze	Span	WM
	a. NA Sample (n = 91)					
H	Oral Prof.	−0.08	−0.23**	0.30**	0.14	0.09
E	Words	0.36***	0.21*	0.39***	0.35***	0.28**
B	Non-words	0.42***	0.30**	0.31**	0.25*	0.20*
R	Cloze	−0.06	−0.30	0.44***	0.16	0.21*
E	Span	−0.05	−0.02	0.18*	0.49***	0.16
W	WM	−0.12	−0.34**	0.41***	0.29**	0.28**
	b. LD sample (n = 18)					
H	Oral Prof.	−0.47*	−0.08	−0.04	−0.39	−0.05
E	Words	−0.29	0.32*	0.36*	−0.02	0.07
B	Non-words	0.04	0.42*	0.25	0.07	0.12
R	Cloze	n.a.	n.a.	n.a.	n.a.	n.a.
E	Span	0.03	0.32*	0.67**	0.27	0.52**
W	WM	0.01	0.29	0.67**	0.26	0.52**

* $p < 0.05$; ** $p < 0.01$; *** $p < 0.000$.

underlying differences in non-verbal ability do not explain the correlations among L1 and L2 reading and language measures.

The second set of analyses involved listwise multiple regression analyses (with backwards elimination) in which non-verbal ability, WM and span were regressed on each of the reading and language measures in L1 and L2. The top half of Table 4 presents results of the regression analysis pertaining to the L1 dependent measures. What we learn from this analysis is that: (a) a combination of E-Span and E-WM explains a third of the

TABLE 4
Summary of Multiple Regression Analysis (Listwise)

Dependent variables	Independent variables	Step 1: T	Sig	F	R^2	Subsequent steps	R^2
English (L_1)							
Non-words	E-Span	3.84	0.001			/	
	E-WM	2.18	0.032			/	
	Non-verbal	1.46	0.148			eliminated	
				16.16 $p < 0.001$	0.36		0.34
Words	E-Span	3.35	0.010			/	
	E-WM	4.55	0.001			/	
	Non-verbal	2.56	0.12	31.47 $p < 0.001$	0.52		0.52
Cloze	E-Span	1.65	0.100			eliminated	
	E-WM	3.28	0.010			/	
	Non-verbal	1.29	0.010			/	
				16.99 $p < 0.001$	0.36		0.35
Hebrew (L_2)							
Non-words	H-Span	0.06	0.950			eliminated	
	H-WM	1.43	0.160			/	
	Non-verbal	1.29	n.s.			eliminated	
				2.90	0.09		0.08
Words	H-Span	0.33	n.s.			eliminated	
	H-WM	2.123	0.050			/	
	Non-verbal	2.50	0.010			/	
				9.25 $p < 0.01$	0.24		0.24
Cloze	H-Span	0.54	n.s.			eliminated	
	H-WM	8.99	0.001			/	
	Non-verbal	1.41	n.s.			eliminated	
				58.83 $p < 0.001$	0.67		0.66

variance associated with basic "word attack" skills as measured with the E-Nonwords task; (b) likewise, variance in performance on the E-Words task, depends on both memory measures (i.e., E-Span E-WM). Yet, non-verbal ability also plays a significant role; a combination of these three measures explains half of the variance; and (c) linguistic-syntactic skills required to deal with the E-Cloze task depend on working memory capacity (E-WM) as well as on non-verbal ability, but not on memory span. The first two cognitive measures explain jointly a third of the variance.

The bottom part of Table 4 presents results of the analysis of the L2 measures. This analysis revealed the following: (a) The Hebrew span measure is not a significant predictor for any of the Hebrew dependent measures; (b) H-WM is the only significant predictor of basic "word attack" skills in Hebrew, explaining a small proportion of the variance; (c) Reading "real" Hebrew words is best predicted by a combination of working memory capacity and non-verbal ability. Jointly these two measures explain a quarter of the variance; and (d) Syntactic-linguistic knowledge, as measured by the H-Cloze, is explained exclusively by working memory capacity, which accounts for two-thirds of the variance.

Considered in conjunction with conclusions drawn from the examination of the correlations in Table 1 and 3, these results suggest that individual differences in cognitive processing capacity, conceptualized in terms of individual differences in working memory and non-verbal ability explain to a certain extent the positive relations between L1 and L2 measures of basic decoding and linguistic skills in NA and LD children, alike.

CONCLUSIONS

On the surface, analyses of data reported in this chapter seem to support the central processing hypothesis: Linguistic skills in L1 and L2 are related through underlying cognitive constructs such as working memory capacity and non-verbal ability. Those children who have deficient reading skills in English experience similar problems in Hebrew, and conversely, those who make few decoding errors in their L1 make few errors in their L2. This is so even though English and Hebrew do not employ the same alphabets, and they vary considerably in terms of their orthographic depth and the complexity of demands they present to these young learners. Furthermore, children's performance on other components of linguistic processing such as the utilization of syntactic knowledge is also related in L1 and L2. That is, notwithstanding linguistic proficiency (which is clearly higher in L1 than in L2) there is a positive relationship between performance on linguistic and reading skills in L1 and L2.

At the same time it is important to note that the correlations among the Hebrew and English reading tasks were only moderate. Additional research is needed to tease apart the relative contribution of underlying cognitive abilities and unique orthographic characteristics to understanding the source of reading skills and reading disabilities in monolingual and bilingual contexts. In fact, it is quite feasible that skilled and less skilled decoding in monolingual and bilingual learners can be better understood in terms of the combined effects of underlying cognitive and linguistic mechanisms and script characteristics.

In a more comprehensive paper based on research using identical methodology to the one described here, Geva and Siegel (1991) conclude that the script dependent and central processing theoretical frameworks are complementary. Geva and Siegel studied the reading skills of 245 children in grades 1–5, learning to read concurrently in English, their first language (L1) and Hebrew, their second language (L2). The central processing hypothesis was supported by the finding that memory was consistently a significant predictor of accurate reading skills, regardless of orthography, and that L2 oral proficiency also played a significant role in predicting L2 reading. However, support for the script dependent hypothesis was also noted: At each of these grade levels children could read more accurately voweled Hebrew words than English words, and the developmental trajectories were much steeper for English than for Hebrew. In addition, decoding error types were orthography specific. For example, vowel related reading errors were much more prevalent in English than in Hebrew, whereas word-stress and visual letter confusions were more prevalent in Hebrew than in English. These results suggest that as children gradually develop mastery of specific features of each orthography, script dependent component processes are dominant. When these component processes are less complex (e.g., vowel related grapheme-phoneme correspondences in Hebrew), they may be acquired with relative ease, even in the absence of linguistic proficiency. When these component processes are more complex (e.g., vowel related grapheme-phoneme correspondences in English), they take longer to master, even when the target language is the learners' first language. All along, however, underlying linguistic and cognitive individual differences continue to play a complementary role in explaining accurate and less accurate word recognition skills in L1 and L2.

ACKNOWLEDGEMENTS

I wish to thank Linda S. Siegel for her invaluable contributions to the research and the preparation of this manuscript.

REFERENCES

Azzam, R.: 1993, 'The nature of Arabic reading and spelling errors of young children', *Reading and Writing: An Interdisciplinary Journal* **5**: 355–385.

Berman, R.A.: 1978, *Modern Hebrew Structure*, University Publishing, Tel-Aviv.

Bialystok, E. and Ryan, E.B.: 1985, 'Toward a definition of skills', *Merrill-Palmer Quarterly* **32**(3): 229–264.
Carlisle, J.F.: 1993, 'The influence of study of a second language on improvement in spelling: A longitudinal study', *Reading and Writing: An Interdisciplinary Journal* **5**: 339–353.
Cuetos, F.: 1992, 'Writing processes in a shallow orthography', *Reading and Writing: An Interdisciplinary Journal* **5**: 17–28.
Cummins, J.: 1984, *Bilingualism and special education: Issues in Assessment and Pedagogy*, Multilingual Matters, Clevedon, Avon.
Daneman, M. and Carpenter, P.A.: 1980, 'Individual differences in working memory and reading', *Journal of Verbal Learning and Verbal Behaviour* **19**: 450–466.
Fang Hu, Ċ. and Catts, H.W.: 1993, 'Phonological recoding as a universal process/', *Reading and Writing: An Interdisciplinary Journal* **5**: 325–337.
Frost, R. and Bentin, S.: 1992, 'Reading consonants and guessing vowles: visual word recognition in Hebrew orthography', in R. Frost and L. Katz (eds.) *Orthography, Phonology, Morphology, and Meaning*, Elsevier Science Publishers B.V., Amsterdam, the Netherlands.
Geva, E. and Clifton, S.: 1994, 'The Development of First and Second Language Reading Skills in Early French Immersion', *Canadian Modern Language Review* **50**: 646–667.
Geva, E. and Ryan, E.B.: 1993, 'Linguistic and cognitive correlates of academic skills in first and second languages', *Language Learning* **43**(1): 5–42.
Geva, E. and Siegel, L.S.: 1991, 'The role of orthographic and cognitive factors in the concurrent development of basic reading skills in bilingual children', presented at the Bi-Annual Meeting of the International Society for the Study of Behavioral Development, Minneapolis, Minnesota.
Geva, E., Wade-Woolley, L., and Shany, M.: 1993, 'The concurrent development of spelling and decoding in two different orthographies', *Journal of Reading Behavior* **25**(4): 383–406.
Gillooly, W.B.: 1973, 'The influence of writing-system characteristics on learning to read', *Reading Research Quarterly* **8**(2): 167–199.
Gough, P.B., Juel, C., and Griffith, P.L.: 1992, 'Reading, spelling and the orthographic cipher', in P.B. Gough, L.C. Ehri, and R. Treiman (eds.), *Reading acquisition*, Erlbaum, Hillsdale, NJ, pp. 35–48.
Jastak, J. and Jastak, S.C.: 1978, *The Wide Range Achievement Test*, Jastak Associates Inc., Wilmington, Delaware.
Katz, L. and Frost, R.: 1992, 'The reading process is different for different orthographies: The orthographic depth hypothesis', in R. Frost and L. Katz (eds.) *Orthography, phonology, morphology, and meaning*, Elsevier Science Publishers B.V., Amsterdam, the Netherlands.
Leong, C. K.: 1986, 'What does accessing a morphemic script tell us about reading and reading disorders in an alphabetic script?', *Annals of Dyslexia* **36**: 82–102.
Liberman, I.Y., Shankweiler, D., Fischer, F.W., and Carter, B.: 1974, 'Explicit syllable and phoneme segmentation in the young child', *Journal of Experimental Child Psychology* **18**: 201–212.
Lindgren, S.D., De Renzi, E., and Richman, L.C.: 1985, 'Cross-national comparisons of developmental dyslexia in Italy and the United States', *child Development* **56**: 1404–1417.
Liu, I.: 1988, 'From print to meaning: Logographs versus alphabetic words', paper presented at the McLuhan Conference on Literacy, Toronto, June.
Makita, K.: 1968, 'The rarity of reading disability in Japanese children', *American Journal of Orthopsychiatry* **38**: 599–614.
McKeough, A.: 1982, 'The development of complexity in children's narratives', unpublished M.A. thesis, University of Toronto (OISE).
McLaughlin, B., Rossman, T., and McLeod, B.: 1983, 'Second language learning: An information processing perspective', *Language Learning* **33**: 135–158.
Obler, L.K.: 1989, 'The boustrophedal brain: Laterality and dyslexia in bi-directional readers',

in Kenneth Hyltenstam and Loraine K. Obler (eds.) *Bilingualism Across the Lifespan: Aspects of Acquisition, Maturity, and Loss*, Cambridge University Press, Cambridge.

Peereman, R.: 1992, 'Lecture, ecritures, orthographes' [Reading, writing and orthographies], in P. Lecocq (ed.) *La Lecture: Processus, apprentissage, troubles* [Reading: Processes, Learning and Difficulties], Presses Universitaires de Lille, Lille, France, pp. 55–77.

Petrie, A. and Geva, E.: 1991, 'A framework for second language remediation of reading disabled adults: Implications from a case study', *Journal of Dynamic Assessment* **2**(1): 67–80.

Raven, J.C.: 1965, *The Coloured Progressive Matrices Test*, Lewis, London.

Rozin, P. and Gleitman, L. R.: 1977, 'The structure and acquisition of reading', in A.S. Reiber and D. Scarboorough (eds.) *Reading: Theory and practice*, Erlbaum, Hillsdale, NJ.

Rozin, P., Poritsky, S. and Sotsky, R.: 1971, 'American children with reading problems can easily learn to read English represented in Chinese characters', *Science* **171**: 1264–1267.

Shimron, J. and Navon, D.: 1982, 'The dependency on graphemes and their translation to phonemes in reading: A developmental perspective', *Reading Research Quarterly* **17**(2): 210–228.

Shohamy, E.: 1984, 'Toward a valid and reliable measure of oral proficiency: From research results to educational policy', manuscript.

Siegel, L.S.: 1994, 'Phonological processing deficits as a basis of developmental dyslexia: Implications for remediation', in J. Riddoch and G. Humphreys (eds.) *Cognitive Neuropsychology and Cognitive Rehabilitation*, Erlbaum, Hillsdale, NJ (in press).

Siegel, L.S. and Ryan, E.B.: 1984, 'Reading disability as a language disorder', *Remedial and Special Education* **5**: 28–33.

Siegel, L.S. and Ryan, E.B.: 1989, 'The development of working memory in normally achieving and learning disabled children', *Child Development* **60**: 973–980.

Stanovich, K.E.: 1986, 'Matthew effects in reading: Some consequences of individual differences in the acquisition of literacy', *Reading Research Quarterly* **21**: 360–407.

Stevenson, H.W., Stigler, J.W., Lucker, G.W., Hsu, C.C., and Kitamura, S.: 1982, 'Reading disabilities: The case of Chinese, Japanese and English', *Child Development* **53**: 1164–1181.

Turvey, M.T., Feldman, L.B., and Lukatela, G.: 1984, 'The Serbo-Croatian orthography constrains the reader to a phonologically analytic strategy', in L. Henderson (ed.) *Orthographies and reading*, Erlbaum, London, pp. 81–89.

Wiss, C.A.: 1987, 'Issues in the assessment of learning problems in children form French immersion programs: A case study illustration in support of Cummins', *The Canadian Modern Language Review* **43**(2): 302–313.

Woodcock, R.W.: 1988, *Woodcock Reading Mastery Test*, American Guidance Service, Circle Press, MN.

Wong, B.Y.: 1986, 'Definition, identification, and assessment', in J.K. Torgesen and B.Y.L. Wong (eds.) *Psychological and Educational Perspectives on Learning Disabilities*, Academic Press, New York.

PART IV

COGNITIVE AND METALINGUISTIC IMPLICATIONS OF LEARNING TO READ

JYOTSNA VAID

19. SCRIPT DIRECTIONALITY AFFECTS NONLINGUISTIC PERFORMANCE: EVIDENCE FROM HINDI AND URDU

All writing systems are written in a specific linear order; some are written from top to bottom, others from left to right, and still others are written from right to left. Because of this fact about written language, users of scripts with different directionalities acquire differential directional scanning biases arising from their reading/writing experience (van Sommers, 1991). The influence of directional scanning tendencies has been amply documented in studies of verbal memory and perception comparing readers of left-to-right versus right-to-left scripts (see Nachshon, 1985, for a review).

Whether reading habits also influence cognitive processing of nonverbal information has been less well studied, although there is scattered evidence to support such an influence, based largely on readers of Hebrew or Arabic. The aim of the present research was to examine directional scanning effects in a population that has not so far been studied, namely, Hindi and Urdu readers. For reasons that will shortly be discussed, this language pair is perhaps better suited than Hebrew-English for research on the scope of directional scanning effects.

Demonstrating that reading habits "invade" the nonlinguistic domain (Bertelson, 1972) would be of intrinsic interest. However, such a demonstration would further be important because of its implications for the interpretation of perceptual asymmetries observed in tasks purporting to measure cerebral lateralization of function. Just as studies of cerebral lateralization of language using the visual half-field method of stimulus presentation have been scrutinized for the influence of directional scanning effects (e.g., Tramer, Butler, and Mewhort, 1985), so too is it necessary to examine whether scanning biases might also explain, at least in part, performance on measures intended to assess hemispheric specialization for nonlinguistic functions. Even if directional scanning does not provide a sufficient explanation for asymmetries in verbal laterality tests, one cannot thereby conclude that scanning effects are an unlikely source of bias on measures of *nonverbal* laterality. Whether scanning effects do or do not influence nonverbal functioning is an independent, empirical question. Surprisingly, this question has rarely been raised, let alone studied, in the nonverbal laterality literature.

I. Taylor and D.R. Olson (eds.), Scripts and Literacy, 295–310.

SOME EXAMPLES OF DIRECTIONAL SCANNING EFFECTS

Let us begin by considering the existing literature on scanning effects on tasks involving nonverbal stimuli and tasks. Most studies of this type have compared Israeli with American subjects (e.g., Nachshon, Schefler, and Samocha, 1977), while some have used Japanese or Chinese readers (e.g., Chen, 1981). Subjects in these studies have been asked to copy geometrical shapes (e.g., circle, triangle, horizontal or vertical line), draw objects with an intrinsic front/back (e.g., a dog, a flag), and recall linearly arrayed stimuli.

In one of the earliest studies of figure drawing, for example, it was found that English and Cambodian readers tended to start drawing on the top left hand side of the page while Iranian and Israeli readers started on the top right (Dennis and Raskin, 1960). Using a very different task (inductive reasoning), Harsel and Wales (1987) examined directional differences in problem solving among Japanese and Australians as a function of whether the stimuli were presented horizontally or vertically. They found that Japanese subjects performed better on the vertical version of the test while Australian subjects were better on the horizontal version, but only when the groups were timed on their performance. These examples should suffice to illustrate the potential scope and influence of directional scanning effects in nonlinguistic tasks.

ASYMMETRIES IN DIRECTION OF MOVEMENT

It has been suggested that reading/writing habits are not the sole explanation for observed asymmetries in direction of movement. If this were so, one would expect no biases at all in pre-literate subjects, yet these individuals do in fact show directional preferences. An alternative explanation, then, has been proposed, in terms of innate directional tendencies in muscular movement, with a smoother execution of movements that are directed away from the body (tensor to flexor) than that for movements directed towards the body (van Sommers, 1984).

According to this line of reasoning, different directional biases may be obtained depending on whether the left or the right hand is being used to perform the task. Thus, in drawing a horizontal line most right-handers, regardless or whether their predominant language is written from left-to-right or from right-to-left, should favor a left-to-right direction (in line with the outward directed movement preference) while left-handers should favor a right-to-left direction. Such a difference has in fact been observed (e.g., Dreman, 1974). Moreover, when (American) left-handers perform the task with their right hand, they too show a left-to-right movement preference (Snyder, Grackenbach, and Branford, 1983).

That reading habits may interact with muscular movement asymmetries is entirely possible. In development, right-handed Israelis show a shift in their directional preference around a time (7–13 years) when their reading/writing skills are becoming firmly entrenched (see Nachshon and Alek, 1981).

CEREBRAL LATERALIZATION FRAMEWORK

Over the last 30 years, a number of studies have sought to relate perceptual asymmetries to hemispheric specialization of function. One popular measure used in these studies involves presenting a word to the subject's left or right visual field. Because of the way the visual system is organized, the retinal image of a word presented in the left visual field (LVF) is initially projected to the right visual cortex while that presented in the right visual field (RVF) is initially projected to the left visual cortex. This means that the left hemisphere has access to the RVF before the right hemisphere does since it takes some time for information to cross the corpus callosum. Right handed people are much better able to read the RVF than the LVF word. This observation is usually interpreted as an indication of a left hemisphere superiority in language processing. Conversely, when non-verbal stimuli, such as faces, are used, a LVF superiority is often observed. This, in turn, is thought to reflect a right hemisphere specialization for facial recognition.

It should be clear from the above discussion that, in readers of a left-to-right script, a RVF superiority for words can be interpreted either within a laterality framework or within a scanning framework. Since both accounts would predict a RVF bias in left-to-right readers, one does not know which is the real explanation or whether both contribute to the asymmetry observed.

TACHISTOSCOPIC STUDIES USING HEBREW SUBJECTS

To disentangle the effects associated with reading habit from those associated with hemispheric specialization of function, some researchers have sought to compare readers of Hebrew (a language read from right to left) with readers of English on a laterality task. The results from these studies present a mixed picture. Some studies obtain a scanning effect independently of a laterality effect; others obtain the reverse, and still others find a joint influence of scanning and laterality.

Apart from methodological differences perhaps contributing to the diversity of the findings, there are potential problems inherent in the use of Hebrew subjects. For one thing, Hebrew does not offer a clear contrast to English since individual letters in Hebrew are written from left to right. Furthermore, arithmetic notation is written from left to right in Hebrew, as is musical notation. While not many students learn how to read music, almost all learn arithmetic, so that they are exposed fairly early to a left-to-right direction in at least one domain. Moreover, many of the subjects tested in these studies are familiar to some extent with English, having been taught it from fifth grade onwards. They are thus better viewed as "bidirectional" readers. It is not surprising, then, that the evidence from the Hebrew literature is, in fact, mixed.

Fortunately, there exist a few studies conducted with Arabic, Persian and Urdu readers which bear on the question at hand. These languages may be considered to impart a stronger right-to-left scanning bias inasmuch as single letters and words in these languages are written and read from right to left. Moreover, in studies of behavioral differences, Arabic subjects exhibit stronger directional effects than do Israeli subjects (Nachshon, 1985). The results from available verbal laterality studies with readers of Persian, Urdu or Arabic suggest that a laterality explanation is appropriate, for a right visual field (left hemisphere) superiority is found even in these right-to-left readers (e.g., Coulter, 1982; Belin, Pionner, Perrier, and Larmande, 1988; Vaid, 1988).

DIRECTIONAL SCANNING EFFECTS IN A NONVERBAL LATERALITY CONTEXT

The question remains, however, whether directional scanning effects may influence performance on nonlinguistic laterality tasks. This question has never been systematically studied, although researchers have acknowledged this possibility (see Levy, 1976; and Freimuth and Wapner, 1979, in the context of asymmetries in aesthetic preference; and Gilbert and Bakan, 1973, in the context of face perception). As stated earlier, the outcome of this question is independent of the outcome of the scanning effect in laterality studies using verbal stimuli.

To study this question properly, one faces a problem when one considers the pairs of languages normally used in studies of directionality effects. This problem was acknowledged by Dennis who, as early as 1958, remarked:

> While the data . . . are consonant with the handwriting hypothesis, they are not entirely conclusive. The two groups compared no doubt differ in other respects as well as in regard to handwriting. It is unlikely that one can find two groups differing in handwriting but identical in all other respects (p. 294).

In what follows I will present data from two groups – Hindi and Urdu readers – that come closest to meeting the criterion that Dennis advocated. Findings from two studies are summarized. The first study compared the performance of Hindi, Urdu and Arabic readers on a nonlinguistic production task (figure drawing), and the second compared these readers on a nonlinguistic perception task (facial affect judgment) that has been used as a measure of right hemisphere involvement.

Before presenting the studies, a brief overview of the historical and structural properties of Hindi and Urdu is provided.

HISTORY AND CHARACTERISTICS OF HINDI AND URDU

Urdu and Hindi are the languages of two different groups originating from the same geographical area – North India – or Delhi, to be more specific. Both are non-colloquial languages created out of the same speech – *Khari Boli* – spoken in the Delhi area several centuries ago. Urdu emerged as the language of contact between Hindu inhabitants and Muslim invaders to India in the 11th century. From this early role, Urdu eventually attained the status of a literary language in the 15th century and by the 17th century was adopted by Muslims throughout India as the language of Islam, thanks to the efforts of wandering mystics, or *sufis*.

Urdu was used alongside Persian, then the language of the courts, and eventually replaced it after the fall of the Mughal empire in the middle of the nineteenth century. The British rulers enforced Urdu as the court language and as the medium of instruction in several states in India.

While Urdu flourished in India for several centuries, modern Hindi was created within the last century when, as Grierson (cited in Narula, 1955: 83) remarked, "Hindi (fell) under the fatal spell of Sanskrit." Furthermore, as Narula (1955) points out, communal sentiments against Urdu, which had been declared the court language of areas with predominantly Muslim populations, also played a part in the evolution of modern Hindi (see Rai, 1991, for a more detailed history).

In current usage, Hindi and Urdu are widely spoken in a core form known as Hindustani in North India and in pockets of south India among Muslims and the descendants of those Hindu castes which once came into intimate contact with them. Urdu is the national language of Pakistan used by over 80 million speakers and, in India, Urdu is one of the 15 regional languages, used as a native language by well over 30 million speakers. Hindi is one of the two official languages of India, the other being English, and is used as a native language by more than 40% of the population.

CHARACTERISTICS OF THE WRITING SYSTEMS OF HINDI AND URDU

Hindi uses the Devanagari writing system which characterizes many of the languages used in North India, and is derived from Sanskrit. Urdu is written in *Nasta'liq*, a form of the Arabic script that was developed in Iran and was adopted in India as the favored style several centuries ago. See Figure 1 for a display of the alphabets of each of the two scripts.

The Hindi writing system is considered to be semi-syllabic, since it has syllable-like properties as well as properties of an alphabetic script. There

Hindi

ः ḥ						
अ a	आ ā	इ i	ई ī	उ u	ऊ ū	ऋ ṛ
ए e	ऐ ai	ओ o	औ ai	ं ṅ		
क k } क़ q	ख kh } ख़ x	ग g } ग़ ġ	घ gh	ङ ṅ		
च c	छ ch	ज j } ज़ z	झ jh	ञ ñ		
ट ṭ	ठ ṭh	ड ḍ } ड़ ṛ	ढ ḍh } ढ़ ṛh	ण ṇ		
त t	थ th	द d	ध dh	न n		
प p	फ ph } फ़ f	ब b	भ bh	म m		
य y	र r	ल l	व v			
श ś	ष ṣ	स s	ह h			

Urdu

ا	—	*alif*	د	d	*dāl*	ض	*z	*zvād*	م	m	*mīm*
ب	b	*be*	ڈ	ḍ	*ḍal*	ط	*t	*toe*	ن	n	*nūn*
پ	p	*pe*	ذ	*z	*zāl*	ظ	*z	*zoe*	و	v	*vāo*
ت	t	*te*	ر	r	*re*	ع	ʻ	*ʻain*	ه	h	*choṭī he*
ٹ	ṭ	*ṭe*	ڑ	ṛ	*ṛe*	غ	ġ	*ġain*	ی	y	*ye*
ث	*s	*se*	ز	z	*ze*	ف	f	*fe*			
ج	j	*jīm*	ژ	ż	*że*	ق	q	*qāf*			
چ	c	*ce*	س	s	*sīn*	ک	k	*kāf*			
ح	*h	*baṛī he*	ش	ś	*śīn*	گ	g	*gāf*			
خ	x	*xe*	ص	*s	*svād*	ل	l	*lām*			

Fig. 1. Hindi and Urdu Scripts.

is a direct correspondence between letters and sounds in Hindi, with very little ambiguity. This is not the case in Urdu. As described by Narang (1986), Urdu is derived from the Semitic family and represents three phonological layers: the indigenous layer of the Indo-Aryan, and the borrowed layers of the Semitic and Iranian. Since the borrowed Semitic model was deficient in retroflexion, aspiration, nasalization and vocalics, the Urdu system added a total of seventeen sounds to represent these distinctions. It also accepted six new consonantals not present in the indigenous spoken language and retained seven consonantal letters which had lost their distinct sounds. As such, there are many letters in Urdu which refer to the same sound, and which letter one uses depends on knowledge of the context. This makes Urdu a more difficult script to master, relative to Hindi.

On the spoken level, the two languages have the same dialectal base and for the most part the same grammar. They share a core lexicon (Kelkar, 1968) to such a degree that speakers of Hindi from India are thought by Pakistanis to be speaking Urdu, and vice versa. Thus, the major difference between the two languages lies at the written level.

In addition to the orthographic differences mentioned above, a salient difference between the two scripts is in the direction in which they are written: Hindi is written from left to right while Urdu is written from right to left. This striking difference in script direction makes it possible to study the role of directional scanning tendencies directly by comparing Hindi and Urdu readers. Since the two scripts are essentially identical on the spoken level (i.e., in their phonology, semantics, and syntax) any differences in performance must be related to orthographic differences. This provides a much tighter control than has been possible in the existing literature on directionality or laterality differences.

STUDY 1: EFFECT OF SCRIPT DIRECTIONALITY ON ASYMMETRIES IN LINE DRAWINGS

As a first step in studying behavioral repercussions of script direction we chose a task – free hand figure drawing – that has previously been used in the literature to examine both cultural and biological influences. The task simply required subjects to draw some simple line drawings of common objects. In our first experiment (Singh and Vaid, 1987) we compared the performance of three groups of readers (Hindi, Urdu, and Arabic) on this task. A follow-up experiment (Singh, Vaid, and Sakhuja, 1987) compared right- vs. left-handers on a similar task using a different set of figures.

Method

Subjects. Subjects for the primary study included 55 male and female Hindi-English readers, 38 male and female Urdu readers with little knowledge of written Hindi and 82 predominantly female Arabic readers with no knowledge of English. All subjects were right-handed adults. For the follow-up study, subjects included 16 Hindi right-handers, 16 Hindi left-handers, 16 Urdu right-handers and 16 Urdu left-handers. All subjects in the follow-up study were girls ranging from 9–13 years of age.

Stimuli and Procedure. Subjects were given a sheet divided into six sections. At the top center of each section was the name of an item that they were to sketch in that section of the page. The items to be drawn were written in English for the South Asian sample and in Arabic for the Arab sample. The items to be drawn included three non-directional, filler items, i.e., a house, a hand, and a tree and three items with a front/back. The directional items in the primary study were: a profile of a face, an elephant, and a bicycle. The directional items in the follow-up study were a fish, an arrow and a flag.

Subjects were instructed to draw each of the six items in the space provided using their dominant hand. They were to draw the figures fairly quickly, without too much attention to detail or elaboration, and could draw the items in any order.

The Arabic subjects were tested in a city in Saudi Arabia by a white, female English teacher. The Hindi and Urdu data for the primary study were collected by a male Indian Muslim in the north Indian city of New Delhi. For the follow-up study, a Hindu female graduate student in Meerut did the testing. None of the examiners knew the purpose or rationale behind the study.

Three dependent measures were of interest: the starting location of the drawings (top left, top right, or other), the sequence of drawing the six items (left to right, right to left, or other) and the direction in which the three directional items were shown facing (leftward or rightward).

Results

Starting Location and Drawing Order. There was a clear difference across groups in the location on the page that subjects began the task. Nearly all the Hindi subjects started their drawings on the top left of the page; this finding is consistent with the observations of van Sommers (1984: 122) using English readers and with findings from three other left-to-right linguistic groups (Dennis and Raskin, 1960). The vast majority of Urdu and Arabic subjects instead began on the top right of the page, consistent with Dennis and Raskin's (1960) finding with Israeli and Iranian subjects.

With regard to drawing order, while nearly 70% of Hindi readers used a left-to-right drawing sequence, this was true of less than 20% of Urdu or Arabic subjects who instead favored some other sequence, typically a right-to-left or zigzag order.

The Facing of Objects. The direction in which the three experimental figures in the primary study (bicycle, elephant, profile) were faced by each group is summarized in Table 1A, along with chi square values. There was a marked difference in object orientation direction of the Hindi subjects versus that of the Arab subjects. The performance of Urdu subjects fell between these two extremes. Specifically, the majority of Hindi subjects faced each of the three directional figures leftward. Arab subjects, in contrast, showed a significant rightward bias on the bicycle and elephant, and showed no bias on the profile drawing. Urdu subjects showed a leftward bias on the elephant and the face, with no significant bias on the bicycle. Comparing across groups, we found that Hindi subjects were significantly more leftward-facing than Arabic subjects across all three items, and were more leftward-facing than Urdu subjects on two of the three items (they did not differ on the profile). Furthermore, Arabic subjects were significantly more rightward-facing than Urdu subjects on all three items (see Table 1B for chi-square values).

The leftward bias on the profile item in both Hindi and Urdu groups and the lack of a rightward bias on this item among the Arabic subjects is noteworthy. It is consistent with Jensen's (1952) report of a marked leftward orientation for profile drawing in a number of linguistic groups, irrespective of script directionality, and may reflect a common convention in face drawing instruction.

While we did not record the starting position of each drawing, van Sommers (1984) has shown that direction of facing of an object reflects the starting position and direction of initial stroke used to draw the object. He further points out that since the directional component (e.g., the trunk of the elephant, or the handle of the bicycle) is usually drawn first, the figure will end up facing left or right simply because the initial stroke is from

TABLE 1

A. Leftward bias in figure drawing orientation

Group	Profile	Bicycle	Elephant
Hindi Ss	89.1%	90.9%	92.7%
(n = 55) chi-sq.	33.6**	36.8**	40.2**
Urdu Ss	86.8%	57.9%	68.4%
(n = 38) chi-sq.	20.6**	0.9	20.6**
Arab Ss	45.2%	34.1%	36.6%
(n = 82) chi-sq.	0.8	8.2*	5.9*

B. Summary of chi squares for group comparisons

	Profile	Bicycle	Elephant
Hindi vs. Urdu	0.1	15.3**	8.4**
Hindi vs. Arab	27.1**	43.3**	33.4**
Arab vs. Urdu	18.5**	6.1*	10.7**

* $p < 0.02$

** $p < 0.01$ or beyond

left-to-right or from right-to-left, respectively, reflecting the direction of writing (Van Sommers, 1984; 1991).

Handedness Effects. Since previous studies of figure drawing with English readers have noted a handedness difference (e.g., Snyder *et al.*, 1983; van Sommers, 1984) we were interested in testing for it as well. In our follow-up study which compared left- and right-handed Hindi and Urdu subjects we found a significant group difference between the right-handers such that Hindi subjects were more likely than Urdu readers to show a leftward figure orientation, consistent with our previous finding. However, the performance of the left-handers was unaffected by reading habits inasmuch as both Hindi and Urdu left-handers tended to orient the figures toward the right (less than 25% of their overall drawings were oriented towards the left).

Thus, the results from our follow-up study suggest that both handedness and reading direction separately influence figure orientation and that the effects of reading direction emerge only among right handers.

STUDY 2: SCRIPT DIRECTIONALITY INFLUENCE ON ASYMETRIES IN FACIAL AFFECT PERCEPTION

To extend the scope of our investigation of script directionality effects, in our next study (Vaid and Singh, 1989) we used a task that has been employed by previous investigators in a laterality context. This task, involving facial affect judgments, was developed by Campbell (1978) and adapted by Jerre Levy and associates (e.g., Heller and Levy, 1981; Levy, Heller, Banich, and Burton, 1983; Levine and Levy, 1986) and has since been used by several other researchers in the laterality literature (e.g., Hellige, Bloch, and Taylor, 1988; Best, 1987; Jaeger, Borod, and Peselow, 1987) as an index of right hemisphere involvement.

The task requires subjects to decide which of two photographs of asymmetrically smiling faces looks happier. Our intention in using this task was to test whether directional scanning effects might be generating the asymmetries otherwise attributed to laterality effects. The possibility of a reading habit bias had been raised only in passing in one of the dozen or more studies that have used this task as a laterality measure but was never studied.

Method

Subjects. Four groups of right-handed adults and two groups of left-handers were tested. Right-handed subjects included 35 left-to-right (Hindi) readers, 57 bidirectional (Urdu/Hindi) readers, 17 right-to-left (Arabic) readers and

22 illiterate speakers of Hindi/Urdu. Left handed subjects included 19 Hindi readers and 12 Urdu/Hindi readers.

Stimuli and Procedure. Stimuli from Levy *et al.* (1983) were used. They consisted of 36 pairs of photos of male faces, prepared as asymmetric composites such that either the left or the right half of the face was smiling. A given pair thus included a left-smile and a right-smile. Subjects were tested individually using a booklet containing the stimulus pairs presented in free vision (as was done in the studies by Levy and associates). The faces were counterbalanced such that the smile was on the left side in the top photo in half the cases and in the bottom photo in the remaining cases. Subjects' task was simply to decide which of the two faces of a given pair looked happier. The experimenter (blind to the purpose of the study) recorded whether the top or the bottom face was chosen.

Data Coding and Analysis. Following Levy *et al.* (1983), a laterality measure was computed per subject. The total number of pairs with a leftward smile were subtracted from the total number with a rightward smile, and this value was divided by the total number of pairs in the test (36). This yielded an asymmetry score varying from negative to positive values, with a negative score signalling a leftward preference. The asymmetry scores were analyzed in an analysis of variance. A frequency analysis, comparing the incidence of leftward versus rightward and no preference across groups was also performed on the data. Finally a reliability test was done.

Results

Reliability. The split-half reliability measure (Pearson correlation) revealed that the scores of all but two groups were reliable (see Table 2). The unreliable groups were the illiterates and the Hindi left handers. The results of these two groups on the other analyses must therefore be regarded as carrying no information with regard to the question at hand.

Asymmetry Scores. The asymmetry scores ranged from –0.286 for the Hindi right handers to +0.072 for the Arabic subjects. The analysis of variance for the right-handers revealed a significant Group effect [$F(3, 130) = 6.05$, $p < 0.007$] such that Hindi subjects were significantly more leftward in their asymmetry scores as compared to all other right-handed groups ($p < 0.01$). Furthermore, there were no differences between the Arab and Urdu subjects' performance (0.072 vs. 0.022, respectively). The analysis of variance comparing left handers revealed a two-way interaction of Group by Hand [$F(1, 119) = 7.33$, $p < 0.007$], indicating a greater leftward preference among Hindi than Urdu right-handers ($p < 0.05$), and a greater leftward prefer-

TABLE 2
Split-half reliability values for facial affect judgment test

Group	N	Pearson r
A. Right-Handers		
Hindi	35	0.71*
Arab	17	0.84*
Urdu	57	0.62*
Illiterate	22	0.02
B. Left-Handers		
Hindi	19	0.18
Urdu	12	0.88*

$p < 0.05$ or beyond.

ence among Hindi right-handers relative to Hindi left-handers ($p < 0.05$). No differences were found between Urdu right and left-handers, or between Hindi and Urdu left-handers.

Frequency of Leftward Bias. Subjects were classified as showing a significant ($p < 0.05$) left bias, a right bias or no bias. Nearly 70% of Hindi right-handed subjects and 77% of Arabic readers manifested a significant bias in either direction, as compared to 42% of Urdu right-handers and 18% of the illiterates. Among the left-handers 33% of the Urdu readers and 26% of the Hindi readers showed a significant preference in either direction.

A chi square analysis of those who showed a significant bias indicated that, among right handers, significantly more Hindi readers ($p < 0.05$) than either Urdu or Arabic readers showed a leftward bias, a leftward bias was found in 83% of Hindi readers versus 54% of Urdu subjects (n.s.) and only 31% of Arabic readers.

Discussion

The results from the facial affect perception task provide partial support for a reading scan hypothesis inasmuch as the observed bias was strongest in Hindi readers and weakest in Arabic readers, being in between for the bi-directional readers. Since the Arabic readers did not show a strong, significant rightward bias, but only a tendency toward a rightward bias, it is not clear whether this reflects the small sample size of this group or an actual interaction of scanning tendency with laterality effect, resulting in the weaker biases observed for this group.

Although handedness was examined, the results from the Hindi groups are inconclusive with regard to the effects of this variable since the performance of the Hindi left handers was statistically unreliable. The fact that there was no difference between right- and left-handed Urdu/Hindi readers is an ambiguous finding: it may indicate a genuine effect of reading scan and a lack of handedness effect on this task, or it may reflect an obscured handedness effect resulting in part from the existence of "hidden lefthanders" in the right-handed group, given the suppression of left-handedness in Muslim cultures. While the latter possibility is plausible we do not think it accounts entirely for the results, since the actual (manifest) left-handers studied might be expected to be particularly strongly left-handed, if they were able to resist societal pressures to be right-handed. Since these left-handers performed in the same way as the ostensibly right-handed group, this may suggest that the task is tapping non-biological differences.

Interestingly, of all of the subgroups that have been studied on the facial affect perception task, the only subjects that have not shown a leftward bias were pre-literate 5 years olds (their mean asymmetry score was –0.092; Levine and Levy, 1986). Only a quarter of the 20 subjects in this group according to Levine and Levy showed a significant asymmetry at all. We submit that a reading-habit interpretation may at least in part account for this group's poor performance on the task, apart from the explanations forwarded by Levine and Levy in terms of fatigue or random responding.

SUMMARY AND CONCLUSION

In our first study (Vaid and Singh, 1987) evidence was presented for an effect associated with script directionality on a nonlinguistic production task. Whereas left-to-right readers (Hindi) began their drawings at the top left of the page and proceeded to draw the other figures in a left to right order, the right-to-left readers (Urdu, Arabic) tended to start at the top right and proceed in a right to left order. Furthermore, the groups differed in the direction in which they oriented the three directional figures, with a leftward orientation favored by the left-to-right readers and a rightward one favored by the right-to-left readers. A follow-up study (Singh, Vaid, and Sakhuja, 1987) corroborated the difference between Hindi and Urdu right-handers but found an overall rightward bias for Hindi and Urdu left-handers.

Although only three figures were used in each of the two experiments, van Sommers (1984) has demonstrated with (right-handed) left-to-right readers that when drawing such objects as cars, fish, shoes, pipes, glasses, cutlery, the spines of books, the quills of feathers, the blades of tools, the fronts of houses, the heads of dogs, crocodiles, birds, etc., the objects' front is drawn first and, given the left-to-right direction of the initial stroke, these objects end up facing left.

The "invasion" of script directionality into a nonlinguistic domain such as figure drawing (at least among right-handers) in our study is particularly striking given that subjects were not aware of the purpose of the study (the experimenters themselves were blind to the purpose) and thus could not be behaving in accordance with any expectations about the purpose, or "demand characteristics". We have since conducted numerous follow-up studies with Hindi and Urdu right- and left-handers using a variety of production and perceptual tasks ranging from line bisection, line length estimations for lines of a targeted length drawn from left-to-right vs. right-to-left and circle drawing direction (Vaid and Singh, 1991). For the most part the results corroborate our figure orientation data.

The second study summarized here showed the operation of scanning biases on a nonlinguistic perceptual task thought to tap hemisphere differences in affect judgment (Vaid and Singh, 1989). Inasmuch as reading habits were indeed found to be present, this study, along with others in the literature should serve to alert researchers to the importance of including readers with different directional scanning biases in laterality studies. That reading habits appear to be more influential on ostensibly nonlinguistic tasks than on verbal laterality tasks is an unexpected but on reflection perhaps not altogether surprising conclusion of the present research.

ACKNOWLEDGMENT

The research reported here was conducted in collaboration with Maharaj Singh and was supported in part by an American Institute of Indian Studies fellowship awarded to J. Vaid.

REFERENCES

Belin, C., Pionner, V., Perrier, D., and Larmande, P.: 1988, 'Tachistoscopic recognition of words in a right-to-left language: Arabic', *Journal of Clinical and Experimental Neuropsychology* **10**.

Bertelson, P.: 1972, 'Listening from left to right versus right to left', *Perception* **1**: 161–165.

Best, C.: 1987, 'Asymmetries in perception and production of infant emotional expressions in chimeric presentation', *Journal of Clinical and Experimental Neuropsychology* **8**.

Campbell, R.: 1978, 'Asymmetries in interpreting and expressing a posed facial expression', *Cortex* **16**: 473–481.

Chen, M.: 1981, 'Directional scanning of visual displays', *Journal of Cross Cultural Psychology* **13**(3): 252–271.

Coulter, L.: 1982 (March), *Brain lateralization for reading in Arabic-English bilinguals*. Paper presented at annual meeting of the Body for the Advancement of Brain, Behavior and Language Enterprises, Niagara Falls.

Dennis, W.: 1958, 'Handwriting conventions as determinants of human figure drawing', *Journal of Consulting Psychology* **22**(4): 293–295.

Dennis, W. and Raskin, E.: 1960, 'Further evidence concerning the effect of handwriting habits upon the location of drawings', *Journal of Consulting Psychology* **24**(6): 548–549.

Dreman, S.: 1974, 'Directionality trends as a function of handedness and of reading and writing habits', *American Journal of Psychology* **87**(1–2): 274–253.

Dreman, S.: 1977, 'A review of directionality trends in the horizontal dimension as a function of innate and environmental factors', *The Journal of General Psychology* **96**: 125–134.

Freimuth, M. and Wapner, S.: 1979, 'The influence of lateral organization on the evaluation of paintings', *British Journal of Psychology* **70**: 211–218.

Gilbert, M. and Bakan, P.: 1973, 'Visual asymmetry in perception of faces', *Neuropsychologia* **11**: 355–362.

Harsel, Y. and Wales, R.: 1987, 'Directional preference in problem solving', *International Journal of Psychology* **22**: 195–206.

Heller, W. and Levy, J.: 1981, 'Perception and expression of emotion in right-handers and left-handers', *Neuropsychologia* **19**(2): 267–272.

Hellige, J., Bloch, M., and Taylor, A.: 1988, 'Multi-task investigation of individual differences in hemispheric asymmetry', *Journal of Experimental Psychology: Human Perception and Performance* **14**(2): 176–187.

Jaeger, J., Borod, J., and Peselow, E.: 1987, 'Depressed patients have atypical hemispace biases in the perception of emotional chimeric faces', *Journal of Abnormal Psychology* **96**(4): 321–324.

Jensen, B.: 1952, 'Left-right orientation in profile drawing', *American Journal of Psychology* **65**: 80–84.

Kelkar, A.: 1968, *Studies in Hindi-Urdu I: Introduction and Word Phonology*, Deccan College, Poona.

Levine, S. and Levy, J.: 1986, 'Perceptual asymmetry for chimeric faces across the lifespan', *Brain and Cognition* **5**: 291–306.

Levy, J.: 1976, 'Lateral dominance and aesthetic preference', *Neuropsychologia* **14**: 431–455.

Levy, J., Heller, W., Banich, M., and Burton, L.: 1983, 'Asymmetry of perception in free viewing of chimeric faces', *Brain and Cognition* **2**: 404–419.

Nachshon, I.: 1985, 'Directional preferences in perception of visual stimuli', *International Journal of Behavioral Neuroscience* **25**: 161–174.

Nachshon, I. and Alek, M.: 1981, 'The development of directional preferences: Cross-cultural differences', *Psychologia* **24**: 86–96.

Nachshon, I., Shefler, G., and Samocha, D.: 1977, 'Directional scanning as a function of stimulus characteristics, reading habits, and directional set', *Journal of Cross-Cultural Psychology* **8**: 83–99.

Narang, G. C.: 1986, 'Development and use of writing system across culture: The case of Arabic-Persian Urdu orthographical model', *Journal of South Asian and Middle Eastern Studies* **10**(2): 64–77.

Narula, S. S.: 1955, *Scientific History of the Hindi Language*, Hindi Academy, New Delhi.

Rai, Amrit: 1991, *A House Divided: The Origin and Development of Hindi-Urdu*, Oxford University Press, New Delhi.

Singh, M., Vaid, J., and Sakhuja, T.: 1987, *Directional scanning and handedness: Influence on the direction and orientation of free-hand drawing*, presented at annual meeting of the National Academy of Neuropsychology, Chicago.

Synder, T., Grackenbach, J., and Branford, C.: 1983, *Directional drawing preferences of the right and left hands of right- and left-handers*, paper presented at the Midwestern Psychological Association, Chicago.

Sommers, P. van: 1984, *Drawing and Cognition: Descriptive and Experimental Studies of Graphic Production Processes*, Cambridge University Press, New York.

Sommers, P. van: 1991, 'Where writing starts: The analysis of action applied to the historical development of writing', in J. Wann, A. Wing, and N. Sovik (eds.) *Development of Graphic Skills: Research Perspectives and Educational Implications*, Academic Press, London, pp. 1–38.

Tramer, O., Butler, B., and Mewhort, D.: 1985, 'Evidence for scanning with unilateral presentation of letters', *Brain and Language* **25**: 1–18.

Vaid, J.: 1988, 'Asymmetries in tachistoscopic word recognition: Scanning effects re-examined', *International Journal of Neuroscience* **42**(1): 253–258.
Vaid, J. and Singh, M.: 1987, *Reading habits influence asymmetries in nonlinguistic perception and production*, presented at tenth annual meeting of the Body for the Advancement of brain, Behavior and Language Enterprises, Niagara Falls.
Vaid, J. and Singh, M.: 1989, 'Asymmetries in the perception of facial affect: Is there an influence of reading habits?', *Neuropsychologia* **27**(10): 1277–1287.
Vaid, J. and Singh, M.: 1991, *Linguistic scanning biases can affect performance on non-linguistic neuropsychological tasks*, presented at annual meeting of National Academy of Neuropsychology, Dallas.

KEIKO KODA

20. COGNITIVE CONSEQUENCES OF L1 AND L2 ORTHOGRAPHIES*

INTRODUCTION

The relationship between orthography and cognition is one of the critical issues in psycholinguistic research. The effects of orthography have been investigated over the past 30 years. The resulting conclusions, nonetheless, are less than certain. Sociologists and historians, on the other hand, approaching the issue from a different perspective, have demonstrated that the evolution of orthographic systems has had a direct influence on social development, especially in the West (Goody, 1968; Goody and Watt, 1963; Olson, 1975, 1977; Gelb, 1963).

In recent times, striking evidence regarding the orthographic impact on cognition has been provided by Scribner and Cole (1981). In their widely-cited study, they explored the consequences of literacy on the cognitive development of an African tribe, the Vai. A series of cognitive tasks was administered to three groups of Vai adults who were literate in different orthographies. The data indicated systematic variations in task performance among the three groups. Scribner and Cole also found that response patterns were correlated with the literacy background of each group. In short, the Vai subjects performed well on tasks requiring cognitive processing similar to the script they usually read. Based on these and other findings, the researchers contend that orthography has some "identifiable cognitive consequences" (p. 125).

One way of investigating long lasting effects of orthography is to examine whether the effects attributable to first language (L1) orthographic systems remain when individuals read a second language (L2) involving a different orthographic system. Recent cross-linguistic studies in reading consistently support the probability that different information processing procedures are involved in reading different orthographies: e.g., Serbo-Croatian (Turvey, Feldman, and Lukatela, 1984), Hebrew (Navon and Shimron, 1984), Chinese (Tzeng and Wang, 1977, 1983), and Japanese (Sasanuma, 1985; Paradis, Hagiwara, and Hildebrandt, 1985). These results suggest that specific skills and strategies are developed through initial literacy acquisition to deal with a particular orthographic system used in the language.

The primary purpose of the present study was to investigate L1 orthographic impact on cognitive strategies used in L2 reading. If the L1 orthographic effects are sustained in L2 processing, two implications arise: (a) cognitive skills and strategies developed through L1 reading are trans-

I. Taylor and D.R. Olson (eds.), Scripts and Literacy, 311–326.

ferred to L2 reading, and (b) L1 orthographic structure has a significant impact on cognitive processes in L2 reading. We can thus make a strong case for orthographic impact on cognitive processing.

ORTHOGRAPHIC TYPES AND COGNITIVE STRATEGIES

Based on the fundamental unit of representation, major orthographic systems presently used in various languages can be classified into two contrasting types: morphography and phonography. In morphography, such as Chinese characters and Japanese Kanji, the representational unit is a morpheme, and thus, semantically-oriented. In contrast, the unit of representation in phonography is phonologically-oriented – a syllable in the syllabary, for example, or a phoneme in the alphabet. Given the contrasting units of representation, we can expect that the cognitive process involved in reading the two types may vary in the following way: (a) the phonological code (i.e., sound representation of individual lexical items) operates differently in each, or (b) contrasting strategies are used to obtain phonological codes.

Function of Phonological Codes

It has been argued that the primary function of phonological codes in reading is to facilitate information register in short term memory (STM) (e.g., Kleiman, 1975; Levy, 1977; Slowiaczek and Clifton, 1980; McCutchen and Perfetti, 1982; Perfetti and McCutchen, 1982). A number of STM studies have demonstrated that phonologically encoded materials are better retained in STM than those encoded visually, suggesting that the phonological code is more suited than the visual code for representing linguistic information in STM (Conrad, 1964; Eriksen, Pollack, and Montague, 1970; Baddeley, 1966; Cimbalo and Laughery, 1967). When comprehending longer and more complex linguistic units, segmental information must be held in STM for higher order processing such as syntactic and discourse analysis. In the reading comprehension process, therefore, visually presented materials must be converted into their phonological form so that they can be efficiently processed in STM (Just and Carpenter, 1980, 1987; Kintch and van Dijk, 1978; Perfetti and Lesgold, 1977; Daneman and Carpenter, 1980).

Interestingly, recent STM studies with Chinese speakers have shown that (a) their memory performance is impaired more by phonological than graphic similarity (Yik, 1978; Mou and Anderson, 1981), and (b) STM capacity for phonologically encoded materials is greater than that for non-phonologically encoded materials (Zhang and Simon, 1985; Yu, Zhang, Jing, Peng, Zhang, and Simon, 1985). These findings seem to indicate that morphographic readers also use phonological encoding to access STM. In short, phonological encoding is apparently the most effective method for STM information register regardless of the orthographic type.

Logically then, phonological code should play an equally important role in the reading process of both phonographic and morphographic orthographies. A number of reading studies, in fact, have demonstrated that phonological coding interference seriously impaired reading comprehension of both phonographic and morphographic readers (e.g., Kleiman, 1975; Levin, 1977; Tzeng *et al.*, 1977). The function of the phonological code thus does not seem to differ in the reading process in the two types orthographies. What can be said, then, about the second alternative – strategies for phonological coding?

Orthographic Representation and Phonological Coding Strategies

A basic assumption is that phonological coding strategies employed in a particular orthographic system are largely determined by the internal structure of the word in the system (i.e., how phonological code is reflected in the graphemic representation). In phonographic orthographies, for example, phonological information is represented graphically, and thus visually accessible. Since the regularity of correspondence between graphemic and phonemic representations varies from one system to another among phonographic orthographies, phonological recoverability (i.e., how systematically the graphemic representation can be converted into the phonological representation) differs from one system to another (Henderson, 1982, 1984; Coltheart, 1984). In order to accommodate different degrees of phonological recoverability, alternative strategies – e.g., lexical analogy (Glushko, 1979; Henderson, 1985), grapheme-phoneme translation (Coltheart, 1978; Patterson and Morton, 1985), and combination of both (Rosson, 1985) – are used for phonological coding by phonographic readers. Irrespective of the strategies employed, however, phonological coding in phonographic orthographies always involves the direct analysis of phonological elements embedded in the graphemic representation. It has been reported, in fact, that unpronounceability impedes the reading comprehension process of English speakers (Cunningham and Cunningham, 1978), which is not the case for Japanese subjects reading English as an L2 (Koda, 1987).

Conversely, in morphography, phonological information is not represented graphically. It has been noted that in morphography, a sound used in speech is arbitrarily assigned to the graphemic representation (Kaiho and Nomura, 1983; Shirakawa, 1978). In Chinese, for example, the same writing system is used across dialects which, in their spoken form, are mutually unintelligible. Consequently, the most common phonological coding strategy among morphographic readers is memory search, using the graphemic representation as the primary activator, and, when necessary, the meaning as a mediator. Although it is sometimes claimed that morphographies have a radical (i.e., an element of a single character) which provides phonological information, the phonetic radical itself is usually an independent character. The radical cannot provide adequate information until its phonological code is first retrieved from memory. Phonological coding for morphographic orthographies thus takes place with virtually no requirement for phonetic representation (Gleitman, 1985; Gleitman and Rozin, 1977; Mann, 1985).

It is highly unlikely, however, that memory search is the only strategy available to morphographic readers. If the phonological code were obtained through memory search alone, we would need to assume that the phonological code for all symbols is stored in memory, and linkages between the phonological code and the graphemic representation, as well as those between the phonological code and the meaning, are relatively permanent. Obviously, such an assumption is psychologically untenable. In reality, morphographic readers encounter many symbols they have never seen before, as well as symbols whose pronunciation they cannot recall. It is conceivable, then, that an alternative strategy is available to morphographic readers when they must deal with characters not referenced in their memory. Deducing from the arbitrary nature of the sound assignment, morphographic readers presumably *invent* a sound for a character and assign it to the character as its phonological code. At least two distinct strategies are thus used by morphographic readers to obtain phonological codes. The characteristic common to both is that neither involves the direct analysis of the graphemic representation – a striking contrast with the phonological coding strategies used by phonographic readers.

To recapitulate, in phonographic orthographies, phonological information is always available in the graphemic representation. The phonological code, therefore, is usually attained by analyzing phonological elements in the graphemic representation. In morphographic orthographies, where phonological information is not visually accessible, analysis of the graphemic representation is circumvented. The comparative analysis of phonological coding strategies thus demonstrates that a major distinction between the two types of orthographies lies in the extent to which readers make use of phonological information in the graphemic representation. In sum, phonographic readers rely on what is available in the graphemic representation, while morphographic readers may form a phonological code – whether or not phonological information is present in the graphemic representation. It was hypothesized, therefore, that phonological inaccessibility would have differential effects on the reading process among phonographic and morphographic readers.

To test the hypothesis, two cross-linguistic experiments were conducted with adult L2 learners of English (n = 83) with contrasting L1 orthographic backgrounds (Arabic, Spanish, Japanese,[1] and English for native control). Since it was essential that all subjects be skilled readers in their L1 and that the non-native speakers of English have sufficient knowledge of written English to perform experimental tasks, the following criteria were established: (a) a college-level education in the native country, and (b) at least six years of formal English instruction.

Since the experimental data was to be subjected to group comparisons, it was imperative that the three non-native English speaking groups be relatively similar in their English proficiency. Two forms of an English proficiency test – cloze[2] and listening comprehension – were given to all non-native English speaking subjects. The results of the two tests indicated that no statistically significant difference existed among the three groups either in listening comprehension [$F(2, 61) = 1.82$, $p > 0.1$], or in cloze test [$F(2, 61) = 1.82$, $p > 0.1$].

Experiment 1

Experiment 1 investigated the effects of phonological inaccessibility on reading performance among the four language groups. For this experiment, two passages of approximately 350 words were constructed: one describing the characteristics of five imaginary fish,[3] and the other describing the characteristics of five fictitious cocktails.

In the control condition, pronounceable English nonsense words were used as names for the fish and cocktails, while in the experimental condition, Sanskrit symbols were substituted for the nonsense English words. Since the subjects had no knowledge of Sanskrit, or its writing system, the symbols presumably represented a phonologically inaccessible element in the experimental condition.

In the experiment, the subjects were asked to read two passages silently at a comfortable speed for comprehension. They were told that the reading time would be measured and also that they would be asked to take a short recall test for each passage. Upon completion of the timed reading, the subjects were given the recall test for the first passage. Once the administration of the first passage was completed, instructions for the second passage were given and the procedure repeated.

The means and the standard deviations of the two outcome measures – i.e., reading speed and recall test scores – are presented in Table 1.

First, differences in reading speed (i.e., reciprocal = 1/reading time) were analyzed using a two-way ANOVA. The analysis revealed that subjects in the all four groups spent significantly more time reading the Sanskrit passages than the nonsense English passage [$F(1, 82) = 54.67$, $p < 0.0001$]. This result suggests that phonological inaccessibility interfered the reading process regardless of orthographic backgrounds. The degree of decrement in reading speed, however, varied among the four groups. The greatest magnitude of decrement occurred among English speaking subjects, followed by Spanish, Arabic, and Japanese in this respective order (see Figure 1). Importantly, the difference in the reading speed decrement between the phonographic (Arabic, English, and Spanish) and morpho-

TABLE 1
Means and standard deviations of three outcome measures

Group	*n*	Condition			
		Control		Sanskrit	
		M	*SD*	*M*	*SD*
Reading Time (in seconds)					
Arabic	20	212.16	62.68	244.64	72.75
English	21	100.71	36.49	147.29	68.85
Japanese	22	205.08	65.06	210.62	67.76
Spanish	20	143.78	43.08	178.29	46.54
Recall Test Scores (Maximum score = 10)					
Arabic	20	6.78	2.65	6.23	2.81
English	21	9.41	1.54	9.17	2.13
Japanese	22	8.93	2.13	8.03	3.23
Spanish	20	8.18	2.54	6.88	2.98

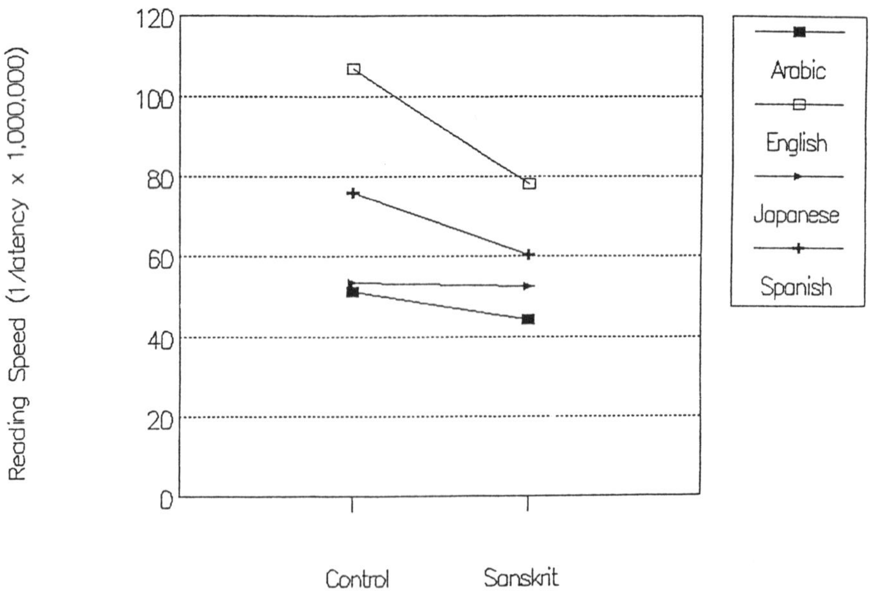

Fig. 1.

graphic (Japanese) groups was found to be significant [$F(1, 82) = 15.72$, $p < 0.0003$]. These results clearly indicate that the subjects with the two contrasting orthographic backgrounds responded differently to phonological inaccessibility in their reading process.

In a subsequent analysis, the recall test scores were examined using a two-way ANOVA. Although the main effect of Condition was significant [$F(1, 82) = 2.55$, $p < 0.0001$], the Group × Condition interaction effect was non-significant ($p < 0.05$). Thus, unlike reading speed, the degree of the decrement in the recall test scores did not differ among the four groups. The fact that the condition × group interaction effect was found non-significant seems to suggest that the subjects, as instructed, read the passages carefully for comprehension. It appears reasonable, therefore, to conclude that the differences in the reading speed decrement among the four groups reflect the differential effects of phonological inaccessibility on reading performance among the four groups.

To summarize, the data form the experiment indicated that the reading efficiency of the three phonographic groups was handicapped by the absence of phonological information to a much greater extent than that of the morphographic readers, and that phonological inaccessibility has differential effects on reading performance between phonographic and morphographic readers. The findings of the experiment thus supports the primary hypothesis, suggesting that different reading strategies are used by L2 readers of English with contrasting L1 orthographic backgrounds. One could argue, however, that the Japanese subjects are simply better at dealing with visually complex figures, and the date do not necessarily indicate differential strategies involved in phonological coding. Experiment 2 was conducted to more directly examine alternative strategies for phonological coding between phonographic and morphographic readers.

Experiment 2

In this experiment, the effects of phonological coding interference on STM recall performance were compared among the four groups. It has been claimed that a phonological code is suited not only for representing linguistic materials in STM but also for retaining ordered information (Hanson, 1982; Baddeley, 1978; Crowder, 1978; Healy, 1975). Previous STM studies have reported that STM performance is seriously impaired by phonological interference (Conrad and Hull, 1964; Rubenstein, Lewis, and Rubenstein, 1971; Wickelgren, 1965), but not by visual interference (Baddeley, 1966; Cimbalo and Laughery, 1967). Consistent results have been provided by STM experiments with Chinese speakers (Mou and Anderson, 1981; Yik, 1978; Zhang and Simon, 1985), suggesting that phonological encoding is the most preferred strategy for STM information register regardless of orthographic backgrounds.

Given that interference with phonological encoding results in poor STM recall performance, this experiment compared the effects of two types of phonological interference on STM performance, using the ordered recall paradigm.

First, two interference stimulus sets were constructed with (a) phonologically similar letter-strings and (b) unpronounceable letter-strings. The third set was constructed with phonologically dissimilar but graphically similar letter-strings. Since, as has been noted, visual confusability has limited effects on STM performance (Baddeley, 1966; Cimbalo and Laughery, 1967), this set presumably served as a control. Each set consisted of eight four-letter strings. In the phonologically similar set, eight letter-strings were composed so that they were all pronounced /keis/, such as CAIS, KEIS, KACE and CACE. In the phonologically dissimilar/graphically similar set, four pairs of graphically similar letters, such as C and G, I and L, O and D, E and F, were combined to make eight four-letter strings which looked alike, while maintaining distinctiveness in their underlying phonological codes (e.g., CIOE, CLOF, and CIDE). In the unpronounceable set, letters were combined so that each string violated English orthographic rules (e.g., XJWZ, QNWF, and QZJN).

The effects of two phonological encoding interference sets were also examined in Japanese. In order to make claims about long-lasting orthographic effects, it was necessary to obtain information about STM encoding strategies used by Japanese subjects when processing their L1.

The three Japanese sets, corresponding to the three English sets, were constructed with pseudo-Kanji characters. In the phonologically similar set, pseudo-Chinese characters were constructed by combining non-phonetic/non-semantic radicals and two types of syllabary symbols (Hiragana and Katagana) which carry the same phonological value /ji/ (see Figure 2). In the phonologically dissimilar/graphically similar set, non-phonetic radicals which looked alike were combined with syllabary symbols which were graphically similar but phonologically dissimilar. The unpronounceable set consisted of characters constructed by combining two non-phonetic/non-semantic radicals (see Figure 2).

Finally, a Sanskrit set was constructed to control for linguistic knowledge among subjects with different language backgrounds. If no significant difference were found among the four groups in STM performance of this set, we could claim that STM capacity among the four groups is not significantly different, and therefore, differences found in other stimulus sets would be attributable to strategy variation rather than differences in STM capacity.

In the experiment, a series of five words was presented, followed by a probe (one of the five words), and the subjects were asked to respond by indicating the word following the probe word in the series. In each trial, prior to presentation of stimulus cards, a 3 × 5 index card displaying eight

1. English Phonologically Similar

1. CATS 2. KEIS 3. KACE 4. CACE
5. KAIS 6. KAYS 7. KASE 8. CAYS

2. English Phonologically Dissimilar/ Graphically Similar Set

1. CIDE 2. CIOE 3. CIOT 4. GIOF
5. CLOE 6. CLOT 7. GLOF 8. GIDE

3. English Unpronounceable Set

1. XJWZ 2. WNGZ 3. QNWF 4. QZJN
5. XPLJ 6. QSZF 7. WXKJ 8. XRQN

4. Japanese Phonologically Similar

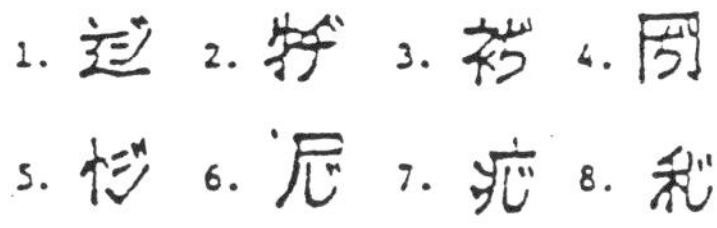

5. Japanese Phonologically Dissimilar/ Graphically Similar Set

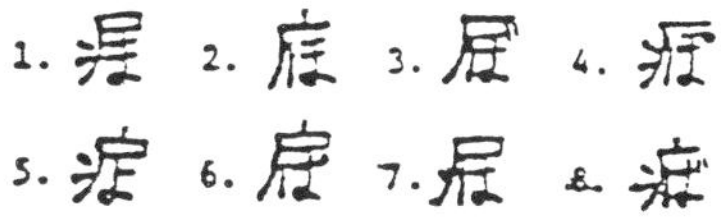

6. Japanese Unpronounceable Set

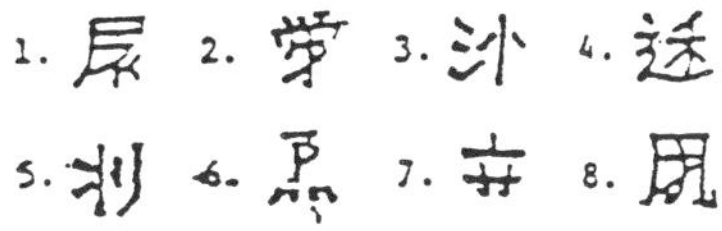

7. Sanskrit Set

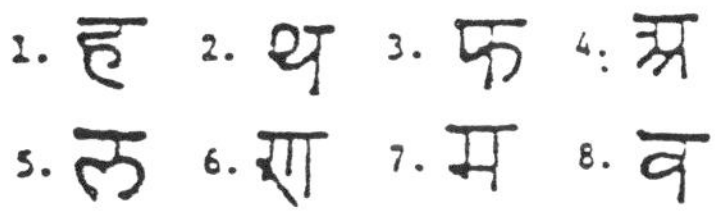

Fig. 2. Stimulus sets used in the experiment.

stimuli used in a set was given to the subjects. Each of the eight stimuli in the trial was numbered so that subjects could use the numbers (1–8) for response. These numbers were randomly assigned and the numbers were reassigned for each trial to prevent the subjects from using the numbers for encoding. Each subject received a different quasi-random sequence with the restriction that each stimulus appeared once in each serial position in each set. The eight stimuli in a set were each used once as a probe and once as an answer.

Stimuli cards were shown manually at a rate of 1.2 seconds per stimulus. The probe word was presented 3.6 seconds after the final stimulus card. The subjects responded with the stimulus that followed the probe in that trial, writing the number of the stimulus presented on the display card. The presentation order of the seven stimulus sets was randomized across subjects.

After receiving instructions, the subjects were given four practice trials, immediately followed by actual trials. Upon completion of the task, a debriefing interview was given to most of the subjects to learn about the strategies they had used to perform the task in each set. The experiment was carried out individually.

The means and the standard deviations of STM recall test scores in the three English and Sanskrit sets are presented in Table 2.

TABLE 2
Means and standard deviations of STM recall test scores in English and Sanskrit conditions

Conditions	Group			
	Arabic (n = 18)	English (n = 21)	Japanese (n = 22)	Spanish (n = 20)
English stimulus sets				
Phonologically similar				
M	2.44	3.05	2.56	2.94
SD	1.04	1.24	1.59	1.64
Phonologically dissimilar/ Graphically similar				
M	2.56	4.29	3.50	3.20
SD	1.58	1.23	1.47	1.79
Unpronounceable				
M	2.22	2.93	3.05	2.33
SD	1.06	1.02	1.50	1.45
Sanskrit stimulus set				
M	4.28	5.81	5.14	4.85
SD	2.22	1.78	1.58	2.37

Note: Maximum score = 8.0.

First, to test the effects of phonological interference on STM recall performance, a two-way ANOVA was performed with the recall test scores in the three English stimulus sets. It was found that subjects performed significantly better when no phonological interference was present [$F(1, 80) = 8.79$, $p < 0.001$]. The data thus demonstrated that STM performance was seriously impaired by phonological interference while graphic similarity had limited effects on STM performance. These findings are consistent with previous research findings, confirming that phonological encoding is used more dominantly than visual encoding (Levy, 1971; Conrad, 1964; Murry, 1965; Baddeley, 1978).

Second, to examine whether different phonological coding strategies are used between morphographic and phonographic readers, the effects of two types of phonological interference – i.e., phonological similarity and unpronounceability – on STM performance were compared. The difference in recall test scores between the two groups (morphographic vs. phonographic) in the two phonological interference sets was found to be significant [$F(1, 80) = 5.19$, $p < 0.05$]. As evident in Table 2, Japanese subjects performed better in the unpronounceable set than in the phonologically similar set, while the three phonographic groups did better in the phonologically similar set than in the unpronounceable set. These results, as predicted, indicate that different phonological coding strategies are used by morphographic and phonographic readers.

Third, to obtain information about phonological encoding strategies among the Japanese subjects in their L1, their STM recall performance in the three Japanese sets was analyzed using a one-way ANOVA. The means and standard deviations of the recall test scores of the Japanese subjects in the three Japanese and corresponding English sets are presented in Table 3. Among the three Japanese sets, the highest mean score was found in the phonologically dissimilar/Graphically similar set, and the lowest in the phonologically similar set. The post-hoc analysis (Student-Neuman-Keules) revealed that the difference in recall test scores between the phonologically dissimilar/graphically similar set and the unpronounceable set was not significant, but the difference between these two sets and the phonologically similar set was significant. These results suggest that phonological coding among Japanese subjects was seriously impaired by phonological similarity, but not by either graphic similarity or unpronounceability.

TABLE 3
Means and standard deviations of STM recall test scores among Japanese subjects

Stimulus conditions	Language			
	Japanese		English	
	M	SM	M	SD
Phonologically similar	4.91	1.44	2.56	1.59
Phonologically dissimilar/ Graphically similar	6.09	1.44	3.50	1.47
Unpronounceable	5.82	1.59	3.05	1.50

Note: Maximum score = 8.0.

The debriefing interview revealed that phonological coding strategies used by Japanese subjects to encode unpronounceable pseudo-characters include: (a) using a reading of real characters which contain the same radicals, (b) using a name of the radicals, and (c) naming a character using its physical attributes, such as 'four dots', 'box', and 'square'. The data thus demonstrated that morphographic readers do form a phonological code without conducting a direct analysis of phonological information in the graphemic representation. Importantly, the response pattern among Japanese subjects was remarkably consistent when processing their L1 and L2 (see Table 3). These findings clearly indicate that L1 strategies are transferred to L2 processing.

Lastly, the data from the Sanskrit set was analyzed using a one-way ANOVA. It was found that the English group performed best, followed by the Japanese, Spanish, and Arabic groups in this respective order. The difference among the four groups, however, was not significant ($p > 0.1$). In the debriefing interview, subjects reported that they processed Sanskrit stimuli as a picture. They first identified physical characteristics of each stimulus and then associated them with something familiar to them. They then encoded stimuli using names of familiar objects. The fact that the STM performance of the four groups did not differ when stimuli were processed as non-linguistic material suggests that there is no significant difference in the basic STM capacity among the four groups. It seems reasonable, therefore, to claim that the differences found in other stimulus conditions are due to alternative strategies used in encoding processes rather than differences in basic STM capacity.

SUMMARY AND CONCLUSIONS

The effects of the L1 orthographic structure on phonological coding strategies involved in L2 reading were investigated through two cross-linguistic experiments. Previous research findings suggest that phonographic readers obtain the phonological code through a direct analysis of phonological information in the graphemic representation, whereas morphographic readers can form a phonological code regardless what is present in the graphemic representation. Given contrasting L1 phonological coding strategies, it was hypothesized that the absence of phonological cues in the graphemic representation would cause differential degrees of interference in the reading process of L2 learners with contrasting L1 orthographic backgrounds.

The data from Experiment 1 showed that the reading speed of the three phonographic groups (Arabic, English, and Spanish) decreased considerably when Sanskrit symbols, or phonologically inaccessible elements, were present in the reading passage, while the reading speed of morphographic readers remained somewhat constant between the two conditions (Sanskrit vs. Nonsense English). In fact, 13 of the Japanese subjects (out of 21) spent less time reading Sanskrit passages than Nonsense English passages. These findings seem to indicate that the reading effectiveness of the three phonographic groups was impaired by Sanskrit symbols, or phonological inaccessibility, more seriously than that among morphographic readers.

In Experiment 2, the effects of different types of phonological coding interference – i.e., phonologically similar and unpronounceability – on STM recall performance were compared among the four orthographically diverse groups. It was found that (a) STM recall performance of the all four groups was seriously impaired when phonological interference was present, and (b) the two interference sets (phonological similarity and unpronounceability) had differential effects on STM performance between morphographic and phonographic readers. These results seem to suggest first, that a phonological code is dominantly used in the STM encoding process regardless of the orthographic background, and second, that different phonological coding strategies are used by morphographic and phonographic readers.

The data from the three Japanese stimulus sets showed that (1) phonological coding of Japanese subjects were seriously inhibited by phonological similarity, but not by unpronounceability; and that (2) their response pattern was parallel between the three Japanese and the corresponding English sets, implying that L1 phonological coding strategies are utilized in L2 processing.

Finally, the result of the Sanskrit set demonstrates no significant difference among the four groups. This result indicates that difference sin STM performance disappear when subjects had no knowledge of stimulus languages. This finding suggests that individual differences in STM performance are resulting from strategic variation rather than difference in basic STM capacity.

The date from the two experiments thus support the primary hypothesis that different phonological coding strategies are used among L2 readers of English with contrasting L1 orthographic backgrounds. Importantly, the response pattern of the three non-native English speaking groups was consistent with the procedural behavior which could have been predicted from their L1 orthographic structures. Hence, the experiments provide strong empirical evidence of cognitive strategy transfer in L2 processing, and demonstrates that native-language orthographic structure does have long-lasting effects on cognitive processing. The present findings thus suggest that linguistic knowledge, – orthographic knowledge in particular – in both L1 and L2 has a significant impact on cognitive strategies involved in L2 proccssing.

NOTES

[*] Parts of the data were previously reported in Journal of Psycholinguistic Research (1989) and Studies in Second Language Acquisition (1990).

[1] When errors in word recognition tests in English among Japanese ninth graders were analyzed (Koda, unpublished data) and compared with those in Kanji among Japanese children (1–6 graders; Japanese National Language Research Institute, 1964), a remarkable similarity was found in types of errors in English and Kanji. These data seem to indicate that strategies developed to deal with unfamiliar Kanji are used to guess the meaning of unfamiliar English words. It was also found that reading comprehension in English among Japanese college students was unaffected by unpronounceability (Koda, 1987), which again suggests that Japanese readers use Kanji strategies (i.e., relying little on phonological information in the graphemic representation) when reading in English.

[2] The cloze test used in the present study was originally developed by Professor Bachman (1982). The test had been used as a part of the English placement test for foreign students admitted between Spring 1980 and Fall 1981 to the University of Illinois at Urbana-Champaign. The subjects who entered the university during the period (n = 3) were all asked whether they remembered the test. None of them reported that they did.

[3] Fish passage was originally deviced by Cunningham and Cunningham in their 1978 study. In the present experiment, the original passage was slightly shortened.

REFERENCES

Baddeley, A.D.: 1966, 'Short term memory for word sequences as a function of acoustic, semantic, and formal similarity', *Quarterly Journal of Experimental Psychology* **18**: 362–365.

Baddeley, A.D.: 1978, 'The trouble with levels: A reexamination of Craik and Lockhart's framework or memory research', *Psychological Review* **85**: 139–152.

Cimbalo, R.S. and Laughery, K.B.: 1976, 'Short term memory: Effects of auditory and visual similarity', *Psychonomic Science* **8**: 57–58.

Coltheart, M.: 1978, 'Lexical access in simple reading task', in G. Underwood (ed.) *Strategies of information processing*, Academic Press, London.

Coltheart, M.: 1984, 'Writing systems and reading disorders', in L. Henderson (ed.) *Orthographies and reading: Perspectives from cognitive psychology, neuropsychology, and linguistics*, Erlbaum, Hillsdale, NJ.

Conrad, R.: 1964, 'Acoustic confusion in immediate memory', *British Journal of Psychology* **55**: 75–84.

Conrad, R. and Hull, A.J.: 1964, 'Information, acoustic confusion and memory span', *British Journal of Psychology* **55**: 429–432.

Crowder, R.C.: 1978, 'Language and memory', in J.F. Kavanagh and W. Strange (eds.) *Speech and language in the laboratory, school, and clinic*, MIT Press, Cambridge, MA.

Cunningham, P.M. and Cunningham J.W.: 1978, 'Investigating the "print to meaning" hypothesis', in P.D. Pearson and J. Hansen (eds.) *Reading: Disciplined inquiry in process and practice* [27th Yearbook of the National Reading Conference], The National Reading Conference, Clemson, SC.

Daneman, M. and Carpenter, P.A.: 1980, 'Individual differences in working memory and reading', *Journal of Verbal Learning and Verbal Behavior* **19**: 450–466.

Eriksen, C.W., Pollack, M.D., and Montague, W.E.: 1970, 'Implicit speech: Mechanisms in perceptual coding?', *Journal of Experimental Psychology* **84**: 502–507.

Gelb, I.J.: 1963, *A study of writing*, University of Chicago Press, Chicago.

Gleitman, L.R.: 1985, 'Orthographic resources affect reading acquisition – If they are used', *Remedial and Special Education* **6**: 24–36.

Gleitman, L.R. and Rozin, P.: 1977, 'The structure and acquisition of reading, I: Relation between orthographies and the structure of language', in A.S. Reber and D.L. Scarborough (eds.) *Toward a psychology of reading: The processings of the CUNY conference*, Lawrence Erlbaum Associates, Hillsdale, NJ.

Glushko, R.J.: 1979, 'The organization and activation of orthographic knowledge in reading aloud', *Journal of Experimental Psychology: Human Perception and Performance* **5**: 674–691.

Goody, J.: 1968, 'Introduction', in J. Goody (ed.) *Literacy in traditional societies*, Cambridge University Press, Cambridge.

Goody, J. and Watt, I.: 1963, 'The consequence of literacy', *Comparative Studies in Society and History* **5**: 303–345.

Hanson, V.L.: 1982, 'Short-term recall by deaf signers of American sign language: Implications of encoding strategy for order recall', *Journal of Experimental Psychology: Learning, Memory, and Cognition* **8**: 572–583.

Healy, A.F.: 1975, 'Coding of temporal-spatial patterns in short-term memory', *Journal of Verbal Learning and Verbal Behavior* **14**: 481–495.

Henderson, L.: 1982, *Orthography and word recognition in reading*, Academic Press, London.

Henderson, L. (ed.): 1984, *Orthographies and reading: Perspectives from cognitive psychology, neuropsychology, and linguistics*, Erlbaum, Hillsdale, NJ.

Henderson, L.: 1985, 'Issues in the modeling of pronunciation assembly in normal reading', in K.E. Patterson, J.C. Marshall, and M. Coltheart (eds.) *Surface dyslexia*, Erlbaum, London, NJ.

Just, M.A. and Carpenter, P.A.: 1980, 'A theory of reading: From eye fixation to comprehension', *Psychological Review* **87**: 329–354.

Just, M.A. and Carpenter, P.A.: 1987, *The psychology of reading and language comprehension*, Allyn and Bacon, Boston, MA.

Kaiho, H. and Nomura, Y.: 1983, *Kanji Johoshori no shinrigaku* [The psychology of Kanji processing], Kyoiku Shuppan, Tokyo.

Kintch, W. and van Dijk, T.A.: 1978, 'Toward a model of text comprehension', *Psychological Review* **85**: 363–394.

Kleiman, G.M.: 1975, 'Speech recording in reading', *Journal of Verbal Learning and Verbal Behavior* **14**: 323–340.

Koda, K.: 1987, 'Cognitive strategy transfer in second language reading', in J. Devine, P.L. Carrell, and D.E. Eskey (eds.) *Research in reading in english as a second language*, TESOL, Washington, DC.

Levy, B.A.: 1971, 'Role of articulation in auditory and visual short-term memory', *Journal of Verbal Learning and Verbal Behavior* **10**: 123–132.

Levy, B.A.: 1977, 'Reading: Speech and meaning processes', *Journal of Verbal Learning and Verbal Behavior* **16**: 623–628.

Mann, V.A.: 1985, 'A cross-linguistic perspective on the relation between temporary memory skills and early reading ability', *Remedial and Special Education* **6**: 37–42.

McCutchen, D. and Perfetti, C.A.: 1982, 'The visual tongue-twistereffect: Phonological activation in silent reading', *Journal of Verbal Learning and Verbal Behavior* **21**: 672–687.

Mou, L.C. and Anderson, N.S.: 1981, 'Graphemic and phonemic codings of Chinese characters in short-term retention', *Bulletin of the Psychonomic Society* **17**: 255–258.

Murry, D.J.: 1965, 'Vocalization-at-presentation and immediate recall with varying presentation rates', *Quarterly Journal of Experimental Psychology* **17**: 47–56.

Navon, D. and Shimron, J.: 1984, 'Reading Hebrew: How necessary is the graphemic representation of vowels?', in L. Henderson (ed.) *Orthographies and reading: Perspectives from cognitive psychology, neuropsychology, and linguistics*, Erlbaum, Hillsdale, NJ.

Olson, D.R.: 1975, Review of *Toward a literacy society* (ed. J.B. Carroll and J. Chall), *Proceedings of the National Academy of Education* **2**: 109–178.

Olson, D.R.: 1977, 'From utterance to text: The bias of language in speech and writing', *Harvard Educational Review* **47**: 257–281.

Paradis, M., Hagiwara, H., and Hildebrandt, N.: 1985, *Neurolinguistic aspects of the Japanese writing system*, Academic Press, New York.

Patterson, K.E. and Morton, J.: 1985, 'From orthography to phonology: An attempt at an old interpretation', in K.E. Patterson, J.C. Marshall, and M. Coltheart (eds.) *Surface dyslexia*, Erlbaum, London, NJ.

Perfetti, C.A. and Lesgold, A.M.: 1977, 'Discourse comprehension and source of individual differences', in M.A. Just and P.A. Carpenter (eds.) *Cognitive processes in comprehension*, Erlbaum, Hillsdale, NJ.

Perfetti, C.A. and McCutchen, D.: 1982, 'Speech process in reading', in N. Lass (ed.) *Advances in speech and language* (Vol. 7), Academic Press, New York.

Rosson, M.B.: 1985, 'The interaction of pronunciation rules and lexical representation in reading aloud', *Memory and Cognition* **13**: 90–99.

Rubenstein, H., Lewis, S.S., and Rubenstein, M.A.: 1971, 'Evidence for phonemic recording in visual word recognition', *Journal of Verbal Learning and Verbal Behavior* **10**: 647–657.

Sasanuma, S.: 1984, 'Can surface dyslexia occur in Japanese?', in L. Henderson (ed.) *Orthographies and reading: Perspectives from cognitive psychology, neuropsychology, and linguistics*, Erlbaum, Hillsdale, NJ.

Scribner, S. and Cole, M.: 1981, *The psychology or literacy*, Havaes University Press, Cambridge, MA.

Shirakawa, S.: 1978, *Kanji hyakuwa* [Hundred stories of Kanji], Chukoshinsho, Tokyo.

Slowiaczek, M.L. and Clifton, C., Jr.: 1980, 'Subvocalization and reading for meaning', *Journal of Verbal Learning and Verbal Behavior* **19**: 573–582.
Turvey, M.T., Feldman, L.B., and Lukatela, G.: 1984, 'The Serbo-Croatian orthography constrains the reader to a phonologically analytic strategy', in L. Henderson (ed.) *Orthographies and reading: Perspectives from cognitive psychology, neuropsychology, and linguistics*, Erlbaum, Hillsdale, NJ.
Tzeng, O.J.L., Hung, D.L., and Wang, W.S.-Y.: 1977, 'Speech recording in reading Chinese characters', *Journal of Experimental Psychology: Human Learning and Memory* **3**: 621–630.
Tzeng, O.J.L. and Wang, W.S.-Y.: 1983, 'The first two R's: The way different languages reduce speech to script affects how visual information is processed in the brain', *American Scientist* **71**: 238–243.
Wickelgren, W.A.: 1965, 'Acoustic similarity and retroactive interference in short-term memory', *Journal of Verbal Learning and Verbal Behavior* **70**: 102–108.
Yik, W.F.: 1978, 'The effect of visual and acoustic similarity on short-term memory for Chinese words', *Quarterly Journal of Experimental Psychology* **30**: 487–494.
Yu, B., Zhang, W., Jing, Q., Peng, R., Zhang, G., and Simon, H.A.: 1985, 'STM capacity for Chinese and English language materials', *Memory and Cognition* **13**: 202–207.
Zhang, G. and Simon, H.A.: 1985, 'STM capacity for Chinese words and idioms: Chunking and acoustical loop hypotheses', *Memory and Cognition* **13**: 193–201.

KWONSAENG PARK AND JYOTSNA VAID

21. LEXICAL REPRESENTATION OF SCRIPT VARIATION: EVIDENCE FROM KOREAN BISCRIPTALS

There exist many different writing systems in the world. This variety of the writing systems raises several important questions related to reading. Do different writing systems entail different forms of information processing in reading? What are the effects of script variations on the processes involved in reading: do they simply constrain peripheral perceptual processes or do they challenge central cognitive processes also? How do script variations affect the organization of lexical representation? etc. In our study, focusing on the latter issue, we sought to explore whether script information is represented in the mental lexicon. We attempted to resolve this problem by studying Korean biscriptals.

The fundamental question as to the organization of lexical representation concerns the defining characteristics of the entries in the mental lexicon (Kirsner, 1986; Kirsner and Dunn, 1985). Specifically, are lexical entries defined in terms of phonological and/or morphological characteristics per se, or is orthographic or script-related information also represented? The fact that children can talk before they learn to read forces us to regard phonological features as essential in lexical representation (e.g., Ehri, 1980). Our ability to recognize homophones (e.g., *right*, *write*, *rite* and *wright*; *crews* and *cruise*) without contextual assistance also makes it clear that orthographic features are used to define some lexical units. (e.g., Baron and Treiman, 1980; Henderson, 1984; Koriat, 1984). Feldman and Moskovljevic (1987) showed that morphology also plays an important role in delimiting boundaries between these units. Indeed, some have argued that morphology may be the primary basis for lexical organization (Kirsner, 1986).

When it comes to the question of the role of script in lexical organization, the answer is not immediately forthcoming in part because this question has been difficult to study, given that orthographic differences between languages are usually confounded by phonological and syntactic differences. Nevertheless, two opposing views can be identified on the basis of existing research on this issue: one is that script information is preserved at the lexical level and the other is that formation of lexical entries is based on phonological/morphological information alone, and thus, that script information does not provide either a necessary or sufficient basis for defining boundaries between the lexical units. In support of the first view, a number of clinical cases show that Kanji (logography) and Kana (syllabary) are selectively impaired in Japanese aphasic and acquired dyslexic patients (Sasanuma, 1974; 1984; Sasanuma and Fujimura, 1971; Yamadori, 1975),

I. Taylor and D.R. Olson (eds.), Scripts and Literacy, 327–339.

indicating that different modes of storage and/or information processing may be used for the two scripts. Similarly, using a number Stroop task, Besner and Coltheart (1979) showed that depending on how we represent numerical information (e.g., as words or as numerals), different types of mental operations may be operative (see also Gonzales and Kolers, 1982; Vaid, 1985a). In addition, the memorability of a word has been found to depend on the form of script (Hanzza – Chinese logography or Hangul – Korean alphabetic syllabary) in which the item was presented (Park and Arbuckle, 1977; but see Taylor, 1980). These results support the hypothesis that script variations do provide a sufficient basis for forming separate units in the lexicon. In fact, some investigators have claimed that different scripts even entail different information processing mechanisms (e.g., Tzeng and Hung, 1980).

On the other hand, studies using the repetition priming paradigm appear to suggest that script information is *not* preserved at the lexical level. In this paradigm, subjects are shown a list of items and asked to indicate whether each item is a real word or not. Repetition effects are examined by presenting the same or similar item twice and comparing the decision latency on the first presentation (the prime) with that on the second presentation (the target). Usually, decision on the target takes much less time than that on the prime. This saving is attributed to the repeated presentation of the same item and is referred to as a repetition (priming) effect. Repetition priming effects on lexical decision latencies have been found to be insensitive to case (upper or lower) variations (Scarborough, Cortese, and Scarborough, 1977): even when prime-target pairs are in different cases, the same amount of facilitation is observed as that observed when the prime-target pairs are in the same case. Similarly, in a study using Serbo-Croatian readers, Feldman and Moskovljevic (1987) showed that presenting the target in a different alphabet (Roman vs. Cyrillic) from the prime does not change the amount of facilitation on lexical decision latencies. Moreover, transfer of repetition effects has been found across languages which are orthographically different but phonologically identical (Brown, Sharma, and Kirsner, 1984: Experiment 1). Using Hindi-Urdu bilinguals, Brown *et al.* observed a similar amount of repetition facilitation on lexical decision tasks between two conditions: one in which the target-prime pairs were presented in the same language (script) and the other in which they were presented in different languages (scripts).

In order to resolve the problem of script difference effects on lexical organization, we need to study languages which vary only in script so that we can observe the effects of script variations alone leaving other linguistic factors intact. As already indicated, the Hindi-Urdu language pair used in Brown *et al.*'s study meets this criterion. The two languages have a common phonology and morphology but are represented in two entirely different writing systems (see Vaid, this volume). Since the words are represented in two different types of visual symbols while other factors such as phonology, morphology, and syntax of words are held relatively constant in this language pair, Brown *et al.* were able to examine the effects of script differences independently of other factors. Therefore, their conclusion on the basis of their repetition priming study that script differences do not provide a sufficient basis for forming separate lexical entries would seem to be justified. With an attempt to secure converging evidence, Brown *et al.* in their second experiment had Hindi-Urdu bilinguals and Hindi-English bilinguals read aloud a mixed language list (Hindi and Urdu, or Hindi and English). In the second part of the experiment, an unexpected memory test was given in which subjects were to recall the language in which the words were presented in the study phase. Brown *et al.* observed that performance on this incidental memory test was around 70% in accuracy when script was the only difference between two languages (Hindi-Urdu pair) but subjects' performance was much better (about 86% correct recall) when the languages differed in their phonology/morphology as well (Hindi-English pair). Brown *et al.* (1984) concluded that script variations do not play a functional role in defining the units of lexical entries.

However, in another study which also tested Hindi-Urdu bilinguals, this conclusion has been called into question. Vaid (1985b) found that her subjects' incidental memory for script was enhanced when the words were to be copied relative to when they were simply to be named out loud (over 80% accuracy for copied words). A similar above-chance memory for format was observed by Vaid and Frenck-Mestre (1991; 1994) using number stimuli. These findings would suggest that script variations in interaction with encoding context may in fact provide a sufficient basis for forming separate lexical units.

Clearly, this conflicting state of research on the role of script in lexical organization requires further investigation. In the present study, using Korean biscriptals, we intended to expand the empirical base of this issue by investigating yet another script pair. Korean readers were selected because a subset of content words in Korean may be written either in Hangul or in Hanzza with equal probability of occurrence without affecting their pronunciations and meanings (see Taylor, 1980, for a detailed analysis of the Korean writing systems). As previously mentioned, it is important to use languages differing only in script to investigate the problem of script variation effects on lexical organization. In reference to this criterion, Korean provides an ideal condition to study the problem.

EXPERIMENT 1

The primary aim of this experiment was to determine the extent to which subjects remember script-related information after working through a mixed script list of words. As in Brown *et al.* (1984: Experiment 2) and Vaid's

(1985b) studies, an incidental memory paradigm was used. According to the hypothesis that script information does not provide a sufficient basis for forming separate units in the lexicon, performance on the incidental memory test for script should be about chance level. Without a separate representation of script-related information in the lexicon, subjects are assumed to decide between the two scripts based on other information (presumably, phonological or/and morphological) that is preserved in the lexicon. Since this other information is the same in the language under study, memory for script should be about chance level. On the other hand, if script information *is* preserved in the lexicon, then memory for the script should be above chance.

According to the principle of encoding variability, memorability of an item changes with variations in the mode of encoding the item. A secondary aim of Experiment 1 was to examine how this principle operates in the incidental memory paradigm. Two encoding conditions (naming out loud vs. copying) were compared with each of the two different scripts in this experiment.

Method

Subjects. Thirty-two speakers of Korean (including 28 males and 4 females) served as subjects. They were graduate students enrolled in a university in southwestern United States. The majority were in their early 30's. All reported that they did not have any difficulty in reading Korean newspapers in which many words are printed in Hanzza. Subjects were subdivided into two groups according to their self-ratings of ease of reading Hanzza, on the basis of criteria described below. Subjects were paid for participating in the experiment.

Stimuli. Forty-eight common bisyllabic nouns were selected by consulting Korean newspapers. An attempt was made to choose those words that are frequently used and found commonly in both scripts. The words were divided into two lists (List 1 and List 2), each containing 24 words. Each word in turn was written twice, once in Hangul and once in Hanzza, at the centre of separate 4×6 inch white index cards. From these 96 cards two stimulus sets, each consisting of 48 cards, were prepared. The words in List 1 written in Hangul and the List 2 words written in Hanzza comprised one set, and the other was composed of the List 1 words written in Hanzza and List 2 words written in Hangul. Thus, each stimulus set consisted of 24 words written in one script and another 24 words written in the other script. Appendix A provides a list of the stimulus words.

Procedure. Subjects were tested individually. In the study phase of the experiment, one of the two decks of stimulus cards was placed on a table in front of the subject. Immediately before they viewed a given card, subjects were instructed as to how they should encode the word, i.e., they were either to read the word aloud or to write it down in the same script. Since the speed of reading and writing may vary across subjects, they were allowed to work at their own pace. Subjects were asked to read the words as clearly as possible so that a recording of their voice could be comprehended by someone else. They were also asked to copy the words so that someone else would be able to read them. Upon completion of this portion of the experiment, subjects were given a brief questionnaire on their language background and familiarity with Hanzza script. They were asked to rate their reading proficiency in Hanzza and their ability to write Hanzza from dictation. The self-ratings elicited from subjects were in terms of the percentage of characters commonly written in Hanzza, from a total corpus of 2,000, that they were able to read or write relatively effortlessly.

Self-ratings of competence in writing words in Hanzza from dictation ranged from 10% to 90%. In order to examine possible effects of this marked difference in self-reported proficiency, subjects were divided into two groups. These included 16 subjects whose scores were 40% or below, and 16 subjects whose self-ratings were 60% or above. The mean percent ratings were 20% for the former group (low proficiency) and 72% for the latter group (high proficiency).

At the completion of the questionnaire, subjects were administered an incidental recognition test. A post-experimental interview indicated that no subject anticipated this text. For the recognition test, four different test lists were prepared, two for each stimulus set. Of the 48 words in a test list, half were presented in Hangul and the other half were presented in Hanzza. Half of the Hangul words and half of the Hanzza words were in the same script as in the stimulus list and the remaining words were in the other script. Thus, four test lists were required to ensure that each word in the stimulus lists appeared equally often in the same script.

Upon presentation of the recognition test, subjects were instructed to note for each word on the list whether it was in the same or different script as that in the learning list. As in the study phase, they were allowed to work at their own pace.

Results and Discussion

The memory data were entered into an analysis of variance as a function of Group (high vs. low proficiency in Hanzza), Script (Hangul vs. Hanzza), and Encoding Condition (read aloud vs. copy). The results showed no significant effect of Group. Script emerged as a main effect [$F(1, 30) = 64.95$, $p < 0.00001$] and in interaction with Encoding Condition [$F(1, 30) = 30.75$, $p < 0.00001$]. The data are presented in Figure 1.

The Script effect indicated that memory for script was better for Hanzza

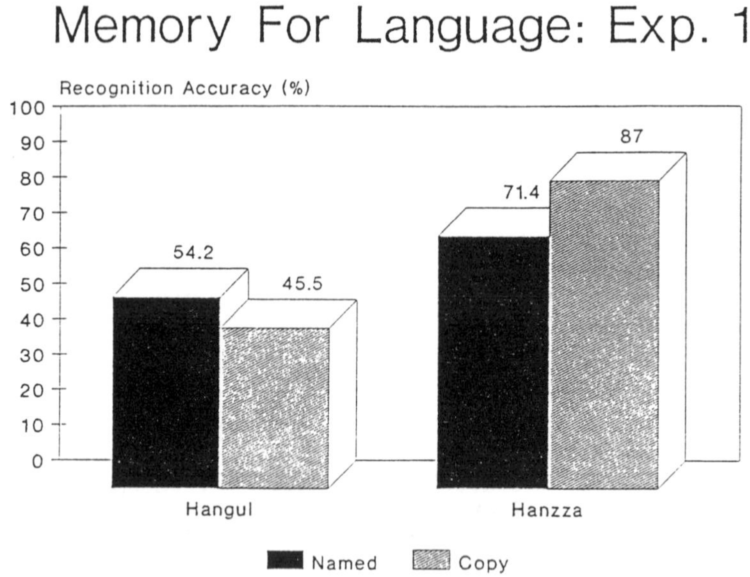

N=32

Fig. 1. Mean percent correct recognition of language (script) as a function of Script and Encoding operation (Experiment 1).

than Hangul (percent correct recall of script was 79.2% vs. 49.9%, respectively). As can be seen from Figure 1, the Script by Encoding Condition interaction mainly resulted from encoding variation effects on Hanzza words. That is, copying the words boosted recognition of script primarily for words that were written in Hanzza.

Since different effects were found for the two scripts, the present results do not provide conclusive evidence for either of the hypotheses previously proposed. The finding that Hanzza was remembered far better than chance level appears to support the position that script information is preserved at the lexical level. Nevertheless, it could be argued that the above chance level of script recognition observed is unique to Hanzza and reflects the fact that Hanzza is "visually more complex" than Hangul. To the extent that Hanzza is thought to be "visually more complex" than Hangul, processing a Hanzza word would presumably involve more effort than the same word in Hangul. In this way, better memory for Hanzza than Hangul can be explained without having to resort to postulating a separate lexical representation for Hanzza script in general.

Even if it seems appealing, an effort-based explanation leads to a problem. Effortfulness may be operationalized in terms of the time taken to complete the task (Carr, 1987; personal communication). Most would agree that copying a word takes more time/effort than naming the word, no matter what the script in which the word is printed. It then follows that copying the words should result in better memory than naming the word. With respect to Hanzza, this prediction was supported; however, it was not supported for Hangul. Therefore, effort per se may not provide an adequate explanation.

There is yet another way to explain the finding that Hanzza was remembered above chance level without resorting to the hypothesis that script information is preserved in the lexicon. Each Hangul character (syllable) is constructed by combining 2–4 out of 24 plausible alphabetic components. In contrast, most Hanzza characters do not share the same components. As a consequence, most Hanzza words are visually distinctive in the sense that they do not often share the same components. The items used in Experiment 1 in both study and test phase were presented visually. Therefore, if the subjects performed the test by relying on their visual memory of the words rather than the words' lexical status, their performance should be above chance and should be better for Hanzza than Hangul because Hanzza is visually more distinctive than Hangul. Moreover, copying Hanzza should serve to enhance visual memory for Hanzza, whereas copying Hangul would interfere with visual memory for Hangul. This possibility is tested in Experiment 2.

EXPERIMENT 2

The results of Experiment 1 showed that Hanzza was remembered far above chance level, while memory for Hangul was about chance level. These findings partially support the hypothesis that script variations provide a basis for forming separate lexical units. However, a possible alternative explanation requires further investigation before this conclusion can be reached. The primary aim of Experiment 2 was to examine whether the results of Experiment 1 can be replicated in a different experimental condition. The other aim was to determine whether visual distinctiveness is solely responsible for the superior memory for Hanzza. Again, incidental memory for script was tested. This time, the recognition list was presented auditorily rather than visually to discourage subjects from relying on visual memory of the word's form and to encourage them to perform the memory test on the basis of the lexical status of the word.

Method

Subjects. A total of sixteen Korean students (14 males and 2 females) were selected from the same population as that used in Experiment 1. An attempt was made to select individuals who judged themselves to be fairly comfortable with Hanzza. Subjects' self-rating of competence in Hanzza ranged between 6.0 and 9.5 with a mean of 7.7 on a scale ranging from 0 to 10. The subjects' ages ranged from 27 years to 42 years with the median age being 33 years. All subjects were paid for their participation in the experiment.

Stimulus and apparatus. A total of 50 new common bisyllabic nouns were selected using the same method as that in Experiment 1. As in Experiment 1, two sets of stimulus words were prepared. Each stimulus set consisted of all the 50 words, half of which were written in Hanzza and the remaining half in Hangul. The words written in Hanzza and those in Hangul in one stimulus set were written in opposite scripts, VIZ., in Hangul and in Hanzza, respectively, in the other stimulus set. Each stimulus word was hand-written and mounted on a 35 mm slide.

A Kodak slide projector was used to present the stimulus words at the subjects' eye level at a viewing distance of about 1.5 m. A digital timer with millisecond precision was connected to the projector in such a way that opening the shutter triggered the timer. The timer was stopped by a Gerbrands voice activated relay, triggered by subjects' vocal response. In this way, naming latencies could be measured from the onset of stimulus presentation.

Procedure. Subjects were tested individually in a dimly illuminated room. In the study phase of the experiment, subjects were told that their task was to read aloud the word on the screen as quickly as they could. Prompt responses were encouraged by telling them that one purpose of the experiment was to examine how quickly we can identify visually presented words. Subjects familiarized themselves with the task using four practice words, two of which were written in Hanzza and the other two in Hangul. The stimulus words were presented one at a time on the centre of the screen. The exposure duration of each word was 1 second and the inter-stimulus interval was 6 seconds. Half of the subjects were given one stimulus set of 50 words and the other half were given the other set.

At the completion of the study phase, subjects were required to perform a Stroop color naming task, which took about 2–3 minutes to finish. In this task they were asked to name aloud, as quickly as they could, four colors in rows of colored dots. As soon as they finished this task, an incidental memory test was administered. Subjects were given a blank sheet of paper, on which the numbers 1 to 50 were printed in order. They were asked to indicate on the sheet for each of 50 words, read aloud by the experimenter, the script in which the words were written in the study phase. They were given as much time as they needed for each word. As a precaution against choosing Hangul for words which subjects did not remember well, they were encouraged to write down "x" if they did not remember having seen a specific word in the study phase.

Results and Discussion

The mean naming latency for Hanzza words was 742 milliseconds (ms) and that for Hangul words was 576 ms.

The number of items correctly recalled was averaged across subjects. The means of accuracy values were 21.8 (87.25%) and 18.2 (72.75%) for Hanzza and Hangul, respectively (see Figure 2). Separate t-tests showed that these accuracy levels were far above chance [$t(15) = 15.78$, $p < 0.0001$, for Hanzza and $t(15) = 3.62$, $p < 0.005$, for Hangul]. Thus, script recognition was above chance and Hanzza was remembered better than Hangul. The latter finding replicates our first experiment. Unlike Experiment 1, however, even Hangul was remembered above chance level in our second experiment. As such the results support the view that script information is preserved in the lexicon.

An alternative explanation for superior memory for Hanzza over Hangul found in Experiment 1 was that the subjects might have performed the memory task on the basis of visual memory of the word's form rather than on the lexical status of the word. This interpretation cannot be applied to the similar results of Experiment 2, since the memory test used in this experiment requires that an auditorily presented word first be recognized as the word visually presented in the study phase, and then the script in

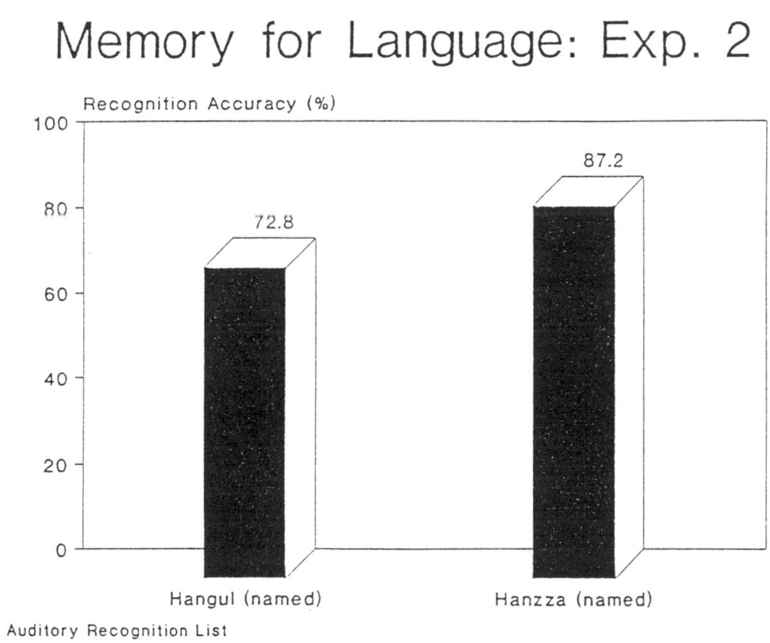

Fig. 2. Mean percent recognition of Script for auditorily presented words (Exp. 2).

which the word was presented be determined. In other words, individual word recognition is mandatory in performing the incidental memory test of Experiment 2. Since word recognition requires lexical access, the lexical status of the word must be addressed in performing this memory task; thus, it is unlikely that the superior memory for Hanzza over Hangul found in Experiment 2 simply reflects subjects' visual memory of the words' surface form. Therefore, it seems safe to conclude that the results of Experiment 2 support the hypothesis that script variation provides a basis for forming separate lexical units. This conclusion is bolstered by other findings from our laboratory: in one study, for example, we found greater repetition priming effects for same-script than for different-script pairs in Korean readers (Vaid and Park, 1988). Cross-language priming effects were also found to be larger for Hanzza than for Hangul target words. In another study (Vaid and Park, 1989) employing an incidental memory paradigm for randomly presented Hangul and Hanzza stimuli that were to be classified into each script, we found below chance recognition accuracy. That is, when the task does not require lexical access, memory for script is not preserved; interestingly, more commission errors were found for Hangul than for Hanzza stimuli, consistent with our other findings of greater memorability or distinctiveness of Hanzza words.

Thus, it would appear from Experiment 2 and related studies that separate lexical units are activated by different scripts of the same word. However, one may well ask why Hanzza is remembered better than Hangul in general. Script variation may be partially responsible for this different memorability. Hanzza is a logography in the sense that the written symbol and meaning of the word are directly mapped. Naming a word presented in Hanzza may automatically activate the semantic code of the word. Put another way, naming (phonologically recoding) a Hanzza word may be post-lexical in the sense that access to the semantic code is a prerequisite to accessing its phonological code. On the other hand, Hangul is an alphabetic syllabary. Access to a semantic code may not be necessary in naming the word when presented in Hangul. Moreover, the subject's task in Experiment 2 was naming. Therefore, it seems reasonable to assume that semantic level processing for the Hangul words was absent or less extensive than that for Hanzza words. These different levels of processing due to script variation may be responsible for the superior memorability of Hanzza words over Hangul words.

Yet another explanation mentioned earlier for Hanzza superiority was that more effort/time is spent for naming words in Hanzza than naming Hangul words. The results of Experiment 2 show that naming Hanzza words does in fact take longer than naming words in Hangul (a similar result was found in Vaid and Park, 1988). However, it is not necessary to assume that Hanzza memory superiority reflects the longer time spent in performing the task, as it is quite possible that naming Hanzza took more time just because Hanzza in general was less familiar than Hangul to the subjects.

SUMMARY AND CONCLUSION

Our first experiment explored incidental memory for the script of words that were visually presented in the study and test phase. The results from this experiment demonstrated an above chance level incidental memory for the script of Hanzza words, and a chance level recognition of the script of words written in Hangul. Moreover, memory for Hanzza script was significantly enhanced when the words had been visually encoded (i.e., copied) in the study phase, as compared to that when they had been named out loud. However, this effect of encoding condition was absent for words written in Hangul.

Our second experiment sought to replicate the results of the first, using new stimuli and subjects. The visual component of the task was minimized by asking subjects only to name the words out loud as quickly as they could, and by presenting the recognition list auditorily. Once again, memory for Hanzza was superior to that for Hangul. Unlike Experiment 1, though, memory for Hangul was above chance in Experiment 2. Moreover, Hangul words were named much faster than words in Hanzza.

Various interpretations of the observed superiority of recognition of Hanzza over Hangul were discussed. It is concluded that rather than reflecting an overall "visual complexity" difference or a visual distinctiveness effect, the results can best be viewed in terms of the structural properties of the two scripts. Specifically, the logographic nature of Hanzza may have facilitated a deeper, semantic encoding of words presented in Hanzza, whereas the phonetic character of the Hangul syllabary may have prompted a non-lexical processing of Hangul words, resulting in their poorer recognition. At any rate, this study provides converging evidence with the results of a previous study, employing Hindi-Urdu biscriptals (Vaid, 1985b), and argues in favor of a scriptal presence in the lexicon.

ACKNOWLEDGEMENTS

This research was supported by a Faculty Summer Research grant awarded to the second author at Texas A and M University. The first author may be contacted at Dept. of Psychology, Keimyung University, Daegu, Korea. Correspondence to J. Vaid may be sent to the Dept. of Psychology, Texas A and M University, College Station, TX 77843-4235. E-mail: jxv@psyc.tamu.edu.

APPENDIX A

Hangul	Hanzza	Hangul	Hanzza
문화	文化	물질	物質
기능	機能	독서	讀書
통계	統計	실습	實習
평등	平等	종류	種類
감각	感覺	발견	發見
부모	父母	이득	利得
시험	試驗	농촌	農村
분별	分別	생명	生命
양심	良心	상업	商業
사회	社會	윤리	倫理
안전	安全	내용	內容
동양	東洋	조건	條件
형식	形式	연구	研究
의미	意味	노력	努力
국민	國民	예술	藝術
교육	敎育	정치	政治
외교	外交	결과	結果
자연	自然	인권	人權
법원	法院	현재	現在
근본	根本	품목	品目
설명	說明	희망	希望
행복	幸福	투표	投標
성당	聖堂	운동	運動
지식	知識	개념	概念

REFERENCES

Baron, J. and Treiman, R.: 1980, 'Use of orthography in reading and learning to read', in J.K. Kavanagh and R.L. Venezky (eds.) *Orthography, Reading, and Dyslexia*, University Park Press, Baltimore, MD.

Besner, D. and Coltheart, M.: 1979, 'Ideographic and alphabetic processing in skilled reading of English', *Neuropsychologia* **17**: 467–472.

Brown, H., Sharma, N.K., and Kirsner, K.: 1984, 'The role of script and phonology in lexical representation', *Quarterly Journal of Experimental Psychology* **36A**: 491–505.

Ehri, L.: 1980, 'The role of orthographic images in learning printed word', in J.K. Kavanagh and R.L. Venezky (eds.) *Orthography, Reading, and Dyslexia*, University Park Press, Baltimore, MD.

Feldman, L.B. and Moskovljevic, J.: 1987, 'Repetition priming is not purely episodic in origin', *Journal of Experimental Psychology: Learning, Memory, and Cognition* **13**: 573–581.

Gonzales, E.G. and Kolers, P.A.: 1982, 'Mental manipulation of arithmetic symbols', *Journal of Experimental Psychology: Learning, Memory, and Cognition* **8**: 308–319.

Henderson, L.: 1984, 'Introduction', in L. Henderson (ed.) *Orthographies and Reading*, Lawrence Erlbaum Associates, Ltd., London.

Kirsner, K.: 1986, 'Lexical function: Is a bilingual account necessary?' in J. Vaid (ed.), *Language processing in Bilinguals: Psycholinguistic and neuropsychological perspectives*, Lawrence Erlbaum Associates, Hillsdale, NJ.

Koriat, A.: 1984, 'Reading without vowels: Lexical access in Hebrew', in H. Bowna and D.G. Bouwhuis (eds.), *Attention and Performance X*.

Park, S. and Arbuckle, T.: 1977, 'Ideograms versus alphabets: Effects of script on memory in "biscriptual" Korean subjects', *Journal of Experimental Psychology: Human Learning and Memory* **3**: 631–642.

Sasanuma, S.: 1974, 'Kanji versus Kana processing in Alexia with transient Agraphia: A case report', *Cortex* **10**: 89–97.

Sasanuma, S.: 1984, 'Can surface dyslexia occur in Japanese?' in L. Henderson (ed.) *Orthographies and Reading*, Lawrence Erlbaum Associates, Ltd., London.

Sasanuma, S. and Fujimura, O.: 1972, 'An analysis of writing errors in Japanese Aphasic patients: Kana vs. Kanji in visual recognition and writing', *Cortex* **8**: 265–282.

Scarborough, D.L., Cortese, C., and Scarborough, H.: 1977, 'Frequency and repetition effects in lexical memory', *Journal of Experimental Psychology: Human Perception and Performance* **3**: 1–17.

Taylor, I.: 1980, 'The Korean writing system: An alphabet? A syllabary? A logography?', in P. Kolers, M. Wrolstad, and H. Bouma (eds.) *Processing of Visible Language* (Vol. 2), Plenum, New York, pp. 67–82.

Tzeng, O.J.L. and Hung, D.L.: 1980, 'Reading in the non-alphabetic writing system: Some experimental evidence', in J.K. Kavanagh and R.L. Venezky (eds.) *Orthography, Reading, and Dyslexia*, university Park Press, Baltimore, MD.

Vaid, J.: 1985a, 'Numerical size comparisons in a phonologically transparent script', *Perception and Psychophysics* **37**(6): 592–595.

Vaid, J.: 1985b, *Memory for script in Hindi-Urdu biliterates*. Paper presented at annual meeting of the South Asian Languages Analysis Roundtable, University of Michigan Ann Arbor.

Vaid, J. and Frenck-Mestre, C.: 1991, 'Incidental memory for format of number presentation: Evidence from monolinguals and bilinguals', *Brain and Cognition* **17**: 272–284.

Vaid, J. and Frenck-Mestre, C.: 1994, *Incidental memory for input format of number words*, Poster presented at annual meeting of the Psychonomics Society, St. Louis.

Vaid, J. and Park, K.: 1988, *The role of script and phonology in lexical representation: Korean data*, Poster presented at annual meeting of the Psychonomics Society, Chicago.

Vaid, J. and Park, Yehsoon: 1989, 'Poor incidental memory for script on a script classification task, unpublished manuscript, Texas A and M University.

Yamadori, A.: 1975, 'Ideogram reading in alexia', *Brain* **98**: 231–238.

JOHN W. BERRY AND JO ANNE BENNETT

22. SYLLABIC LITERACY AND COGNITIVE PERFORMANCE AMONG THE CREE AND OJIBWE PEOPLE OF NORTHERN CANADA

INTRODUCTION

In this chapter we present an overview of our findings from a study of the syllabic literacy found among indigenous peoples in Northern Canada. The project has examined the historical and cultural dimensions of this form of literacy, its current distribution in four communities, and some perceptual and cognitive test performances that may be associated with it.

It seems likely that, seventy or eighty years ago, the Cree-speaking people of Northern Canada had one of the highest literacy rates in the world. They were able to read and write in their own language in a syllabic script which had been invented for them in the 1830s by a Methodist minister, James Evans, working in Norway House, Manitoba. (For a detailed account, see Murdoch, 1981: 20–33). After its initial dissemination, knowledge of the script spread rapidly, by a process of person to person instruction, so that by the 1850s Oblate missionaries on the James Bay Coast, a canoe journey of approximately 1500 miles, reported that all adults among the local Cree population were able to read and write "une espece de stenographie" (Laverloche, 1851; Garin, 1855).

Early accounts of the success of the script abound with descriptions of its rapid transmission and ease of acquisition (see for example, Murdock, 1985 and McLean, 1890). These accounts are more remarkable when one considers the total lack of "institutional" supports for literacy. There were no schools, no teachers in the common sense of the word, no paper, no pens or pencils. And there was very little available to *read* in the script. Hymnals and portions of the New Testament were among the earliest texts to be printed. Nevertheless, it appears that almost everyone over the age of forty or forty-five in the four communities we studied is literate in the syllabic script. Nearly all of these claim that it was their parents who taught them to read.

We have been investigating Cree syllabic literacy in four communities in Northern Ontario (see Figure 1): the Cree-speaking[1] communities of Attawapiskat and Fort Albany on the James Bay Coast, and the inland communities of Big Trout Lake and Kasabonika. People from the two latter communities generally refer to their language as "Oji-Cree". In the *Handbook of North American Indians* (see Helm, 1979) they are described, partly on a linguistic basis, as "Northern Ojibway" although this term has nothing like a consensus among researchers (see, for example, Rogers, 1983;

I. Taylor and D.R. Olson (eds.), Scripts and Literacy, 341–357.

Fig. 1. Map of Ontario showing locations of four Cree communities (with asterisk).

Honigmann, 1979; and Rogers and Taylor, 1979). When speaking English the "Northern Ojibway" further complicate matters by referring to themselves as "Cree", a practice which we will follow throughout the rest of this paper. There *are* differences between the Cree of the James Bay Coast and the inland "Northern Ojibway" of Northwestern Ontario. However, with respect to the distribution and knowledge of syllabic literacy, the two groups are very similar and will be considered together here.

ETHNOGRAPHIC BACKGROUND

The Cree were traditionally a nomadic people, relying mainly upon hunting and fishing for their subsistence. For several centuries they also formed the backbone of the Canadian fur industry. They followed annual cycles of movement (Rogers, 1962; Hallowell, 1949; Dunning, 1958; and Honigmann, 1956) which alternated between residence in relatively large groupings during the summer months and isolated dispersal in the bush during the remaining ten months of the year. Summer groupings were often located near a Hudson's Bay trading post. Often a church, too, was close by. Over time these summering places developed into small year-round communities. With the coming of treaties in 1929 many of these communities became the focus for the designation of "bands". Administrative offices, nursing stations, schools, airstrips, electrical power, etc. all followed in due course and most people now spend most if not all of the year living "on reserve".

Such communities, however, were not part of traditional native life. As little as forty years ago most people lived for the greater part of the year in the bush in small, isolated hunting groups which tended to centre on pared-down versions of the extended family: for example, parents plus a married child; or two married brothers with their wives and children. Within these hunting groups each nuclear family tended to have its own dwelling (Bishop, 1974; Dunning, 1959; Rogers, 1962; but see Honigmann, 1956). The relative scarcity of game, the low "carrying-capacity" of the boreal forest environment, required human populations to spread out thinly over the landscape (Rogers, 1969; Steegman, Hurlich, and Winterhalder, 1983). It was impossible for large groups to live together for any extended periods of time. Even the short collective groupings of summer were made possible only by the dependable presence of thriving fish populations in certain lakes and rivers.

Incursions of southern, Euro-Canadian culture into northern native communities have occurred at an ever-increasing rate. Generally speaking, the process has been slower in the inland communities of Big Trout Lake and Kasabonika than it has for the coastal communities of Fort Albany and Attawapiskat. But all four communities now have year-round live-in health professionals, daily scheduled air service, private telephones and electricity. Federally funded schools have been in place for between 25 and 35 years, depending upon the community. There were summertime mission schools available before that and in Fort Albany there has been a year-round mission school of sorts since the early years of this century.

Increasing contact with southern Canada and southern Canadian ways has been accompanied by an economic shift away from the traditional subsistence occupations of hunting, trapping and fishing and towards an increasing reliance upon wage labour and government funds of various sorts: job training, family allowance, unemployment insurance, etc. However, while far fewer people engage in trapping, hunting and fishing still remain popular. Wild fish and game form a significant proportion of the diet in many households and wild food is widely shared and valued.

THE SYLLABIC SCRIPT

In the Cree language the majority of syllables consist of a single consonant followed by a single vowel. Rev. Evans took advantage of this pattern when he devised the Cree syllabic script.

The Cree syllabarium (see Figure 2) consists of a small number of characters (usually between nine and twelve, depending upon the dialect). Each character is associated with a sound that can be thought of as a single consonant, for example "T", "B", or "M", etc. These consonants form the initial sound of the syllables. The vowel quality, which follows the consonant, is given by the orientation of the character. Each character is presented in one of four orientations roughly corresponding to our notions of north, east, south and west. Thus, reading across to the right from the English letter "T", on Figure 1, the characters read "te" (tay), "ti", "to", "ta".

In addition to the dozen main characters, the Cree syllabarium employs some additional signs: dots over the character to lengthen the vowel, a series of diacritical marks (some dialects use smaller versions of the main

	E	I	O	A	Finals	
	ᐁ	ᐃ	ᐅ	ᐊ		
T	ᑌ	ᑎ	ᑐ	ᑕ	ᐟ	ᑦ
K	ᑫ	ᑭ	ᑯ	ᑲ	ᐠ	ᒃ
N	ᓀ	ᓂ	ᓄ	ᓇ	ᐣ	ᓐ
M	ᒣ	ᒥ	ᒧ	ᒪ	ᒼ	ᒻ
Ch	ᒉ	ᒋ	ᒍ	ᒐ	ᐨ	ᒡ
S	ᓭ	ᓯ	ᓱ	ᓴ	ᐢ	ᔅ
Sh	ᔐ	ᔑ	ᔓ	ᔕ	ᐡ	ᔥ
P	ᐯ	ᐱ	ᐳ	ᐸ	ᑊ	ᑉ
Y	ᔦ	ᔨ	ᔪ	ᔭ		
L	ᓓ	ᓕ	ᓗ	ᓚ	ᐪ	ᓪ
R	ᕃ	ᕆ	ᕈ	ᕋ	ᕑ	ᕐ
W	·ᐁ	·ᐃ	·ᐅ	·ᐊ	•	•

Fig. 2. Cree Syllabarium.

characters) to denote the insertion of a final consonant at the end of the syllable – to change "ka" to "kak" for example.

The Cree used their script in much the same way we use our own Roman script. They sent letters, kept diaries, wrote notices, recorded family births and deaths. They did *not* use it to create for themselves a body of "literature". Nomads would have a limited use for such a creation and in any case there wasn't really time for forms and genres to establish themselves. However, there is now a substantial body of mainly religious and educational material available in the script (see Murdock, 1984).

Today much of the traditional work of the syllabic script has been replaced by modern telecommunications. Telephone is the most popular means of conveying messages within and beyond the community. Local radio stations also serve this function.

In the area of record-keeping the use of syllabic script is giving way to the use of English, particularly as younger, English speaking and writing, people replace their elders in various positions within the community. Knowledge of English and the Roman script is necessary for interaction with the various branches of provincial and federal governments dealing with the reserves.

Although older people continue to use the syllabic script, those under forty rely upon English. Public notices are more likely to be posted in English than in syllabics. Even those notices generated within the community are likely to be written out in English first and translated afterwards into Cree syllabics for the sake of older residents.

There has always been a strong association between the syllabic script and the Christian religion. Rev. James Evans was, after all, a missionary. It is not surprising that the first books printed in the syllabic script were hymnals, prayer books and portions of the Bible – as were the majority of books to date. The syllabic script continues strong in both the Church of England and the Roman Catholic church which were the first two Christian religions to proselytize among the Cree. Even today most church services are conducted in Cree with a sizeable array of liturgical books available in the syllabic script.

Recently, however, an increasing number of people have become involved with pentecostal and fundamentalist sects which often conduct at least part of their services in English and in any case place no reliance upon the syllabic script. Church of England and Roman Catholic clergy have begun to conduct some services in English to cater for the needs of the younger people, many of whom cannot read any of the syllabics material sprinkled around the pews.

Thus, with the religious use of syllabics as with record-keeping, there appears to be a generational split. Older people know and rely upon the syllabic script. Younger people are more at ease with English and Roman orthography.

THE COMMUNITY LITERACY SURVEY

In order to obtain a more formal understanding of syllabic literacy, and to cross-validate the material collected through ethnographic methods, a survey instrument was developed. It was administered (in Cree) as an interview by trained assistants who were members of the communities.

The sample was drawn from the Band Lists of the total population of each community. After eliminating those "Off Reserve" and those under 16 years of age, we selected every fourth person for the sample. A total of 480 names were obtained in this way and of these we interviewed 419 individuals. There is: a moderate level of formal schooling (8.3 years) and a low level of parental schooling (3 to 4 years); a high proportion of life spent in an Indian (rather than in a predominately European) community; few years spent working for wages (and low level of current "employment"), but also a low level of trapping and hunting ("this year").

With respect to Cree language, all respondents use Cree in the home and, on average, rate their Cree ability as 4.9 on a 5-point scale; syllabics knowledge and use is self-rated lower (3.4); most respondents' parents know syllabics, while only about half of their siblings know them; and syllabics were learned around the age of ten on average. With respect to English language, self-rated knowledge runs around 3.2 to 3.5 on the same 5-point scale (about the same level as self-rated knowledge and use of syllabics), and about two-thirds read English language newspapers and magazines.

As part of the survey, a brief reading test was administered in both Cree syllabics and English (two passages in each script/language). Accuracy was rated by the Cree interviewer on a 5-point scale, and speed on a 4-point scale. Since high intercorrelations (all above +0.9) were found among the four ratings of ability in each language (two ratings on two passages) a total score with a maximum of 18.0 was created for each individual.

For syllabics, the mean score was 11.0 (sd = 6.44) in the whole sample. Older respondents were more able than younger to read the passages ($F = 24.72$, $p < 0.001$) and females were more able than males ($F = 39.60$, $p < 0.001$). This pattern held true in each community. The correlation of syllabics ability, and schooling in the total sample was −0.47.

The lack of syllabics ability among younger people is almost certainly the result of the introduction of full-time western schooling in the four communities. Schools initially forbade not only the teaching of syllabics but the use of the Cree language within their walls. Thus, an entire generation was raised with minimal knowledge of the script their parents and grandparents had been using for generations. Some families continued to insist that their children learn the syllabic script at home but many took a more lenient course with the result that most people between the ages of sixteen and thirty-five performed poorly on the test of syllabic reading ability. The introduction of syllabics instruction programs in the schools in the early seventies does not appear to have reversed the trend towards declining syllabics ability among the young in any effective manner.

The difference in performance between males and females (with females doing better) is most dramatic among people in their thirties and it may be that more males than females of this age actually attended school, thereby decreasing their chances of learning syllabics. However the superior ability of females persists in a less dramatic form across all ages. Whether this is a product of differential access to western education or of some other factor we are not able to say.

For English, the mean score was 12.9 (sd = 5.9) in the whole sample (This should not be compared to the mean on the syllabics score, since Cree assistants may not have used the rating scales in the same way when rating reading performance in the two languages). Contrary to syllabics reading ability, younger respondents were more able than the older ($F = 37.23$, $p < 0.001$) and males were somewhat better than females ($F = 5.05$, $p < 0.05$). Age differences held in each of the four communities but males were better than females only in one community (BTL). The correlation between English ability and schooling in the total sample was +0.76.

English reading ability was the mirror image of syllabic reading ability, this time with age inversely related to ability. Young people did well while older people did poorly. The distribution of English reading ability was directly related to the history of western education in the four communities with more schooling leading to better performance on the English reading test. The most dramatic differences between the performance of young and old occurred in the inland communities of Big Trout Lake and Kasabonika. Differences were less pronounced on the coast where contact with southern Canada started earlier and educational opportunities, albeit of a limited kind, have been available for a longer time.

The mean age at which syllabics was learned was 10.3 (sd = 4.9). Overall, older people in the sample reported learning syllabics at a younger age ($F = 3.01$, $p < 0.001$), but analysis by community indicates that this is true only in ATT and FTA. There were no sex differences in the age at which syllabics were learned. It seems probable that here again we are dealing with the influence of western schooling, with schooling postponing the age at which syllabics were learned. It is precisely among those in their late twenties and early thirties (who would have been attending school at the time syllabics were 'outlawed') that we find the highest reported ages for starting to learn syllabics. For example, in both Big Trout Lake and Fort Albany the average age given by young men in their late twenties for starting to learn was twenty. In Kasabonika it was eighteen. It looks very much as though people of this age group put off learning syllabics, if they learned them at all, until they had finished with western schooling.

Those in the youngest age groups (16–20 and, to a lesser degree, 20–25) would all have received syllabic instruction at some point in their school careers and the average age they give for starting to learn syllabics is considerably lower than the age group immediately above them.

With respect to frequency of writing in syllabics (self-rated on a 5-point scale of 0 to 4), the mean was 1.05 (sd = 0.92), older people overall write more than younger people ($F = 11.28$, $p < 0.001$), and females overall write more than males ($F = 21.59$, $p < 0.001$). These age and sex differences exist in all four communities (except that there is no sex difference in FTA) and directly reflect the pattern of distribution of syllabics reading ability.

For syllabics reading (self-rated on a 7-point scale of 1–7), the overall mean was 2.37 (sd = 3.9). Older people overall read more ($F = 11.41$, $p < 0.001$) as do females ($F = 23.46$, $p < 0.001$). These age and sex differences exist in all four communities (again, except that the are no sex differences in FTA). Again these differences directly reflect the distribution pattern of syllabics reading ability.

People who had acquired at least a minimal proficiency with the syllabic script were asked whether they had learned syllabics at school or had been taught elsewhere by a priest, a minister, a relative, or some other person. Most people claimed to have learned from either a teacher or a close relative and the number of responses was almost evenly divided between these two (138 and 133 respectively). However the pattern of responses varied markedly with age, younger people usually claiming to have learned from a teacher and older people saying they were taught by a member of their family. In Fort Albany a sizeable proportion of older people broke the prevailing pattern by claiming to have learned syllabics from a teacher. This undoubtedly reflects the fact that the Oblate missionaries ran a school of sorts in Fort Albany from the early years of this century and that syllabics were taught in that school until 1965 at which time they were dropped only to be picked up again in 1975.

A small minority (seven percent of responses) said they had learned syllabics from a priest or minister. The remainder (also a small minority) claimed either to have taught themselves, to have learned from friends or elders, or said they just could not remember.

Syllabic literates were asked when they had last written something in the script. Following the general pattern of distribution of syllabic knowledge, older people were more likely than younger people to have used the script in the recent past. In fact 38% of the younger people (ages sixteen through twenty-five) said they had never written anything in the script. A slight tendency for the use of syllabics to drop off in extreme old age is probably related to declining visual and motor faculties.

Turning from script use to the use of the Cree language itself (with 7 possible targets, self-rated on a 7-point scale, yielding a maximum score of 49), overall mean was 29.84 (sd = 11.4). Older people used Cree more often ($F = 5.81$, $p < 0.001$) and there were no sex differences. Older people rely upon Cree almost exclusively. Many, in fact, can speak no other language. The lower scores of young people reflect an increasing use of English vis a vis people who are outsiders to the community: teachers, nursing staff, government officials, researchers, etc., all of whom may be presumed not to know or speak Cree. It is only with those under thirty or thirty-five that we see people admitting to using English with other native-speakers of Cree, for example classmates or visitors from a neighboring community. The nuclear family remains a stronghold of native language although here, too, English is becoming more common.

The drop-off in scores among the oldest respondents (fifty-six and over) reflects a tendency to avoid interaction with several categories of non-Cree speakers. Older people were quite explicit about this. They said they could not talk with outsiders. Neither side would understand what the other was trying to say. Others said they could do so only with the help of an interpreter.

COGNITIVE CONSEQUENCES OF SYLLABIC LITERACY

The cognitive consequences of literacy are widely presumed to be substantial, including increased abstraction in thought, greater logical precision, and higher general intelligence (see Olson, 1986 for a review). In turn, socioeconomic and cultural development are thought to be the eventual outcome of literacy (Goody and Watt, 1968). These presumed intellectual and social consequences, however, are largely undocumented (see Scribner and Cole, 1981, for a critical review).

A central theoretical and methodological problcm is that literacy and formal education (schooling) are usually confounded as individual experiences and as social institutions. To examine the consequences of literacy *per se*, one needs to find a population in which literacy has become widespread in the absence of schooling. Further, such an ideal population should provide four categories of individuals: those with and without schooling, crossed with those with and without literacy. However, the category "schooled, non-literate" is virtually impossible to find even though there are a few examples of the opposite category ("non schooled, but literate") available for study.

The one completed research project on this latter category (by Scribner and Cole, 1981, among the Vai people of Liberia) concluded that there is no evidence for general cognitive consequences of literacy in the absence of schooling, but there were some specific consequences directly related to the type of script used by the Vai.

As we have noted, across Northern Canada a broad range of Native Peoples became literate in a syllabic script that was introduced in the 1840s. This script was transmitted without benefit of formal schooling, so that by early in this century literacy rates in these areas were probably close to 100%, and certainly higher than among non-Native sectors of the Canadian population. Previous research on syllabic literacy has been sporadic, and psychological research has been absent. The present research (modelled on the study of Vai literacy by Scribner and Cole) has employed a two phase strategy in four Cree and Ojibwe communities. In the first phase, ethnographic methods (including a survey of 419 persons) established the distribution of knowledge of the script, how it was learned, the uses to which it is put, and the current value placed on the script. In the second phase, a sub-sample of 150 persons (selected for a literacy *vs* schooling contrast) were administered a battery of psychological tests; these include reading tests in Syllabic and Roman script (three passages in each), a Cree/Ojibwe Picture Vocabulary Test (Creebody, from Mawhinney, 1983), an English version of the same (Engbody), two spatial tasks (from PMA, one involving rotation, a basic process in the use of the script), and an extended version of Ravens Matrices (A, Ab, B, C, D, E).

RESULTS

Table 1 is the distribution of participants in the psychological testing sample (n = 148) arranged according to experience of schooling (< 4 years *vs* 5^{+} years) and performance on the initial syllabics reading test. There is clearly an imbalance in the intended design, with virtually no participants available in the no school/no syllabics cell. This had meant a shift away from a 2 × 2 design to a multivariate one.

TABLE 1
Psychological test sample categorized by schooling and syllabic reading
(Total n = 148)

	Schooling	
Syllabics reading	Yes (5 yrs +)	No (0–4 yrs)
Yes	47	52
No	47	2

A display of test means by the original 2 × 2 design is presented in Table 2. Because one cell is virtually empty, no statistical tests are attempted on these data and because syllabics reading was one of the category variables, no means are reported for the Syllabics Reading test.

Because of the impossibility of carrying out 2 × 2 analyses, we performed a series of multiple regression analyses to answer the question: what can be held to account for the distribution of test scores? In Table 3 are the simple correlations between predictor variables (age, sex, grade, and accul-

TABLE 2
Mean test performance by schooling and syllabic reading categories

Test	Syllabics reading	Schooling	
		Yes	No
Spatial	Yes	20.8	17.8
	No	20.0	–
Rotation	Yes	98.4	83.2
	No	95.4	–
Matrices	Yes	43.9	32.5
	No	43.4	–
Engbody	Yes	36.6	27.9
	No	36.1	–
Creebody	Yes	37.4	35.5
	No	36.8	–
English reading	Yes	25.9	11.4
	No	24.9	–

TABLE 3
Simple correlations among predictor variables and test scores

Test	Predictors				
	Age	Sex[1]	Grade	Accult	Syllabics
Spatial	–0.27	–0.22	+0.33	+0.28	–0.08
Rotation	–0.28	–0.22	+0.41	+0.35	–0.12
Matrices	–0.41	–0.05	+0.50	+0.49	–0.20
Engbody	0.57	–0.07	+0.64	+0.75	–0.31
Creebody	–0.16	–0.31	+0.35	+0.34	–0.11
English R	–0.62	+0.04	+0.79	+0.81	–0.39
Syllabics R	+0.52	+0.01	–0.43	–0.45	–

Note: [1] Male is coded 1; Female is coded 2;
[2] A correlation of 0.23 or higher is significant at the 0.05 level.

turation) and the test scores; and in Table 4 are the simple correlations among the predictor variables.

The multiple regression analyses themselves are in Table 5. All five predictor variables are listed for each test, even though they do not all contribute to the variance explained.

TABLE 4
Simple correlations among predictor variables

	Age	Sex[1]	Garde	Accult	Syllabics
Age	–				
Sex	–0.27	–			
Grade	–0.68	+0.01	–		
Acculturation	–0.75	+0.10	+0.79	–	
Syllabics	+0.52	+0.01	–0.43	–0.45	–

Note: [1] Male is coded 1; Female is coded 2

DISCUSSION

On the basis of the community survey results, it is fair to say that syllabic literacy is *not* a "restricted literacy" in the sense employed by Goody (1968). For a long time, for a wide variety of purposes, and among most of the population, syllabic script use has been clearly in evidence. We thus have a situation where a test of the literacy *vs* schooling issue is possible, since there can be no recourse to the "restricted" argument. While it is true that among younger people (who are learning syllabics in school), and among the "missing generation" (who did not acquire syllabics either traditionally or in school) there is less than full syllabic literacy, it is still possible to claim, at a population level, that syllabic literacy is widespread and widely used in these communities; it is part of the *bricolage* of these peoples (Berry and Irvine, 1986).

The distribution (Table 1) of participants by schooling and syllabic literacy, while imbalanced (and preventing the intended 2 × 2 analyses), is revealing: virtually no one is illiterate in these four communities. Approximately one third can read Cree syllabics, one third are schooled (and presumably able to read in English), and one third can read both. No direct comparisons are possible with recent national data for Canada as a whole (conducted by Southam News); however, it may be fair to say that Cree literacy levels match or surpass national norms.

When using tests developed in one culture in another, we need to check the internal consistency of the tests; the Cronbach Alpha coefficients are generally satisfactory (all between 0.71 and 0.99), indicating that the use of total scores is justified.

While no tests of distribution anomalies are presented, all psychological tests were not notably skewed; however, the two reading tests were bimodal in distribution, with large and roughly equal numbers in the highest and lowest score range and, as noted, there is a problem with Creebody. Thus the use of correlational statistics with these two reading tests need to be treated with caution (and perhaps interpreted more as a biserial cor-

TABLE 5
Multiple regression analyses of psychological tests

Test	Predictor	R	Rsq	Beta	Rsqch	F
Spatial	Grade	0.33	0.11	0.22	0.11	4.18
	Sex	0.40	0.16	−0.30	0.05	13.47
	Age	0.43	0.18	−0.29	0.03	6.04
	Syllabics	0.45	0.20	0.17	0.02	3.54
	Accult.	0.45	0.20	0.01	0.00	0.00
Rotation	Grade	0.41	0.17	0.29	0.17	5.50
	Sex	0.47	0.22	−0.28	0.05	12.37
	Age	0.48	0.23	−0.16	0.01	1.50
	Syllabics	0.49	0.24	0.13	0.01	2.06
	Accult.	0.49	0.24	0.09	0.00	0.43
Matrices	Grade	0.50	0.25	0.26	0.25	4.18
	Accult.	0.52	0.28	0.23	0.03	2.91
	Sex	0.53	0.28	−0.12	0.00	2.29
	Age	0.53	0.28	−0.14	0.00	1.33
	Syllabics	0.54	0.29	0.09	0.01	1.08
Engbody	Accult.	0.75	0.56	0.67	0.56	43.84
	Sex	0.77	0.59	−0.17	0.03	8.08
	Grade	0.77	0.59	0.08	0.00	0.83
	Syllabics	0.77	0.59	0.08	0.00	1.54
	Age	0.77	0.59	−0.09	0.00	0.97
Creebody	Grade	0.35	0.12	0.19	0.12	2.38
	Sex	0.47	0.22	−0.33	0.10	17.36
	Accult.	0.49	0.24	0.30	0.02	4.84
	Syllabics	0.50	0.25	0.08	0.01	0.90
	Age	0.50	0.25	0.06	0.00	0.22
English R	Accult.	0.81	0.65	0.50	0.65	36.26
	Grade	0.85	0.72	0.42	0.07	31.80
	Age	0.85	0.72	0.04	0.00	0.29
	Syllabics	0.85	0.72	0.00	0.00	0.00
	Sex	0.85	0.72	0.00	0.00	0.00
Syllabics R	Age	0.52	0.27	0.46	0.27	16.19
	Sex	0.54	0.30	0.15	0.03	3.81
	Accult.	0.55	0.30	−0.08	0.00	0.33
	Grade	0.55	0.30	−0.08	0.00	0.22

relation), while those with Creebody may not be sensible, given limited variance.

Inspection of the test score means by schooling and syllabic reading categories (Table 2) suggests that schooling, rather than syllabic literacy is the important predictor: the means on all tests for the two schooled samples (with and without syllabic reading ability) are virtually identical, while the means of the non-schooled/syllabic literate sample are numerically lower in all cases than their schooled counterparts. The relative importance of these factors will be assessed statistically later in the correlational and multiple regression analyses.

Test intercorrelations reveal a matrix of positive coefficients, almost all significant, but with Syllabics Reading being negatively correlated with all other tests. A factor analysis shows one factor (accounting for 49% of variance) with all tests loading positively except Syllabics Reading (–0.32). The effects of partialling age, grade and acculturation are not substantial, indicating a rather robust set of basic relationships among test scores.

Simple correlations between predictor variables and test scores (Table 3) suggest a powerful role for schooling and acculturation (positive and significant for all tests except Syllabics Reading, where they are significantly negative), a strong role for age (the reverse pattern to that found for schooling and acculturation), and limited roles for sex (with males tending to score higher than females on three of the tests, but significantly so on only one), and Syllabics Reading (where only two relationships are significant: negative with Engbody and English Reading).

The correlations among the four predictor variables (Table 4) indicate a strongly negative relationship between age and grade (–0.68) and acculturation (–0.75), while the latter two are strongly positively correlated (+0.79). Sex is unrelated to either grade or acculturation, but there is a sex imbalance by age.

Results of the regression analyses (Table 5) generally reveal the expected pattern. For the three non-language tests (Spatial, Rotation, Matrices), there is a common pattern: grade is the most important predictor of high performance, while age is a predictor of low performance; this pattern is strongest for Matrices, (especially Analytical), and less so for Spatial and Rotation. Sex is a predictor, but is not strongly related to test performance (corresponding to earlier findings with hunter-gatherers; see Berry, 1966).

For the four language tests, the same patterns obtains for Engbody and English Reading. However, a distinct pattern is present for the other two tests: Creebody displays an attenuated version of the pattern for the English tests, but there exists a different pattern for Syllabics Reading: age is a predictor of higher performance, while grade and acculturation are unrelated once age is taken into account. Once again sex is not a major predictor.

CONCLUSIONS

The central question addressed in the community survey part of this study is the distribution, knowledge and use of the Cree syllabic script. It is clear that script knowledge is widespread (if not universal), and that it is employed for a wide variety of purposes; it is highly valued by the Cree, and forms part of their identity (see also Darnell and Vanek, 1973). Thus its vitality seems to be assured. Given this result, questions about its future in a variety of domains (education, administration, communication) will need to be addressed, and answers need to be framed within this generally positive context. In our view, the syllabic script is likely to be part of the Northern scene for generations to come.

The central question addressed in the psychological testing portion of this study concerns the relative effects of schooling and syllabic literacy on cognitive test performance. From the regression analysis, it is clear that schooling has a major influence on Engbody and English Reading, with a lesser influence on Spatial, Rotation, Matrices and Creebody. In contrast, Syllabics Reading is unrelated to schooling, once age is taken into account. Thus, there is a clearly stronger relative degree of influence in favour of schooling, over syllabic literacy, in controlling test performance.

A second issue is whether the relatively high level of spatial (and related abilities) reported in the literature for hunter-gatherers in the Arctic (Berry, 1976; McShane and Berry, 1988) might be a consequence of the widespread syllabic literacy found in the population, rather than to ecocultural adaptation (as proposed by Berry, 1966; 1976). It is evident that the influence of syllabic literacy on the present set of psychological tests is minimal. Hence, earlier arguments about the role of ecological and cultural factors in the psychological development of Arctic hunter-gatherers appear to stand.

ACKNOWLEDGEMENTS

The research reported in this paper has been supported by the Social Sciences and Humanities Research Council of Canada, and by a Northern Science Training Grant from the Department of Indian and Northern Affairs, Government of Canada. A pilot study was initially supported by a grant from the Advisory Research Committee, Queen's University.

NOTES

[1] The term "Cree" in this paper is used in a generic sense, and covers Cree speakers proper, as well as Northern Ojibwe and Oji-Cree speakers.

[2] In some cases the same assistants were involved in several phases of the project; in other communities they were not. We worked with a total of thirteen assistants in the four communities but special mention should be given here to Evelyn Nanokeesic of Big Trout Lake and to Elizabeth Gull of Attawapiskat, who assisted with survey data collection and psychological testing as well as seeing to our physical well-being and providing invaluable community introductions. The psychological tests were administered by Karen Parsonson; she also assisted with filling in the gaps in the survey data, and carried out many of the computer analyses. Pat Brown scored and coded most of the data, and checked the files for accuracy. To all we extend out thanks.

REFERENCES

Berry, J.W.: 1966, 'Temne and Eskimo perceptual skills', *International Journal of Psychology* **1**: 207–229.

Berry, J.W.: 1976, *Human ecology and cognitive style: Comparative studies in cultural and psychological adaptation*, Sage/Halsted, New York.

Berry, J.W. and Irvine, S.H.: 1986, 'Bricolage: Savages do it daily', in R. Sternberg and R. Wagner (eds.) *Practical intelligence: Nature and origins of competence in the everyday world,*, Cambridge University Press, New York, pp. 271–306.

Bishop, Charles A.: 1974, *The Northern Ojibwa and the fur trade: An historical and ecological study*, Holt, Rinehart and Winston of Canada Ltd., Toronto.

Darnell, R. and Vanek, A.L.: 1973, 'The psychological reality of Cree syllabics', in R. Darnell (ed.) *Canadian languages in their social context*, University of Alberta Press, Edmonton, pp. 171–192.

Dunning, R.W.: 1959, *Social change among the Northern Ojibway*, University of Toronto Press, Toronto.

Garin, R.P.: 1855, 'Lettre du R.P. Garin, O.M.I., à un Père de la même Société', in *Propagation de la Foi, No. 11*, Mars, pp. 4–17.

Goody, J.C. (ed.): 1968, *Literacy in traditional societies*, Cambridge University Press, New York.

Goody, J. and Watt, I.: 1968, 'The consequences of literacy', in J. Goody (ed.) *Literacy in traditional societies*, Cambridge University Press, New York.

Hallowell, A.I.: 1949, 'The size of Algonkian hunting territories: A function of ecological adjustment', *American Anthropologist* **51**: 35–45.

Helm, June (ed.): 1979, *Handbook of North American Indians*, Smithsonian Institution, Washington.

Honigmann, John J.: 1956, 'The Attawapiskat Swampy Cree – An ethnographic reconstruction', *Anthropological papers of the University of Alaska* **5**(1): 23–82.

Honigmann, John J.: 1979, 'The Westmain Cree', in J. Helm (ed.) *Handbook of North American Indians Volume 6, Subarctic*, Smithsonian, Washington.

Laverloche, R.P.: 1851, 'Lettre du R.P. Laverloche a un Père de sa Congregation Moose Factory, 30 Aout, 1850', in *Propagation de la Foi*, No. 9, Mars, pp. 99–104.

Mawhinney, T.A.: 1983, 'A picture vocabulary test for the Eastern James Bay Cree', in S.H. Irvine and J.W. Berry (eds.) *Human assessment and cultural factors*, Plenum, New York.

McLean, J.: 1890, *James Evans-Inventor of the syllabic system of the Cree language*, William Briggs, Toronto.

McShane, D. and Berry, J.W.: 1988, 'Native North Americans: Indian and Inuit abilities', in S.H. Irvine and J.W. Berry (eds.) *Human abilities in cultural context*, Cambridge University Press, New York.

Murdoch, John: 1981, *Syllabics: A successful educational innovation*, Unpublished Master's thesis, University of Manitoba.

Murdoch, John: 1984, *A bibliography of Algonquian syllabic texts in Canadian repositories*, Gouvernement du Québec, Project ASTIC, Ministeres des Affaires culturelles, Direction regionale du nouveau Québec et service aux autochtones, Québec.

Murdoch, John: 1985, 'Syllabics history: The Spread of native literacy', *Education Manitoba* **13**(2): 9–11.

Olson, D.: 1986, 'The cognitive consequences of literacy', *Canadian Psychology* **27**: 109–121.

Raven, J.C.: 1963, *Raven's Progressive Matrices*, Lewis, London.

Rogers, E.S.: 1962, *The Round Lake Ojibwa*, The Royal Ontario Museum, Toronto.

Rogers, E.S.: 1969, 'Natural Environment – Social Organization – Witchcraft: Cree Versus Ojibwa – A Test Case', in D. Damas (ed.) *Contributions to anthropology: Ecological essays*, Bulletin #230, National Museum of Canada, pp. 24–39.

Rogers, E.S.: 1983, 'Cultural adaptations the Northern Ojibwa', in A.T. Steegman, Jr. (ed.) *Boreal forest adaptations: The Northern Algonkians*, Plenum Press, New York.

Rogers, E.S. and Taylor, G.: 1979, 'Northern Ojibwa', in J. Helm (ed.) *Handbook of North American Indians Volume 6, Subarctic*, Smithsonian, Washington.

Scribner, S. and Cole, M.: 1981, *The psychology of literacy*, Harvard University Press, Cambridge.

Steegman, A.T., Jr., Hurlich, Marshall G., and Winterhalder, Bruce: 1983, 'Challenges of the Boreal Forest', in A.T. Steegman, Jr. (ed.) *Boreal forest adaptations: The Northern Algonkians*, Plenum Press, New York.

Thurstone, L.L.: 1938, *Primary Mental Abilities*, University of Chicago Press, Chicago.

ROBERT J. SCHOLES

23. ORTHOGRAPHY, VISION, AND PHONEMIC AWARENESS

I. INTRODUCTION; SETTING THE CONTEXT

Our interest in orthography is, we like to think, in the Whorfian tradition of studies of the ways in which our conceptions and uses of language determine the cognitive and perceptual constructs by means of which we know the universe around us.

In this present work we will consider some research on literacy and phonemic awareness within this Whorfian context. Specifically we ask if there is any evidence that variance in the orthographic representation of words plays a role in phonemic awareness and if internal visual representation of speech is necessary for phonemic analysis. We will, in addition, have some things to say about the influence of orthography on linguistic science and language description.

These questions are here considered in the context of a tripartite typology of orthographies, such as is widely used (e.g., Coltheart, 1984) and was suggested in the call for papers for this conference, namely: alphabetic, syllabic, and logographic. Our criticisms of this typology will be addressed in Section IV of this paper, but for the purpose of the exposition in the following two sections, we will use it in the usual sense.

In the next two sections we present the results of some experimentation relating to orthography and phonemic awareness. In the first of these (Section II), we show that phonemic awareness is directly linked to spelling in literate users of English. In the second (Section III), phonemic awareness is investigated as a function of whether lexical items are orthographically represented alphabetically, syllabically, or logographically and, concurrently, if phonemic awareness is related by the ability to internally visualize speech.

II. THE ORTHOGRAPHIC BASIS OF PHONEMIC AWARENESS IN LITERATE ADULTS

A. *Phoneme Deletion and visualized Spellings*

The extent to which the speech perception of literate adults is based on spelling was here investigated in two studies: a phoneme deletion task and a phrase matching task.

In a phoneme deletion task (Bruce, 1964), subjects are asked to mentally delete a speech sound from a word and report the result. In the experi-

I. Taylor and D.R. Olson (eds.), Scripts and Literacy, 359–373.

ment reported here the stimuli were presented orally and the subjects wrote down their responses. For the purposes of this present discussion, we will report the responses of a group of 90 university undergraduates.

The stimuli were of three types. In one type, the sound to be deleted corresponds to a single letter in the spelling of the word. There were three stimuli of this type: 'raft' take away [f] (= 'rat'), 'quick' take away [w] (= 'kick'), and 'quite' take away [k] (= 'white'). In the second type, the sound to be deleted is not uniquely represented by a letter in the spelling of the word. There were two stimuli of this type: 'mixed' take away [k] (= mist, missed) and 'taxed' take away [s] (= tact, tacked). In the third type two different responses could be given depending on whether the subject dealt with an (internalized) phonetic representation or an (internalized) visual representation. They were: 'thought' take away [t] and 'liked' take away [k]. In the case of 'thought', if the subject is performing the deletion task on the basis of sound, then the response should be 'thaw'; if, however, the subject is working with a visual mental representation, then the response should be 'though'. In the case of 'liked', phonic processing yields 'light' while orthographic processing yields 'lied'.

Subjects were given ten seconds to respond to each stimulus and failure to respond in that time was, along with inappropriate responses, treated as incorrect.

For the three stimuli of the type where the sound to be deleted corresponds to a letter in the spelling, the 90 university students gave the correct response in 77% of the trials. For the two stimuli where the sound to be deleted is not directly represented in the spelling, correct responses fell to just 35%. In the two cases where phonic and visual processing yield different answers, the phonically based answer was given in 46% of the trials and the visually based answer was given in 37% of the trials.

These results seem clear enough. Literate speakers of English are able to do phoneme deletion quite easily when the sound to be deleted is represented by a letter in the spelling of the word, but find the task difficult when the sound to be deleted is not orthographically opaque. Further, there is evidence from the 'thought' and 'liked' cases that an internalized visual representation is employed in phoneme deletion equally as much as an internal auditory representation (a fact verified by subjects' informal reports that they "look at the word and take out the letter").

B. *Orthography and Allophones*

A second experiment investigated a different aspect of the way in which knowledge of English orthography affects auditory comprehension. In this case, we were interested in the perception of post-[s] voiceless stops and how this perception may be influenced by knowledge of writing. It is generally held that post-[s] stops are allophones of the voiceless stops even though they sound like voiced stops. Thus, for example, the stop consonant in 'spin' is treated as a variant of the phoneme /p/ (often said to be "unaspirated") rather than the phoneme /b/, to which it is much closer auditorialy. As this identification has long been a matter of some curiosity to us, we wondered if the phonemicization might possibly have something to do with spelling (i.e., that 'spin', 'strip', and 'screw' are the spellings, rather than 'sbin', 'sdrip', and 'sgrew').

To investigate this curiosity, nine different phrases were recorded once and this recording was then dubbed, cut and spliced so as to construct a set of 15 pairs of phrases. The phrases were:

the cat's pit	the cats bit	the cat spit
the cat's trip	the cats drip	the cat strip
the cat's core	the cat's gore	the cat score

In six of the 15 pairings, the phrases were identical. In the other nine pairings, the phrases were paired as follows: in three cases word initial voiceless stop was paired with word initial voiced stop (i.e., 'pit' with 'bit', 'trip' with 'drip', and 'core' with 'gore'); in three cases word initial voiceless stop was paired with post-[s] stop (i.e., '-s pit' with 'spit', '-s trip' with 'strip', and '-s core' with 'score') and in three cases word initial voiced stop was paired with post-[s] stop (i.e., '-s bit' with 'spit'. '-s drip' with 'strip' and '-s gore' with 'score').

The 15 pairs were presented twice to a single group of 17 university students (none of whom were subjects in the phoneme deletion experiment). In the first run the subjects were told that they would hear pairs of phrases and that they should judge each pair as the same or different and to respond S (same) or D (different) to each pair.

In this run the six pairs that were the same were judged to be the same in 100 out of the 102 trials. For the pairings of different stimuli, initial voiceless and initial voiced stop pairs were judged to be the same in 10 of 51 trials, initial voiceless stops were judged to be the same as post-[s] stops in 14 of 51 trials, and initial voiced stops were heard as the same as post-[s] stop in 16 of the 51 trials.

For the second run, the phrases used were written on a blackboard, the subjects were given a few minutes to read over the phrases, and the exact same tape was replayed with the same instructions.

For this run, same pairs were judged to be the same in 90 of the 102 trials, initial voiced and initial voiceless pairings were heard as the same in just one of the 52 trials, initial voiceless and post-[s] stops were heard as the same in 5 of the 52 trials, and initial voiced and post-[s] stops were not once heard as the same.

The first thing that can be seen in these results is that the pairs of phrases (of which 6 of 15, or 40%, were actually the same) were judged to be the same more often in the first run (55%) than in the second (38%).

That is, when the listeners didn't know how the phrases are written, they judged them to be the same in the majority of cases: when they did know the orthography they judged phrases written differently to sound different more often and more accurately. Of especial interest is the extent to which post-[s] stops are identified with word initial voiceless and voiced stops. In the first run, without knowing the orthography of the phrases, the subjects identified phrases with word initial voiced stops and phrases with post-[s] stops as sounding the same in 16 of the 51 trials (over 31%, and more often than they made the same identification of initial voiced and voiceless stops or post-[s] stops with word initial voiceless stops). Once they knew the orthography, however, this identification was not made once in the 51 chances. These results would suggest that auditory phonemic discrimination is highly influenced by knowledge of orthography.

The situation in phonemics with respect to Post-[s] stops has always been somewhat puzzling. The general view taught to students of phonetics and linguistics is well represented in Smalley (1961). Smalley posits three types of voiceless stops in (American) English: voiced, voiceless aspirated, and voiceless unaspirated. Noting that the stops after [s] do in fact sound like the voiced stops (a fact easily verified with a reel-to-reel tape recorder and a tape-splicing kit – record the words 'spill', 'still', and 'skill', excise the [s], and ask people what words they hear; they will generally respond 'bill', 'dill', and 'gill', respectively), he nonetheless follows the standard practice of saying that the stops after [s] are allophones (nondistinctive variants) of the voiceless stops. This leads him to the quite bizarre claim that ". . . the distinction between aspirated and unaspirated is not phonemic. That is why as speakers of English we do not need to be conscious of the /p/ in *spill* being different from the /p/ in *pill*" (1961: 108). But of course, as the results of our little experiment show, we are conscious of the difference – so conscious, in fact, that we hear it as [b].

If, as Smalley (and other phonemicists) claim for post-[s] stops and word initial voiceless stops, a distinction is not phonemic (i.e., is allophonic), then the two variants separated by this distinction should be heard as the same. The perceptual identity of allophones is documented in a wealth of excellent research on the general topic of perceptual phonemicization of phonetic continual reviewed in, for example, Fry (1964) (for consonants) and Scholes (1967) (for vowels). Why, then, should a phonetic feature of no use anywhere else in the phonology of English be invoked in order to preserve the identity of post-[s] stops with /p/, /t/, and /k/? The answer is, we think, clear (if somewhat destructive of 20th Century linguistic science): because that's the way they are spelled!

Just to drive the point home, we would ask the reader to consider which of the following two descriptive statements best fits the data (we realize that neither is exact):

1) After word initial 's' the letters 'p', 't', and 'k' are pronounced [b], [d], and [g], respectively.

2) After word initial 's' the phonemes /p/, /t/, and /k/ are pronounced [b], [d], and [g], respectively.

The evidence in favor of the first statement is not only behavioral. Fred Householder (Householder, 1971) has presented demonstrations of the superiority of written form over spoken form in simplicity and efficiency of description in constructing the generative rules of English grammar.

The results of both the phoneme deletion work and the phrase matching experiment do not, by any means, indicate that phonemic awareness and alphabeticity is an all-or-none linkage. What they do fit very nicely, indeed, is the original concept of *litera* which David Abercrombie (1949) reminds us is "... a thing with three attributes, *nomen, figura*, and *potestas. Figura* was the letter as written, *potestas* as pronounced, and by its *nomen* it could be identified for discussion or teaching." Such a trinity appears to be exactly the sort of conception needed to account for the phonemic awareness of the literate speaker as well as the phonemic ignorance of the illiterate speaker; i.e., that for literates (and phoneticians) phonemic manipulation of speech is based on the *potestas* of the *litera* – an aspect, being one of an inseparable three, which cannot be divorced from the *figura*, and, for non-readers, lacking the knowledge of the *nomen* and *figura* of *litera* there can be no knowledge of *potestas*.

What's more, the idea provides an explanation for an otherwise incomprehensible set of facts. The facts are: 1) in the phonic method of reading instruction, the child is presumed to be learning the graphic shapes that correspond to the speech sounds she already knows, 2) the pre-reading child has no phonemic awareness, 3) the phonic method works – children exposed to it do learn to read. This dilemma is now cleared up by the more accurate statement of what is being taught and learned in the phonic method; namely, *literae*.

III. ORTHOGRAPHY AND PHONEMIC AWARENESS IN BRAILLE READERS

A. *The Questions*

There is a methodological problem inherent the quest for relationships between orthographic types and other aspects of language and cognition; namely, the fact that in most cases both the language and the orthography vary. That is, to determine how script type affects the reader's linguistic awareness, we would need to find a single language which some of its speakers write alphabetically, some write with a syllabic script, and some write in a logographic way, or a case in which a single group of users sometimes use alphabetic, sometimes syllabic, and sometimes logographic scripts. The second case exists for a group of native speakers of English who employ a Level II Braille. The existence of this group makes it possible to ask if the ways in which lexical material is represented affects the reader's awareness of the oral components of this material.

In addition, the existence of congenitally blind readers makes it possible to investigate the claim – based on phone manipulation performance by alphabetically literate seeing subjects – that phone manipulation is done largely on the basis of an internally visualized representation of the heard material.

Additional exposition of our research with blind braille readers is given elsewhere (Scholes and Willis, 1989). Here, we review those results most directly relevant to the focus of this conference; specifically, the affect of orthography on phonemic awareness.

The ability to deal with an utterance as a concatenation of phonic segments is here tested by means of a phoneme deletion task. While sighted readers of alphabetic orthographies are able to do phoneme deletion well and as early as 3rd grade, neither pre-reading children nor adult illiterate speakers of English can do it (Scholes and Willis, 1987b; 1988). There is, moreover, a suggestion that the ability to perform this task is a function of the alphabeticity of the orthography employed by the language user in that Read et al. (1987) found the skill to be absent in young Chinese readers. Finding that literate native speakers of English had great difficulty with the phoneme deletion task when the sound to be deleted was not directly represented in the word's spelling (Section II), we have hypothesized (1988) that such tasks are at least facilitated by, if not dependent on, an internal representation of the alphabetically written form of the word.

B. *Braille and its Readers*

Braille orthography is based on a matrix of six raised dots (called a *cell*) arranged and numbered as shown below.

1 o o 4
2 o o 5
3 o o 6

With this matrix it is possible to construct 63 unique single-cell configurations, of which, for English, 26 are used for letters of the alphabet. With the use of dot #6 as a capital letter sign, only 27 cells are needed for English letters (as opposed to the 52 different graphs used in standard printed orthography).

There are three different levels or grades of braille writing. Grade I is a one-to-one transliteration of standard spelling. Since this form was found to be slow and laborious for blind readers, Grade II was developed (Ashcroft and Henderson, 1963). In Grade II braille. A complex system of 189 whole-word and part-word signs are employed. Some of these signs are syllabic representations of words, as, for example, in bl = blind, grt = great, and brl = braille; others are logographic, as in b = but, y = you, and p = people. Whole and part word signs can be used inside words if the normal pronunciation of the sign is maintained in that word. So, for example, the whole word sign for 'and' can be used in 'bystander' but the whole word sign for 'name' cannot be used in 'ornament'.

Grade III braille is a shorthand system not relevant to the present discussion.

For most uses and in most reading programs for the blind, only Grade II is used. Children in residential schools, including the one in this present research, begin reading instruction with Grade II. Consequently, there is no stage during which children learn to read a completely alphabetic orthography.

Grade II braille writing of English (known as English braille, American Edition, 1959; revised 1962), referred to hereafter as EB, maintains the normal conventions of left-to-right horizontal writing, word boundaries, and punctuation.

While showing some delay and deviance in the earliest stages, the acquisition of language and literacy in blind children appears to be quite parallel to that of sighted readers (Landau and Gleitman, 1985; Lowenfeld, Abel, and Hatlen, 1968; Tomkins and McGee, 1986). At later stages, blind children ". . . may even surpass their sighted peers in the complexity and variety of language" (Rogow, 1986: 298).

C. *The Research*

The subjects of the present report were 15 congenitally blind students of the Florida School for the Deaf and Blind in St. Augustine, Florida. This group ranged in age from 14 to 18 and in grade in school from 7th to 11th. Nine of the 15 were white, six were black; seven were male and eight female. By standard assessment instruments (adapted for the blind) their average reading comprehension grade level was 8.4, their spelling 8.3, and their vocabulary 9.2. They were then, a pretty typical group of teenagers save for the fact that they could not see and they read English with their fingers.

Three sets of three words each were used in the phoneme deletion task. The words in the first set, 'raft', 'grow', and 'spin' are represented alphabetically in EB (that is, with separate cells for each of the four letters of the standard spelling), the words in the second set are represented syllabically – 'great' written 'grt', 'braille' written 'brl', and 'quick' written as 'qk', and the words in the third set are represented logographically – 'still' represented by a special symbol for the digraph 'st', 'quite' written with just the 'q' cell, and 'many' written as 'lm'. The EB representation of each

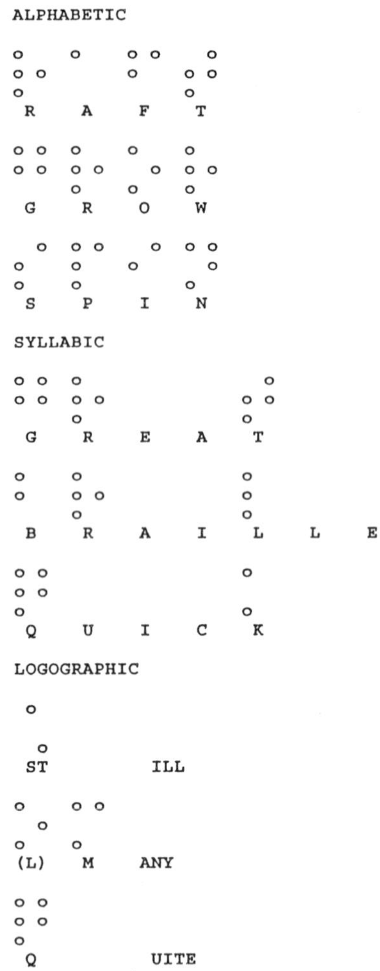

Fig. 1. Phoneme deletion stimuli for EB readers.

word is shown in Figure 1. The phoneme deletions to be performed were: 'raft' minus [f] (= 'rat'), 'grow' minus [f] (= 'go'), 'spin' minus [p] (= 'sin'), 'great' minus [r] (= 'gate'), 'braille' minus [b] (= 'rail'), 'quick' minus [w] (= 'kick'), 'still' minus [t] (= 'sill'), 'many' minus [m] (= 'any'), and 'quite' minus [k] (= 'white'). The actual question was of the form, "What word do you get if you take the sound [x] away from the word 'y'?" In some cases the question was repeated, but never more than once.

For the 45 trials involving alphabetic stimuli, the subjects responded correctly 34 times; for the syllabic stimuli, there were 37 correct responses; and for the logographic stimuli, 36 correct responses. There were, then, no obvious differences in phoneme deletion performance as a function of the orthographic type of the stimulus words. Three of these same stimuli ('raft', 'quick', and 'quite') occurred in the test of sighted, literate university undergraduates reported above and for these stimuli, the EB readers performed as well as the sighted group.

We are led to conclude that neither the ability to internally visualize an alphabetic spelling nor the type of script are crucial to performance on phoneme deletion tasks.

There are, however, two problems with interpreting these data. First, with respect to the orthographic variable, these students are quite familiar with typewriter and computer keyboards – a skill which could well provide a way of internally representing words alphabetically (through tactual memory for key positions, for example), even when the words are not so represented in EB. Secondly, on the question of internal visualization, the students' personal reports, as well as certain research results (Easton and Bentzen, 1987) indicate that the blind retain an ability to internally visualize.

In view of these caveats, about the best that can be said of our research is that phonemic awareness in blind braille readers shows no evidence of an orthographic variable nor any deficit that can be assigned to the visual impairment.

IV. ORTHOGRAPHY AND GRAMMAR

The search for relationships between the ways in which languages are written and such important concerns as the acquisition of reading skills, the awareness of the constituents of oral language, and the development of cognition in general is hampered by a number of obstacles. Not the least of these is that the linguistic science to which we look for accurate descriptions of language knowledge and use has grossly misguided us – linguistics has presented a picture of language acquisition and use that has largely denied any role played by reading and literacy. We now know that much of the dramatic development in linguistic competence and performance by children previously described simply as "language acquisition after the age of five" (Palermo and Molfese, 1972) does not take place in persons who do not learn to read (Scholes and Willis, 1987a, 1987b). Recent work on phonemic awareness in literate and illiterate native speakers of languages dramatically vindicates the insight of Fred W. Householder, who suggested that in describing phonological competence the linguist should "... require for languages like English the orthographic form, and ... make use of economical rules to derive most of the phonological features from that form" (Householder, 1966: 487).

In addition to its teaching that language acquisition and competence are independent of the literacy of the native speaker, linguistics has also tended to ignore the probability that the description of the structure of any language is a function, at least in part, of the grammar of the linguist's native language, including the constructs gained through use of its orthography. Although the works of Benjamin Lee Whorf are widely read and even sometimes admired, few linguists seem to have grasped the fact he so eloquently demonstrated (e.g., Whorf, 1940) that descriptions of other languages are very likely to show elements and processes our native languages constrain us to expect to find. It is certainly the case that the mainstream of linguistic teaching in this country (e.g., Fromkin and Rodman, 1988) more often reflects the literacy of the linguist than the language of the speaker. One would do well to take seriously the suggestion of Ranko Bugarski:

> It seems plausible that insights of relevance to grammatical description and theory alike may be derived from a systematic study of the nature and scope of the units themselves, not necessarily as identified by the investigating linguist but as recognized by speakers of different languages using different writing systems (Bugarski, 1970: 458).

With the teachings of Whorf and Householder and Bugarski affixed to our field methods manuals, we should significantly improve our chances of finding intellectual satisfaction and perhaps even practical significance in our search for the answer to what, we think, is the question many of us really want to ask: namely, in what ways does our literacy (presence or absence, degree, and orthography) influence how we conceptualize the world around us – including the languages we speak?

Even with a more informed understanding of the impact of literacy on oral language, however, we would still need an heuristically valid typology of writing systems. The questions dealt with here were addressed in the context of a widely used (e.g., Coltheart, 1984) tripartite typology of orthographies suggested in the call for papers for this conference: namely, alphabetic, syllabic, and logographic. Using this classification would seem to pretty well insure that answers of interest would not be forthcoming; the taxonomy simply doesn't allow for clear identifications and comparisons. The concept of a logographic orthography, if the meanings of logos and graph are to be understood as comprising the compound, suggests that a system of writing that utilizes visual symbols representing ideas ('ideas' being a better English rendering of logos than, say, 'word' – cf. the first sentence of Genesis) would then be logographic. Having defined it in this way, it is still not at all clear what orthographies would be classified as logographic and which ones not. The spacing and punctuation conventions of English would, we think, make its orthography logographic in that units of thought correspond to visually defined (by spacing, capitalization, and other punctuation) units of writing. The term, then, does not appear to provide a clear and motivated means of distinguishing, say, English script from that of Hebrew or Chinese which also isolate lexical and semantic gestalts.

"Syllabic" is even worse. The syllable, as Bugarski pointed out (Bugarski,

1970) is not definable orthographically. It is a unit of speech (loosely, acoustic energy bounded by minima of amplitude) and has no relation of any kind to the orthographic representation of language. English words such as 'bored' and 'board', 'waded' and 'waved', 'tacked' and 'tact' adequately demonstrate that spelling and syllabic structure are quite unrelated.

When is an orthography alphabetic? The general understanding of the term (and the one clearly intended for this conference) is that of an orthography in which there is a one-to-one (or nearly so) correspondence between units of writing and speech sounds. Here, again, the concept does not allow us to say anything very informative about the relationship between writing and speech simply by knowing that the writing system is derived from and based on the orthography created around 740 BCE in Greece. Written English is alphabetic; yet the information conveyed by the orthography is far more indicative of morphological identity than of spoken form. Consider, for example, the graphic to phonic relationship of "Did you eat yet?" pronounced "Jeetjet?", or our ability to identify the titles of children's stories (by reading them aloud) when they are written as, say, *Ladder Rat Rotten Hut* and *The Thrill It Up Eggs*, or the morphological identity (but phonological differences) of such pairs as 'night' and 'nocturnal', 'fight' and 'faction', etc.

What one knows, then, on being informed that English orthography is alphabetic is largely limited to historical derivation (that it is based on the Greek model), and not a great deal about the extent to which it represents speech.

It seems, then, that starting a search for orthographic affects on various aspects of language acquisition and use with a classification of orthographies as alphabetic, syllabic, or logographic is not likely to lead to interesting conclusions. Less in the belief that we can solve the problem than in the desire for discussion, we offer one of our own. The first and probably most relevant distinction to be made of orthographies is into those which are linguistic and those which are not. By a non-linguistic orthography we mean a communicative graphic system that bears no relation to the language spoken by its users. The two obvious examples are pictography and symbolic logic, examples that suggest that this category might be subdivided into representational and non-representational types. A pictograph denoting a dog, for example, is quite independent of how 'dog' is expressed in the language. Further, such a picture might show considerable detail even though the individual elements (hairs, facial features, etc.) may well have no lexical representation in the language of the artist. As for symbolic logic (or related subjects such as foundations of mathematics) readers are generally warned not to confuse the written propositions with the (imprecise and vague) natural language by which they may be read aloud.

Any writing system that is linguistic is necessarily morphemic since the defining property of language – i.e., the relations between form and meaning or function – is manifested in the morphemes of the language. A logical next step is, then, to look at how morphemes are represented in the writing system. Here, two dimensions would seem to be needed: one dealing with the visual representations of the morphemes; and the other dealing with the pronouncability of these representations. Borrowing the terminology from Sapir (1921) we propose three types of morpheme representation: *Isolating*, in which each morpheme is represented as a spatial entity (the only example of such a system we are aware of is Signed Exact English); *Agglutinative*, where morphemes are concatenated in lexical gestalts (words, generally, although word and agglutinative here become tautological) although they remain graphically identifiable by virtue, usually, of fixed shapes and positions (for which examples are numerous); and *Synthetic*, where individual morphemes are not graphically identifiable.

On the second dimension, orthographies need (as demonstrated by the research above) to be distinguished in terms of phonological opacity. There are cases such as Italian where words cannot (we're told) be misspelled nor misread aloud. Such an orthography is *phonetic* in that for any written symbol there is one and only one speech sound and for any speech sound there is one and only one letter (or combination of letters). An orthography that is *phonemic* but not phonetic is widely represented in western languages, as when Russian final stops are written (with the Cyrillic graphs for) b, d, and g while pronounced as [p], [t], and [k], respectively (the phonemic voicing of the stops shows up when there is a following suffix; cf. [sat] 'garden' but [fsadu] 'in the garden'). Similarly, final stops are written in English even though the distinction between pairs such as 'bad' and 'bat' is phonetically conveyed by vowel length (the final stops are not generally articulated in American dialects, but we know they are phonemically "there" because they appear in 'badly' and 'batter').

A third possibility is that the orthography is totally independent of the spoken form of the language even though it is clearly linguistic (morphemic). American Sign Language (AMSLAN) and other sign languages employed by the deaf would appear to be of this type.

Finally, we close with an observation that may be regarded as discouraging by some, but which we feel is entirely consistent with the evidence and argument presented during the course of this conference. This observation is that there is no reason to suppose that the overt visual properties of an orthography have any impact on the linguistic processing of that orthography. In fact, available evidence strongly suggests that any given body of sense data can be processed in a number of ways and it is more that the psychological properties of the processing system will determine the perceived physical properties of the sense data (as in the phrase discrimination experiment presented above) than that the physical properties of the sense data will determine the psychological properties of perception. In studies of cerebral asymmetry, for example, a common aspect of the findings is that a given signal is processed differently by the dominant left hemisphere of the brain than by the right. A right ear superiority may be seen when speech is to be judged for phonemic properties, but not when it is to be judged on acoustic dimensions such as amplitude and duration. A right visual half field superiority may be observed when dioptically presented words are to be processed in terms of their linguistic function but not when the judgment is made on non-linguistic properties such as length or letter height. And, of course, whole sentences are dealt with differently by the isolated right hemisphere than by the isolated left hemisphere. (See Krashen, 1976, for a readable review of laterality studies.) Similarly, visual shapes such as drawings of liquid-filled beakers can be processed in different ways (the famous conservation of quantity task). If the taller of the two beakers is judged to hold the greater amount of liquid, the subject is said to be employing concrete operational cognition; if the volume is judged on the basis of more abstract properties of the beakers (cubic capacity of the beakers and height of the liquid) then the subject is said to be employing formal cognitive processing; but it is not the visual representations that change or, therefore, determine the cognitive analysis that is applied to them. The same principle holds for language representation and language processing. Spoken or written sentences of English can be processed in at least two qualitatively distinct ways – ways we call *extensional* and *intensional* (Scholes, 1988; Scholes and Willis, 1988; 1991). In extensional processing only the order and adjacency of extra-linguistic referents of morphemes are utilized in comprehension; whereas in intensional processing the linguistic functions of morphemes are employed in syntactic analysis. In some cases of extensional processing, intensional morphemes are simply ignored, as in the case of 1) and 2) below where many users of English (particularly, non-readers) will parse both sentences to mean that the girls are the ones who play.

1) The boys watching the girls played ball.
2) The boys watched the girls play ball.

In other cases, a single overt shape is processed intensionally by some language users and extensionally by others, as in 3) where 'by' may be read (or heard) as 'near' or 'beside' (extensional) or as 'subject marker in the passive construction' (intensional). (See Willis, 1988, for an extensive treatment of this phenomenon.)

3) John was discovered by the White House.

We know, then, of no reason to suppose that the overt physical properties of some body of sense data (e.g., orthography) constrains or even strongly influences the cognitive processing that may be applied to that data.

ACKNOWLEDGMENT

I would like to acknowledge the contribution made to this research and to earlier versions of this document by Brenda J. Willis of Central Florida Community College.

REFERENCES

Abercrombie, D.: 1949, 'What is a "letter?"', *Lingua* **II**(1): 54–64.

Ashcroft, S.C. and Henderson, F.: 1963, *Programmed instruction in Braille*, Stanwix House, Pittsburgh.

Bruce, D.J.: 1964, 'The analysis of word sounds by young children', *British Journal of Educational Psychology* **34**: 158–159.

Bugarski, R.: 1970, 'Writing systems and phonological insights', papers from the Sixth Regional Meeting of the Chicago Linguistic Society, Chicago Linguistic society, Chicago.

Coltheart, M.: 1984, 'Writing systems and reading disorders', in L. Henderson (ed.) *Orthographies and reading: Perspectives from cognitive psychology, neuropsychology, and linguistics*, Lawrence Erlbaum Associates, Hillsdale, NJ.

Easton, R.D. and Bentzen, B.L.: 1987, 'Memory for verbally presented routes: A comparison of strategies used by blind and sighted children', *Journal of Visual Impairment and Blindness* **81**(3): 100–105.

Fromkin, V.A. and Rodman, R.: 1988, *An introduction to language* (Fourth Edition), Holt, Reinhart and Winston, New York.

Fry, D.B.: 1964, 'Experimental evidence for the phoneme', in D. Abercrombie, D.B. Fry, P.A.D. MacCarthy, N.C. Scott, and J.L.M. Trim (eds.) *In honor of Daniel Jones*, Longmans, London.

Householder, F.W., Jr.: 1966, 'Phonological theory: A brief comment', *Journal of Linguistics* **2**: 99–100. Reprinted in V. B. Makkai (ed.): 1972, *Phonological theory: Evolution and current practice*, Jupiter Press, Lake Bluff, IL.

Householder, F.W., Jr.: 1971, *Linguistic speculations*, Cambridge University Press, Cambridge.

Krashen, S.D.: 1976, 'Cerebral asymmetry', in H. Whitaker and H.A. Whitaker (eds.) *Studies in neurolinguistics* (Vol. 2), Academic Press, New York.

Landau, B. and Gleitman, L.R.: 1985, *Language and experience: Evidence from the blind child*, Harvard University Press, Cambridge, MA.

Lowenfeld, B., Abel, G.L., and Hatlen, P.H.: 1968, *Blind children learn to read*, Charles C. Thomas, Springfield, IL.

Palermo, D. S. and Molfese, D.L.: 1972, 'Language acquisition from age five onwards', *Psychological Bulletin* **78**(6): 409–428.

Piaget, J.: 1955, *The language and thought of the child*, New American Library, New York.

Read, C.A., Zhang, Y., Mie, H., and Ding, B.: 1986, 'The ability to manipulate speech sounds depends on knowing alphabetic writing', *Cognition* **24**: 31–44.

Rogow, S.M.: 1986, 'Semantics and the blind child', *Semiotica* **62**(3–4): 297–312.

Sapir, E.: 1921, *Language* (Harvest Books Edition), Harcourt, Brace and World, New York.

Scholes, R.J.: 1967, 'The categorization of synthetic speech sounds as a predictive device in language teaching', *Studies in English as a Second Language* **11**(2): 1–16.

Scholes, R.J.: 1988, 'Language, literacy, and LAD: An exposition of the intensionality hypothesis', *Occasionally* (the Newsletter of the Mcluhan Foundation for Culture and Technology and the Consortium on Quality and Literacy), Ontario Institute for Studies in Education, Toronto.

Scholes, R.J. and Willis, B.J.: 1987a, 'Language and literacy', *Journal of Literary Semantics* **XVI**(1): 3–11.

Scholes, R.J. and Willis, B.J.: 1987b, 'Age and education in oral language skills', *Developmental Neuropsychology* **3**(3–4): 239–253.

Scholes, R.J. and Willis, B.J.: 1988, 'The illiterate native speaker of English: Oral language and intensionality', in J. Klesius, M. Radencich, J.J. Coye, and A.J. Lowe (eds.) *Links to Literacy*, Proceedings of the Florida Reading Association 1987 Conference, pp. 33–42.

Scholes, R.J. and Willis, B.J.: 1989, 'Invisible speech: Oral language skills of blind braille readers', *Interchange* **20**(1): 1–13.

Scholes, R.J. and Willis, B.J.: 1991, 'Linguists, literacy, and the intensionality of Marshall McLuhan's western man', in D.R. Olson and N. Torrance (eds.) *Literacy and Orality*, Cambridge University Press, Cambridge.

Smalley, W.A.: 1961, *Manual of articulatory phonetics*, William Carey Library, South Pasadena, CA.

Tomkins, G.E. and McGee, L.M.: 1986, 'Visually impaired and sighted children's emerging concepts about written language', in D.B. Yaden, Jr. and S. Templeton (eds.) *Metalinguistic awareness and beginning literacy: What it means to read and write*, Heinemann, Portsmouth, NH.

Whorf, B.L.: 1940, 'Science and linguistics', *Technological Review* **42**(6): 229–231; 247–248. Reprinted in 1955, *Language, thought, and reality: Selected writings of Benjamin Lee Whorf*, The MIT Press, Cambridge, MA.

Willis, B.J.: 1988, *Aspects of the acquisition of orality and literacy among Kenyan Primary School children*, PhD dissertation, University of Florida.

AUTHOR INDEX

SUBJECT INDEX

NEUROPSYCHOLOGY AND COGNITION

The purpose of the Neuropsychology and Cognition series is to bring out volumes that promote understanding in topics relating brain and behavior. It is intended for use by both clinicians and research scientists in the fields of neuropsychology, cognitive psychology, psycholinguistics, speech and hearing, as well as education. Examples of topics to be covered in the series would relate to memory, language acquisition and breakdown, reading, attention, developing and aging brain. By addressing the theoretical, empirical, and applied aspects of brain-behavior relationships, this series will try to present the information in the fields of neuropsychology and cognition in a coherent manner.

Series Editor

R. Malatesha Joshi, *Oklahoma State University, U.S.A.*

Publications

1. P.G. Aaron: *Dyslexia and Hyperlexia.* 1989 ISBN 1-55608-079-4; 1994, ISBN Pb 0-7923-3155-9
2. R.M. Joshi (ed.): *Written Language Disorders.* 1991 ISBN 0-7923-0902-2
3. A. Caramazza: *Issues in Reading, Writing and Speaking.* A Neuropsychological Perspective. 1991 ISBN 0-7923-0996-0
4. B.F. Pennington (ed.): *Reading Disablities.* Genetic and Neurological Influences. 1991 ISBN 0-7923-1606-1
5. N.H. Hadley: *Elective Mutism.* A Handbook for Educators, Counsellors and Health Care Professionals. 1994 ISBN 0-7923-2418-8
6. W.C. Watt (ed.): *Writing Systems and Cognition.* Perspectives from Psychology, Physiology, Linguistics, and Semiotics. 1994 ISBN 0-7923-2592-3
7. I. Taylor and D.R. Olson (eds.), *Scripts and Literacy*: Reading and Learning to Read Alphabets, Syllabaries and Characters. 1994 ISBN 0-7923-2912-0
8. V.W. Berninger (ed.): *The Varieties of Orthographic Knowledge.* I: Theoretical and Developmental Issues. 1994 ISBN 0-7923-3080-3
9. C.K. Leong and R.M. Joshi (eds.): *Developmental and Acquired Dyslexia.* Neuropsychological and Neurolinguistic Perspectives. 1995 ISBN 0-7923-3166-4

KLUWER ACADEMIC PUBLISHERS – DORDRECHT / BOSTON / LONDON